ALSO BY ANTHONY HEILBUT

Thomas Mann: Eros and Literature

*Exiled in Paradise: German Refugee Artists and Intellectuals in America
from the 1930s to the Present*

The Gospel Sound: Good News and Bad Times

The Fan Who Knew Too Much

The Fan Who Knew Too Much

Aretha Franklin, the Rise of the Soap Opera,
Children of the Gospel Church, and
Other Meditations

Anthony Heilbut

Alfred A. Knopf NEW YORK 2012

Copyright © 2012 by Anthony Heilbut
All rights reserved. Published in the United States by Alfred A. Knopf,
a division of Random House, Inc., New York, and in Canada by Random
House of Canada Limited, Toronto.
www.aaknopf.com

Knopf, Borzoi Books, and the colophon are registered trademarks of
Random House, Inc.

Portions of this book appeared in The Believer, Harper's Magazine,
The Los Angeles Times Book Review, The Nation, The New Yorker,
The New York Times Book Review, *and* Truthdig

Library of Congress Cataloging-in-Publication Data
Heilbut, Anthony.
The fan who knew too much : Aretha Franklin, the rise of the soap opera,
children of the gospel church, and other meditations / by Anthony Heilbut.
p. cm.
"This is a Borzoi Book"—T.p. verso.
Includes index.
ISBN 978-0-375-40080-3
1. Popular culture—United States. 2. Gospel music—United States.
3. United States—Civilization—1945– 4. United States—Social
conditions—1945– 5. Celebrities—United States.
6. Fans (Persons)—United States. I. Title.
E169.12.H435 2012
973.91—dc23 2012003699

Jacket design by Carol Devine Carson

Manufactured in the United States of America
First Edition

7/12

IN MEMORY OF OTTO HEILBUT (1891–1970)
and BERTHA HEILBUT (1911–2003)

Contents

I. ALL GOD'S SONS AND DAUGHTERS

All God's sons and daughters
Drinking of the healing waters
Are going to live, are going to live,
Live on up in glory
After awhile.

W. HERBERT BREWSTER,
"Move On Up a Little Higher"

THE CHILDREN AND
THEIR SECRET CLOSET

Some years ago PBS ran a special on Dr. Alfred Kinsey and his investigations of homosexuality in American society. One historian was less than persuaded. He admitted that Kinsey had been impressively thorough in his considerations of business or the military or education. But he had ignored certain groups, the scholar argued. "What if he had interviewed the members of a Pentecostal church?"

Having been a close observer of African-American gospel music for almost fifty years, I decided to ask the same question of several singers and musicians, and got the following responses:

"They woulda lied."

"From the pulpit to the door."

"Baby, those figures would have gone up the roose-rooftop."

"Church? That's the children's home away from home."

But most often, the response was simple laughter. They heard the question as rhetorical; everyone knew better than the quizzical professor. They also knew that it is impossible to understand the story of black America without foregrounding the experiences of the gay men of gospel. From music to politics their role has been crucial; their witness, to quote their mother's Bible, prophetic.

That witness has not always been acknowledged. Occasionally it has been suppressed. One of Glenn Beck's arch black supporters happens to be Martin Luther King's niece Alveda. She denies any connection between civil rights and homosexuality. "The civil rights movement was born from the Bible," she insists, and everyone knows that "God hates homosexuality." She neglected to mention that two of the movement's greatest architects were gay men, Bayard Rustin, a former singer, who made his recording debut with a gospel quartet, and Alfred A. Duckett, who was, among many other roles, Mahalia Jackson's publicity agent.

From the storefront church to the courts of Europe, from the poorhouse to the White House, the gay men of gospel have, as the songs say, opened doors that were closed in their face, and made a way out of no way.

"WE BUILT THIS CHURCH"

Truman Capote once said that a faggot was a homosexual gentleman who had just left the room. In church circles, gay and bisexual men are regularly identified as "sissies" or "punks"—terms sometimes used, and often not more kindly, by the men themselves. Almost as common and much friendlier is the appellation "the children," a term rich with its allusion to the lifetime quest of a mother's favorite son. Thus, Evangelist Willie Mae Ford Smith might slyly recognize the members of her congregation, "It's so good to see the children . . . and the children."

For well over a hundred years, these men have been, along with their mothers and sisters, the black church's rock and shield. They have been among the most faithful members and the most vivid celebrants:

"Nobody shouts like the children," said an old church mother, alluding to the folkloric term for holy dancing. With eyes shut, gay men have danced steps that would both anticipate and transcend the partiers in any club. They have brought such imaginative and critical resources to the church that for many years—and even now during the homophobic reaction that has swept fundamentalism—they have been the unacknowledged arbiters of the culture.

They have been the master orchestrators of the Spirit. Most preachers could not survive without the young, underpaid keyboard man underlining his words with rhetorical stabs and moanlike runs. Evangelist Ernestine Cleveland grumbled, "You all can't have church unless you got some punk on the organ." Along with the women members of the congregation—all of them pledged to their pastor and many, according to legend, romantically attached as well—gay men have helped conduct the Spirit. "When the sissies jump out of their seats, folks know to stand up." Their worship is gracefully athletic. I've seen gay men stand and move rhythmically through most of a pastor's message, anticipating the communal shout that may be a sermon's length away, that may never even occur. I've seen dancing leaps that can only be compared to broad jumps—while running, Reverend Isaac Douglas is said to have leapt over a small pond.

The children have also brought the cold eyes of a professional to the ritual and ceremony. "If you ain't moved them," says DeLois Barrett Campbell, "you ain't done nothing." Mahalia Jackson was the world's gospel queen, but her gay pals could always upset her by saying that her best singing days were over. The critics were nice, and the fortune she earned spoke for itself. But she knew that the children were the real judges.

They have also made the church their special arena. As recently as 2007 I saw a middle-aged man dance around a Harlem church with a fire that no hip-hopper could approach. I asked Brother Charles if he had ever danced in a club. "Sir, they tried to make me a soul singer. They said I had the looks and the voice. But soon as that band started up I got as stiff as a white boy. I lost all my rhythm." Perhaps because it wasn't *his* blues. I long ago concluded that gospel music was the blues of gay men and lesbians. This may explain why so many great singers either didn't go into pop or failed in their trying. Bishop Carl Bean, a former Motown artist, says, "I just never felt right up there, singing about my girl." The late Gloria Griffin, who made a stab at club singing, in emulation of her great friend Aretha Franklin, gave it up. "I can sing about the love of God. The love of man, I don't know too much about that."

However, the first time I heard the word "soul" as it is currently used, it was in a gay context. In 1957 Sam Cooke confounded the church by moving from gospel to R&B. "He'll do fine," a clerk at Harlem's Record Shack assured me. "He's got soul." He then informed me that Sam liked men as well as women. "Sure he's gay, how else could he have that much soul?" (I next heard the term used by Malcolm X, who asserted that soul was black people's contribution to America.)

One of gospel's great appeals to this nonbeliever has been the vast emotional territory it claims for itself. I first learned this at the Apollo Theater in 1958. At that time local disc jockeys would rent the place for a week and present "gospel caravans" featuring the leading stars in "programs" that ran for ninety minutes, three times a day. The last night was always the most memorable, the occasion for the singers to let out all stops, and programs might last for two or three hours—three times as long as a typical blues show. The 1958 Easter caravan had many highlights, among them Marion Williams and Clara Ward's hair-raising duet of the seasonally appropriate "Old Rugged Cross." But earlier, Julius Cheeks, a male quartet singer, had "plumb demolished the place" with a tribute to mothers. Nowhere in the lyric was a baldly religious image. The song was all about a mother working herself to death for her children.

> *Sometimes I get to wonder,*
> *Did I treat my mother right?*
> *She used to moan early in the morning,*
> *She used to groan very late at night.*

The weeping and wailing had nothing to do with scripture, and yet would not have been countenanced in any other setting. Several years later, another last night coincided with the attacks on civil rights marchers. Prompted by the moment, Johnny Martin of the Mighty Clouds of Joy rushed to the microphone: "I wanna say this for the folk in Alabama . . . 'There's a Bright Side Somewhere.'" The theater erupted; he seemed to leap out of himself, and the other Clouds could barely hold him down. All over the theater, men and women were running up the aisles, hollering their rage and despair.

There might have been a biblical implication to the events down south; Dr. King had certainly insisted on that. But back in 1958, I saw something more surprising. As a novelty attraction, the caravan's sponsors had hired a professional actor named Gilbert Adkins to recite part of James Weldon Johnson's *God's Trombones,* a faux-naif sermon called "The Creation." Adkins's performance would have been old school in the 1920s; the only appealing note came from the organist Herman Stevens, who accompanied the sermon with every noise a Hammond could make. But the Apollo audience was not used to Broadway, and they experienced Adkins's performance as a treat.

On the last night, Fred Barr, the disc jockey–promoter, summoned Adkins back to the stage and handed him a large bouquet of flowers, the contribution of a group of church ladies who had attended every program. The actor was overcome. He started to laugh and cry. "You know," he said—and you could only reckon the difficulties of being an actor in those days—"my mother told me something that has stayed with me down through the years. She said, 'Boy, you can go a lot of places. But people don't have to love you.'"

He shook his head and left the stage. But the moment was not complete. Suddenly young people all over the Apollo rose to their feet and started to shout. Some singers onstage got happy as well. The shouting continued for twenty minutes, as ushers dashed around the floor, snatching the bodies of men and women overcome by the spirit. It was black church at its highest, and there had been nary a word spoken about Jesus. The point I derived was that gospel's emotional borders were almost limitless. Everything that Adkins had intimated—and surely this was a time when each person had a story to tell—could be comprehended in the form. In retrospect the particular appeal of gospel music to gays and lesbians was manifest. Why sing disingenuously about one kind of emotion—sexual love—when all the others were yours to intimate, convey, and command?

The church and its gospel music have offered a second home, and often a friendlier place than the homes where boys might face ridicule or worse. (Though, as many have reported, the physical abusers could also be sexual predators.) Gospel has allowed the worship of a loving male—as we'll see later, a theme that has inspired numerous white writers. But the children, battered by poverty, racism, and homophobia, may have the richest testimonies. I have seen five-man groups weep and stagger as they sang, "When sorrow has taken my heart by surprise, He never has left me alone," or "I do not know how long it will be, or what the future holds for me." They'll wave glad hands when some old mother exhorts them, "Children, take it to Jesus, you don't need to tell nobody else. Just step into your secret closet."

That secret closet is a constant in Protestant worship, most evident in the extremest form of Protestantism—Pentecostalism. (Matthew 6:6: "But thou, when thou prayest, enter into thy closet, and when thou hast shut thy door, pray to thy Father which is in secret; and thy Father which seeth in secret shall reward thee openly.") The scripture also says that God resides where two or three are gathered. But the Pentecostal believer, more commonly known as a "saint" (whereby the Pentecostal-type churches have long been called "sanctified"), can reduce the number to one. The secret closet resembles the gospel highway in that old song, "On the Jericho road, there's room for just two, / No more and no less, / Just Jesus and you."

A closet is where you shut yourself off from the world. And just so the church has always loomed as "the arc of safety"—even more a safe harbor when it's the place most identified with mothers and grandmothers. Bishop Carl Bean says, "It's always been that way. The straight boys who play around with girls, and make babies, and break their mothers' hearts, they live in the streets. The well-behaved boys, the sensitive, quiet kids, the ones we now call nerds and sissies, they've always landed in church. Church or the street, take your pick."

He implies the great and constant battle within American fundamentalism between muscular Christianity and a womanly faith. Or, as figured in biblical imagery, between the gentle Shepherd and the Warrior on a battlefield. Obviously, for many hyperbolically butch preachers from Billy Sunday (pitching for Jesus) to Bishop Eddie L. Long (muscle building for the Lord), the religious vocation had to appear a guy's thing. For such men, even tears can seem virile.

Carl Bean's flock considers this a false dichotomy. Their faith borders on the androgynous, even as their gospel music has always welcomed male sopranos and female basses. I once heard a young Carl Bean, years before he had founded Unity Fellowship, the first black gay denomination, when he was still a seminarian. Facing a small storefront church, filled inevitably with a pastor, a pianist, a guitarist, older women, and younger men, he declared, "In heaven they tell me there won't be no day or night. And there won't be no man or woman. Don't you want to go? Don't you wanna go?" He too advised the saints to hold fast before that glorious, postsexual morning. "Look to the hills, children. And stay in your secret closet."

Those who find consolation in the secret closet find it large enough to include any burden and every trial—"Just take it to the Lord in prayer." That other closet, the space from which the children move in and out, is also a place of secrets. "If I want a secret kept, I can tell this friend," sings Marion Williams. "I know that I will never ever hear it again." Some things needn't be uttered aloud; save them for your secret closet.

This may partially explain why gospel lyrics are rarely as graphic or poetic as blues lyrics—though without calling names, they certainly expose unpleasant realities. "Your enemies cannot harm you," wails Inez Andrews. "Keep an eye on your close friend." Dorothy Love Coates—Dot Love—sings of enemies "inflicting all the hurt they can, / Throwing their rocks and hiding their hands." It's up to every mother's child to fill in the details, imagine the particular betrayals. At choir rehearsals,

I've seen men step away and cry to themselves. "I'm sorry, children. I was just thinking about some folk who did me so bad." You could make a blues out of that, or simply abstract it into a gospel metaphor. If the deepest gospel songs tell of oppression, it's always overcome. Mahalia Jackson liked to say that a blues singer dwelled at the bottom of a pit, and she simply didn't live there.

But many gospel singers have, including Mahalia herself at times, and many of the church children who followed women like her or Marion Williams, Inez Andrews, and Dorothy Love Coates. For all of them, church was the one place to express your sorrows, and trust in a spiritual catharsis, its sign, "The Lord has brought me out." For generations, virtually up to the homophobic present, the secret closet has allowed the faithful children the safest place to leave and return.

The role of gay men in the church has long been common knowledge. In the early twentieth century, the great contralto Marian Anderson left Philadelphia's largest black Baptist church, where she had been performing since her childhood, and, accompanied by the city's finest church musician, began to tour the country. But her career was momentarily sidetracked when he was arrested for soliciting (as was her next pianist, a white European). Anderson would become famous for her concertized arrangements of spirituals, many of them the products of gay musicians, who flocked around her as later men would adore Mahalia Jackson or Marion Williams. In the stereotype, conducting a gospel choir became a gay specialty—as still seen in the Tyler Perry films with their sissified choir directors.

If you were known by your company, it took a brave man to admit membership in a choir. Reverend Jesse Jackson told the *New Yorker*'s Marshall Frady that he had been scared to join a choir in college until his mother joked that he must be very uncertain of his masculinity. (The implication may have sailed past Frady—just as it may have when Mahalia Jackson told Nat Hentoff that you didn't need to be a "sissy" to sing gospel.)

Frequently, gay men raised in the church who retained their love of the ritual and ceremony while despising the fundamentalist ideology have played heroic roles in public. From George Washington Carver (Marian Anderson's greatest fan) to Bayard Rustin, from Langston Hughes to James Baldwin, it's impossible to imagine African-American culture without the children's active participation. These men would be the church's proudest and most prodigal sons.

And yet by the early twenty-first century, the black church had risen against its very own. The two dominant themes of the megachurches, all of them Pentecostal or charismatic, have been the prosperity gospel and vehement opposition to gay rights, most particularly but hardly limited to gay marriage. The most outspoken warriors have been new-breed sanctified preachers like T. D. Jakes, Creflo Dollar, and Paul Morton.

The paradox is that both white and black Pentecostalism have been the stomping grounds of gay men since at least 1900, the year when a white Kansan pastor, Charles Fox Parham, ushered in the practice of glossolalia, speaking in tongues. Among certain Christians, this would prove to be the long-anticipated sign of Jesus' imminent return. Parham was a somewhat unsavory vehicle; he was violently racist, and shared the hoary belief that the twelve tribes of Israel had landed in Great Britain. All the same, his most notable disciple was a black preacher named William Joseph Seymour, who would show up a few years later in Los Angeles, where he conducted a revival at the Azusa Street Baptist Church. Parham had initially elicited the Holy Spirit in one person, a woman named Agnes Ozman. But in Seymour's two-year revival, thousands of people were led to the mountain heights of religious ecstasy, contorting in their seats, spasming on the floor, and speaking in unknown tongues, most of them unique to the speaker.

The Azusa Street revival is generally considered ground zero in Pentecostal history—though members of some small black congregations had been speaking in tongues for years, while the term "holy rolling" had been extant since at least the 1840s. The church drew worshippers from all over America and even Europe (Ukrainian Pentecostals would spring up in the years before the 1917 revolution). As bemused reporters noted, black and white saints were joined in one accord; class and race were dissolved in the spirit. Veterans of Azusa Street would start various Pentecostal denominations, such as the Assemblies of God. Charles Parham heard the news, traveled to Los Angeles, and decried the nightly revivals as nothing but sensation. He condemned the events as "holy rolling," specifically in the time-honored style of black churches. He considered the variety of tongues a travesty, since in his view there was but one heavenly language: one English, one Unknown Tongue as discrete as English or, better yet, Hebrew, which it often sounded like. Seymour paid him no mind.

But within a few years their careers would anticipate the history of many gospel children. Seymour, granting himself messianic powers, had a throne installed on the altar. His church was not prepared for such displays, and banished him to an early death. (In a few years, the African-American Father Divine, Daddy Grace, His Grace King Louis H. Narcisse, and Pope William O' Neal would make him appear modest, while the Korean ex-Pentecostal Reverend Sun Myung Moon would pronounce himself Christ's more highly favored brother.) Charles Parham would be accused of sodomy with young boys: a charge for which he was never tried. There were also rumors that he had solicited a policeman in a public restroom. In later years many of the children would undergo similar trials. Well into the 1980s, a major choir director would be arrested for soliciting a white cop in a Memphis urinal.

When I told the story of Parham and Seymour to some older gospel singers, they all jumped to the conclusion that the two must have been lovers. It was just too unlikely that a white man, particularly a racist, and a black man would have drawn so close in early-twentieth-century Kansas. What leaps out for me is Parham's dismissal of the noisy revivals. "It's not real, it's not of God": this would become a standard line among highly competitive gospel singers. They alone are "real"; all the others, show-boating clowns. When the people shout off their song, "the Lord has blessed." If a rival singer, preacher, or choir tears up, it's "just a circus," "they brought their families," "the women shout so those quartets will see them," or "you know the sissies will shout for each other." I detect the cry of a wounded artist, seeing his public abandon him.

The next major name in Pentecostalism was Aimee Semple McPherson, the famous pastor of the Church of the Foursquare Gospel. Her Los Angeles–based Angelus Temple drew thousands of poor whites, many of them recently arrived from the Bible Belt, but also some blacks and Mexicans. Her church fed the hungry and sheltered the homeless. (This largesse should not be confused with liberal politics. She was fiercely anti-union, and Irving Berlin would introduce his "God Bless America" at her Temple during an event honoring a congressional investigation of left-wing Hollywood.)

But she was cursed with notoriety. During the 1920s, her famous kidnapping turned out to be a bogus event; she had been on a spree with her lover. After that she became a figure of scorn to the world. But the saints did not abandon her, and she lived on until 1944, by which time she had broken relations with both her mother and her daughter.

This is a story that would be repeated many times, from Jimmy Swaggart to Jim Bakker to Ted Haggard, the Pentecostal icons exposed as rank hypocrites. Except that none of them were simple charlatans, and, invariably, some saints welcomed them home, figuring that the Lord will forgive anyone four hundred and ninety times a day. Sister Aimee was the first of the flamboyant female evangelists. She was also the first to introduce frilly uniforms for her Angels, the women in her choirs. This sanctified lingerie would later be adopted by Gertrude Ward, the founder and manager of the greatest of all gospel groups, the Famous Ward Singers. And just as the Ward Singers drew many gay fans, gay men flocked to the Angelus Temple. Some were preachers, who were occasionally photographed grinning deliriously while "slain in the Spirit" on the altar. As early as the late 1920s, gay members of her church would be interviewed by academic sociologists. But just as many came to admire the handsome young preachers, the homespun fashion, and Sister Aimee's brand of sacred camp. She was the farthest thing from a feminist, but she made preaching a womanly vocation.

She helped introduce the Pentecostal convention of laying hands on women and men alike, causing them to fall back in convulsions, "slain in the Spirit." This was a whole new womanly power. "This tiny woman leaves men rolling in the aisles!" After Aimee, a saint didn't have to remain a cheerleader. She could become captain of the team.

Within the black church, new-breed pastors far surpassed Sister Aimee's flamboyance. The Baptist Church continued to attract gay men. Eugene Smith, an original member of the Roberta Martin Singers, modern gospel's premier group, observed the children's role for most of his eighty-eight years. Toward the end, I asked Gene why there seemed to be so many gays in the church. He replied reasonably, "Well, in most of our neighborhoods, there are more churches than anything else. Except for bars." He paused. "And then again, some jump from one to the other."

Because well until the late twentieth century the Baptist Church dominated African-American religion, it probably attracted the most gay worshippers. Some of them acquired a shamanic authority. J. Robert Bradley, a native of Memphis, was raised in extremest poverty, "born in an alley, raised in an alley . . . My mama dressed me in the worn-out drawers of boys who had been blessed with a living father." He was also the victim of childhood bullies; when he was eight, another boy hurled a stone at him, blinding him in one eye. His mother withdrew him from school. Yet he was a child prodigy, and both black and white Baptists saw that he had a thorough musical education. By his late teens, he had a huge, robust bass-baritone, capable of singing lieder and gospel songs with equal aplomb.

He was Paul Robeson with soul. Except instead of the football-playing Othello, Bradley was a short, effeminate Mr. Five-by-Five. It didn't matter; it may have contributed to his power with the people. (The male star of the Roberta Martin Singers was a short, thin, and very homely man named Norsalus McKissick. But as the critic John Hammond noted, his gorgeous vocals made women respond as if he were Billy Eckstine.) Every year Bradley would perform a concert at the annual meeting of the National Baptist Convention. He would begin with Schubert and Schumann, and the audience would applaud respectfully. Then he'd sing some concert spirituals, and they would applaud louder. Then he'd start talking about his widowed mother and sing a hymn or gospel song. He would rear back, stroke his lapel, make the expressive "ugly face" of a mourning-bench moaner. And with a world-class voice, he would become a pure gospel singer, phrasing with such power that women threw hats and pocketbooks, and men would run around the aisles and jump over balconies.

In 2005, a couple of years before his death, Bradley returned to the convention, a stout but frail old man, no more virile than before. "They said, 'J. Robert Bradley is in the house,'" he recalled, "and eight hundred Baptists started waving their handkerchief." He sang an old gospel song, "He'll Understand and Say Well Done," and people began to fall out. Reverend Clay Evans, Jesse Jackson's former pastor, leapt from his seat. "You ain't getting out of here before you sing that verse about 'But if you try and fail in your trying.'" And rolling his two eyes, the real one and the artificial, Bradley sang until "all those high and mighty were running about like little babies just received salvation." Some years earlier, Clay Evans had recorded a sermon lamenting "Homosexuality in the Church." But for the moment, his musical witness was Bradley, the great singer who'd lost an eye for being a sissy boy.

Yet for all the famous Baptist gays, the myth has always placed the children in the newer and smaller churches. Fifty years ago, a Baptist singer joked, "There are more sissies and bull daggers in the sanctified church, and they all think they the only ones going to heaven." He was just speaking a received truth. But when I quoted his words in my first book, *The Gospel Sound: Good News and Bad Times,* many pastors were enraged. I was informed that some had preached sermons against that nasty little jewboy from New York. On the other hand, I was also told that the book was among the most stolen in the Chicago library system.

It's easy to see why the small churches would welcome a talented gay musician. The church didn't judge him, and in turn he gave it his all and all. "Onliest thing, those preachers would never pay," Alex Bradford remembered. "They'd always say the same thing—the Lord will bless you, and Payday's coming after a while."

The biggest Pentecostal denomination, the Church of God in Christ (COGIC), adhered to a stern, unforgiving theology. Homosexuality was another sin that COGIC saints were expected to overcome. "I put off the old man and put on the new," a saint told me. "They say they was born a sissy. I tell 'em, you need to born again." Yet the church was raised on the loving arms of gay men. Dr. Wilbert Jordan, a member of the huge West Angeles Church of God in Christ, says, "When did you know a Church of God in Christ without the children?" An eighty-two-year-old musician, who spent years at one of New York's biggest churches, says that the pastor (a bishop within the Church of God in Christ) would "preach against the homosexuals every Sunday, and twice a week he'd have some young kid show him a good time."

The most flamboyant ministers were in smaller denominations, particularly the Spiritual Church (services of which often invoke the spirits of dead saints and involve rituals that resemble Santeria, African cults, and Roman Catholicism). Chicago's most famous preacher was Clarence Cobbs, pastor of the First Church of Deliverance. His radio choir was the first to perform the newer gospel songs, composed by writers like Thomas A. Dorsey, in the early 1930s. Just as it embraced new musical forms, it opened its doors to outlaws and strays. It became the home church of policy queens and numbers runners. Cobbs was quietly gay, and his church became the place where talented lesbians and gay men could worship without being 'buked and scorned. First Church reflected its city, both in its cosmopolitanism and in its undercurrent of vice.

In Oakland, California, a spiritual pastor began healing the sick and causing the poor to prosper. Too driven for modesty, he dubbed himself His Grace King Louis H. Narcisse (love that "H"). Narcisse, a native of New Orleans and distant cousin of the singer Bessie Griffin, was a notable singer himself. His style was drawn almost completely from New Orleans's greatest gospel woman, Mahalia Jackson. Paraphrasing the question "What would Jesus do?" he'd think, "What would Mahalia do?" and echo her, albeit in a strong baritone voice.

When he was growing up in Alabama, Alex Bradford was inspired by a local spiritual church leader. "Prophet Jones started in Bessemer. He was the first man I saw to play piano with his feet. He started with the spirituals, and wore those fabulous robes. Aimee Semple couldn't touch him. He inspired all the young folk." Prophet Jones later switched to the Church of God in Christ and then founded Triumph the King of Christ Universal Dominion Kingdom of God and Temple of Christ, International Fellowship. For a while, he owned Detroit. "I saw women throw their minks down for Prophet Jones to walk across." Such gestures expressed their gratitude, since apparently Jones's words and advice, his anointed oil, and his spirit-filled services had caused "heaven's doors to open and pour down a blessing you won't have room to receive." But their garments mimicked his; "nobody could wear minks and furs and diamond rings like Prophet. He bought 'em up and wore 'em up." It was his habit to interrupt a sermon, speak in tongues, and then interpret the message—standard sanctified behavior, except that it would be specifically addressed. Listeners heard his words not as holy generalities but as practical directions. (New York's Reverend Ike would carry on in the same tradition.)

This was an early, purer version of the prosperity gospel. In Jones's churches, some members might shout, but others promenaded as if they were at Buckingham Palace. The members of Jesse Jackson's Operation Push declared, "I Am Somebody." Prophet Jones's flock weren't just somebodies; they sang, "I'm a royal child." The promenade made explicit the deliverance from bondage to freedom, "out of darkness and into the marvelous light." It was a message that spoke to his own heart. Singers who visited his home would comment on the world's largest toy railroad, a track as wide as a room. "You know, babies," he told them. "When I was coming up, I never had a thing, no toy, no choo-choo train, no nothing." He left implicit that as an effeminate kid, he wouldn't have had many friends. So now he had more of a train—a *gospel* train—than any boy in the land.

Prophet Jones would be arrested in an adult-movie theater, although the only activity he performed appeared to be voyeurism. Still, it was damaging. He died in 1971, aged sixty-three, leaving no biological children but many descendants. They would gentrify his rituals, but they'd stick with his message "God wants his children to have life more abundantly," and no, that abundance was not simply the peace that surpass-eth understanding. It was the stuff promised a royal child, singing in full voice, "My father is rich in houses and lands."

—

Gospel music has always been divided into a minimum of two genres, two kinds of practitioner—very simply, into two aesthetics. The oldest style is represented by male quartets, which may include as many as seven or eight members but adhere to the rules of four-part harmony. These men wear "uniforms," suits and ties. At first quartets sang a cappella, somewhat in the style of barbershop quartets, though with much greater fervor and individuality. To these ears the quartet lost much of its charm when instrumental accompaniment was introduced. This is particularly the case because the preferred quartet instrument is guitar, and as Mahalia Jackson once said, "Singing by the gee-tar just hems you in." Music, at least in the form of guitars, foreclosed the harmony. The bass voice, for one, was virtually obviated by the bass guitar.

There have been many famous quartets. Most of the members were not only great singers but stupendous showmen. Ira Tucker of the Dixie Hummingbirds once said, "If you ain't run down the aisles and caused some folks to shout, you ain't done nothing." And famously, quartet singers would induce a pandemonium that bordered on the erotic. Since the lead singers were often very handsome, the ecstatic response of their female fans invited a worldly interpretation. "They shouting for their boyfriends" became a very familiar complaint.

Like vagabond blues singers, quartet leads were professional heart-breakers. In one famous story, a celebrated quartet singer attended a church program only to discover five of his girlfriends in the front row, accompanied by his unacknowledged children.

Sex appeal became a quartet lead's ticket. Some of the greatest sing-ers in rock and roll—men like Sam Cooke, Wilson Pickett, and Al Green—grew up as quartet singers, and they brought all the emotional and erotic power of their former metier into pop. It almost writes itself that quartet singers were universally identified as "good country mens," even though Sam Cooke, for example, was raised in Chicago. It became a point of pride that such fellows were adamantly straight. "They ain't sissies. They men."

Gospel's other branch is called simply, and not very clearly, gospel. It has evolved into at least two styles, traditional and contemporary. The distinctions between gospel and quartet are so great that they qualify as separate genres, which may share a certain repertory and church setting but not much else. To begin with, gospel's greatest practitioners have been women and the men who sing like them. From the start in the early 1930s, gospel was always accompanied by a keyboard instrument. (So it was that for one of her gospel sessions, Aretha Franklin recruited Joe Ligon, the quartet lead of the Mighty Clouds of Joy. Ligon found himself in musically unfamiliar territory. He apologized to the church for not being "a piano singer." Aretha hastened to console him: "You don't need no piano to sing.")

Even though gospel's first star, Sister Rosetta Tharpe, was a remarkable guitarist—who would influence rockers from Chuck Berry to Johnny Cash, not to mention Ira Tucker, who she contended sang just like her—she was an equally gifted pianist. And as I learned working with her, Rosetta's great ear heard far more music than her guitar could provide. Paradoxically, her harmonies and singing were freer in her early days, when she accompanied herself exclusively on guitar, than when she was accompanied by the boogie-woogie pianist Sammy Price. Their records were commercial hits but he didn't always complement the orchestration she carried within.

Gospel's greatest divas—Mahalia Jackson, Marion Williams, Clara Ward, Dorothy Love Coates—all depended on the keyboard. One of Mahalia's first hits, "Even Me," featured only her voice and the organ of Professor James Herbert Francis (also known as Blind Francis). The record swept the church, not merely because of her inspired song, but because his accompaniment was so well attuned to her spirit. As in jazz, the instrumentalist answered the singer—only, because of the church's tradition of call-and-response, gospel's musicians were far more rhetorically explicit. To say of some gifted musician "That boy can make an organ talk" was to say the obvious.

When the women first hit what I've dubbed the Gospel Highway—a network of churches and small arenas scattered all over the country—the men gave them a hard time. Wilson Pickett's inspiration, Reverend Julius Cheeks, once said, "I used to think a woman couldn't sing. Then I saw how Ruth Davis and Dot Love and Marion Williams could get into a church. Those girls changed my mind." R. H. Harris, the Soul Stirrers' first and finest lead, was just as dismissive. In the mid-forties, his group toured with the Georgia Peach, a New York contralto, and her female group: "Just hard, mannish-looking women. They ran around the church, acted like they were men." Whenever I've told that story, gospel singers have given the same reply: "He's mad because them girls took the house."

For many reasons the gospel women exhibited an individual excellence that surpassed any of their quartet foes. (An objective factor may be that each quartet member is a team player, whose first loyalty is to the ensemble. A gospel soloist answers only to herself . . . and perhaps her instrumentalists. This may resemble the difference between Alex Rodriguez and Roger Federer.)

And yet they had modeled themselves on their male rivals. Mahalia Jackson spent most of the thirties singing with the Johnson Singers, a quartet with male and female members. For her first recordings, in 1937, she chose some of their songs, simply singing the background chorus along with the lead vocal. "God's Gonna Separate the Wheat from the Tares" and "O My Lord (Sing On, My Singer)" were quartet standbys; in fact, the second record begins with her command:

Now you sing on, sing on, my tenor,
You sing on, sing on, my baritone,
You sing on, sing on, my basso,
I know the Lord will hear you sing,
Now you sing on, sing on, my tenor,
And don't you worry about your leader!

It is no small irony that a woman who later inspired so many gay men had learned much of her craft from male quartet singers, the children's archenemies.

Because they were singing to people who worshipped God with both soul and body, gospel women allowed themselves physical liberties that might appear shocking. Indeed, the young Mahalia Jackson was considered too physical. Eugene Smith remembered, "My pastor wouldn't let Halie nowhere near his church. You know why, it's the way she shook that butt." At her glorious peak, she would perform her biggest hit, Reverend W. Herbert Brewster's "Move On Up a Little Higher," in which each line imagines an upward climb through the New Jerusalem:

Move on up a little higher, meet my loving mother,
Move on up a little higher, meet the lily of the valley.

The lyric called for eight post-mortem encounters. But on nights when she'd meet the Hebrew children or the Twelve Tribes of Israel, the bluesy riff on "move" could be reiterated twenty or thirty times. And with each move her hips would rotate, as though she were stepping in place. Similarly, when Marion Williams sang "Surely God Is Able," another Brewster composition, she would run down aisles roaring "surely," on some nights fifty or a hundred times. Because she had a big-hipped strut, likened by one fan to Mae West's, she managed to swivel as she ran. The physical freedom that led Mahalia and Marion down the church aisles provided a model for their ecstatic fans. One singer remarked, "I'd have gotten into some houses myself if I'd had a booty like those girls."

These two had been preceded on the highway by Sallie Martin, Thomas A. Dorsey's first vocalist, and Willie Mae Ford Smith. Mother Smith had the most powerful contralto of early gospel. Dorsey felt that she could have surpassed Bessie Smith, whom he knew from his blues-singing days as Georgia Tom. Her volume was so great that an engineer said she required the mike setup of a five-piece chamber group. But she was even more known for her showmanly gestures. When in doubt she resorted to agile semaphor: sing "fly," and she'd flap her arms; sing "bow on my knees," and she'd descend to the floor.

Such women became the models of gay men. Mother Smith would out one of her greatest disciples in a circuitous fashion. "Sallie Martin says Brother a carbon copy of Willie Mae—ain't that just like a sissy!" As many men emulated her as women.

Gospel is one of the rare forms where women have provided the role models for men. Yet the borrowing had begun earlier. Louis Armstrong was much noted for his wide and generous smile. Compare his photo with one of Ma Rainey and the resemblance is startling. He claimed her smile, if not her persona. So it was not unprecedented that Mahalia's disciples tended to be men. Very few women singers resemble her closely, while Brother John Sellers, Singing Sammy Lewis, Reverend Jodie Strawther, Cleophus Robinson, and King Louis H. Narcisse all resembled her in male drag. To a man, they mocked her. The word is used in the old English sense of imitation (as in mock apple pie), but I've always heard an ambivalent note in its usage. John Sellers, whom she had helped raise, could hold his shoulders, neck, and even cheekbones exactly like her. In 1945, a good year before she cut her first postwar records, he waxed covers of her debut performances of "God's Gonna Separate the Wheat from the Tares" and "Oh My Lord," thereby demonstrating that she had become a church-sanctioned model—and more specifically, a model for men rather than women.

Back in the 1930s, when John Sellers was still a schoolboy, he used to battle the fans of Roberta and Sallie Martin. Robert Anderson, later one of Mahalia's dearest friends, was then wholly enthralled by Roberta, his mentor. Roberta was subdued but incisive—"she'll make you hurt yourself," remembered Madame Ernestine Washington, "if you don't watch out." But Mahalia was loud and bold, Bessie Smith to Roberta's Ella Fitzgerald. So Roberta's boys delighted in aggravating Brother John: "You know Halie's diction ain't right . . . You know Halie fuck up the time." He'd reply, "But she'll take the program from any of 'em." All of this was true; she could outsing her competition, and she would mispronounce her words and mess up the time throughout her career.

Mahalia knew how to play the children. In her great biography, *Just Mahalia, Baby*, Laurraine Goreau describes a church program when Mahalia sang "I Bowed on My Knees and Cried Holy." Exhibiting some Mother Smith showmanship, she descended to her knees, but found herself unable to rise again. Robert was in the Spirit and didn't hear her requests for aid. Finally she burst out, loud enough for all the church to hear, "Help me up, you bubble-eyed nigger!"

He could hold his own. One time they traveled to Brooklyn's Washington Temple, where Mahalia recruited the church pianist, Blind Francis, to accompany her. But the pastor's wife, Ernestine Washington, got up first and shouted the house, and did it with Robert's composition "Prayer Changes Things," a song Mahalia had recently recorded herself. The queen was outdone. "Robert, I'm gonna show them. This is Chicago's night!" But everyone shoutable had cut a step already, and none of her songs got over. Finally she sashayed over to the piano and addressed the musician. "Francis, you sound like a Mississippi mule clomping up a country road. You ain't playing worth a damn." "Madame," the blind man replied, "I'm playing the way you're singing." Robert burst out laughing—his laugh notes soared into the seventh octave—so dramatically that he had to mime getting happy, and let himself be laid out as if slain in the Spirit. "Beloveds, isn't that beautiful?" said Madame Washington, going along with the program. "Brother Anderson was so Spirit-filled we just had to pray over him."

They traveled together for years, often sleeping in the same bed. She also recorded six of his compositions, and informed Hollie West of the *Washington Post* that Robert was her "idol." With her actions she demonstrated that she preferred the company of gay men. The other kind only brought her grief. Or, as Marion Williams once said, "there's two kinds of men. A good man won't understand your career. And the kind that understand ain't always all that good." Ironically, her last years would be ruined by a nasty divorce trial, in which her second husband's lawyer would ask her organist about his sexuality, as if to damage her credibility as a holy woman.

She could be very hospitable: J. Robert Bradley remembered staying at her house and being awakened so she could bake him a cake. When Dr. Martin Luther King, who had called Bradley his favorite singer, died, Bradley didn't have enough money to attend the funeral, "and Halie bought me a ticket." She protected some of her friends, bailing out a few when they were arrested on morals charges. Bradley remembered her telling a judge about one of her clones: "Your Honor, have mercy, please. I know he's a po' sissy, but he love the Lord." But she could also be curt and dismissive; you could be either her walking cane or her footstool. There's a famous tale, long told in gospel circles, that was finally printed in a recent history. Since the story is out, I thought it worth being told completely.

Mahalia was driving to a concert in Chicago. The other passengers were some of her closest friends—Robert Anderson, Alex Bradford, James Lee (the accompanist on "Move On Up a Little Higher"), and two others. She was driving too quickly, and a cop stopped her. Immediately she tried to charm him. "Officer darlin', you please let Halie go to her program."

"Your what? You're who?"

"Officer darlin', I'm Mahalia Jackson, the world's greatest gospel singer, and I'm going to my . . . concert."

"But ma'am, if you're such a great gospel singer, why are you riding in a car filled with men?"

"Officer darlin', these ain't men. These sissies!"

The published tale goes something like that. But two of the passengers completed the story for me. Once they drove off, a properly offended Robert Anderson said, "After all, Halie, couldn't you do no better than that?" And her regal reply was, "What the fuck, you want me to say you're cocksuckers?" On an equally unsympathetic note, she advised Carl Hall, a singer with the range of a lyric soprano and the lungs of a male, "Baby, you need to stay clear of those funny people. They'll steal your substance."

Mahalia's men took it all, the hospitality and the rude taunts. At her funeral, Robert Anderson sang "Move On Up"; his reading of the lines "It will be always howdy, howdy / And never goodbye" can freeze my bones forty years after. But the highest moment occurred when J. Robert Bradley was called upon to sing. He turned "I'll Fly Away" into a slow, emotionally devastating funeral dirge. By the time he had reached the verse "When the shadows of this life have grown, I'll fly away, / Like a bird from prison bars has flown, I'll fly away," there was no stopping the people. Reverend Cleophus Robinson, seated directly in front of Mayor Richard Daley, spun around in his mink coat. James Lee wound up collapsed on the floor.

During her tenure with the Ward Singers, the only group to match Mahalia's popularity during the early 1950s, Marion Williams acquired a slew of male fans. Just as her voice ranged from near-operatic soprano to the heavy growls of a storefront preacher, she combined the flair of both gospel and quartet. "I liked the way she'd drop from that light voice to that heavy quartet bottom," said Alex Bradford. The radio host Leonard Lopate has quipped that Marion was the greatest of all male quartet singers.

So the many men, from Bradford to Little Richard, who "mocked" her growls and notes were answering one kind of musical androgyny with yet another. This became clearer to me long after Marion had left the Ward Singers. In 1976 she appeared at New York's Town Hall for a Thanksgiving concert. Trying to induce the audience to sing along with her, she chose the hymn "Come, Ye Thankful People, Come," but they called out, "Too high!" "Too high?" she pondered, and dropped the song an octave. Now, obviously nobody would care to sing along with that kind of virtuoso—until a voice called from the balcony, "I'll help you, honey." A regal church lady stepped down and proceeded to take the mike from her hand. She sang like a taller Marion, rearing back, hitting notes with a hand on her left hip. Then, demurely, she returned the mike: "Here she is, the world's greatest." Only as she returned to her seat, grandly acknowledging the applause from every side, did I realize she was a man.

She was a well-known drag queen nicknamed Ruth Brown, whom I next saw a few years later when Marion sang at the New York club Sounds of Brazil. I had produced an album by Marion, *I've Come So Far,* and had invited some critics. There were several white fans, a scattering of modestly attired COGIC saints, and another group notable

Alex Bradford and Marion Williams, 1961. The great gospel men loved and learned from the great gospel women.

for its maternal elegance. "Look at those distinguished-looking church ladies," observed the writer Vivian Gornick. "They're not church ladies," I replied.

But they acted like them. During the first set, Marion turned *I've Come So Far* into an impassioned testimony. I scanned the room to see how the church saints were responding. As so often when the Spirit moves, it moves with speed. Two women stood, their eyes stabbed shut, their arms held erect above them. But standing between them, miming the same gesture, was Ruth Brown. Whether or not he was faking it, he had caught the Spirit as quickly as the saints . . . or understood that it was there for the capture.

Most of the crowd and all of the critics left after the first set. The audience for the second set included me, white fans like Leonard Lopate, and the drag queens. And for them, the same audience who had always been her most loyal and acute fans, Marion sang better than I'd heard her do in years. Lopate requested "The Day Is Past and Gone," an English hymn that Thomas A. Dorsey had turned into a brooding, bluesy vision of death. As she reached the song's most indelible line, "Death may soon disrobe us all of what we now possess," her neck began twitching. Leonard observed, "I don't know how anything can be so vulgar and so sublime."

She next sang "Farther On Up the Road," a Brewster composition from the Ward Singers days. The song climaxes with a run up the scale, "Farther on, farther on, farther on, whoo." As she neared the money note, all the church queens began clearing their throats. "No, babies," she commanded. "This one's for Mother. 'Farther on, farther on, farther on, farther on, WHOOOOO," and then, just to exert the power of ownership, she added her patented "WHOOO-HOOO." After that, all the children, led by Ruth Brown, got up and did the holy dance.

Ruth began to call me. She spoke of a troubled career, divided among the Gospel Highway, drag bars, and jail. She also recounted her adventures and run-ins with performers like Johnny Cash, who she said had spoken fondly of his episodes with men while in prison. She recalled being at Stonewall: "You know, some of those colored girls had come up in the church." I began to wonder if some of those brave queens proudly strutting up Christopher Street hadn't been summoning the image of their earliest models, the great gospel women. It seemed reasonable.

All the time Ruth kept saying, "I can sing, Mr. Tony. You need to hear me." Finally I accepted an invitation to a set she would perform at a pub called Sally's. This turned out to be a drag bar on Forty-third Street, diagonally across from the New York Times. I found the place forbidding. The drag queens were astonishingly pretty black and Puerto Rican youths. The bouncers, white and Puerto Rican, looked like murderers. Sally turned out to be Sal, a Louis Prima look-alike, and I began to think that I was not on holy ground, but mafia soil. I sat by myself and must have looked uncomfortable. But Ruth was gracious. She grandly offered a church welcome: "I want to introduce to some and present to others Mr. Tony. He work with Inez Andrews and Shirley Caesar and my heart, Marion Will'am'. Say hello, Mr. Tony." I stood, knees trembling, and waved to the children.

Fortunately, Ruth began to sing. She was indeed a powerhouse, a combination of Wilson Pickett and Little Richard, but better than either. She sang a typical soul repertory, including songs that predated her young audience. Her housewrecker was Sam Cooke's "Ain't That News" (adapted from an old spiritual with the same name). She called on Sal to join her, and while he gave it his Atlantic City all, she hit some gospel whoop notes—not quite Marion, but very superior Little Richard. During the instrumental break, Sal began to dance, an avuncular twist. Ruth did the only thing she knew how to do, the holy dance, executed with delicacy and finesse. After that she descended to her seat, from which she sang a brilliant if anomalous version of Otis Redding's "Try a Little Tenderness." The young ones began to surround her, smile modestly, and drop bills down her bodice. "Thank you, baby," she replied, very much the church's first lady.

After the set, I walked up to her. A middle-aged friend had gotten there first and was speaking church talk. "Child, you . . . sang, you sang for Jesus." "Ain't nobody mad but the devil," Ruth replied with a shrug. I bid her farewell: "You're terrific. You're better than most of the guys out there. You could bury Richard and Wilson and Al Green and . . ." Not for the first time, my responses, while heartfelt, may have been a tad hyperbolic. She simply shrugged. "Yeah, I know, I know, baby. I'd have been a star if I hadn't put on this dress."

—

During what I've defined as gospel's golden age (1945 to 1960), most of the male gospel stars were gay. Because their voices were as immense and virile as any quartet lead's, the quartets were not pleased by their arrival. Homophobic comments were rampant. Even if somebody stole the show, the quartets would mutter, "He ain't nothing but a sissy." Yet because quartet singers and gospel singers traveled together, their relations were usually amicable. A gospel keyboard man might sometimes accompany a quartet; a quartet guitarist might help a female group. When the various groups and quartets appeared together, they provided a cheering section for each other, ignoring genre divisions.

Despite the quartets' reputation as uninflectedly straight, the gospel singers insisted otherwise. As in culture after culture, the queens make fun of the butch guys' disdain. A prominent East Coast musician says, "The quartets always made themselves available." In some instances the men of both genres would engage in a sexual rivalry. One time in 1958 Sam Cooke began flirting with a teenage boy. Alex Bradford told him to watch out. "Sam, he may have his mother's features, but he have his father's fixtures."

Though gay men and lesbians had always been among gospel's greatest stars, Alex Bradford was the most flamboyant performer the church had yet seen, a Prophet Jones who could sing, play piano, compose hit songs, and direct choirs. He had a huge, gruff voice and the irrepressible urge to hit top notes like Marion Williams. He could also strut, Suzy-Q, and wiggle like her—a tape of the two performing in the gospel musical *Black Nativity* shows the two big-bottomed stars strutting in unison, as if they shared twin rear ends. Bradford's Alabama pal Dot Love said, "Junior always been the same. Always had showmanship, always mocked Marion."

Bradford was raised in Bessemer, Alabama, and was something of a wunderkind. He discovered certain things while very young. He was a local star before his voice changed. He had also been spotted and outed even earlier. When he was three an uncle raped him. Though he would be married twice, the second time to Marion's accompanist Alberta Carter, Bradford was the most famous gay man in gospel. "Junior could fool you," remembers one of his co-workers. "He could outsing any man, and then turn around and be such a girl. He could just be so *pure*." He had the huge neck of a stevedore and the exquisite manners of, as the idiom goes, "a great white lady." When he joined the army, an officer asked his post-service ambition. "Well," Bradford liked to recall himself saying, "I told him, 'I'd really like to be an . . . actress.'" He wasn't being cute; he simply didn't know the other word.

After years of directing choirs for churches that underpaid, and composing songs for Roberta Martin, who bought them for twenty-five dollars apiece, Bradford finally struck gold. He signed with Specialty Records, perhaps the finest gospel label of the day (its R&B talent included Little Richard and Roy Milton). His first record was his own composition, "Too Close to Heaven," a gospel blues that swept the nation; everyone sang it, quartet, choir, group, soloist. It remains a standard, and it was enough to push him onto the Gospel Highway.

Specialty's biggest artists were male quartets like the Soul Stirrers and the Pilgrim Travelers. Bradford had previously recorded with female groups, but he now assembled a male group, the Bradford Specials ("Specials" connoting their distinction from the all-female Bradford Singers). The members included Jonathan "Joe" Jackson, a former high-school athlete with a ringing, almost operatic tenor and a short but very powerful build; Louis Gibson, a dapper, light-skinned man with limited vocal abilities but physical charisma; and Charles Campbell, a large man, also light-skinned, who sang a steady and piercing alto. To say the least, they didn't look like good country mens. Putting them on the road with the Stirrers and the Travelers was a calculated risk.

They distinguished themselves from the street-garbed quartets with their gospel choir robes. One of their first gigs was in New Orleans at a concert promoted by Bessie Griffin. The mikes were set up on an islet surrounded by a few feet of shallow water. When the Specials walked on, the response was unfriendly. "Those country womens died laughing," Bradford recalled. "They saw our robes and thought they were dresses." He could feel the audience rejecting him and his group, a failure they couldn't afford so early in their career. He also knew that up close, he would have no problem. Facing a church, he would veer from glowing smile to Spirit-filled ugly face. He had dreamed up a form of choreography for his group, usually miming the gestures they might be describing in song ("running" they'd sing, and running they'd do). It seems banal and obvious today, but it was regarded as innovative in 1954. So there was only one solution. Charles Campbell loved to tell the story. "'All right, you bitches,' Miss Bradford said, 'a dollar a holler,' and we waded through de mud."

After that Bradford would hold his own with the quartets. One night when the church was his, Albertina Walker of the Caravans walked up to the Pilgrim Travelers' manager: "How 'bout that, Alexander? Sissies on fire tonight."

Bradford remained an elusive, chameleonic figure. He was a man of many faces and many names, referred to as Alec (usually pronounced "Elec"), Alex, Bradford, Junior, and quite often as Pearl or Pearlie Mae, in homage to Pearl Bailey, who had introduced the sharp, cutting tongue of a sanctified matron, Mahalia talk, to the world. He might speak proudly about opening doors for his brothers: "I think a lot of boys took heart after they saw me." But then he would try to behave conventionally, join a Masonic lodge and boast about his stepchildren. In 1963, he released a single titled "Am I Wrong." He enumerated his faults: "I like good liquor, am I wrong?" and "I like pretty women, Lord, am I wrong?" He had sailed too far into the vanguard. Disc jockeys broke the record into little pieces. Forty years later, that kind of self-examination would be all over the gospel charts. Kirk Franklin would confess his love of pornography, Donnie McClurkin would recount his childhood rape by an uncle, Bradford's testimony.

Yet the division between quartet and gospel remained intense. Quartets and their fans tended not to like the women singers—Dorothy

Love Coates, Ruth Davis, and Marion Williams might pass muster, but grudgingly—and actively disliked the males, excepting Brother Joe May, a former quartet singer himself with enough volume for Willie Mae Ford Smith to dub him "the Thunderbolt of the Middle West." Generally, they were dismissed as "singing like women."

The women recognized the gay men as their colleagues and allies, their mentors and musicians—but also their rivals. Bradford once informed Inez Andrews, "You girls have to hate me. I can scream like you or Marion and still got me what you all will never have . . . Ain't the Lord good!" A young Chicago tenor committed himself to imitating Inez, a tall, stately woman with the noble bones of her Indian ancestors and a four-octave range. Spotting him at a program, she'd send notes: "Which one of my records are you gonna sing tonight? Just so I can prepare my musician." Bessie Griffin put one wannabe in his place: "Baby, don't you forget that I'm real. You may be for real. But I'm real." Yet more often, the women recognized their need for gay fans. "Those quartets had the programs sewn up with all their girlfriends screaming as soon as somebody hollered 'Jesus.' If it wasn't for the children, we might not have gotten any shouts at all."

Particularly rich alliances were forged between gay men and lesbians. The church had always attracted forceful women. During the late 1920s, sanctified women like Sister Jessie May Hill and Reverend Mary Nelson growled and squalled like backwoods preachers. By the 1920s, such women had begun outsinging all the men. Madame Emily Bram, a sanctified contralto who lived into her nineties, began her travels team-preaching with her first husband. She'd begin the message; he'd continue. But she outdid him, and the sermon always ended with her.

Gospel's most famous lesbian was Ruth "Baby Sis" Davis. Where Bradford basked in his campy overkill, Baby Sis assumed a butch guise. She sported a short-cropped hairdo, whether processed or natural, indistinguishable from a man's. Beneath her choir robe, she might wear jeans and men's shoes (when Mahalia or Clara Ward were sporting rhinestone gowns and high heels). People said she sang as hard as a man. But with matchless charm she dared them to love her. Quartet women cheered her whenever she hit a stage, recognizing her as a female emissary from the guys' side. (She told me that her idol had been Dinah Washington, but her style resembled more that of Ira Tucker, lead singer of the Dixie Hummingbirds.)

There were also female quartets, who cultivated the same kind of a cappella or guitar-based harmonies as the men, and many of their performing traits. R. H. Harris's second wife, Jeanette, was the lead singer of a female quartet, the Golden Harps. To my mind, no quartet singer has ever outsung the young Harris. But he cut a clumsy figure onstage, and rarely moved from the microphone. "Jet" would romp around a church, working very much harder than her husband. Perhaps that's why many Chicagoans said that she was the better quartet singer.

This intramural battle had its sexual connotations. Hard-singing women were dismissed as "bull daggers." A woman couldn't win; she was either a "ho" or a "bull dagger," when all she wanted to do was sing gospel. By no means were female quartet singers invariably lesbian; many of them married preachers and/or quartet singers. But there was one who surpassed even Baby Sis when it came to taking on the men.

Willmer Broadnax was a very short, high tenor, nicknamed "Little Ax," in part because of his size, in part because his older brother, "Big Ax," was a popular baritone. Little Ax sang with many quartets. Initially his voice was as sweet, clear, and poignant as that of his model R. H. Harris. Then, as quartet singers grew louder and blunter, he became a heroic screamer, holding his own with some of the strongest leads, Archie Brownlee or Silas Steele.

I never saw Little Ax in person, though I admired his records, largely because there was something nonquartet about his delivery. It was impassioned in a way that I associated with women singers of his generation (he was born in 1915). Publicity photos showed a very petite fellow, inches shorter than his quartet colleagues, with the smoothest of complexions. In standing shots it was clear that his bottom could give Mahalia's or Marion's a run for the money.

Therefore I was not surprised that when, after Ax was killed by his girlfriend at the age of seventy-seven, the autopsy revealed he was not an anatomical male. A few quartet singers tried to say he hadn't fooled them. JoJo Wallace of the Sensational Nightingales said, "I always wondered about Ax." Claude Jeter of the Swan Silvertones remembered touring with Ax's various quartets when segregation meant that singers often couldn't use public bathrooms. (Marion Williams once said, "I've used many a leaf in my day.") But when the fellows stopped to urinate, Jeter says, "Ax'd always go off by himself." This is not wholly dispositive evidence; I might have been as gun-shy as Ax.

But the reality was that he had fooled almost everyone. The gospel children had imitated women for years, sang like them, performed like them. But even in fiercest drag, nobody hearing Ruth Brown would think her a woman. Many a fellow could sing as high as a lyric colora-tura, but none of them could pass as women, or even try. Ax, then, was exemplary. She sang as powerfully as any man; and if she didn't have a guy's volume, listeners could blame it on her lyric tenor and the reduced volume associated with light-voiced singers. If Ax had been a runner and a jumper, her big hips might have given her away. But she chose to be a "flat-footed singer" and not a "quartet clown"—a strategic choice, under the circumstances.

The division between quartet leads and gospel singers involved more than voice or vocal style or even performing outfits, suits versus robes. It was also inherent in their self-presentation and display of emotion. Outside of some storefront churches, men tended not to shout, and cer-tainly did not fall out or display extravagant emotion. It's true that their performances were very bold. Quartet leads would run down aisles as if lost in the Spirit. They would roar like preachers, each growl a mark of "sure 'nuff soul." But the audience expected them to behave like men and know when to stop. If their routines appeared a show, it's because most times they were. (This changed when Wilson Pickett's idol Julius Cheeks began to shout—a gesture he considered revolutionary: "I was the first one to cut the fool for the people." A few years later the Mighty Clouds of Joy, a group formed very much in Cheeks's image, became the kings of the Gospel Highway. After that, all the quartets began to shout, though usually in ways that seem far too synchronized to be spiritually inspired.)

But if the quartets were sober, the male singers grew drunk in the Spirit. Joe May and Alex Bradford ran around churches, dancing with a lissome grace that belied their huge butts and bellies. Young gay fans, many of them products of the more uninhibited smaller churches, got with the program. When the Spirit ran high, they would fall out as dra-matically as the women. One could see athletic contortions that almost defied a body's capacity, as if they were being drawn and quartered in the Spirit.

Quartet fans didn't like the male gospel singers' sound and were unsympathetic to their presentation. This would be true for white fans as well. One time the critic Jon Landau, speaking with a strong Boston accent, said, "I don't like Alex Braaaadford. He doesn't seem real to me." Bradford's vocal quality and his historical significance—in a word, his brand of "realness"—were lost on him.

Meanwhile, gospel singers didn't enjoy the quartets. If you like piano accompaniments, and piano-derived harmonies, the quartets may sound limited and uncreative. The English critic Simon Albury once asked James Cleveland whether he liked quartets. "I hate them," Cleveland replied. "But some of them have great harmony." "So? What is that?" Cleveland was that blasé because harmony is universal in the black church. The grand, sweeping sound of an instrumentally unaccompanied congregation has thrilled listeners for centuries. English tourists raved about it in the nineteenth century.

Though I love the top quartets, I can appreciate the gospel fans' dismissal of the lesser acts. Listening to *Fire in My Bones,* a three-disc anthology of local and amateur gospel singers, I felt myself thwarted and constricted. After several songs accompanied by plangent electric guitar, a piano and organ suddenly appeared, setting things up for a performance by a church congregation. There was no more talent exhibited, but the expansion of harmonic and melodic possibilities seemed like a deliverance.

Gay musicians and singers had grown up in small churches, attending free-will-offering programs, where local quartets sang like their heroes and like each other. "No individuality whatsoever," James Cleveland would mutter. (Of course, the local gospel acts fed off their heroes and heroines. There simply were fewer of these local groups.) And even if their vocal qualities were indisputable, the quartets were noted more for their clowning, for their transparent commitment to shouting the house.

If you were a smart young musician, you could easily grow sick and tired of quartet after quartet, running down aisles, summoning up memories of dead mothers, appealing to the most basic emotions simply to make a buck. During the golden age, all the singers, gospel or quartet, worked very hard. They would leave the stage raining down sweat. But within a moment, the same quartet lead who had caused a sanctified pandemonium would be cursing, drinking, and flirting with his local girlfriend. It was a game—hard, fascinating work, but still a game.

Herbert "PeeWee" Pickard, a brilliant Detroit pianist, had only cordial relations with the Pilgrim Travelers or Soul Stirrers while traveling with Brother Joe May, Dorothy Love Coates, and Alex Bradford. But the ubiquitous quartets rubbed his ears raw. "I'm through," he now says, "as soon as I hear a "We—e—ell" (the standard quartet opener that establishes a song's key and tempo).

Both quartets and gospel singers would accuse the other team of shamming. "They're not real, all they do is clown": the same complaint from either side. But since gospel plays such a saving role for the children, I'm willing to grant that their emotional involvement was more authentic. Quartet singers might cry in songs about their mother. But they tended to approach their vocation as a fun job, far better than work in a factory. The gospel singers, and particularly their gay musicians, saw their work as an evangelical art form, with some singers enjoying more the evangelism ("See how the Lord blessed us this evening!"), and others the art ("I don't want to brag, but we sang tonight!").

For many years gospel's biggest star was James Cleveland, a native of Chicago, and intermittently one of Alex Bradford's best friends. Both were gifted pianists (Cleveland being perhaps the superior) and singers (Bradford having by far the better voice), arrangers (again Cleveland) and composers (evenly split). For a while they led a local Chicago group, the Bradford-Cleveland Singers. Bradford had volume and range, but, as he admitted, "James is the quicker thinker on his feet." As gospel made its transition from traditional to contemporary, Cleveland—who as a child had become the mascot of Thomas A. Dorsey's church choir, and as a teenager had run errands for Mahalia—would become a superstar.

Cleveland projected a more conventional image than Bradford. Though he was widely recognized as gay—and would die of AIDS—he never "would switch [the church word for "swish"] like Bradford. James could make you think he was a man." In the early 1960s, Bradford dreamed up an annual convention of younger singers, a modern alternative to Thomas A. Dorsey's National Convention of Gospel Choirs and Choruses, where they still sang as if it were 1939. But Cleveland had greater organizational skills, and ran with the idea. He became the Workshop's founder, director, president, and symbol.

Whether or not he intended it, the Workshop famously became the annual convocation of gospel's gay youth. Good-looking young men would show up for a week's convention with enough clothes to last them a month. As the attacks on gay rights grew more virulent, the Workshop became the subject of nasty jokes. Even though many straight women and men showed up every year, the Workshop effectively institutionalized the gay gospel world. Now there was a time and place that the children could call theirs—even if it were never identified as that.

Some months after his death in 1991 Cleveland was outed in the national press with a *Jet* magazine article, "James Cleveland Infected L.A. Youth with HIV, $9 Mil. Lawsuit Claims." Yet an experienced

James Cleveland, 1970: the presiding figure in gospel between 1960 and 1980. Photograph by Stephen Paley

reader had been there before. Years earlier *People* had profiled Cleveland, and noted that the never-married artist had lived with a series of "nephews." *60 Minutes* had been contemplating a sequence on Cleveland and the Workshop, but after the allusion to "nephews," Ed Bradley decided to withdraw. (It was still a time when gay activities were regarded as shameful and, more particularly, an embarrassment to the race.) Unwittingly, *People* had revealed one of the gospel singers' most hallowed formulas: that a woman's significant other was not her "lover," much less "partner," but her "sister." The family metaphor didn't fool everyone. One great singer introduced a young man to his pastor's wife: "This is my son," he announced. "And moon," she added.

Cleveland also had a peculiar revenge on the quartets; he turned them into gospel groups. He did it all when he rearranged the old spiritual "I've Been in the Storm Too Long" for the Mighty Clouds of Joy. As he conceived it, the lead singer, Joe Ligon, would sing long passages without any vocal background, thereby making the whole idea of "quartet" irrelevant. Then he introduced chords and harmonies identified with choirs. Since then all the younger quartets pay homage to contemporary gospel in their arrangements or in their use of clichéd gospel devices. I have called these vocal tricks and overblown melisma "the gospel gargle" and "the Detroit disease." The quartets don't do them quite as often, but their sound has been transformed. Cleveland won the battle.

Something similar had occurred fifteen years earlier. When quartet leads like Sam Cooke, Johnnie Taylor, and Lou Rawls switched to rhythm and blues, they were stymied by the new musical demands. Singing for most of their careers either a cappella or with guitar accompaniment, they were unprepared to sing with pianos or female backup singers. All three turned to Robert Anderson—James Cleveland's mentor, Mahalia's close friend—for instruction. Thanks to his coaching, their ears opened, their styles evolved, and they became far more flexible and chromatic than they had been with the Soul Stirrers or the Pilgrim Travelers "clank-a-lanking" behind them. (They had also been more soulful in their quartet incarnations, but all three were glad to bid hard-singing days adieu.)

None of the Sam Cooke biographies mentions his debt to Robert Anderson. But then rock critics might be deaf to the distinction between singing "by the gee-tar" and singing "by the piano." My point is that Cooke and his friends were not; that's why they needed Robert Anderson. As he used to boast, "I took those quartet boys and introduced them to *melody*."

Perhaps it happens elsewhere—possibly in a battle between, say, the fans of *American Idol* and fans of heavy-metal music. But gospel gives a rare example of an aesthetic division that is also political, sexual, and ideological.

The closest analogy may be the late-seventies reaction against disco. Like a less pernicious version of Hitler's book burning, record albums were destroyed because they represented a music dominated by keyboards rather than guitars, and where the singers were not earnest, thin young white men but full-figured, ex-gospel divas—and, not incidentally, a form where the most loyal fans were gay men. About the time of the mass record burning, Ira Tucker complained to me that gospel had gone bad: "The sissies and bull daggers done took over." He displayed the same animus as the rock fans.

In the Bible, David says, "Weeping may endure for a night but joy cometh in the morning." So it was that in the discos, the children danced until dawn. Some former church boys admitted that when they cut loose, they were reviving the shout steps of their youth. They idolized the former gospel singers Patti LaBelle and Jennifer Holliday, not to mention Aretha Franklin, with the same fervor Ruth Brown had felt for Marion Williams. In terms of cultural dynamics, it was a startling replay: gospel divas and gay men working together to achieve a public and universal catharsis. In both places, a fellow could lose himself in his secret closet, dance with his eyes stabbed shut, stay in the Spirit for as long as he chose, and then leave, ready for life in an unfriendly land. In both places, the aim of the music was the same: transcendence, to be defined and measured individually. As Margaret Allison and the Angelic Gospel Singers sang,

> *You don't know what the Lord told me,*
> *You don't know, you weren't there.*
> *You don't know how and you don't know where,*
> *You don't know what the Lord told me.*

In both places, the children were fervently listening. The difference was that the disco offered the catharsis without the doctrine; all release, no self-hatred. By transporting the church's joy to the club, the children had given it a new life.

Just as the gospel world began to turn on its own, the children found a new place to have church.

The exchange of love between gospel divas and the men of disco became a phenomenon fully comparable to that between guitar heroes and their devotees. The difference—not a small one—was that while Pete Townshend sidewinded, his flock made ugly faces and played air guitar; when Patti LaBelle emoted, her flock started to dance, with as much elegance and abandon as their uncles had displayed, shouting off Dot Love or Marion Williams. There have been famously stressed moments. In a major rhetorical gaffe, the newly born-again Donna Summer (who had modeled herself on Mahalia Jackson) advised her flock that God had not intended Adam and Steve. She was obliged to apologize, poorly but often.

One of the most gifted singers was Loleatta Holloway. She was such a teenage wonder in Chicago that after Shirley Caesar left the Caravans, the group's founder and manager, Albertina Walker, chose Loleatta to replace her. With her corybantic showmanship and evangelical talents—as she once said, "My preaching is much more dynamic than my singing"—Shirley would subsequently become Evangelist Shirley Caesar, Pastor Shirley Caesar Williams, and, for over thirty years, the First Lady of Gospel. At seventy-three, she still retains the passion and most of the voice of her youth. Loleatta had the more impressive chops; in 1967, Shirley observed wryly, "She's selling voice. I'm selling virtue." But her tenure with the Caravans didn't last long, and in fairly short order she had followed Aretha Franklin into the secular field.

Another contrast would be the two women's attitude toward their numerous gay fans. Shirley Caesar has given altar calls, beseeching the "sissies and bull daggers" to "come up and be saved," and warning that homosexuals were "stealing our children." She has done so at major festivals in New Orleans and Boston, to some controversy. Loleatta was quite her opposite. Until her death at sixty-four, she too retained most of her youthful power. But she expressed only contempt for the tradition exemplified by her predecessor. She told reporters that she despised the church, with its abundance of hypocrites and backbiters. Instead, when she wanted to feel the Spirit, she preferred a gay club. That's where the people were "real."

And the interplay continues. In the late 1990s New Orleans hip-hop introduced a new dance step known as the Bounce, involving athletic spins of the gluteus maximus. A more extreme variant would be called the Sissy Bounce. Shades of all the choir directors who had strutted and sashayed like Mahalia and Marion, the Sissy Bouncers gave pride of place to the children: a former choir director renamed Big Freedia became a star of the movement. And harking back to the women audiences who flocked around Bradford and Cleveland, some of the Sissy Bouncers' greatest fans were women, emulating the men who were ostensibly emulating them.

The way Big Freedia presides over his flock recalls the activity in countless storefront churches, where the membership is almost exclusively female and the only men present are the pastor and the pianist. The women feel physically liberated in these men's presence; there is no sexual threat or tension. That's because it's *holy* ground. Freedia offers his girls deconsecrated holy ground, a place to be sexual where no man can harm them. To make this clear, he declares that he's big and very strong; he'll watch over them.

Actually, Loleatta had anticipated Big Freedia. There exist YouTube clips of her bouncing around a stage—in her exuberance, she may do a couple of push-ups—while young men dance beneath her. Both of these former gospel singers invoke a realm in which the representative of one sex beckons the members of another to express themselves more completely than they ever could in a strictly heterosexual context. In both cases, sexual segregation is necessary but not sufficient.

Once Marion or Dot Love had been obliged to outsing and outclown the quartet singers. Now the female Sissy Bouncers have added a new chapter to the battle of "real" and "for real."

———

I began attending gospel concerts at the Apollo Theater when I was fourteen, not perhaps the typical behavior of a son of German Jewish refugees. But my parents had a great respect for the culture; like many émigrés, they had visited Harlem soon after they arrived in New York. By seventeen I had acquired enough nerve to meet the singers, the men and women who have remained my idols. Many would remain in my life for years; and I even had the immense good fortune to produce a few, women like Marion Williams, Inez Andrews, and Dorothy Love Coates, men like Claude Jeter, Ira Tucker, and Alex Bradford.

About that time I began to visit the Hotel Cecil, a shabby hotel right next to the famous jazz club Minton's, where gospel and rhythm-and-blues talent would stay when they couldn't afford the classier Hotel Theresa. It was there that I was introduced to the very complicated gospel life. Alex Bradford invited me to his hotel room, where I met a group of elderly men and women, all clearly gay even to my untutored suburban eyes. There was also an effeminate young man with a southern drawl, and his boyfriend, a light-skinned, very handsome youth who looked like a graduate of the High School of Music and Art.

I found Bradford consoling a young woman with two black eyes and a bruised face. She said that a well-known singer and her brothers had attacked her for spreading the word that the diva was a lesbian. Bradford said, "That ain't nothing. Everyone in Harlem knows that child's a bull dagger." I was so green that I didn't know the term. But I could see that Bradford was presiding over proud and open gay people. After that I became very friendly with other denizens of the Cecil, among them Claude Jeter, the hotel's assistant manager and the most influential of all quartet falsettos (Al Green has acknowledged his inspiration). That friendship would last until his death at ninety-four in 2009.

But I pursued another kind of friendship with Bradford's singers—Joe Jackson, Louis Gibson, and Charles Campbell. Though I was not a complete novice, they introduced me to the range and variety of "the life," at least the gay life in Harlem. Once, Little Joe was showing me around the neighborhood when we passed a stout, light-skinned fellow weeping profusely. He was being led away by a stern, distinguished-looking man, a Ralph Bunche type. Joe informed me that he was "one of Harlem's top numbers runners," and that his companion had once been "the most beautifullest boy in New York." Here was a more gripping sociology than anything I had studied at Queens College.

Joe and Louis were young and extremely handsome. Bradford may have chosen them in part for their looks; he himself always admitted that "I may not be pretty but I've got *personality,* and the Lord stays faithful." Charles Campbell was the fattest man I'd ever met. And with my unerring lack of tact (my father often said, "My son is no diplomat") I asked him, "Charles, are you wearing a brassiere?" "Yes, baby," he said in a soft, womanish drawl. "I need to, son. My titties are too big."

Joe and Louis exposed me to a fast, glamorous circle, in which pride of place was offered to "freaks." They put a pressure on the word that I would hear later in the expression "down low," the term for men who sleep with men but don't consider themselves homosexual. A freak was someone who could do anything with anyone. Louis, like many gay men in gospel, had fathered at least one child. Joe advised me that nowadays advanced people had bid farewell to the old categories. That quartet singer who liked to have his dick sucked wasn't gay, he was "just a freak." All the singers seemed to agree that the old behavior had changed as well. A famous diva was "a freak. She'll give a man head before she'd give him her body." One fellow made the piquant observation, "Honey, fucking's gone out of style. It's too hard work."

The Bradford Specials didn't earn much, but they had their fun. Just as the quartet stars boasted about their women—and some of the most beautiful women I've ever seen would hang around the Soul Stirrers—the children had their own precious memories. As a track star in high school, Joe Jackson claimed to have slept with the great Jesse Owens, and he also boasted of a ménage à trois with a famous diva and Joe Louis.

Charles was very much less graphic. He was the house mother, invariably well behaved when not drunk. He was also Bradford's best friend, even though Alex would often spend the group's money on booze, boys, and song. "I'll always forgive him. That's the onliest man who ever gave me

something." But what about Smitty—
his partner—I'd ask. "I had to fuck for
that," he'd explain. Later I would learn
Charles's story. He had been raised by
a single mother, who occasionally supported them with sex work. As a boy
he had gone to the House of Prayer for
All Nations, the megachurch presided
over by Elder Lucy Smith, "and I just
cried like a little baby. She got up and
said nobody switching would ever go
to heaven. And that meant I might not
never make it in." He might have lost
his religion until he discovered Clarence Cobbs's church, where outlaws
and freaks of all kinds would have
a spiritual home. While some of the

*Charles Campbell as part of Alex
Bradford's group, 1955: a pillar of
the Chicago gospel community*

younger guys in Bradford's ensemble offered me a more glamorous tour
(and I would engage in some very tentative experimentation with two of
them—actions I never repeated with any of the singers I would later produce), Charles was offering me a rare form of wisdom. He liked me, too.
Many years later he would tell people, "Miss Bradford had gone off with
her trade and left Joe Jackson and me to starve at the Cecil—until that
cute little jewboy Tony Halyoubut went out and bought us pork chops. I
remember those things, I'm not easy to forget."

Bradford's singers came and went. None of that first crew of Specials
appeared with him in *Black Nativity*, the gospel musical in which he
co-starred with Marion Williams. By the seventies, he was appearing on
Broadway in shows like *Don't Bother Me, I Can't Cope* and *Your Arms Too
Short to Box with God*, both directed by Vinnette Carroll, one of *Black
Nativity*'s creators. Charles had returned to Chicago and was working as
a practical nurse when "Bradford summon me to Broadway. I told him,
'I can't half sing and you know I can't act.'" But Bradford needed his
buddy. He became involved in contractual battles with Vinnette Carroll
and believed that she and the producers had stolen his copyrights.

He could duke it out with Mahalia or Roberta Martin, and give con-
niptions to women like Dorothy Love or Marion Williams, who were
simultaneously his idols and rivals. But Carroll and her lawyers were

too big for him. He gave an angry interview to *The New York Times,* and Carroll patronized him by not replying. She wouldn't answer "Alex" because it would not be dignified. She knew those words would torment him. Bradford always said, "Don't rob a sissy of his dignity." In the midst of his lawsuit, he suffered a stroke. He lingered for a couple of weeks. But one morning Alberta Carter Bradford woke me up. "Tony, Alex passed." Without thinking I asked whether Charles was there. "Of course." He had flown in from Chicago, along with Smitty. I asked to speak with him. "Well, sir, you stayed true to the end." "Thank you, baby," he crooned. "I tried to."

That was 1978. It would be a good ten years before we met again. Robert Anderson volunteered to drive me to the home Charles and Smitty shared. I saw that he had lost a good hundred pounds and was drunker than ever. "Unh-uh," he said, smiling. "No, honey, you ain't my husband no mo'. Look at you, gotten old and almost bald as me. No, baby, you ain't my husband no mo'."

Clearly he felt I had neglected him while recording "ev'ry tired old sissy and bull dagger in Chicago." When I vouched my affection, he kept replying, "No, child, you ain't my husband no mo'." He then took to chastising me for my unbelief. "You say you an atheist. You stay with me, Tony Halyoubut, and you won't be no atheist. Robert know what I'm talking about. Mama gone." In other words, when you'd lost your only steadfast friend in the world, you would need somebody else to go your bond. Robert looked serious.

But I'd had enough. "Charles, I love you. You're one of my oldest friends. But you can't drink like this." "You can't tell me nuttin'. You ain't my husband no mo'." I decided to run with that. "Sorry, Charles," I said. "When I married you, I married you in sickness and health, for better and worse. And I traveled all these miles just to carry you from sickness to health . . . and from worse to . . . better." Everyone laughed, Robert Anderson was so tickled that he fell to his knees. Charles gave me a dirty look.

Bless his heart, he did hear me. Within a few months he called to say that he'd quit drinking. "You got to me, son." After that our friendship was rekindled. He would attend my record sessions, encouraging his old friends, many of whom had sung at First Church when he was a boy. I learned that he and his niece Patsy, another practical nurse, had taken on themselves the home care of some of their fallen brothers, "the children dying of the virus." Nothing bothered him. They cleaned the sheets and bodies, humored the men in their dementia, told dirty stories and played old records.

Sometimes Charles couldn't make it to a session. "You tell them a tired old lady says you go on and sing your song." The singers would laugh, and somebody invariably said, "Charles is such a sissy." I'd grow irate. "He shows me more religion than anybody in Chicago," and somebody else would say, "That's right."

As his health grew weaker, Charles would cherish his memories of Bradford. I began to understand the nature of their friendship. "I know he loved me. When he was living in Newark, we'd go to bars and some dude would say some shit about me, and Brad would leap over the bar and bust his head. America knew she was a woman, but Miss Bradford could fight." He spoke of nights when they'd sit together, not drunk, and reminisce about being Mother's children, little sissy boys without any visible support. How they'd come up without a father and without money, been 'buked and scorned, "called everything but a child of God." (And that meant "sissy" and "punk" along with all the racial epithets.) How they'd wept together over the sheer fact of their survival.

But he also had an unblinkered vision of his friend's follies. Bradford recorded a gospel blues that begins:

Some say the dead knows what the living is doing,
But to that school of thought I do not agree.
For if the dead knew what the living was doing,
There'd be someone worried about me.

Then he moans, Mahalia-style, and sings a magnificent gospel blues:

If my mother knew the trouble I was in, she'd comfort me,
If she could cross the river of Jordan,
She'd help me bear this old heavy burden.

"That's great, Charles," I'd say, noticing his unsympathetic face. "That's the song Bradford sang at a party at the Newport Folk Festival, and Joan Baez cried like a baby."

"It still ain't shit."

"What do you mean?"

"Olivia [Mrs. Bradford] knew what Junior was doing. Olivia wasn't going nowhere."

He exhibited a parental care for the other Bradford singers. Only two had lucked out: Rolland Hinton had become a school principal, and Carl Bean, one of Bradford's last singers, had recorded a disco hit, "I Was Born This Way," that qualified as a gay anthem, complete with a storefront testimony about the life he had been leading "since I was a little boy." (The title would be echoed thirty years later by Lady Gaga.) After an unsatisfying round in show business, he would start Unity Fellowship, the first black gay church, as well as the Minority AIDS Project. I asked Charles whether Bradford would have been proud of the group's "Baby Boy." "You never knew with her. She played games. But I'm proud as I can be." He still wept over the fates of one Bradford Special, a drug addict who spent years in jail, and another who wound up a drunk, freezing to death on the streets of Chicago.

He had never been impressed by their famous conquests. "So what if Joe had Sam Cooke. Sam turned around and got him hooked on dope. Thanks for nothing." Jesse Owens? Joe Louis? "Shit, when I was a little boy, selling my body, I had more football players and aldermen than . . . Sheeish! I was smooth and light-skinned and I had my girlish titties. I'll match my trade with them any day of the week. I don't care who they fucked. They still wound up on the streets." He managed to send money across town to Little Joe, who had been reduced to selling pencils on the street while seated in a wheelchair. Perhaps coincidentally, Joe died a few days after Charles.

After Charles's death I became friendly with his partner, Smitty, a well-spoken man who had held a government job for forty years. The two behaved like any old couple, constantly sniping at each other. Carl Bean said there were knock-down fights over which one was truly saved: Smitty, a stalwart, old-school Baptist, or Charles, who had come up in the wild and woolly Spiritual Church. I told Smitty that such debates didn't interest me: "You know I'm not really a believer." "I think Charles was like that," he'd say, not in judgment. Instead he suggested that Charles had made church his secret closet. Toward the end Charles told me, "I can go into those little churches and see all those poor women and sissy boys shouting and praising God. Like my grandma sang, 'Tell God all about it after a while.' And I'll just cry and cry for the people. Don't know why."

He had devised a solution for dealing with the backbiters and hypocrites. "I just know 'em . . . and they know that I know 'em. And I see them. And like Mama said, I love 'em right on." Once I was riding to a session with Charles and two of First Church's grandest stars, the pianist Ralph Goodpasteur and the contralto Madame Irma Gwynn. I mentioned one of Chicago's most famous sanctified families, paying particular tribute to their mother. "Yes, yes," said Irma, "that's a God-sent preaching woman." Charles was equivocal. "All right, maybe so. But to me she always been offish. In fact that whole sanctified troupe strike me as offish."

He paused contemplatively. "That's all right. I'm offish too." Irma chimed in, "I *know* I'm offish." Charles looked at me. "Yes, boy?" "All right," I said, paraphrasing a gospel hit, "sign me up for that offish jubilee."

Without lesbians and gay men there could be no gospel music. I'd known it for years but had avoided discussing it in print. But after the church abandoned its responsibility toward gay men suffering from AIDS and, adding insult to injury, began to swim in homophobia, I resolved to write this essay.

Charles had told me so much over the years. Nobody had ever doubted he was gay, but homophobia was pouring forth from men whose histories were virtually indistinguishable from his. Could I tell his story and quote him? "Sure, baby. I think it needs to be told. It all needs to be told." He paused. "You write on, son. Nothing can harm me now. Mama's gone."

AIMEE'S SONS

The gay contribution to black gospel is crucial and fundamental. Even the straight singers were productively engaged with the children. But for many years it struck me as unlikely that similar behavior existed in white gospel. The white Pentecostal churches appeared so moralistic and puritanical, and their members so staunchly red-state American. In such an unfriendly environment, gays couldn't thrive, could they?

So most of America thought until the scandal of Ted Haggard. As the head of the National Association of Evangelicals, the Colorado Pentecostal was the most influential evangelist in America—far more so than the loopy Pat Robertson or the discredited Oral Roberts. Like Robertson with his Family Network or Paul and Jan Crouch with their Trinity Broadcast Network, Haggard used the media to spread his message throughout the world; he boasted of disciples in the Ukraine, churches that shared his intense dislike of socialism and homosexuals, hatreds that he considered equivalent.

Haggard's exposure by a male prostitute whom he had patronized for years was a real shocker. Not merely to the saints, who had lifted holy hands while he decried the feminists and homosexuals who were ruining God's country. Jeff Sharlet, a very bright observer of the religious right, admitted that he had not seen it coming; homosexuality was the one element he had never considered. Caleb Crain offered a sympathetic but wrongheaded view that Haggard was a man too naive to recognize his own sexuality. In his view, such a man could well believe that he might pass unharmed through a fire ten times hotter than it ought to be. As one of the chosen, he could allow himself what he'd forbid any other man.

The news stunned Haggard's flock. One black gospel singer was less surprised. "Soon as I saw Ted I knew that was my white sister." When Brother Walter Stewart saw a video clip of Haggard embracing hunky young members of his congregation, and chuckling over the abundant sex lives they had enjoyed since Jesus came into their hearts, he couldn't stop laughing. "You see those holy hands stroking those fine young men? They know what they doing!" But Haggard's own members swore they hadn't picked up on the signs.

One tormented young gay man took a horrible revenge. Matthew Murray, a twenty-four-year-old from Englewood, Colorado, had gone through several intense and unavailing attempts to deliver him from his sexuality. He began posting comments on an online site, ex-pentecostals .org, about the blazing hypocrites who had driven him mad. In May 2007, he wrote that he didn't need the prospect of eternal punishment. "I already live in Hell every single miserable day. Yeah, no matter what, I'll be going to Hell, and many pastors, including Ted Haggard, will be down their [sic] in chains, to be my sex slaves." On December 9, he killed two people at Youth with a Mission in Arvada, Colorado, two at New Life Church in Colorado Springs, and then himself.

As mentioned earlier, the white Pentecostal church's roots begin with the putative homosexual Charles Parham. Gay men and lesbians have played a leading role ever since. For example, A. A. Allen was once a world-famous evangelist and healer, the immediate forerunner of Jimmy Swaggart (who recently compounded his disgraces by observing that if a man gave him a suggestive look, "I'd kill him and tell God I lied").

His audience comprised poor southern whites and blacks. Indeed, his services were integrated from the start. On YouTube, you can see clips of his choirs from the 1960s, filled with cute, innocent-looking whites singing black gospel in an idiomatically correct fashion, usually led by the African-American Gene Martin, who recycled the styles of Ruth Davis and Jackie Verdell of the Famous Davis Sisters. While Janis Joplin was trying to sing black, these youngsters were succeeding at the task.

Allen was a classic American type. He resembled a young James Cagney in good fighting form, and enjoyed playing the gospel wild man. Church communities were split between those who thought he was God-sent and those who considered him a transparent charlatan. Allen liked the notoriety, basked in the ambiguity. He dared his critics to expose him. But, as Thomas A. Dorsey wrote, "Your sins will find you out." When he died, the autopsy revealed that he was suffering from cirrhosis of the liver. Somebody observed, "That liver must have been marinating for years, seeing how much whiskey Allen consumed." He also liked men—not exclusively, since he too had a wife and children. (By now, you will have gathered, that has never thwarted the children in their pursuits.)

One night Allen and a black boyfriend wound up in a Philadelphia club that had begun featuring gospel groups. The leader spotted him and recognized his date. "I got devilish. I said, 'We want to acknowledge the presence of that great man of God A. A. Allen. We're gonna sing for Brother Allen a song made famous by Philadelphia's own Clara Ward . . . 'Let Us All Go Back to the Old Landmark.' I promise you Allen and his trick were out of there before we finished the song."

Gays played a formative role in the Jesus movement that swept working-class, hippie communities in the late sixties. No product of the movement was more evident than a young man evocatively named Lonnie Frisbee. He had a reputation for drawing in street kids and surfers, having found a voice and tone that could appeal to a drug-saturated generation. His responses were as often "Wow!" and "Outtasight!" as "Praise the Lord!" He was ambitious enough to move from the Jesus movement's arena of former drug addicts and street people to the more bourgeois circle of Kathryn Kuhlman, a healer famous for pointing her hand at whole rows of people, who proceeded to fall back in their seats, slain in the Spirit.

Eventually Frisbee aligned himself with the Vineyard Movement, a newfangled church founded by John Wimber, the onetime pianist for the Righteous Brothers, a place that welcomed the latest signs of charismatic blessing, holy laughter and Spirit-filled aerobics. (It was in this church that Bob Dylan was briefly saved and sanctified.) Frisbee then had covered all the Pentecostal bases. But Wimber dropped him after he was outed. In his final years, like many a former gospel star, he was reduced to small-time revivals. Like Sister Rosetta Tharpe in her last days, reminding the storefront churches that once she'd been their queen, Frisbee told his flock, "I need to tell you, I moved in big circles." His death from AIDS was most notable for allowing some pastors to gloat over the passing of the original Jesus Freak.

They were equally dismissive of two gospel stars. Ray Boltz is middle-class, middle-of-the road, a singer more out of Billy Graham than Oral Roberts. His friendly songs about Christian family life would fill a particular niche, and his albums have gone gold. When he came out recently, his fans were thoroughly shocked. Many of the comments on YouTube after he posted his latest single, "Don't Tell Me Who to Love," warned that God was not mocked, and invoked Sodom and Gomorrah. A more musically intriguing figure is Kirk Talley, who began singing with a southern gospel group, the Talleys, comprised of himself, his sister, and his brother. White Pentecostals made the Talleys an iconic group. Many years ago I saw Kirk share a TV camera with his sister and whistle "Just a Closer Walk with Thee" with soul and finesse. His sweet alto, a down-home countertenor, was unusually expressive.

In recent years he began to perform songs I found maudlin, all about sad, lonely people, praying themselves through nights of sorrow. I heard in them a Pentecostal Rod McKuen, and perhaps my instincts didn't betray me. In retrospect his songs were an honorable *cri de coeur*. His coming out was a profounder shock than Boltz's, but only to the extent that Pentecostals are so vocally homophobic. It was as if the church's fairest boy had betrayed them all. His dates were canceled, and his family refused to speak with him.

Almost as scandalous as Ted Haggard's exposure was the revelation that Paul Crouch, co-founder with his wife, Jan, of the aggressively anti-gay Trinity Broadcast Network, had paid $425,000 to his black chauffeur. Crouch declared that he was spotless, but as in Michael Jackson's twenty-million-dollar payout to the family of a young boy who had shared his bed at Neverland, the money belied his words. Another Paul, the Pentecostal guru Paul Cain, one of the last surviving colleagues of the prodigious faith healer William Branham, would be obliged to come out in his mid-seventies, admitting that he was both an alcoholic and a homosexual. (As the best-known prophet of the Vineyard Movement, Cain often spoke of his private chats with angels, his secret closet being just that capacious. Some of his followers considered him an "apostle," a title he shunned, though many black evangelists have claimed it.)

For many years the most loving historian of the early Pentecostal leaders was a writing pastor named Roberts Liardon. He especially celebrated those figures with a checkered past—a surprisingly large number—titling his book *God's Generals: Why They Succeeded and Why Some Failed.* Kathryn Kuhlman, Lonnie Frisbee's friend, ended her life on a note anticipated by Aimee Semple McPherson. For years she had featured on her television programs a young Greek pianist named Dino, who brought Liberace to the revival arena. "Here he is," she'd introduce in her Carol Channing contralto, "Dee . . . noooo." But he was unkind enough to accuse her of hitting on him, making her seem a lecherous old lady. She became sick and, ignoring the commandment "Physician heal thyself," entered a hospital, where neither prayer nor the doctors could save her. Roberts Liardon was particularly moved by her story. He wrote widely read passages about her lonely death, and mildly chastised her for marrying a divorced man with two children—not Aimee Semple hijinks but still morally questionable, though he gave her the benefit of the doubt. If he didn't, all those healings and deliverances would lose their savor.

He also became a star within the circuit of megachurches, black as well as white, by recounting his dream vision of heaven. There he had found a room filled with spare body parts, all of them unclaimed by those of little faith. (This tallied with the Word of Faith movement's belief that all things good, from houses to healing, await the enlightened saints.) He too would be forced out after he was accused of sleeping with his church's youth pastor. But disgrace wouldn't make him lose his religion.

He would return, preaching now to gay fundamentalist congregations, even though the concept seemed like a contradiction in terms, along with Tammy Faye Bakker, who had managed to move from the severe right-wing strictures of the 700 Club to become a kind of earth mother in gay circles. Of course, as a type she was almost too ideal, a female Liberace, exulting in her excesses and bad taste. Her son, Jim Jr., would eschew the rococo excesses of his parents' PTL Club. He targeted punk kids and became a vehement supporter of gay rights. (Similarly,

Bishop Carlton Pearson, a light-skinned black Pentecostal and graduate of Oral Roberts University, was once a star of the religious right and had contemplated a career in Oklahoma Republican politics, thereby allying himself with far-right figures like Senator James Inhofe. But as rumors swirled that he was coming out, he began preaching "a gospel of inclusion." That meant a nonjudgmental gospel, in which homosexuality was no longer a sin, the cross having vanquished sin. He said that his deepest spiritual experience occurred when Bishop Yvette Flunder, a black former Pentecostal preacher, laid hands on him and washed his feet. Virtually his entire following fled. He was reduced to preaching to the faithful albeit "inclusive" few.)

But Liardon abandoned the inclusive movement. Along with Paul Cain and Ted Haggard, he underwent a process of "restoration," a program of fasting, prayer, and steady consultation with the elders of the church that promised to remove every homosexual impulse. At least in Haggard's case, it didn't take. Sounding like the abandoned Lonnie Frisbee, he told *GQ* magazine, "People are, at their core, hateful," and he compared New Life, his old church, to "the Soviet Union," strong words from the old red-baiter. He and wife would open a new "inclusive" church that welcomed gay members, though it would not marry them. As for himself? "I think that probably, if I were twenty-one in this society, I would identify myself as a bisexual."

—

In their devotion to Kathryn Kulhman, Lonnie Frisbee and Roberts Liardon resembled the black gospel children, men who have devoted themselves to a sacred diva. The dynamics were astonishingly alike. And to find an equivalent of the gospel singers' worship of their Mahalias, in 2008 one of YouTube's most popular clips showed an effeminate young man named Chris Crocker screaming in evangelical fashion, "Leave Britney alone." He was on Holy Ghost fire for his diva, and his delivery was almost a caricature of a black drag queen, Ruth Brown born again as a skinny white boy. He boasted that he spoke fluent "ghetto as a second language," and dared black "girls" to call him a racist. It's almost too perfect to learn that he had been raised by his Pentecostal grandparents.

This has proved a worldwide phenomenon. During the early nineties the biggest star in Brazilian pop music was Edson Cordeiro, a short, campy man, who gloried in his vocal range from baritone to coloratura soprano. He scored a huge hit with his version of one of Mozart's Queen of the Night arias . . . and to extend the unwitting similarities with black gospel music, his co-star was a butch singer named Cássia Eller, singing "Satisfaction" in a deep contralto. Cordeiro too had been raised in a Pentecostal church, the São Paulo branch of Aimee Semple McPherson's Church of the Foursquare Gospel. He too had rolled for Jesus and spoken in tongues—until the pastor molested him.

But he retained the church's fire. He recorded a disco album, including the universal gay anthem "It's Raining Men." At its conclusion, he began to mutter in English, "Thank you, Jesus—thank you, Lord." When I told that to Bishop Carl Bean, he said, "Sounds like something Bradford would say." Or, for that matter, Father Mychal Judge, the priest martyred on 9/11. He used to stand on a corner in New York's Chelsea, speaking to his good friend the gay activist Andy Humm. As each night's flock paraded by, he'd say, "Isn't God wonderful?"

For another half-devout, half-blasphemous recasting of Pentecostalism, consider the avant-garde artist Rod Athey, whose risky exploration of body art drew the condemnation of Senator Jesse Helms. Scourging his body, broadcasting his HIV-positive status, Athey has attempted a mind-boggling synthesis of love, pain, and deliverance. It would be familiar to any born-again believer: "No cross, no crown." Athey too was raised in a Pentecostal church. He has condemned everything about its theology but retained a fascination with its flamboyant women, the McPhersons and Kuhlmans. At the end of his 2005 "opera," *Judas Cradle,* he one-upped Edson Cordeiro by actually speaking in tongues.

The wiliest survivor may be a singer named Larry Hart. Like Kirk Talley, he was a boy wonder, traveling with the Hart Family Singers and winning crowds with an Alex Bradford–like form of anointed camp; his rangy tenor flew into a soprano register, and he strutted more than Vestal Goodman, the idiom's house mother. By his early twenties, he was the biggest name in white Pentecostal music, winning a Grammy award for a switched-on version of "What a Friend We Have in Jesus"; he accepted the award garbed in an outfit that outflanked Liberace and Elvis Presley. Fast-forward thirty years, and he was now calling himself "the gay Martha Stewart of Las Vegas."

His mother, once a Pentecostal evangelist, now ran a bed-and-breakfast for newlyweds. Their house was a meta-Graceland, a miracle of hyperventilated rococo, of cheap goodies that he had stapled, glue-gunned, and reconfigured into a phenomenon worthy of attention in *The New*

York Times. To a reporter he confessed a childhood that would be most familiar to any of the gospel children. "The little time I had in school, I was the one who never got picked for anything—the outsider, most certainly the ugly and fat duckling." (This elaboration of the idiom bespeaks an uncauterized wound.) "Part of the attraction to the shiny and beautiful is maybe an externalization, maybe feeling there was nothing I could do about me." So instead he became a child star of the church, white gospel's answer to Michael Jackson. And then he became too real for the saints. "The world of gospel music set their crosses on fire." Where Ted Haggard discerns the Soviet Union, he sees the Ku Klux Klan.

Only someone who has escaped to tell the tale would dare to say that.

By 2010 Hart was still singing and composing gospel musicals (one of them partially bankrolled by Michael Jackson), but he and his lover were also producing events and still dabbling in the wilder forms of interior design. In a demo video for a proposed TV show called *The Harts of Vegas,* he can be seen performing for his mother in their home. As she stares bemused, he sings a bawdy tune entitled "Cock Talk." The old saint replies, reasonably, "That's really dirty. You all go to hell over that, Larry." "No," he replies. "It's really funny."

My guide to the gay life within white Pentecostalism was a young Tennessean named Shannon Williams. For me, the child of émigrés, Shannon had the sunny, all-American look of a Huck Finn or Tom Sawyer. His father was killed while serving in the army during World War II, and he was raised in the country by a single mother, a hardworking woman, active in her church. He would play tapes where the trumpets and accordions reminded me of Aimee Semple McPherson services. "Oh, no, Tony, we weren't that rich. I'd say we were one step above snake handler." I once tried to draw a complicated distinction between white and black Pentecostalism. "That's too deep, Professor. I'd say they were emotionally about the same." But, I argued, black gospel is the music of people who have nobody to depend on—no government, no social institutions, no friends, no—

"I'd say," he shut me off, "it's about the same."

We also had dissimilar views of the gay role in gospel. Where I saw it as a world gays had made their own, he foregrounded a sexual appeal. "Oh, I don't know, Tony. You got this beautiful man, with those fine features, and he's your lover for life. All that holy stuff is so sexy. Laying holy hands on somebody's body. Letting him use you, and come into

your heart, and just go all *through* you. Now, you know that's hot!"—
and he'd conclude with a giggle. Even to a nonbeliever, his analysis
seemed blasphemous. Surely all that passion couldn't be reduced to a
willful sublimation!

But his analysis chimes with the memories of Professor Michael
Warner, a leading figure in queer studies. He was yet another fatherless
child, raised by a Pentecostal mother, and spent much of his youth in
church. Though he admits that it sounds very "superstitious," he too
would receive a pastor's touch and fall back on the floor—except that
whenever he heard the words "In the name of Jesus," he imagined the
beautiful actor Jeffrey Hunter laying holy hands on his adolescent body.
(Smitty, Charles Campbell's partner, would not have been susceptible.
About Hunter's performance of Jesus in *King of Kings,* he said, "That's
some Hollywood shit—a blonde Jesus. Don't they know he had hairs
like lambswool and feet like polished brass?") The more common dismissal of charismatic ecstasy is that it's a kind of sanctified foreplay. For
generations outsiders have drawn a connection between holy rolling and
sex: according to the myth, nine months after the spring revival, all the
young women started having babies.

Shannon began playing piano for the traveling evangelists ("those
cute, stout guys with their marcelled hair waves," the male equivalent of
the women with "Pentecostal hair," a rather derogatory and class-based
description of holy women who shun makeup and save their vanity for
their abundant hairdos—campy Larry Hart even wrote a song about
them, "Big Hair Gets You Closer to God"). In his eyes, they all seemed
gay—or at least much more flamboyant than the next fellow. "They
looked like Liberace, and the women loved them like they was their
sons." They would be his first lovers. I spoke to one, who had left the
church and become a shoe salesman in Times Square. He still remembered his most famous sermon, "When God Gave Some Pigs a Permanent Wave." He also said that Shannon could play a better Pentecostal
piano than Jerry Lee Lewis.

Mrs. Williams worked hard to send Shannon to Lee College, a Pentecostal school; he remembered nightly prayer services that invariably
ended with his classmates lying slain in the dormitory hallways. "I had
to creep over the boys. Yeah, sure, I had me a few." He might have had
himself a few more. On a YouTube clip, an angry graduate, still smarting
from the years of institutionalized homophobia, claims that everyone
knows that Lee is filled with gay men. ("As a former student I wish I had

a nickel for every guy I knew in the Lee Singers who was queer as the day is long but stayed closeted for their parents' sake and to finish their degree.")

But Shannon had discovered that he preferred black men, not the boys of Lee. He found himself in the happy position of A&R man of Nashboro Records, the South's biggest gospel label. Initially he followed the money, preferring the contemporary choirs and the hit-making male quartets to the older traditional singers. After Nashboro folded, and he became the store manager of a Radio Shack, his tastes realigned. Now Clara Ward, Marion Williams, and Mahalia Jackson filled his dreams; and the Roberta Martin Singers' *Prayer Meeting* was his desert-island disc.

Shannon was quiet, dry, constantly laughing but not witty himself, and excruciatingly honest. He had one of those voices with a limited emotional range. Whether he was telling me something funny or horrifying (his former lovers dying of AIDS, his own emotional breakdown), his tone never varied. When one of his lovers quit him for a wealthy black doctor, he went "half-crazy" and saw a psychologist, who to his extreme surprise kept asking about his dreams. He was shrewd but not sophisticated, and his politics were extremely right-wing. When we met in 1970, he kept informing me that Richard Nixon was our greatest president and that the student movement made no sense at all. I used to joke that he'd have been a Klansman if he hadn't fallen in love with the black penis.

He had many lovers, as many quartet singers as gospel. At first I assumed that he was simply servicing the good country men of quartet. But Shannon, who had made me his confidant, described the activities. Though he invariably played the bottom role, he made it clear that the quartet singers were fully engaged, not supercilious straight boys "giving up nothing." In early 2003, he was gladdened when a local quartet singer asked to see him and thanked him for revealing a world of pleasure he had never found with his wife. "One of those good country boys, and he ain't never forgot me."

After his beloved David left him for the doctor in D.C., his sex drive shut down. As we neared our sixties, I asked him which was better, the strength of youth or the wisdom of age. "I don't know," he said, as emotional as I'd ever heard him. "But I'll tell you this. I wouldn't want to go back there again." Instead, he spent his nights playing poker on the computer, or joining some of Nashville's best gospel musicians in card games, where he'd continue to lament David. He used the Internet to track down his father's army records. He'd have dinner with his cousins, two women who had also grown up in the Pentecostal Church but were proud backsliders. "They say it was all just lies." He hadn't quite given up on the church. When extended, universal outbursts of laughter became a Pentecostal phenomenon, he showed up to see for himself. "Tony, I know what you'll say. And I guess it *was* ridiculous. But it's contagious." Sure, I'd reply, laughter will open those pores.

Such were our semiannual chats over a period of thirty years. Shannon told me that he had begun expressing symptoms of high blood pressure. But I was most unprepared when David called me. Though they were no longer together, the two spoke every morning, and it was after Shannon failed to pick up the phone that David pleaded for cops to break down his door. They found him dead in his bed. David and the cousins gave him a most private funeral, burying him next to his mother. A few days later some of his black soulmates called me, furious that they, who had laughed and drunk and wept with him, had not given him a true gospel funeral: "Every singer and musician in the South would have shown up." To my distress, they assumed that I had been Shannon's best friend, which indicated that those semiannual calls had been perhaps the only revealing moments of his life.

When I began this essay I asked Shannon to include his story. "Sure, help yourself."

"And call your name, too. Are you okay with that."

"Sure, just make sure to publish it before I pass"—words that seemed a joke, considering that he was a year younger and very fit. But, like Charles Campbell, he didn't get to read about himself. And, just like Charles, he had offered me carte blanche. I could tell it all, he said, because—well, because "Mama's gone on home."

WRITING IT OUT

At the end of *Paradise Regained,* after rhetorically vanquishing Satan, Milton's Jesus returns to his "mother's house." This is a typically daring invention, granting a human identity to a character who has only begun to view himself as his Father's son. It is also a witty allusion to the famous passage where Jesus says, "In my father's house there are many mansions." The divine Milton tells us that after forty days and nights in the desert, the son of man heads for a woman's abode. In my father's house may be many mansions, but in my mother's house are secret closets.

The literary trope linking mother, Christ, and same-sex love exists well outside the storefront church. A homoerotic vision of the Bible is at least as old as Michelangelo and Caravaggio. If anything, it has persisted even after the loss of faith. This became clear to me when I started writing about Thomas Mann's *Joseph and His Brothers.* Mann always delighted in finding homoerotic tendencies in great men. He had no trouble imagining the mythically vain Joseph as a beautiful seventeen-year-old, lusted after by his father, Jacob, just as Mann had once flirted with his thirteen-year-old son Klaus. He also, impishly but correctly, imagined God as a jealous and spiteful companion, demanding his beloveds' foreskins as a token of ultimate faith.

Mann's son Klaus, openly gay and sadly partial to sentimentality, imagined a pantheon of great men presided over by an "incredibly handsome" Christ. Mann's son-in-law W. H. Auden wound up in church, though it seems that, much like Charles Campbell, what drew him was the spirit and fellowship; instead of Catholicism, the most popular religious port of call, he chose the smaller Russian Orthodox Church, the equivalent of the storefronts where Charles found his spiritual home. As campy as any gospel singer, Auden would refer to the temper tantrums of "Miss God."

Constantine Cavafy, the Greek poet championed by Auden, wrote a startling poem titled "In Church." As G. W. Bowersock has noted, Cavafy loves the ritual and ceremony of Byzantium, but he is equally charmed by its exclusively male atmosphere, the monasteries closed to women. Bowersock wittily compares the twentieth-century poet with an eighth-century forerunner, Abu Nuwas, writing "in luminous Arabic" about a desirable young man. First he wishes to be his priest—or better yet, the metropolitan of his church (as King Louis H. Narcisse would preside over young members of his congregation). But then he wishes to become the Bible itself, or the eucharist he swallows, or the chalice from which he drinks. This resembles Prince Charles's desire to be reincarnated as his lover's tampon.

The most famous of Catholic poets, Gerard Manley Hopkins, demonstrates a similar confusion of faith and desire, though his is a far less joyous experience, riddled with guilt and self-hatred. At the age of twenty, he would be drawn to the church by a sixteen-year-old boy named Digby Mackworth Dolben, who had composed Cavafy-like poems about a hunky Christ ("Then, my own Beloved . . . Lay me on thy Breast"). Ashamed of his desire for Dolben, Hopkins joined the Jesuits at twenty-one and wrote a friend that from now on "my sap is sealed. My Root is dry." Toward the end of a short life, harrowed by shame and disease, he composed "Thou Art Indeed Just, Lord."

> *Why do sinners' ways prosper? and why must*
> *Disappointment all I endeavor end?*
> *Wert thou my enemy, O thou my friend,*
> *How wouldst thou worse, I wonder, than thou dost*
> *Defeat, thwart me? . . .*

Any gospel lover will recognize the eschatology of "Farther Along" ("Then do we wonder why others prosper, / Living so wicked year after year") and the yielding masochism of both hymns ("Whatever my lot thou has taught me to say, / it is well, it is well with my soul") and gospel songs ("I am in want almost every day / But it may be the best for me"). The apposite text would be Job's affirmation "Yea, though he slay me, yet shall I trust him," a confession once parodied as "Kick me, Jesus, down to my knees" (sung to the tune of "Beat Me, Daddy, Eight to the Bar"). Both Cavafy and Hopkins share a vision of religion without women, church that is a men's club rather than a mother's house. (That may simply mean it is not Protestant, and thunderously not Pentecostal—no women sobbing and shrieking, no feminine distraction from the displays of male power and beauty.)

In America the fundamentalist church is regarded as vehemently anti-intellectual. Its most illustrious figure is the Assemblies of God hero John Ashcroft. But, most likely because Pentecostalism in Great Britain is identified with the charismatic invasion of the Anglican Church, that country has produced several eloquent apostates. The critic James E. Wood has written of services in his father's church, at which overweight teenagers would dance throughout. Jeanette Winterson has written more affectionately about her working-class mother's Pentecostal church. But Sarah Kane spoke witheringly of her early years in a charismatic church. She loved the words Samuel Beckett gives Hamm in *Endgame* when he realizes that his prayers will not be answered: "The bastard! He doesn't exist!" According to friends, when she visited New York, she might see a black street preacher in Times Square screaming about the sinner's terrible fate. Most people would pass him by; a surprising number, while not sharing his belief, would find him quaint and folkloric, a charming piece of local color. But she would scream right back at him that he was preaching a kind of madness. Her terrifying depictions of physical violence are thematically similar to the grotesqueries of Rod Athey's body art. Both expose the visions of apocalypse as inherently sadomasochistic, and the Pentecostal faith as a license to torture. A friendlier, lapsed-Catholic version occurs in John Rechy's *The Sexual Outlaw,* in which leather is offered in prayer: "Bless the sacrifice prepared for the glory of your holy name." But that's schoolboy blasphemy compared to Sarah Kane.

In recent years, several novelists have reckoned with the enduring infatuation of gay men with Jesus Christ. It has particularly compelled novelists who were raised as Roman Catholics. Two gifted novelists are both named Thomas, a badge of their doubt. Thomas M. Disch's *The Priest: A Gothic Romance* (1995) barely manages two contradictory impulses: a flair for the grotesque, deployed with a blithe disregard for verisimilitude, and a red-hot anger at the church, a rage that turns any non-gay-affirming priest—virtually all of them turn out to be queer—into a monster. Disch's eponymous priest is too vile to be gay; his love for altar boys is a diversion from "woman-hating," misogyny gone rogue. At times Disch offers a lively, sociological examination of the modern church, in which gay identity is drowned in psychobabble. "The new breed of seminarians did not come right out and declare themselves gay. They used other code words for their own transgressions. They spoke of a need for intimacy, of the joy to be realized by becoming 'available' to others." In other words, the church is populated by knaves and fools.

The hero of Thomas Mallon's *Fellow Travelers* also ends up an apostate, but his loss of faith is deeply moving. Tim Laughlin, a good Catholic boy from the Bronx, has a low-level government job in mid-fifties Washington, D.C. He knows very few things, except that he hates communism as much as he loves God and the male sex. He has a clandestine affair with Hawkins Fuller, an upper-class, married Wasp, who is far more experienced and promiscuous, but also far less honorable. Expressing the same impulse that led Edson Cordeiro to end his recording of "It's Raining Men" with "Thank you, Jesus," as Tim begins to worship Hawk he also comes to recognize that he has "always been in love, physically and particularly, with Christ, whose dark, haloed image on every calendar and classroom glowed more handsomely than any man walking His Earth."

Desire turns the altar boy blasphemous—his cuff links bear the initials HF for both his lover and the commandment "Have faith." But love grants him a vision that is uniquely his in that closeted, self-hating era. He will not confess to having "impure thoughts," won't bear "false witness" against a love that was "literally divine." He loses his religion but not his faith or fidelity, deciding that his spoken vow of love, "unlike, it seemed, the catechism . . . would remain in effect forever." After Hawk, to avoid being red- and fag-baited out of the foreign service, abandons him, Tim is left bereft of God and man. Precisely then, he devises a god of his own. "I'm still taking communion, just making up my own rules." Realizing what Montaigne would call a *soumission désabusée* (a devotion stripped of illusion), Tim decides that the two truths of his life are that he loves Hawk as deeply as he once loved God.

He even stops hating the Communists, in part, after finding someone both red and queer, a figure even lower in the hierarchy than Tim himself. Mallon allows Tim to parody scripture—he likens a ménage à trois to the Trinity, clearly a habit not exhausted by Auden when he claimed that "Miss God is keeping me celibate." More sensationally, he realizes that, in the stages of first love, he had dreamed of consuming two bodies of flesh: Christ in communion and Hawk in his arms. "This is my body" acquires a double meaning that the two born Pentecostals Shannon Williams and Michael Warner would affirm. It must be a sign of gay Catholic liberation—and of Mallon's narrative tact—that the novel did not inspire enraged attacks.

Tim also quotes the daily news: when Hawk fondles him, he replies, "Have you no decency, sir?" As fits the locale and the times, Tim is always thinking about politics. The unspoken irony is that the mighty men of his time, the stalwart anti-Communists—Joe McCarthy, Bishop Fulton Sheen, Francis Cardinal Spellman—would all be revealed as gay. Knowing and not knowing the specifics, he resembles the gospel children gossiping about the COGIC bishop caught with a football player, or the gay-baiting minister with his own criminal record. Far more than Thomas Disch, Thomas Mallon evokes the loss to body and soul of a true believer's faith. Tim dies in middle age, leaving the far older Hawk to shed a few dry tears in his memory. Tim's only friend, typically, is a woman, who says that he ended his days alone, too "nervous" (clearly

Shannon Williams and the Barrett Sisters (l. to r., Rodessa Barrett Porter, DeLois Barrett Campbell, Billie Barrett GreenBey, 1972. Raised in the white Pentecostal Church, Shannon became an important record producer during the 1960s.

shell-shocked from Hawk's betrayal) to find new lovers, not "the least bit religious in any ordinary way."

Mallon has admitted that he regrets his loss of faith, and that his sexuality helped make it inevitable. "I still miss the wonder of it, still miss the possibilities it had to explain the world to me." Or, as James Baldwin's young hero John tells his brother in *Go Tell It on the Mountain,* "No matter what happens to me, where I go, what folks says about me, no matter what anybody says, you remember—please remember—I was saved, I was there." Just as some of Thomas Mann's readers always knew that *Death in Venice* was not an exercise in myth and symbol, Baldwin's finest readers have known from their own experiences why John can't stay there.

Baldwin is, of course, the great writer about growing up sanctified. At the same time that he was a whiz kid in high school ("the most Jewish black you've ever seen," recalled one of his classmates), he was exercising his verbal talents as a boy preacher. In *Go Tell It on the Mountain,* his first novel, the church world is a sanctuary that John must leave but can never escape. Baldwin often wrote that he loathed the patriarchal theology, identified most personally with a stepfather who made the lives of him and his family a constant torment, and who ridiculed his intellectual ambitions and effeminate behavior. But he also wrote that no sound had ever stirred him more than the church mothers' moans. One of the happiest film clips of Baldwin shows him and his contemporary the nightclub star Bobby Short (whom I consider vaudeville's answer to the child prodigy Alex Bradford) singing Rosetta Tharpe's first hit, "Rock Me" (aka "Hide Me in Thy Bosom").

I met Baldwin in the mid-1970s. He was a fan of *The Gospel Sound,* and we met several times while he was composing his own novel about gospel singers, *Just Above My Head* (an echo of Tharpe's "Up Above My Head I Hear Music in the Air"). It turned out that he was rooted and grounded in mid-1940s gospel music. His brother David had sung in a local quartet, the Thrasher Wonders, along with a teenage Clyde McPhatter. And realizing that I found cultural kaleidiscopes irresistible, he showed me a placard of a gospel fund-raiser for Congressman Benjamin Davis, a Communist, that featured, among others, Paul Robeson, his brother's quartet, and Sister Rosa Shaw, the poor man's Rosetta Tharpe. I delighted him with something I once saw at Harlem's Hotel Theresa. An old white evangelist asked if she could pray with a Puerto Rican dishwasher. Within a few seconds, she was speaking in tongues at the top of her voice, while he stood, hands raised, eyes shut, caught up in her fire. When she finished, she turned to two Irish cops, probably on the lookout for some local numbers runner, and declared, "It's a wonderful thing, a God that lets you speak in unknown tongues."

At that time Jimmy was facing enemies seen and unseen—as Reverend Brewster would say, "reeled and rocked from side to side." Philip Larkin would write nastily about "Negro homosexuals and religion." Richard Wright and Ralph Ellison wrote each other that Jimmy had made religion a faggotty enterprise. (Of course, Baldwin had written unkindly about Wright, and published his critique.) Norman Mailer, who by the late sixties confessed that he had grown tired of "Negroes and their rights," also implied that Baldwin's art had given way to agitprop. Truman Capote wrote harsh letters about "Jimmy's fiction; it is crudely written and balls-achingly dumb." He might also have given derogatory information to the FBI. J. Edgar Hoover, who shared very little with Baldwin but a sexual persuasion, targeted him for years. According to James Campbell, he may have used Baldwin's homosexuality to discredit the writer. Eldridge Cleaver, on his circuit from cultural nationalism to right-wing politics, wrote that Baldwin was yesterday's news, and declared that his sexuality alone rendered him unreliable.

In our chats Jimmy alluded to his enemies, usually rolling those great eyes. He was much more interested in discussing the gospel singers and preachers; when I described some of the savage put-downs, he would nod fiercely and point his finger at me. "Yes, baby, I know it all. I know them, I was raised with them." One evening he invited me to join him at Trader Vic's for cocktails with a friend, who turned out to be, of all people, Truman Capote. Whether because it was his nature to dominate a conversation, or whether he felt guilty about undermining Baldwin, he wouldn't let that world-class talker say a mumbling word. Instead we heard a long monologue about James Jones and Katherine Anne Porter. Occasionally, out of politeness, Jimmy would point a finger at him, as if he had nailed the question. But when Capote took a brief trip to the john, he rolled his eyes profusely.

A couple of weeks later, he asked me to join him at the apartment of a famous vocal coach, whose star pupil, Roberta Flack, had decided that she would play Bessie Smith in a movie to be written by Baldwin himself. The coach was a well-bred, light-skinned man. Baldwin arrived with a tall, very handsome man who was often in his company. Lacking perfect pitch, I couldn't tell whether John was Jimmy's inamorato; my instinct was to think not, and that he was similar to the nice Irish family who had been Truman Capote's companions, a salt-of-the-earth type who just happened to be eye candy.

After Flack left, the coach grew progressively drunker. He spoke about working with Pearl Bailey in a film. She had indulged in the full range of low-church dishing; she had been a "bitch on wheels." But when she grew impatient with the rehearsals and began to walk out, he bowed down on his knees before her. "Oh no, Miss Bailey, you can't leave us. You're the only real thing we have!" He turned to John, visually toured his body, and gave him a list of things he would need to do if he wanted to climb out of his rut. I forget the specifics, but do remember his saying, "I don't care how tall and fine and beautiful you are, baby, and how big a dick you have." Jimmy started pointing at him, and then turned to John, "Baby, he's telling you how to *last*."

It was vastly too complicated for me, a crash course in class and intraracial politics that made me very uncomfortable. So I left, and Jimmy walked me to the door. As was his wont with almost everyone, he hugged me, and I said, "That man is something. What do you think would happen if he'd lock horns with one of the dangerous gospel singers, with an Alex Bradford or James Cleveland?" He had appeared untroubled by his literary rivals, the Capotes and Mailers, perhaps seeing them as the heirs of his high-school classmates, fellow bookworms. But for the first time I saw a look of fear on his face. "That . . . would be terrifying."

Baldwin was the greatest writer to come out of the gospel church. But his immersion in the world went far beyond a love of its music and fellowship; he also knew the complicated strategies that generations of the children had mastered. In 1969, he wrote a revealing letter to his brother David, the former quartet singer. By then he had concluded that his personality consisted of a "mad man," a zealot and political activist, a "fragile, gifted child," and a "superbly paranoiac intelligence." I've tried these adjectives out on some of the smartest gospel singers, men who recognized the word "paranoid" but didn't always know the name of James Baldwin. All of them—in Chicago, Detroit, Atlanta, Los Angeles—have said the same thing: "But, baby, that's us." The child prodigies who learned to survive by expecting everyone else to fight dirty . . . who took it for gospel that "if you dig one ditch, you better dig two."

WAR ON THE CHILDREN

For generations gay men have endured the occasional attack from the pulpit. It didn't drive them away; when it was necessary, they could be as sanctimonious as every other church member who swore off alcoholism or adultery, but just not now. Alex Bradford, in his swinging youth, composed the fearsome "Turn Away from Sin." When James Cleveland was in his late fifties, he returned to the Apollo Theater, the site of his early triumphs. He chastised those in the audience who "say you've lost your joy. Well, maybe it's because of that raggedy life you've been living." He then shook himself, as if jolted by the Holy Ghost.

(Gay self-hatred has long been a constant. In 1963, a well-known singer disappeared from the home he had shared with his accompanist. He wrote a letter saying that nothing had gone wrong. "But the Lord spoke to my heart that if I didn't give it up, I'd soon be dead." His lover attempted suicide; and the singer went on to marry, found a church, be taken up by white evangelists, and die young. Another singer informed his friends that holiness could overcome any temptation. He would found a megachurch in Jamaica, New York—and be one of the first to die of AIDS.)

Everyone understood that gospel depended on the labor and talent of its gay practitioners. If everything wasn't spoken aloud, it didn't always need to be; Don't Ask Don't Tell has rarely been so painless. But that has changed. The family secret has become public knowledge, and the black church, once the very model of freedom and civil rights, has acquired a new image, as the citadel of intolerance. This development would have national repercussions, particularly on the career of President Barack Obama. It would introduce an ugly but not uninformed term, "black redneck."

And yet, just as gays have dominated gospel music, so they had been among the most significant players in the civil rights movement. (There have long been rumors that J. Edgar Hoover was nursing tapes of Dr. Martin Luther King in bed with his colleague Ralph Abernathy.) If James Baldwin was the movement's scribe, its leading tactician was Bayard Rustin, a proudly open gay man, who had also been a professional singer, specializing in spirituals and an occasional gospel song.

In 1940 Rustin recorded as a member of a quartet supporting Josh White, a folk singer, steeped in church music, who had made his recording debut as Brother Joshua, the Singing Christian. They performed a rearrangement of a song Mahalia had recorded three years earlier, "Sing On, My Singer." Rustin's sweet, high tenor was both soulful and idiomatic; thanks to him, the background sparkled. Twenty years later I would hear him perform a recital for the students at my college. He gave a stern impression, insisting that the spirituals were the deepest expressions of Negro life, and chastising the members of the school's NAACP for not respecting their heritage. When it came to the musical legacy, he was an unashamed cultural nationalist.

He had been equally unashamed of his nature. A TV documentary showed Rustin as a member of his high-school football team, surrounded by young white students, who he would tell his grandmother were also his first lovers. In his twenties he began an affair with a young white pacifist. Interviewed decades later, the man spoke movingly of their years together. And then, to my surprise and pleasure, I heard a familiar voice on the soundtrack. It was Marion Williams singing "There's a

Man Going Around Taking Names," a record I had produced in 1989. The choice pleased me a lot, especially since the song had been a Josh White specialty.

In 1963 Rustin was the architect of the March on Washington. We now know that his enemies, from Adam Clayton Powell to Dr. King's right-hand man Stanley Levison, wanted to kick him out of the movement. (Betraying the left's retrograde attitude toward gays, Levison felt that Baldwin and Rustin should stick to the homosexual movement and leave civil rights to the real men.) Three years later, I attended a debate between Rustin and Stokely Carmichael, in which he defended the principles of integration, much to the hostile response of a black-power audience. Several young men in the audience kept pointing at him and saying, "Look at her. Shut up, you old sissy!" Rustin, at one moment, did a comical bump-and-grind, as if to say, "You asked for sissy, I'll give you sissy!"

In clips of the march, there's a wonderful, gospel-inspired moment that shows Rustin at his happiest. Mahalia Jackson had rocked the crowd with "How I Got Over." As an encore, she asked everyone assembled onstage to join her singing the old spiritual "I've Been 'Buked and I've Been Scorned." Not for the first time, she forgot a lyric ("There's been trouble all over the land") and ad-libbed familiar words, in this case, drawn from C. A. Tindley's "Stand by Me." If you look at the performance, most of the figures on the podium seem baffled. Either they don't want to sing, or they're confused by her revision. But one man stands beside her, smiling hugely and belting out whatever words she chooses to sing. It's Rustin, whom I like to see as representing all the gospel children who had ever dreamed of singing with their idol. Forget about the naysayers. He had pulled the hugest crowd in civil rights history and was now singing with Mahalia. It must have been the supreme moment of his life.

In later years, drummed out of the movement, he would move to the right, first supporting Lyndon Baines Johnson's war in Vietnam (perhaps because Johnson had supported his own battles) and then aligning himself with the groups affiliated with the magazine *Commentary*. Upon his death at the age of seventy-five, almost all the many paid obituaries in *The New York Times* were from such organizations. But by then he had made his home elsewhere. He went out insisting that the civil rights movement of our time was gay. Had he lived to see civil rights heroes like Walter Fauntroy and Fred L. Shuttlesworth become outspoken foes of gay rights, would he have been astonished? Perhaps, after his years dodging Adam Clayton Powell and Eldridge Cleaver, not.

———

Progressive politics and fundamentalist religion seldom go together. This dilemma was posed for many civil rights volunteers when they attended church services offered "in the name of Jesus, that name alone by which all men may be saved." If you were not a born-again Christian, you simply were not in the holy number, and that meant most of the whites in the church. This also meant that progressives were fighting for the rights of people who preached a righteous intolerance. How often did I hear young whites say they had wanted to blurt out, "But Jesus was a Jew." (As for the misogyny and homophobia rampant in folk culture, the mid-sixties was a time when the rights of women or gays were considered distractions from the main goal. "Keep your eye on the prize" meant staying focused.)

This has remained an enduring factor in black worship. A recent survey asked believing Christians if unbelievers and even atheists had a chance at heaven. Over 50 percent of mainline Protestants said yes. Among black Protestants the chances were zero. There was still no other way to make it in.

But the civil rights era inhabited such a charged moment that theological differences were easily overcome. There were greater commonalities, particularly opposition to the Vietnam War. After Dr. King became identified with the antiwar movement, his enemies, led by J. Edgar Hoover, portrayed him as a dangerous radical. After he was assassinated, Coretta Scott King said that he had died for the Memphis workers and the Vietnamese peasants; quoting her, *Life* magazine left out the peasants and didn't even indicate the omission with ellipses, from which we can infer that the editors felt his martyrdom would be compromised by his antiwar stance. During the sixties, Reverend C. L. Franklin, Aretha's father and the most popular folk preacher in America, was also identified with progressive politics.

Franklin and King were both friends with the remarkable Alfred A. Duckett, a gay man and one of the unsung heroes of the movement. A New York–based publicist, he ghost-wrote Jackie Robinson's biography, and co-wrote many of Dr. King's early dispatches. He also understood the often violent rivalries that roiled through the National Baptist Convention. He was among the first to challenge Dr. J. H. Jackson, the convention's president, an eloquent orator and unabashed reactionary, a combination of Booker T. Washington and Alan Keyes (a comparison he would not disown; along with Zora Neale Hurston and George Schuyler, he was among the first members of the John Birch Society).

Jackson despised Dr. King, saw him as a Communist tool; in later years he would move the entrance of his church so it wouldn't lie on Dr. Martin Luther King Drive. He firmly believed that the race could only move forward economically by mastering red-in-tooth-and-claw capitalism. Therefore, civil rights was a waste of colored people's time, if not outright treason. Duckett begged to differ. He was among the first to argue that black people could have it all, money and freedom. He also understood that this battle had to be fought in the grass roots and not among the talented tenth. (He himself was a poet and one of Langston Hughes's best disciples.) And so he helped plot an insurrection in the Baptist Convention, forming alliances that would allow Dr. King's message to prevail. He knew the gospel scene well, and had served as Mahalia's publicist. Recognizing that only the queen of gospel could defeat the president of the Baptist Convention, he persuaded her to invite Dr. King to Chicago. That helped put the Atlantan on the national map. It also ushered in a sadly brief moment when religion and progressive politics seemed natural bedfellows.

Then as now, the alternative to the activism of Duckett and Dr. King was political quietism, garbed in noisy faith. Franklin confided to the scholar Jeff Todd Titon that he disliked a certain kind of loud religion, especially out of church, and he clearly meant his sanctified rivals. In one reading, the church could have gone in either direction, with King and Franklin's theology of liberation, or with the Pentecostals' theology of hellfire and brimstone. Actually, the dialectic was never that simple. Toward the end of his life, Franklin opened his church to Reverend Leroy Jenkins, a white Pentecostal evangelist who later did time in jail. And Dr. King's last rally was held at the Memphis headquarters of the Church of God in Christ.

Either way, the Pentecostals won the battle. The Church of God in Christ is now the biggest black religious denomination; and its once-contested rituals—speaking in tongues, faith healing, getting slain in the Spirit—have now permeated the Baptist and Methodist churches as well. "They shout more than we do," quips Brother Walter Stewart.

"It's still new to them, but we're used to the Holy Ghost." And just as the charismatic movement in the high churches turned many previously liberal Episcopalians rightward, the sanctified tendency had the same effect in black churches.

What's more, while it's pretty to think otherwise, fundamentalism—especially, alas, at its most attractively folkloric—is naturally hospitable to conservative politics. When my gospel book appeared, a student at the Yale Divinity School observed that if the John Birch Society weren't so racist, most of the black church would sign up. He may have overstated, but he could call on some illustrious witnesses. Utah Smith was the Church of God in Christ's most virtuosic guitarist, a sanctified showman of the first order, who sported huge angel wings as a visual correlative of his biggest hit, "I Want Two Wings to Veil My Face." He was gifted enough to appear at New York's Museum of Modern Art in 1941 and receive solid and respectful attention from Virgil Thomson. A few years later in New Orleans, during a campaign to sign up black voters, he assumed a reactionary stance: negroes didn't need party registration, they "needed to register with Jesus." This is familiar sanctified rhetoric (with multiple variations—e.g., a singer may say, "I'll never earn a gold record, but my witness is in heaven and my record is on high"). But the community didn't find Smith quaint or charming; he was widely deplored as an Uncle Tom.

James Brown, for many the personification of grass-roots soul, campaigned with Richard Nixon. "I'm not selling out," he explained, "I'm buying in," and from a certain, shrewd perspective, it was a reasonable argument: black people have usually taken a sheepish pride in their scoundrels—"At least one of our boys is getting over." And consider Pearl Bailey, the woman who brought the riotous humor of church ladies and gospel sissies into the public arena. She became Mamie Eisenhower's "Ambassador of Love."

As most of America moved to the right, so did the black church. Dr. King's dream of integration became a chimera, with big cities like Chicago and Detroit more segregated than in the days of Mahalia Jackson or C. L. Franklin. But integration could never be the first order of business for an ambitious fundamentalist. After all, the more integration, the more education, and as the saints liked to sing:

Go to the college,
Go to the school,

If you haven't got Jesus,
You an educated fool.

Integration might well mean a farewell to that old-time religion, and empty pews. Sadly, it never arrived and the churches remained full.

Yet while the black church remains a segregated institution, more than ever it bears the influences of white theology. The prosperity gospel—most identified with the Word of Faith movement and its leaders, like Kenneth Hagin and Kenneth Copeland—took over. Now, when evangelists spoke in tongues, their "interpretations" were the visions of an accountant: "Somebody, hallelujah, will be blessed with a new home; you may not have a dime, but name it and claim it. Otherwise you're living beneath your privilege." God may not have wanted you to be free, but he definitely wanted you to be rich. In no ways was this a socialized—much less "socialist"—faith; a typical motto was "Whatever the Lord has in store for you, it's just for you." That meant you didn't have to work for it or fight for it, much less help anyone else achieve it.

The transitive verb was "claim," as in "Name it and claim it" (with the slight variant "Confess it and possess it"). Live right and you might claim anything as yours; after all, your father owned the cattle on a thousand hills. Bad news could be shrugged off: "I'm not claiming this disease." Politics was another claiming ground: after the Obama election, Smokie Norful ad-libbed, "I used to think we'd never get out of the poorhouse. Now I'm claiming the White House."

By some lights, this was an updated version of the Protestantism analyzed by Max Weber. Except back in the day, God had helped those who helped themselves. Now there was no need to spin or toil; blessings untold were just a prayer away; all things were "possible, if you only believe."

Huge megachurches were built on this foundation. Pastors like T. D. Jakes and Creflo (irreverently dubbed "Cash Flow") Dollar offered courses in business and real estate. The saints declared they were "stepping out on faith. Don't have a dime, but I'm claiming a new home in Jesus' name." The results were predictable and terrible. At least a portion of the housing bubble was first inflated and then broken by believing Christians who couldn't pay their mortgages. The whole rotten situation was manipulated by the bankers, who earned commissions on the number of new customers they signed up. But it was greatly abetted by the pastors themselves. In 2009 it was revealed that Wells Fargo had paid $350 to the churches for each new home buyer. Considering a mega-church could have thousands of members, this was a serious inducement to advise somebody's grandmother that she deserved the home of her dreams.

Homophobia, always a background rumble, became a deafening cry. Of all the other sins so bountifully displayed in church, from gluttony to adultery, this was the lone sin that could keep you out of heaven. As many gay men have commented, the rhetorical ploy was to defend the drunk and "whoremonger" with the consoling qualification "At least he ain't a sissy."

How could this happen in churches where the choirs would have folded without gay input? Some of the noise came from outside. The Traditional Values Coalition's Reverend Lou Sheldon, a close colleague of Karl Rove, produced a film caricaturing gay rights as an obscene parody of the civil rights movement, and it was widely distributed in black churches. During a Republican era, it made sense to sound Republican. Shortly after his inauguration in 2001, George W. Bush invited some conservative black preachers to the White House. The voluble Eugene F. Rivers left the meeting "highly encouraged" that the president's first pledge was to oppose same-sex marriage. Rivers, the well-educated pastor of a small Pentecostal congregation in Cambridge, Massachusetts (surely not the best stalking ground for homophobes), became a much-quoted figure in the Bush era. Another Bush ally was the Texan Methodist Kirbyjon Caldwell, who affirmed Bush's positions on same-sex marriage . . . and the economy: after the president commanded the nation to shop, Caldwell's wife preached a sermon to demonstrate that he had scripture on his side. Megachurches benefitted from Bush's policy of faith-based ministries. Their ability to discriminate against gay people while receiving government aid was like manna from heaven: all the benefits without any legal obligations. (While promising to rectify the situation, Barack Obama let it slide, perhaps because his religious director was a Pentecostal.)

In addition there was the popular music that everybody heard on television or coming out of their kids' cassette players, in which words like "ho" and "faggot" were almost as frequent as "nigga."

Gospel music and "the blues" (generically used to mean all popular music) have always reflected each other. It was so when Mahalia Jackson was promoted as the second Bessie Smith. It remained so when pastors preached sermons that turned pop song lines ("I Heard It Through the

Grapevine") into religious metaphors. Rap and the church agreed on two themes, Jesus and bling. The frequent gay baiting of rap (rendered far more violent and downright murderous in reggae) was another welcome note to the new-breed preachers. Prophet Todd Hall acquired tens of thousands of YouTube viewers with his sermons denouncing homosexuals. He trafficked freely in the language of rap. "I don't care how much you shout, if most of your preachers are faggots and punks, your church ain't nothing but a gay bar." There seemed to be an unspoken covenant: we can act and sound as worldly as we please, just as long as we dish the sissies. That, in particular, will prove our anointing, the sanctified mot juste of the last thirty years. (So much for that favorite notion of Michel Foucault that a new language enables a new reality. The homophobes used all the modern terms without changing their stance one whit.)

There remained a constant dilemma of the fundamentalist church, reconciling the Prince of Peace with the warrior on a battlefield. After muscle building became a gay specialty, muscular Christianity had to find a new means of asserting itself. Being tough wasn't enough; you had to be tough on the sissies. So the white Seattle pastor Mark Driscoll dismisses the liberal denominations' Jesus as "a Richard Simmons, hippie, queer Christ," a "neutered and limp-wristed popular Sky Fairy of pop culture that . . . would never talk about sin or send anyone to hell." Reverend Gregory Daniels, a Chicago pastor, told *The New York Times,* "If the KKK opposes gay marriage, I would ride with them." Even the progressive black Baptist Reverend Johnnie Ray Youngblood tried to recruit young men by insisting that "my Jesus didn't have no sissies or punks around him." (Youngblood would eventually become a strong advocate for those of his parishioners stricken with HIV.)

The Promise Keepers were founded by Coach Bill McCartney, who first made his name by opposing gay rights in Colorado; he has spoken of lesbians and gay men as "stark raving mad." He maintains that in a true Christian home, the husband remains lord of the manor. But he has responsibilities; Promise Keepers frequently confess their past failures as fathers and husbands. As they do, men weep and embrace each other. There is much lifting of arms and speaking in tongues; some men, overcome by the Spirit, will fall to the ground, as their brothers pray over them. The meetings are intensely physical, though studiously not homoerotic.

It's all in the eye of the beholder. I was once watching a Promise Keepers rally in Washington, D.C., reportedly attended by over a million men. Ray Boltz, who a decade later would come out as a gay man, sang to his brothers, and they wept and rejoiced. The gospel children didn't spot him, as they would Ted Haggard. Instead they hooted with laughter at the crowd as its members trembled in contrition or shivered in ecstasy. "Uh-uh, baby, they can't do that stuff—that's our shit! Look at those clumsy white boys trying to act like they got the Holy Ghost. When we children got happy, they 'buked and scorned us something terrible. But let a jock do it, let a white jock do it—oh, the windows of heaven are opening and Shekinah Glory's pouring on down."

In other words, a style mastered by gay men was now deployed by their enemies. They had been robbed. I had heard the same note in the 1960s, when singers would laugh dryly at the Beatles imitating Little Richard imitating Marion Williams, or Mick Jagger emulating Tina Turner. "See them white boys," I used to hear, "doing everything those poor girls figured out for themselves—and making all the money."

This impious take reminded me of the actor Roscoe Lee Browne's irreverence toward his co-star John Wayne. The son of a Baptist preacher, Browne had been a national track star in his youth, before turning to the stage. He had retained his love of gospel music, and particularly entertained his friends with imitations of Marion Williams—a bit like the drag queen Ruth Brown, who represented quite the opposite corner of show business, he would attempt her high notes and growls. So you can understand his glee when he learned that the hyper-butch John Wayne's real name was Marion. He reportedly joked about it often. I have to imagine that he appended a "whoo-hoo," and cut a shout step.

Male gospel singers like Alex Bradford were perceived as campy in the extreme; even his physical girth only advanced him to the status of Ferdinand the Bull. The children have always been subject to outrageous stereotype. Back in the fifties, pastors would joke about the wealthy homosexual who had donated amply to the church: "We said, 'Brother Jones, in honor of your contribution, we're gonna let you pick our choir's next hymn. Which hymn would you like?' And him being a sissy, he said, 'I'll take him and him and him.'"

In the films of Tyler Perry and his acolytes, the choir director is invariably a nervous sissy. J. L. King's *On the Down Low* and Terrance Dean's *Hiding in Hip Hop* are popular books by men who sleep with other men but insist they are not gay. Both authors speak contemptuously of "church queens." Whether this is a class bias or the familiar rejection of gay men by their own, the implication is that the children are simply too unguarded for a down-low man to hang with.

If America is a thoroughly mulatto culture, black gays have explored it more fully than their straight brothers. Though I know of no sociological study, my educated guess is that they have had more close nonblack friends and lovers, and that they have moved more freely in a nonblack world. Baldwin or Rustin or Roscoe Lee Browne chose a hard role, to be culturally ambidextrous and to finesse contradictions. They and their nephews were obliged to be very smart—famously so: the gospel sissies are seen as clannish ("Them folk stick together") and strong ("They take care of their own"). Even their enemies allow that they're bright, as even a homophobe will recognize their skills of adaptation and survival. Bishop Harry Jackson, a Washington, D.C., Pentecostal, has fought recognition of gay marriage for years. He grants that homosexuals are not stupid. "Some of the black gays" with whom he studied at Williams College "were off-the-charts smart." But they were also sinners, too smart for their own good. Such observations betray the same anti-intellectualism that reduces bright kids to class and race traitors.

Liberals hope that exposure will lead to increased tolerance and can point to a wider acceptance of gay rights and same-sex marriage among Americans under fifty. But this has not been the case in the gospel church. Instead, the franker the language, the earthier the revelations, and the more fluent the psychobabble, the greater the bigotry. Between 1996 and 2004, black Protestant support for gay rights dropped from 65 to 40 percent, according to a survey conducted by the Pew Forum on Religion and Public Life.

Keeping up with the times meant a vulgarizing of the church testimony. In the past God was thanked for "making a way out of no way," for "being a company keeper in a lonely hour," "a mother for the motherless," "a bridge over deep waters," "food when I'm hungry," "shelter in the time of storm." Now traditional metaphor yielded to specific and intimate detail. So it was that Kirk Franklin, the contemporary gospel star, could talk of being delivered from "the love of pornography," and Shun Pace Rhode, a country girl with an old-timey voice and a face reminiscent of Mahalia's, could testify that despite having been married to a gay man afflicted with AIDS, her HIV report had come back "negative—thank you, Jesus!"

Attacks on homosexuality were, if anything, more graphic. "Adam and Eve, not Adam and Steve" was tame. Raunchy idioms and street talk became the norm in megachurches, a familiar dose of weekly comedy about anal sex. Bishop Paul Morton, who had been noted for his performance of Alex Bradford's "Since I Met Jesus," hounded gays from his pulpit with risqué analogies (e.g., outlets need plugs). Bishop Eddie L. Long raged from the pulpit, "Don't tell me you were born this way. Because if you say you were born this way, you're saying God is a liar." Don't know who you are? "Take your clothes off. I'll tell you who you are!" he promised. The more decorous but no less fiery Bishop T. D. Jakes announced that since gays were "broken people," he would not hire any of them. After his own son was arrested on a morals charge, Jakes—by now one of President Obama's spiritual advisers—begged all the LGBT people in his church to leave, just leave. There was scarcely a megapastor who didn't make gays feel unwelcome, if not the scum of the earth.

The gospel church's immediate response to AIDS was a grievous combination of ignorance and contempt. Reverend Milton Brunson, founder and director of Chicago's most famous choir, the Thompson Community Singers, told the press that the virus was "God's punishment." Shortly thereafter, a local singer died, claiming that Brunson had infected him. Bishop Jeff Banks of Newark's Revival Temple COGIC was perhaps the first to record a warning: "Diseases going round today them doctors don't know nothing about. I tell you, church, God's getting tired of your immori-teh, he's getting tired of your homosexuali-teh." A few weeks after his album's release, I ran into Bishop Banks at the offices of Savoy Records. He greeted me with a holy kiss: "Baby, it's so good to see you." "Jeff," I said, "you look great, as usual. But Jeff, Bishop, how could you treat your own that way?" I didn't have to specify; he understood at once. "Oh," he said, covering his mouth. "I hope I don't get found out." But then, spinning on a dime, his tone turned into a modified preacher's growl: "Yet and still, God's getting tired . . ."

In the past, quartet singers had condemned the standard vices—drinking and gambling and "fooling around with another man's wife." Now they targeted the homosexuals. All their anger since the days when Alex Bradford or James Cleveland had outsung them resurfaced. It was a chance to bury the opposition. Yet the gospel concerts were even more stridently antigay. The Clark Sisters, childhood darlings of the Church of God in Christ, were particularly contemptuous. In one performance, Karen Clark Sheard recounts the wonders of sanctification: "With Holy

Ghost power, the sissies will stop switching." It doesn't faze her that the Clarks' biggest hit, "You Bring Out the Sunshine," was first popularized in gay bars.

At a recent Stellar Awards contest (gospel music's Oscars) the hot singer and choir director Tye Tribbett (who has recorded with Justin Timberlake) led his background singers in a choreographed routine worthy of 1955 Alex Bradford. The young men fell to the ground, then struggled back to their feet. "Come on out, church!" Tribbett commanded. "Come on out of homosexuali-teh, come on out of lesbianism!"

Supposedly these men were indicting something foreign to their nature. The newest variation was for men to admit that they had tasted the forbidden fruit, though always at some other's behest: i.e., they hadn't been born gay, somebody had "turned them out." Donnie McClurkin, with the most ringing tenor since Brother Joe May, wouldn't rest on his vocal laurels. He had to tell the world that he had once been gay, a fate he ascribed to having been sexually abused by a cousin (much as Bradford had been at the age of three). But he had been "delivered—praise God, delivered from the curse of homosexuali-teh." Invariably his thanksgiving would be broadcast in tongues. Following McClurkin's insistence that he hadn't been born homosexual, that pederasts had made him that way, the gay image changed, very much for the worse. No longer were they merely sissies; they were child molesters.

There was even a written text for homophobes to draw upon. J. L. King's *On the Down Low* saturated black America. For months the book rode high on *The New York Times* Best Sellers chart. Considering that its white audience was minuscule, the book must have been the biggest seller in years to a virtually exclusively black audience. King revealed a new group of men, not covered by any previous designation. Men on the down low were men who got away with something. They fooled their friends and families, most particularly their women. They weren't gay, although it wasn't clear whether King simply equated "gay" with effeminate. They were everywhere. And where did they meet most often? Appearing on—where else?—Oprah's show, King said they didn't gather in gay bars, because they weren't gay. Their favorite meeting spot was church.

Whether he intended it or not, this had a devastating impact on black women. Added to all their other problems in finding a mate, now there was a lurking suspicion that Mr. Right might be on the down low. Black women have suffered huge rates of AIDS infection, far greater than their proportion of the population. King's book turned their lovers into potential killers. He had sounded a huge alarm. Women, church women particularly, had a right to feel angry and terrified. It matters little that King fills his book with religious testimonies and praises God for winning him the loving friendship of his ex-wife. (Terrance Dean is equally driven to testify about the joys of worship at the West Angeles Church of God in Christ, whose pastor, Bishop Charles Blake, has invited the arch-homophobe Rod Parsley to preach from his pulpit.)

I suspect that King's book forced many male preachers to take on gay men as a means of demonstrating their distance from their condition. Same-sex marriage became an assault on the black family—apparently because it made a travesty of the institution of marriage. The preachers admitted that most black children were born out of wedlock. But how could young people aspire to something better if even sissies and bull daggers were allowed to marry? Many preachers also resented the comparison of the civil rights struggles of black people and of gays. The argument was that while gays can evade or disguise their identity (which they have willfully chosen, since nobody is born that way), blacks never can. Willie Mae Ford Smith used to say, "Negro blood is like the Holy Ghost—one drop and you're marked for life."

This is undeniable. But isn't it also true that the extent of gay suffering has been very great? In the last hundred years there have been only a few lynchings. But every year hundreds, if not thousands, of black gay men are murdered. The church's children have suffered in particular. Two musicians who performed on albums I've produced were killed by their tricks. In a brutal irony, Reverend Paul Jones, whose big hit, "I Won't Complain," has become the most performed gospel song of the last twenty years, died under similar circumstances.

If you were promoting the black family, didn't it have its large share of gay people? Mother Leola Crosby once said, "We have a race like a flower garden, and each one of our families is like the twelve tribes of Israel. I got one cousin who's a college president and another who's a murderer." In that large crowd have been many single people, at least some of them gay and lesbian. "And, baby, they don't want to tell it," Charles Campbell liked to say, "but we the ones who pay for our nephew and niece education. And who else always be there for Mama? The others always too *busy* to remember the bridge that brought them on over."

The single men who did the heavy lifting for their parents have also supported their idols. Many a gospel diva, like Bessie Griffin, has made sport of the children. But after their careers go south, when the programs are canceled and the phones stop ringing, there's usually some old fan who'll accompany them to the clinic and reminisce about those days when they could tear up any church. I learned recently that one of Chicago's last gospel stars had to undergo radiation treatment. Who nursed her through all the subsequent horrors? Of course, it was one of the children, a man in his early seventies, who had just suffered a stroke. Though he had barely regained the ability to speak, he could still mumble that she was his favorite singer.

But sympathy was seldom extended to men who had contributed so much, musically, spiritually, and personally. Or it came in the guise of hating the sin and professing to love the sinner.

This had a profound effect on black politics, long before the outcry over black political support of California's Proposition 8. There already had been a slew of megachurch Republicans, from Los Angeles's Frederick Price to Philadelphia's Herbert Lusk II. (And even earlier, in 1984, black America's second-favorite presidential candidate after Jesse Jackson for a moment had been Pat Robertson!)

In 2004 the first two black religious leaders to support George W. Bush's candidacy were Detroit's Reverend Marvin Winans, lead singer of the very popular group of brothers called the Winans, and his minister of music, Donnie McClurkin. About that time, Marvin's sisters Debbie and Angie testified before a congressional committee, warning against the dangers of gay rights. They said that their message was inspired by the awful example of Ellen DeGeneres (elsewhere America's sweetheart). I learned that several gospel singers had voted for Bush simply because of his antigay stance. One couple was typical. The husband had grown up imitating Alex Bradford; the wife learned everything she knew from the Davis Sisters. (Talk about loving the sinner . . . !)

It would have been neatly dialectical if the homophobia had emanated only from the Pentecostals, with their religious-right affiliations. But great civil rights heroes like Walter Fauntroy and Fred L. Shuttlesworth were just as vehemently opposed to gay rights. Shuttlesworth, the true hero of the Birmingham, Alabama, movement, would end his days in Ohio confusing everyone by saying that he remained a Democrat for all purposes except for gay rights. Even the legacy of Dr. King was not immune. Three of the four King siblings were progay, as was Coretta Scott King. But Reverend Bernice King adamantly disagreed. She had joined the fourteen-thousand-member New Birth Missionary Baptist

Church of Bishop Eddie L. Long, a Full Gospel Baptist—the term for a charismatic Baptist, i.e., a Baptist who, unlike his forerunners, believes in glossolalia and faith healing, ergo the reference to a new birth. (Long claims to have received the baptism of the Holy Spirit at the hands of the now disgraced Jimmy Swaggart.) On one occasion Bishop Long and Reverend King convened a large number of followers at her father's grave. They then marched back to New Birth, where she attempted to free her father's image of any progay sentiments. Attempting a prophetic stance, she bellowed, "I know from the depths of my sanctified soul that he didn't take a bullet for same-sex marriage." (Her use of low-church boilerplate—"depths of my sanctified soul"—went against the grain of his polished rhetoric.)

By then Bishop Long might have figured as the anti–Dr. King. Where the latter had eschewed worldly goods, Long celebrated them. In the grand tradition of big-time preachers, he boasted about his wardrobe and his expensive colognes. Where Dr. King had been prim and almost pompous, he was frankly "down." Where the older man was modest to a fault, he was an unashamed narcissist. He liked to talk jive, or its modern incarnation, rap. Summoning his younger members to their feet, he'd taunt them, "Where my young people at? Where my little Sporty? Where my little Shorty?" He alluded to marching around the house "buck naked" and made ample reference to his own muscular body. At times he'd challenge women to overcome their love of male flesh: "I *know* how fine a man's body can be." Resist it, he commanded. Pray the lust away. All the while, he continued to damn gay men as the lowest of sinners. Don't you know, he would inform them, that "God wants you dead"? Signing his letters "Amazed by His grace," he told the children that grace alone could save them from their sins.

Coretta Scott King's funeral resembled a scene in Shakespeare. Seated in the congregation were Yolanda (now deceased), Dexter Scott, and Martin Luther III. Much was made of the eulogy of Reverend Joseph Lowery, who stressed Mrs. King's opposition to the wars in Vietnam and Iraq, a forthright position given that President Bush was seated near the altar. But the family drama occurred when Maya Angelou rose to speak. Within her first sentence she declared that "Coretta loved everyone, gay or straight, black or white." It was true, she had compared homophobia to racism, and seen them as equally insidious. But in the context of the King family, Angelou was very obviously separating mother and child. While she spoke, the cameras showed Bishop Long conferring with Bernice, advising her like some anointed Iago. Angelou's eulogy was a brave and bold ploy, at least to those clued in. But since the black church's homophobia was not yet an issue, the import of her words received little attention.

That would change in 2008. The election was notable for shining a national spotlight on the black church's homophobia. To his great credit, Barack Obama attacked the bigotry, lamented the opposition to "our gay sisters and brothers," and did so in Dr. King's home church, Ebenezer Baptist in Atlanta. One assumes that he knew Bernice's position. But the homophobia of some of his other supporters became a real, if temporary, liability for him. It was announced that concerts featuring the biggest stars in gospel would be held in support of his campaign. At first this was seen as a shrewd appeal to the grass-roots types who, supposedly, were still beholden to Hillary Clinton.

But then it was learned that the featured star would be Donnie McClurkin. There was an immense outcry, and the Web was filled with thousands of complaints, most of them from black gay men. Obama's staff had been caught unprepared—so much for their knowledge or love of gospel music, McClurkin's testimony having been widely known for years. In a formulation that would grow very familiar during his first months of office, the candidate declared that he was presiding over a big tent. There was room for all, gay men and the men who hated them. A white gay Unitarian pastor was chosen to speak the benediction at the concerts. (This could not have been more tone-deaf from a fundamentalist perspective!)

McClurkin said he had awakened to find himself a national ogre. He insisted that he had no hatred of anyone, that his experience was unique to himself. He sounded like the very model of tolerance, and may have persuaded those who hadn't attended his revivals, in which the demons of homosexuality were often exorcised. National reporters observed with some surprise that he had done a bizarre kind of Indian war dance. Of course it was the church's holy shout. He had averred that he meant no harm, but since God had "delivered me out of homosexuality," he needed to rejoice in the finest way he knew, cutting a few steps for the TV camera.

Obama's next church-generated nightmare involved his pastor, Reverend Jeremiah Wright. Eventually he would have to disown his "spiritual father" for his more radical statements. It was not mentioned that, unlike many other big-name preachers, Wright supported gay rights, and that Trinity United Church of Christ had been very hospitable to AIDS patients, unlike the churches led by the Milton Brunsons of Chicago. (The United Church of Christ denomination supports gay marriage, which casts a skewed light on President Obama's self-proclaimed religious objections.)

Much was made of Reverend Wright, and Obama would eventually be forced to "turn him loose." Gone too would be his second of three spiritual advisers, Father Michael Pfleger, who became a millstone around the candidate's neck when, in a falsetto voice, he began mimicking Hillary Clinton. Almost nothing was made of Obama's third adviser, Reverend James T. Meeks, the pastor of Salem Missionary Baptist Church. For example, *The New York Times Index* referred to him only as the organizer of a group that had raised funds for the mother of Jesse Jackson's out-of-wedlock child. Many of his positions on education or gun control would chime with Senator Obama's. Indeed, the senator was so drawn to Salem that he ended the night of his election praying in the church. But Meeks would become most known for his opposition to "sissies" and "punks," words he used often, never in jest, and particularly in the pulpit. He made a point of driving the children out of his choir, a quixotic gesture that immediately reduced the male section to something resembling a quartet.

In October 2006 he held a "Halloween Fright Night," a version of the haunted houses conceived by white Pentecostal pastors as a means of drawing youth and then scaring them half to death. In a particularly gaudy version, Salem featured the spectacle of two stereotypically effeminate young men, covered with makeup and glitter, swishing through the church until eventually they were cast into hell, their screams rising higher along with the flames. Meeks also condemned "Hollywood Jews for bringing us *Brokeback Mountain*." (The remark was no less offensive for being incorrect, since the writers and director were all non-Jews.)

He had been elected to the state senate, but briefly considered running for governor (Rod Blagojevich's wife had enjoyed attending his services). He said that he was "the guy" for all the "white conservatives," since he alone of the major candidates opposed both gay and abortion rights. Within the state senate, he attempted unsuccessfully to defeat SB3186, an Illinois LGBT nondiscrimination bill. Once again he went after the "punks and sissies." Then, strangely, after another senator had risen to their defense, Reverend Senator Meeks stepped up and kissed him on the cheek.

Now you cannot attend a Meeks service without hearing him savage gay people. It is as central to his message as Jeremiah Wright's views of black oppression. The exposure of Meeks got some limited press attention, most of it, surprisingly, from Christopher Hitchens. But, perhaps because Meeks sounded like them, the Republicans, who found in Jeremiah Wright a gift that kept on giving, ignored the Salem pastor. I may have been among the very few who were alarmed by Obama's equanimity. Swallowing Meeks should not have been so easy. (Nor is it easy to reconcile the president who taped an "It Gets Better" clip for gay youth and the pilgrim who includes T. D. Jakes and Kirbyjon Caldwell among his spiritual mentors.)

The president's professed sensitivity to all perspectives would next manifest itself at his inauguration, where he once again broke the hearts of his gay supporters—and much of his liberal base—by inviting Reverend Rick Warren to give the opening prayer. He did offer as a compensating factor a benediction delivered by the very progressive and progay Reverend Joseph Lowery. For gospel lovers, it was bracing to hear Lowery speak of an inclusive God, who stood "with a hand of power and a heart of love," words quoted from "Beams of Heaven," one of the first gospel songs, whose composer, C. A. Tindley, also gave us the prototypes of "We Shall Overcome" and "Stand by Me," the song Mahalia quoted at the March on Washington.

For those with a bird's-eye view of gospel history, this was a tribute to traditional gospel, both its tolerance and its musical genius. Alas, the far younger Reverend Warren fitted too exactly with the spirit of contemporary gospel. Lowery summoned Reverend Brewster; Warren, Pastor Marvin Winans. Viewed from another angle, President Obama's confidence that he alone could reconcile left and right, gays and their haters, would seem prototypical. By the end of his first year in office, he would be chastised on all sides for his irrepressible need to split the difference. For many, such attempts at reconciliation were not merely quixotic; they were delusional. But, obviously, any supporter of gay rights who had no trouble attending services at Salem Baptist would disagree.

The continual abuse of gay men by singers and preachers alike would prompt an attack from a surprising witness. Al Sharpton, who had been a boy preacher at Washington Temple, Brooklyn's largest Church of God in Christ, couldn't hold his peace. He had viewed the hypocrisy for years and was now sick of the homophobic preachers who after "the lights go off go cruising for trade." All over America, gay men who knew the score dreamed of outing the pastors who had made a lucrative hustle of burying their own.

Meanwhile, at perhaps some real political cost, the Black Congressional Caucus has been almost unanimous in its support of gay rights. From New York's Governor David Paterson, who attempted unsuccessfully to make gay marriage legal in his state during his brief tenure, to Julian Bond, the chairman of the NAACP, who addressed the 2009 Gay March on Washington and stated forthrightly that, yes, gay rights and civil rights were indivisible, many celebrities made clear their opposition to the saved and sanctified bigots.

All this time, a small but vocal number of the children had decided to leave their former homes and invent a new one. Unity Fellowship Church of Christ, the first black gay church (as opposed to the interracial Metropolitan Community Church, founded by Reverend Troy Perry, a former Pentecostal, who looked eerily like the men Shannon Williams remembered from his youth). In a beautiful evolution, it was founded by Bishop Carl Bean, a very fine singer who spent much of his youth traveling with Alex Bradford and who remains loyal to his baffling memory while cherishing, along with me, recollections of the saintly Charles Campbell.

A couple of years ago I attended a Unity Church convention held at the Newark church of Bishop John Shelby Spong. What struck me at once was that the audience looked almost exactly like the gospel crowds I had first seen in the late 1950s—the hulking men, the outsized women. Even the fashions were traditional; nobody was dressed for his or her close-up. And there was fire, plenty of it, in the house. Men and women wept, shook, and raised holy hands. Finally there was a church march to a new tune, "Hey Now, How You Doing, Since Jesus Came Into Your Heart?" It could have been Daddy Grace's church in 1957. Many people left the marching line to shout on their own. Several fell to the floor, then rose up to shout some more. After the song ended, the dancing grew even more athletic. I remembered the old line "Nobody shouts like the children." Some men went from double to triple time, dancing to a quicker measure than their neighbors. I had come to the ur-source of club dancing at its most inspired.

In a word, it was "sure 'nuff church." Ironically, Bishop Spong had not much earlier attended a conference of African Anglicans, the very group whose extreme hostility to gay men, much less their ordination, would eventually persuade many conservative Episcopalians to leave the

American church and join them: these days homophobia trumps racism every time. (President Robert Mugabe has frequently taken aim at the homosexual pastors he claims to have discovered corrupting the Anglican Church of Zimbabwe.) Spong had been shocked at the evangelical behavior; he compared it to a revivalist meeting gone mad. For this remark the conservative theologian Father Richard Neuhaus dismissed him as unspeakably vulgar. Both men were a mite disingenuous. The right-wing branches of both the Episopalian and the Anglican churches have been neo-Pentecostal since at least the 1960s. Father Neuhaus hated their outbursts, finding them hysterical and primitive. In other words, both sides shouted; politics was the crucial difference. You either shouted because God had made you gay or because he hadn't. (Neuhaus had no doubts, however, about Father Marcial Maciel Degollado, founder of the Legionaries of Christ. When rumors swelled about Maciel, Neuhaus called his innocence "a moral certainty." Eventually he would be publicly disgraced. Among Maciel's many victims had been two of his own sons, a tour de force of child abuse that far surpassed the transgressions of any of the sanctified demons of Carl Bean's youth.)

Carl Bean's memoir describes a transcendent moment, steeped in the church's tradition of cathartic release, yet revolutionary in its expression. Early in the days of his congregation, he was led to testify. But rather than bask in abstractions—the friends who had given him a hard time—he called them by their name: specifically, the uncle who had raped him when he was three and continued to do so for years. Bean knew that he had touched a live wire. He asked the men and women around him to summon up those who had "robbed you of your innocence" and dared them to call the name of Mama, Papa, Preacher, Teacher.

The church went up. One woman screamed that everyone from brother to uncle had been guilty. Within moments dozens of people were hollering, shivering, contorting with a grief that could pass for getting happy. Ushers carried the bodies out as if it were the days of Norsalus McKissick singing "The Old Ship of Zion" and assuring the saints, "Ain't no danger in the water." After that, it took an hour for order to be restored.

Gay-affirming churches, like Unity Fellowship, are still in the vast minority. Another out leader is Bishop Yvette Flunder of Oakland, California, founder and pastor of the City of Refuge United Church of Christ, who sounds like a younger version of Jackie Verdell, a former member of the Davis Sisters. Lately Bishop Flunder has publicly invited all the gifted lesbians and gay men to join her movement. Only in half-jest, she assumes that they keep returning to the big churches because of the music. They may have to sit through Rev's contempt, but those choirs can really sing.

Why not, she asks, form choirs of our own? They could be the sing-ingest groups in town. Instead, in Los Angeles, many members of James Cleveland's church jumped to another City of Refuge, a Pentecostal temple presided over by Noel Jones, not incidentally Grace Jones's brother, a man who had given vocal support to Jamaica's most zealous—and violent—homophobes. How could Cleveland's flock abide this new message? The veteran Walter Stewart quipped, "You know, some gay folks just love being 'buked and scorned." In other words, masochism has its comforts.

If the gospel-singing children were going to rise up against their enemies, the movement would have to come from within. By 2009 there were interesting signs. Tonéx (pronounced Tonay) is one of the new-breed stars. He can rap with fluency, spin, dance, and cartwheel, sing while lying "slain" on his back. He can charm and entertain, and then growl and moan like his bishop father. In the fall of 2009 a You-Tube clip was posted in which a gospel version of Oprah questioned Tonéx. He admitted that he had engaged in "same-sex" episodes. Like Donnie McClurkin and Alex Bradford, he acknowledged that he had been abused as a kid. But he refused to blame his sexuality on a child-hood trauma. What's more, he refused to see it as shameful. A wild man on the altar, he spoke very calmly during the interview. He refrained from supporting gay marriage, since that was biblically reserved for men and women, but found a "covenant" between two men acceptable.

Within a month the clip had 160,000 viewings, a very great number for a gospel singer. There were also thousands of comments. Initially, these were universally negative. Scripture was quoted and quoted again. Tonéx was warned that he risked losing his soul, much less his career. Fans wrote that they felt shocked (given Tonéx's stage demeanor, "shocked shocked" would have been more correct) and betrayed. Most of the messages were irredeemably hostile, remarks that might break a weaker person. Even the kinder ones promised that everything would be all right—as long as Tonéx took back his choice. Because it was obviously his choice. He hadn't been born that way; some devil of a pederast had turned him into a punk, when all he needed to say was "Devil, you're a liar."

A few weeks later Tonéx's good friend Deitrick Haddon checked in. Haddon, another bishop's son, has the stage savvy of a sanctified Michael Jackson. He's also got a fine tenor. Though his version of Sam Cooke's "A Change Is Gonna Come" is overloaded with contemporary-gospel melisma, his ear is so fine that the melisma addresses and flatters the song's chord changes. It's a beautiful update of 1950s gospel quartet, converting even a doubter like myself. Haddon admitted that he and Tonéx were pals, and he wouldn't care to say a thing against him. But, he had to add, they had nothing in common: "I don't have a sissy bone in my body."

Naturally, the Internet lit up. At first there were messages praising God that his sons hadn't all gone worldly. The most interesting response was to Haddon's language. "Sissy," several of the children wrote, is a demeaning insult, as bad as the N word, every bit as hurting. The children were finally instructing their friends in what should have been obvious. Haddon must have been astonished by this reception. He removed the comment from his Web site.

But the word was out. At a convention of the religious right, one of the few black speakers, Bishop Wellington Boone, spoke against gay rights, and then added, "I'm from the ghetto"—one of the oldest ploys of quartet leads, beseeching the women to start responding as if they were still back home in that little wooden church on the hill. And being ghetto, he told it like it is: we call them "sissies" and "punks." After the response to Haddon it would be interesting to see if such language would change. Maybe "queer" or "gay" would be invested with the same hostility.

Tonéx's story swept through the church and even received attention in *The New Yorker*. It was inevitable that Donnie McClurkin respond. At a November 2009 convention of the Church of God in Christ, he spoke—in both English and tongues—for over thirty minutes. He indicted everyone, the errant children and their negligent parents. "We've failed, we've failed, we've failed," he kept repeating, his voice sliding through two octaves of anguished vowels and percussive consonants. We parents have allowed our youth to be led astray by a culture of rampant sexuality. Extending his arm in a healing gesture, he pronounced, "I *loose* you from the computer."

Satan was tempting with imagery. (As tropes go, this one never loses its punch. Jimmy Swaggart says that when Satan appeared before him, he was "the most beautiful thing I've ever seen.") Stay on your knees, pray without ceasing, McClurkin commanded. Since the notoriety of his Obama appearances, he had begun to select his words with care. So, even as he made fun of the "broken and feminine" boys and "hard, mannish" young girls, he advised their parents, "Don't beat them, don't kill them." You might think that parents wouldn't need to hear this. But a few years earlier, Vickie Winans had told the convention how to deal with disobedient children: "Beat 'em, they won't die."

Instead, McClurkin wept, love them into submission. He made an altar call, commanding the young people to "run, run," and dozens of confused-looking youngsters rushed up the aisles. He next asked for a laying on of hands, but only by the "pure." Everyone in the house knew the scriptural verse "Touch not my anointed, do my children no harm." He implied that a mere swipe of a straying hand could violate the "babies" as they submerged themselves in Jesus. There were more tears, more tongues. Once again he announced himself a sinner saved by grace. (At other revivals he has allowed that his chains are still not completely broken. Every now and then the old lusts return: "Diabetics crave sugar, don't they, church?") Without the Holy Ghost he'd still be a "homosexual," the word uttered with blistering contempt. Only the cross had prevented his becoming a "vampire." When he uttered that word, saints lifted their arms, swayed and moaned. He had reached the higher ground of an inspired sermon. Gay men were not merely cradle snatchers and defilers of youth—they drank the children's blood!

Of course his appearance was uploaded on YouTube. And, of course, the saints applauded his holy boldness. With a bow to political correctness, some wrote that there was no hatred in his sermon; he spoke out of "nothing but love." Tonéx didn't hear the love; he demanded that McClurkin apologize. And gay people were mortified. A Web site devoted to black Christians was flooded with eloquent replies. One man wrote, "Organized religion strikes again. When will we realize that it is not our friend?" One went further: "This Donnie guy is so obviously in pain, so very much in pain. And these people are as dangerous as the Taliban."

And so it was finally being told, that the Pentecostal Taliban had ruined countless lives. "Ravenback" spoke a gay man's truth to COGIC power: "Not to lessen the massacre committed by Hasan at Fort Hood, but everyone gets worked up over this man and his Muslim faith as possibly being the impetus for his actions. If that's the case, then I don't see any difference from the Christian faith spewing out hatred against gays and causing many deaths in the wake. Too many of these churches filled with 'good Christian folk' have crammed young folks' heads with despair, shame, and unworthiness that has fueled a high number of suicides, drug usage, and alcohol abuse among our gay youth. How many lives have they cost?"

I found these words chilling. The gospel church was not the only culprit. The misguided words of Sigmund Freud may have caused as many suicides as those found in Leviticus. But in America today, the shame and hatred emanate most powerfully from the fundamentalist churches. Reading these comments, I found myself agreeing. Yes, here was that famous, biblically promised number that no man can number. Not merely all the gay men killed for being themselves. Not merely the church sons dead of AIDS and abandoned in their dying by their mother church. The number included so many others, those beaten but not dead, forced into half-lives. The strongest secret closet would buckle against these words. How many lives ruined, how many dead—all "in the name of Jesus"? If, as Walter Benjamin says, history must be written for its victims, the story of the gospel church's children demands to be told. Perhaps an eloquent youth will tell it. And just as no Holocaust story, whether it be the great memoirs of Victor Klemperer or Fred Wander, can begin to tell it all, so it will need many volumes of testimony to balance the scales in the children's favor.

Or perhaps the prodigal sons will produce another Peter Tatchell, arguably the most radical and courageous gay activist in the English-speaking world, who, among other deeds, has placed Robert Mugabe under citizen's arrest, confronted the mayor of Moscow for banning gay pride parades, and attacked the hate-filled strophes of reggae as "murder music." He was raised, a working-class Pentecostal, in Melbourne, Australia, where he was born again and Spirit slain at thirteen, four years before he stepped out of his secret closet.

———

Everyone expected a megapastor to be exposed, somewhat in the manner of Dr. George A. Rekers, the Family Research Council founder, who was outed after his vacation with a lad he had met on Rentboy.com.

And then in the fall of 2010, with the simple elegance of a fable, Bishop Eddie L. Long himself was outed. First one, then two, then three, and finally four young men declared that he had been their lover, wooing them with generous gifts and trips abroad. He admitted to treating them like his "sons," but only because he was trying to provide a model of male authority for a generation of fatherless boys, who had not known what it's like to have a strong man in the house. He had shown them how to dress, how to bathe, how to conduct themselves in the world. His profit was to have it all coalesce in one unforgettable metaphor, Jamal Parris's remark that "I cannot forget the smell of his cologne."

As I previously noted, gay men and lesbians have long referred to their lovers as their "spiritual" siblings and offspring. Long before Long, men had given a holy gloss to their sexual drive. Backrubs with holy oil had preceded many nights of tropical splendor. (The activity harks back to George Washington Carver, who applied his special invention of peanut oil to the jocks of Tuskegee.) Long's contribution was to make the charade part of a social—indeed, educational—movement.

The next Sunday Bishop Long appeared in church and seemed once more to deny the allegations. He had never claimed to be a perfect person, but "this is not me." He was strong in his faith, and he had not yet begun to fight. The church rose up, cheering and shouting. In subsequent days he denied every accusation, and said he welcomed a chance to prove his innocence.

But then photos of Long posing in form-fitting spandex went viral. The members of New Birth might claim that he was only encouraging the boys to follow him into the virile land of bodybuilding. Most everyone else saw the photos as erotic. By any light, it was a strange and wondrous event that the hallowed tradition of muscular Christianity should reach its apogee with the image of Eddie L. Long snapping himself with his cell phone.

New Birth tarried; America laughed. Especially when Bishop Long decided to go into mediation, thereby avoiding—perhaps only temporarily—a public trial. As every legal commentator observed, you could mediate a lot of things, but not the truth. Either he had slept with the boys or he had not. The Atlanta cartoonist Mike Luckovich drew Long in his pulpit and showed a congregation member hollering out, "Hallelujah! He's received the gift of speaking in legalese!"

That could be construed as intellectual white man's humor. But it was superseded by a riotously filthy YouTube clip, posted by Ms. Cadillac Kimberly, entitled "Dick Sucking Eddie Long, YA WRONG! 'WATCH THIS!!!!'" Given the gravamen of her argument, four exclamation points were not too many. Ms. Kimberly granted Long no mercy, and was equally dismissive of his wife. Many before had questioned why a woman might stay with a man she knew to be gay. Cadillac Kimberly said it was all about money and power.

Within three months, the clip had been viewed over a million times. Since, for all the attention of commentators like Anderson Cooper and Jeffrey Toobin, this remained a story of primary interest within black America, it was safe to conclude that Kimberly's analysis had saturated the community more dramatically than anything since . . . J. L. King's book *On the Down Low.* An educated guess would have the bulk of her viewership African-American, and most of that female.

Long's outing might have been a blip on the screen, as quickly forgotten as the scandal sheets' revelation that James Cleveland had died of AIDS. Except that his ordeal occurred within a few days of Tyler Clementi's suicide. In the next weeks there were a rash of "bullycides," most of them white boys, all of them driven to their deaths by the relentless attacks of those around them. America wept for these lost boys and, for the moment, assigned the face of their tormentor to Bishop Long.

This was a calamitous event within the history of black Christendom. Forty or fifty years earlier, the black church had acquired a wholly other image. Thanks to Bayard Rustin, Al Duckett, and Dr. King, for a few astonishing years it had become identified with the noblest aspirations of democracy. The church may have had its share of fools and knaves, but—much as Duckett had predicted—it now represented the best of America, to paraphrase President Obama, its veritable perfecting. Now all that had changed. The three biggest megachurches were ruled by outspoken homophobes—Bishop Long, Bishop Jakes, and Bishop Blake. And the most egregious forms of bigotry had been exported to the foreign outposts of Pentecostalism, countries like Jamaica or Uganda, where identifying yourself as gay could be a death sentence.

Even white America could not claim so many powerful bigots. (Jerry Falwell was dead; Pat Robertson, largely defanged.) Joel Osteen and Rick Warren were models of tolerance compared to Long or Jakes or the African and Jamaican happy clappers.

There was a historically fraught addendum. Shortly after Long's exposure, another Georgian megachurch pastor was outed, but this time by himself. Jim Swilley, founder of the Church in the Now in Corinth, revealed his sexuality within the pulpit. He had been raised in the Assemblies of God, speaking in tongues long before Eddie L. Long had received the Holy Ghost, through Jimmy Swaggart's intercession. He had grown up knowing that he was called to preach, and that he was a homosexual. That knowledge had nearly broken him. As a teenager, he had been half in love with death; the rapture could not come soon enough. Since his church believed in the exorcism of demons, he rolled on many a floor, hoping to be delivered from his curse. Until he concluded that there was no demon to cast out.

Before that, he had married twice; in a style reminiscent of many black Pentecostals, he made his second wife, Debye, his assistant pastor, and she bore him two sons, biblically named Judah and Jonas. But the style of his church and Long's could not be more different. If the tone at New Birth veers between hip-hop and switched-on Bapticostal, the Church in the Now re-creates the atmosphere of a down-home talk show. Swilley's church, remarkably integrated for the South, is a quieter, more sober place, astonishing enough for a church that still believes in prophecy and miracles: he even has spiritual "sons" in the West Indies and Africa, though whether they will tolerate his gayness remains an open question.

Like a character out of Nathaniel Hawthorne, Swilley stood in his pulpit and declared himself, but not with guilt or shame. He had always been gay—though he didn't mention any sexual episodes. He had informed Debye before their marriage, and she had accepted him anyhow. The television camera showed her assenting, showering him with loving glances. Finally she rose to testify herself. In one of the most astonishing episodes in the history of Christian marriage, she praised him for his courage. Since they were both committed to being honest and "real," he would have betrayed both of them by not admitting what he was, what he had always been. In words that might not have rung from many pulpits, she said, "I'm so frickin' driven . . . I'm your word made flesh."

What had prompted Swilley to risk everything? Most immediately, it had been the deaths of Tyler Clementi and the other boys. He told one local interviewer, "As a *father* . . . " and paused, more emotionally stricken than he had been in the pulpit, "I don't know . . . think about . . . your sixteen-, seventeen-year-old"—he coughed—"killing themselves . . . " and paused again, unable to speak. On another occasion, he warned about places like the one where he had been saved. "Take them to a hellfire-and-brimstone church . . . don't come crying to me when they commit suicide."

But there had been an earlier event in the summer of 2010. He had dined with several of Atlanta's megapastors, men draped in Armani suits and sporting "too much cologne"—nobody could escape the reference. Their waiter had been an effeminate kid, his face covered with acne—implicitly, not one of the comely thugs Eddie Long had called his sons. This was a far more typical church sissy, a real gay boy, not somebody who could be bought or seduced by power, and the aromatic men treated him with contempt. "These pastors were such jerks to him . . . these big successful gluttonous rich nasty preachers." Indicting them, Swilley sounded like some of the enraged men writing on the Internet. The media noted Swilley's story, though mostly as an addendum to the Long saga. Nobody observed the comparative paradox of a white preacher accusing a black preacher of intolerance. Had sexual identity come to supersede racial? Both black and white critics condemned Long for his hypocrisy . . . and the members of New Birth for their blind faith. Greed and ego, those great American standbys, had assumed the garb of evangelical Christianity, a tale at least two centuries old. The only difference was that now gay men were the sacrifical lambs.

In the last week of May 2011, Bishop Long and his accusers settled out of court; their attorney, B. J. Bernstein, pledged absolute silence, though within a few days there were reports of an $850,000 or even a $15 million payout, quite enough to bankrupt most congregations. (At that rate, even the Catholic Church would fold.) On May 29, Elder Bernice King resigned from the church, a fact that Bishop Long deigned not to announce until after Memorial Day, in order not to divert attention from America's servicemen and -women: Is it religion or patriotism that's supposed to be the scoundrel's last refuge?

That very week, Lady Gaga's *Born This Way*—with its acknowledged echo of Bishop Carl Bean—became the fastest-selling album in six years. I could imagine Charles Campbell grinning, "Son, ain't the Lord good?"

———

The black church might not be the same after the fall of Bishop Long. Or the forces of intolerance might win out; they still had a lot working for them—custom, tradition, and simple familiarity. Long might simply end up an outcast; he had already been abandoned by many pastors, including the fiercest ex-gay on the Internet, an evangelist who calls himself DL Foster (and let the devil make something of those initials).

Barely a month after Long's case was settled, the church's persecution of gay people acquired a new dimension impinging on national politics. The victory of gay marriage in New York State on June 24 prompted many calls for President Obama to endorse it as well. His inhibitions were specifically linked to his fear of losing black church support and thereby endangering his chances of re-election. If you wanted evidence, on June 26, the very day of the most exhilarating gay pride march in history, Black Entertainment Television broadcast a salute to the biggest stars in black music. The gospel artists chosen were all outspoken homophobes—Shirley Caesar (who had lately boasted that "we've already killed Saddam," a pun on Gomorrah's twin city), Mary Mary (who had equated their gay fans with murderers), Deitrick Haddon (who had volunteered his services to the National Organization for Marriage), and Donnie McClurkin, the church's most visibly tormented self-hater.

If these were the faces of the black church, Obama would indeed have had cause for alarm. Yet Shirley Caesar performed a pop ballad, "You Have a Friend," dedicated to Patti LaBelle, who, ever since Luther Vandross founded her first fan club, has been the queen of black gay America. McClurkin, Haddon, and Mary Mary performed "Thank You Lord (for All You've Done for Me)," a song composed by the gay-affirming Bishop Walter Hawkins and popularized by Bishop Yvette Flunder, the most outspoken lesbian in gospel.

How could you deconstruct this leviathan? The arch-homophobes were singing the music of gay people, acknowledging with every breath and step that if you banished the sissies and bull daggers, the tabernacle might crumble. It would be like Germany without its Jews.

Perhaps salvation lay in humor, the same humor that minorities have always deployed to keep themselves sane. The thoughts too deep or bitter for tears might just be soothed with laughter; the balm in Gilead restored to those who dwell in secret closets. There might still be spectacles to rival Larry Hart serenading his sanctified mom with "Cock Talk."

A couple of years ago, Donnie McClurkin held a revival in Philadelphia. Though he may tell the world that he's only working out his soul's salvation, in church he engages in full-frontal exorcism. One night he had a prayer line of young men standing, their arms lifted, hoping to be released from their demons. He noticed one guy, Billy, who had fallen out during the choir's last song. As the boy revived, he pointed to him: "I'm spiritually led to recognize a sissy. Boy, come on up. You need a double dose of the Holy Ghost." He then lay his anointed hands on the boy, shaking him so forcefully that he fell out again. After that, Billy returned to his seat. A church mother patted him on the shoulder. "Son, those are some beautiful earrings you got. Now that you've been delivered, you won't need them no more. Why don't you give them to me?"

My favorite retort occurred in the early 1990s. Evangelist Shirley Caesar held a revival in Chicago and pleaded for "all the sissies and bull daggers" to "come up and be saved." One fellow turned to his friend: "You going up?"

"No, baby," was the reply. "If it was good enough for Mother, it's yet good enough for me."

Or scripture might provide the last word. After the young men turned on Bishop Long, he declared himself the little guy in the fight, but just like another small fellow, King David, he claimed to possess five stones, and in God's own time they would all be thrown. He might better have quoted another of David's remarks: "If I cover my head, my feet will show. If I cover my feet, my head will show."

ARETHA: HOW SHE GOT OVER

Two of the most significant public events of our time were graced by the presence of gospel singers. The first was the 1963 March on Washington. Mahalia Jackson sang a triumphant "How I Got Over," recalling the storefront singer of her youth and not the officious matriarch of national television. But she did more than set the crowd up for Dr. Martin Luther King's speech.

When Dr. King's first paragraphs didn't excite, the showman in Mahalia instructed her to go with the hits. "Martin, tell them about the dream," she kept repeating until he got the message. Without her insistence, America would not have heard his most famous words. She might have played another role. Fearing a violent reaction from the crowd, Robert Kennedy had been prepared to have his staff play Mahalia's version of "He's Got the Whole World in His Hands," at such volume that any outbursts would be drowned out. (His taste in gospel was of an order with his knowledge of Dr. King's movement.)

The second event on the podium was, of course, Barack Obama's inauguration, and it included another gospel singer, only nominally ex-, Aretha Franklin. That occasion was marred by the appearance of Rick Warren and his previous comments about gay and women's rights. He was representing—to the huge disappointment of many voters. But so, in her particular way, was she.

Somehow Aretha's appearance, in all its complexity, carried me back to the spring of 1961 and a party given by the publicist Al Duckett.

I was a young gospel fan and had recently heard Aretha singing in Brooklyn's Washington Temple Church of God in Christ. Her co-stars had included her father, Reverend C. L. Franklin, the most popular black preacher in America; Miss Sammie Bryant, a dwarf with more volume than most bass-baritones; and the Davis Sisters, a magnificent female group. Aretha had sung with vigor and spunk. But she had been obviously outclassed by her elders, and the voice seemed precociously fatigued. So I was not prepared to hear, coming out of Duckett's tape recorder, Aretha Franklin singing:

> *Yesterday I sang a love song,*
> *Today, I'm singing the blues.*

The voice was thrillingly clear, combining the beauty of her two favorite singers, Clara Ward and Judy Garland. There was also a note of fearsome urgency, an expressive directness that I had not heard at the Apollo Theater, certainly not during the rhythm-and-blues shows, and not really in the gospel, because it was both angry and introspective.

This was the same Duckett who had ghost-written Jackie Robinson's biography and co-wrote many of Dr. King's early dispatches. But that afternoon his role was to promote the debut of C. L. Franklin's daughter as someone singing "the devil's music," a move as epochal in its way as Dr. King's nascent program. Though in the early days C. L. Franklin was dismissive of Dr. King, he would become his staunchest ally, someone with a grass-roots appeal that the formally educated King had lacked. (He was also, Duckett informed me, a closet blues singer; he claimed to have recordings of the pastor singing Muddy Waters, though I never heard them.)

In retrospect here was the nexus of politics and show business that would define American life for years to come. Here too was a forecast of one singer's immensely complicated career.

It is received wisdom that the Beatles and Bob Dylan helped change the culture, at least during the 1960s. The areas where Aretha did the same go uninspected but are more intriguing. There may be no other show-business saga quite like hers. She is not merely one of the best-selling vocalists of all time; she is also the most purely folkloric to succeed in a worldly context, surely the only pop singer to bring so rich an alternative tradition into the arena.

Thanks to her example, women vocalists of all races were allowed a freedom, a chance at an uninhibited transcendence, that would never have been the option of middle-class Brits or working-class Mexicans or Catholic girls from Newark. Her greatest power of example was within her own community. She introduced forms of self-representation that would profoundly change the way black women lived in the world. Not particularly as a conventional feminist: the message of "Respect" goes only so far. But in other ways, her role was such that a history of black America could well be divided into pre- and post-Aretha.

The rumor that this great woman had been diagnosed with pancreatic cancer devastated her fans, many of whom had never known a life without her voice. Fifty years since her debut, she had become one of America's most famous women, one of the few immediately identified by her first name. Few female performers, and certainly no other black women, have lasted that long, or have continued to claim the spotlight years—visible years, audible years—since their initial glory. Fewer performers of any kind have incarnated so many roles—foxy lady, proto-feminist, earth mother, avatar of high culture from opera to ballet, and storefront evangelist—simultaneously, and insisted on being all of them, at any time, in any place. Likewise, few apart from the similarly mononomial Elvis have gone from sexy svelte to comically obese—and he didn't survive the change. A Sinatra or Dylan might have enjoyed similar longevity, but they both had advantages denied her, starting with their race and sex.

The chorus of "Blessed Assurance" begins "This is my story, this is my song." What may distinguish Aretha from most of the other singing legends is that her story always seems so much larger than her song, no lyric adequate to the breadth of her experience. That is one reason why she could reign, almost without dispute, as Lady Soul, the personification of a feeling larger than mere words (one that perhaps could only be expressed in a wordless moan).

She was born in 1942, the daughter of C. L. and Barbara Franklin. Barbara left home when Aretha was ten and died a few years later without seeing her children again. But Aretha would become a true daughter of the church, with many gospel-singing mothers, and as a father, the dean of Baptist preachers, "the man with the million-dollar voice."

HER FATHER

A few years ago *Mojo* anointed Aretha Franklin the greatest singer of the twentieth century. For all her fame, she would be the first to say that the real star in her family was her father, Reverend C. L. Franklin, pastor of Detroit's New Bethel Baptist Church. During the 1950s, his albums preaching a theology of liberation and racial pride sold millions of copies, and helped prepare the way for Dr. King. Within black America, Reverend Franklin was royalty. That his daughter would become the Queen of Soul was almost inevitable.

In his biography, *Singing in a Strange Land: C. L. Franklin, the Black Church, and the Transformation of America*, Nick Salvatore reveals Franklin to have been a huge character, whose personality comprehended great charm and eloquence, a heroic drive to outrun the miserable circumstances of his youth, and a surplus of energy, more than enough for a political statesman, CEO, or matinee idol. He was also a notorious lover of women and liquor, a Falstaffian padre to astonish Nathaniel Hawthorne and delight Graham Greene.

Salvatore, a labor historian, makes vivid the social networks Franklin inhabited, from Masonic lodge to political backroom; indeed, he makes the annual meetings of the National Baptist Convention, with their fierce battles over ideology and fiefdom, sound like Wild West shoot-outs, particularly since so many of the warring preachers, including Franklin, carried pistols. He traces Franklin from his youth as a sharecropper in Mississippi, where he was born in 1915, to his early preaching days in Memphis and Buffalo and his fat years in Detroit, where he practically ruled the town. He also sees Franklin's life as a pilgrim's progress. He may not always have welcomed his calling—he told a young man considering the ministry, "If you can keep from doing it, then don't"—but never denied it.

Clarence LaVaughn Franklin, known to friend and foe alike as "Frank," was both a master of old-school oratory—he almost never strayed into ebonics—and the most powerful "Mississippi whooper" (a leonine but lyrical growl) of his generation. Exhibiting the same range was his favorite singer, J. Robert Bradley, the soulful Paul Robeson, who could move from concert spiritual to backwoods moan. "Frank had more music in his holler," Bradley remembered, "than any of them out here today; gospel today is just a whole lot of mess."

Franklin's strength came from both mind and voice, a robust rangy baritone that contained traces of blues singers like Muddy Waters and vaudevillians like his special favorite, Al Jolson (even as Judy Garland would become a vocal model for Aretha). He first recorded as a singer, and he was very much part of the modern gospel tradition. Unlike other Baptist men who sang in a cappella quartets, he opted to perform the new, piano-based gospel, a bold choice of genres since the form's earliest stars were primarily women and gay men. In masterpieces like "Precious Lord," "The Old Ship of Zion," and "I Will Trust in the Lord," Frank displayed the melismatic and improvisatory ease of the greatest male singers. Song was crucial to Frank, to his message and his delivery. He played a congregation as if it were his instrument, and their synchronized response, always in tune and tempo with him, outshone any choir. His sermons are transcendentally lyrical because when he soars highest in the Spirit he draws closest to the melodic flow of a gospel song. He hears the piano's chords even when they aren't there.

After she became a star, Aretha delighted in introducing him as "the greatest man I know," and in summoning his presence whenever she had a chance. For example, in her recording of the classic blues "Going Down Slow," she imagines a poor woman on her deathbed, calling for her dad. "Tell him to pray for me, and to forgive me for my sins"—a line she phrases as hard-boiled and conclusive. She imagines her bereft father: "All he can do is stand there and moan," ad-libbing, "And I believe he can do it, yes he can." The lyric posited a moaning parent; it just happened that this one was a moaner second to none—unless it was his daughter herself.

Bradley first met Frank in Memphis, along with his wife, Barbara, whom Bradley remembered as "a beautiful mulatto woman with fine, soft hair." She could sing (on the order of Mary Johnson Davis, who, coincidentally, also inspired Aretha's idol Clara Ward), "play piano while turning toward the people, just sing and entertain . . . and have children. And she was the making of Frank." Given the central place of women in church, that could only mean encouraging her husband to whoop and holler until the sisters fell out. After giving birth to four children, Aretha and her siblings, Erma, Cecil, and Carolyn, Barbara separated from Frank, although they were never divorced. The children would be raised by their grandmother Rachel Franklin, familiarly known as Aunt Rachel, who, according to her son and granddaughter, possessed a mighty hand: i.e., she didn't spare the rod.

In Memphis Frank also encountered his mentor, Reverend W. Herbert Brewster, pastor of East Trigg Missionary Baptist Church and one of gospel's greatest composers, whose songs, like "How I Got Over," usually included coded references to social mobility and political empowerment. Brewster's featured soloist was a stout, light-skinned woman named Candace T. Anderson, who would cut very few records but is remembered as one of the most powerful vocalists in gospel history. It was she who introduced the Brewster compositions that would become the signature songs of Mahalia Jackson, Marion Williams, and Clara Ward. By the late 1930s, she had attracted enough black and white followers to be dubbed "the Queen of the South." After that, Reverend Brewster renamed her Queen C. Anderson. He had also helped raise J. Robert Bradley, who remembered inheriting the "used drawers of Brewster Jr."

That would have been somebody's idea of musical heaven: a church that featured the tyro sermons of a young C. L. Franklin and the early vocals of Queen C. Anderson and J. Robert Bradley, two of the most soulful singers in American history. By the mid-1950s Sam Phillips of Sun Records was recording Reverend Brewster and bringing singers like Elvis Presley to East Trigg. It's fair to say that two superstars, Aretha and Elvis, were among Brewster's acolytes. Presley often acknowledged his Sundays at the church; and Aretha has continued to sing Brewster songs like "Surely God Is Able" and "The Old Landmark." All of Brewster's songs and sermons were steeped in biblical imagery, seldom as wondrously deployed since the days of King James. Among many examples:

Who is this who's coming from Edom
Who lifts up falling men from bondage to freedom?

or

We'll be like a bird set free from his cage,
While red seas and Jordans beneath us do rage.

or

(In glory)
David will be there, playing his harp around the throne,
Jeremiah will be there, with the fire in his bones,
Queen Esther will be there, dressed in royal uniform,
Job will be there, waiting for his change to come.

or

John saw a pale horse,
Death rode his back,
And hell was on his heels
As he dashed on down the track.

Surrounded by Brewster, Queen, and Bradley, Frank received the best tutelage in deep gospel blues. In short order, he became the boy wonder of Memphis gospel, displaying enough fire to wreck houses with his songs and sermons, and yet exhibiting enough cool to host a weekly radio program devoted to local politics.

In 1950 he had a regional hit singing "Give Me Wings"—the gospel diva Willie Mae Ford Smith swore he had stolen her arrangement—but he only became king of the gospel highway with the release a few years later of his sermon "The Eagle Stirreth Her Nest." As Bradley veered from lieder to moans, Frank exploited all the folkloric devices without being quite what academics call a "folk preacher." He both incarnated and transcended what he called, using the jargon of night-school sociology courses, "my traditional upbringing."

He did it by likening captive Hebrews and enslaved Africans to black Americans suffering under the yokes of Jim Crow and exploiting bosses; his flock was now made up, not of farmers, but of factory workers. He thrilled black churches with his ability to make things new by making them plain. The whole point of his long-winded, spoken preambles was the ecstatic song-filled conclusion wherein theology was domesticated. Christ became "our brother" in a literal sense; the Gospel writers, church deacons.

His references included historical figures, biblical scholars, and writers ranging from Countee Cullen to Rudyard Kipling, The subtext was frequently one of cultural nationalism—this is how *we* worship; moaning and shouting brought *us* through—but there was also a spirit of auto-critique. Toward the end of his life he lamented that you could stir a crowd with the "gravy" of a Mississippi growl. But they would be "entertained," and not enlightened, a situation he found "disillusioning."

Am I wrong to also find in Frank's greatest sermons a note bordering on the confessional? Knowing as he did what people said about him, he displayed a delirious chutzpah in titling one of his sermons "The Preacher Who Got Drunk"; and in "Hosea the Prophet and Gomer the Prostitute," after the hero drives away his wife, the mother of his children, he laments what time has done to her "fine lovely hair." Yet, impersonating Hosea, Frank moans, "But I love her just the same . . . O Lord . . . I know she left me alone," in a passage as dense with blue tonality as Robert Johnson at his most despairing. He outdoes himself in "Jacob Wresting the Angel." Jacob was "human, all too human," and he lists a bill of indictment that covers many of his own sins ("a trickster, a deceiver, a supplanter, you understand, a man of extreme selfishness and self-centeredness"). In a Spirit-filled moment, Frank announces that "Jacob was wrestling with Jacob . . . He was wrestling with himself." If, as Yeats says, we make rhetoric out of arguments with the world, and art out of arguments with ourselves, then Frank now becomes a commanding artist, turning his mirey muck into pure gold.

Lofted by "The Eagle," Franklin began touring with the Famous Ward Singers. Salvatore paints an amusing picture of his run-ins with the group's manager, the imperious Madame Gertrude Ward. But it should be remembered that the Wards featured two of the greatest gospel singers, Ward's youngest daughter, Clara, and Marion Williams. When Marion led two of Reverend Brewster's most affirmative anthems, "Surely God Is Able" and "I'm Climbing Higher and Higher," she was singing what Franklin preached. The Wards were equally famous for their flamboyant robes and their architectural hairdos. Salvatore is very alert to Frank's self-presentation, including his thirty-five suits and jazzily conked hair. With their robes and wigs, the Wards were treading the same winepress, setting standards of fashion and performance for men and women alike. Through such tours—and gospel singers still claim that "Clara made him"—Frank became the hero of a generation: according to J. Robert Bradley, "he inspired more black men to preach than anyone in the twentieth century." It was a match of colossi that culminated in the long romance of Frank and Clara Ward, the King of Preachers and the Queen of Gospel.

Starting in the 1950s, Frank took an active role in the civil rights struggle. He allied himself with Dr. King, to the extreme displeasure of

Dr. J. H. Jackson, the National Baptist Convention's president. Most of President Bush's black support came from church folk, who endorsed his conservative politics and seconded his opposition to same-sex marriage. Most of them happened to be Pentecostal, and Franklin had no love for Pentecostals; in 1977 he told Jeff Todd Titon that their noisy faith healing offended him, and he occasionally targeted sanctified preachers as clowns and charlatans. It is doubtful that he would have joined the current gay bashing; his favorite pianist, Herbert Pickard, says "Frank wouldn't even have gone there."

Franklin was physically memorable, with dark African skin, precise Ethiopian lips, and slanted eyes that could seem almost Asian. He can be seen in all his glory in Sydney Pollack's film of the *Amazing Grace* recording session. Frank owns the pulpit and overflows the screen—you wonder if any movie star could match his charisma. He's overjoyed. Not merely has his girl conquered the world, but she hasn't abandoned the church, not one holy bit. "Aretha is just a . . . a *stone* singer," he boasts. Yielding to his scholarly impulse, he imagines her art as a "synthesist" [sic] of all her ancestors—Mahalia, the Ward Singers. Then he mocks himself, spinning half to his knees, "What am I talking about?" Meanwhile, Aretha sits in a state of extreme attention, a small girl desperate for her father's approval. It is that fawn-in-the-headlights look her fans know so well.

While she sings "Never Grow Old," accompanying herself on piano as she had during their first tours, he gazes proudly from his seat. When she comes up with an inspired ad lib, he spins around, looking for someone to giggle with in sheer musical delight. When she starts to sweat, he stands and mops her brow, one of the most poignant paternal gestures I've seen in a movie.

Toward the end, sickness and drink ravaged the once-brave voice. There were unfortunate episodes—run-ins with the IRS, an arrest for drunken driving, etc. He could still astonish one, as when he informed David Frost that he didn't believe in hell—"I'm too good a father"—and on a rare healthy Sunday he could still manage to whoop, holler, and shout the house. In 1979 he was shot by robbers who had invaded his home. He lingered in a vegetative state for over five years. During this period Aretha sacrificed her career to tend him.

The black church could have gone in either direction: the liberation theology of King and Franklin or the social conservatism of the Pentecostals. The musical analogy would be to have stuck with the bluesy tradition of the Wards and Reverend Brewster or succumb to the brittle charms of contemporary gospel. In both cases Frank's side lost. In 2005, J. Robert Bradley sang one final time at the convention. Afterward, people came up to him saying they hadn't shouted so hard in forty years, "not since Frank was our pastor and you were our singer." But he didn't encourage them. "I told them I ain't coming back. Time that's been won't be no more."

HER MOTHERS

Among the several myths Franklin incarnated was a familiar type— Reverend Eatemup, the man with pastoral appetites in food and women. This kind of preacher, according to myth, assumes that he owns the church and the members therein. And as if to confirm the myth, pastors who swindle and ravish their flocks have never gone out of style. It has become a sad kind of ghetto comedy to see the number of newfangled preachers reverting to all the old ways. Even the connection between political radicalism and pulpit chicanery is not new, most famously exemplified by the proudly corrupt Adam Clayton Powell.

The myth of a blues-singing gospel girl was much less familiar. In actual fact, before Aretha, there had only been two, Dinah Washington and Sister Rosetta Tharpe. Like Aretha and her idol Clara Ward, Dinah had been a singing pianist, modeling both of her talents on Roberta Martin. Her early recordings, when her voice was still high and clear, exhibit the elegant, refined but soulful phrasing of her mentor. As the years coarsened her voice, her persona turned into a self-professed Evil Gal. Yet the earthier she got, the more churchy she sounded. For example, listen on YouTube to her great performance of "Come Rain or Come Shine." When she growls out the line "Days may get cloudy or sunny," the previously quiet room erupts. She's taken a supper club back to church, an uncommon event back in that day.

Unlike her peers Ella Fitzgerald or Sarah Vaughan, Dinah was almost never simply pretty. Her slant was wry and unsentimental, matter-of-fact to the point of cynicism. She liked to swallow a word, thereby making any sentiment equivocal. Dinah was the woman who told it like it was, just what you'd expect from a gospel singer. This truth telling was more often than not sensual in the extreme, a fact not mitigated by Dinah's absence of conventional glamour.

In 1969, at the height of Aretha's fame, Albert Goldman wrote that she was the first black woman singer to express "the normal female soul or the free expression of the full range of female feeling." He then made the fairly outrageous observation that Aretha's version of "Satisfaction" was "the greatest proclamation of sexual fulfillment since Molly Bloom's soliloquy." Of course, the difference between James Joyce and Mick Jagger is that one writer evokes pleasure, the other, its exhausting denial. Goldman's pretentious remark betrays his inability to hear the actual lyric. Adding insult to injury, he feared that Aretha would sacrifice this relaxed eros to the strident force of gospel shouting. In fact, her interpretation of the song was steeped in hard gospel, from its shouting tempo to its lilting whoop notes.

He had obviously not heard Lil Green's 1940 masterpiece, "Romance in the Dark," with its juxtaposition of gospel church belting and unabashed lewdness; the song ends with a very sly command, "Turn out the lights." Nor, apparently, had he seen other blues women at the Apollo Theater fellate the microphone. But he could have been expected to know Dinah's fabulous "TV Is the Thing," in which, to a bluesy gospel riff out of the Ward Singers, Miss D lists her repairman's skills: "The way he eased into channel 1, / I knew that this was gonna be fun," etc. With equal nonchalance, she could make an innocuous ballad like "Teach Me Tonight" sound just as "blue." Where the lyric reads "Starting with the ABC of it, / Right down to the XYZ of it," she ad-libs the word "roll" before the "right down," thereby making it a lesson truly worth learning.

Even before Dinah swept black America with songs like "Fat Daddy" and "Long John," another church girl had confounded the public with her daring sensuality. Sister Rosetta Tharpe's career more closely parallels Aretha's. Both women specialize in ambivalence, an erotic gospel, a holy blues. Rosetta's style, as singer and guitarist, was always representative of her sanctified denomination, the Church of God in Christ.

Nineteen thirty-eight was a pivotal year in the rapprochement of gospel and pop music. The Golden Gate Jubilee Quartet recorded Harold Arlen's "Stormy Weather" with the huge blocked chords and bluesy slurs of a Baptist hymn, the kind C. L. Franklin or J. Robert Bradley excelled in singing. I'd rank the Gates's recording as the forerunner of 1960s soul, challenged only by Rosetta's version of "Look Down That Lonesome Road," in which she sings, "Love, oh Love, what have I done," with the anguish of a sinner kneeling at the mourner's bench. She periodically recorded blues, though "only when I'm broke." In 1953 her so-called blues "What Have I Done" was a transparent revision of the old church song "Love, O Love Divine." On the flip side, she begged her man to return, promising him that "the Lord will bless you." Her fans felt betrayed, but as she saw it, she was still walking in the light.

Her first gospel records were even more ambiguous than her blues. Thomas A. Dorsey had written "Jesus, hear me singing"; Rosetta recorded "Won't you hear me swinging?" She retitled Dorsey's "Feed Me, Jesus" "Rock Me," and since she didn't call anybody's name, a listener could take her invocation for a love song. Equally open to interpretation was "My Man and I," her revision of an old hymn, "My Lord and I." In perhaps her most intense early performance Rosetta sings lyrics that could only be construed as religious:

He knows how much I'm longing for
Some souls for him to win;
And so he bids me to go and say
A loving word for him.

But then, lost in a spirit of her own invention, she concludes:

He knows how much I love him,
He knows that I love him well,
But with what love he loveth me
No tongue can ever tell.
It's an everlasting love
With an ever rich supply,
And so we love each other,
My man and I.

Any listener, saved or not, would be confused, especially with her seductive intonation of the words "love" and "supply."

Rosetta always flirted with her audience. She would make transparent love to her guitar, plucking the strings in a kind of foreplay. Frequently, as her husband charged up the electricity, she'd chant, "Oooh, Daddy, fill me up . . . feels so good," while saints chuckled at her holy boldness.

Singers like Mahalia Jackson presented a stolid, almost sanctimonious face to the world (always mitigated, however, in Mahalia's case, by her good humor and earthy charm); Rosetta was more brazen. In Gayle Wald's biography we learn about a time when, unhappy with her husband, she proposed to a French fan. She inquired whether he was saved. "Well, no." Not even a little bit? No, not at all. This didn't faze her; she wasn't a fanatic, and his agnosticism would not be a dealbreaker.

Aretha would never be a show woman like Rosetta or Dinah. During the mid-sixties, her disco moves were polite and timorous—no Tina Turner she. Her favorite dance step would be the church shout. In one clip she performs "Jumping Jack Flash," accompanied by some English musicians. The groove moves her and her group to start shouting, as if they were still church girls getting happy. It was one of her many gifts to the secular world.

—

The church Aretha knew had always been a citadel but not a sanctuary, particularly for its wonder children.

Rosetta Tharpe once told me, "I was just a little innocent babe from Cotton Plant, Arkansas. Then I hit Chicago and they turned me every way but loose." When she hit Chicago, she was all of five years old. A cousin raped Willa and Clara Ward when they were twelve and nine, respectively. Willa endured, perhaps because she quit the church for piano bars, but Clara's life would become a long series of torments. (The cousin later raped one of his daughters.)

Child abuse has been distressingly common. The obituary of Reverend James Bevel noted his legendary role as the organizer of the Birmingham, Alabama, civil rights movement. But it also recorded his time in jail for raping his teenage daughter—only one of the relatives he had abused. Kids growing up in church were exposed to other horrors. When she was nine, Marion Williams saw her father murdered by one of his girlfriends. Many years later, in her recording "Look at the People," she imagined "Robert," her dad, standing at the judgment about to be tried. In another recording she sang, "There's a man going around taking names, / One day he took my father's name and he left my heart in pain," her performance conveying the violent nature of that loss. The Davis Sisters' second lead Jackie Verdell, another of Aretha's inspirations, was a child when she saw her father kill her mother. Years later, she sang the same verse with one word changed: "There's a man going around taking names, / One day he took my mother's name and he left my heart in pain." In this case the male figure wasn't Death.

C. L. Franklin lived very high. His youngest daughter, Carolyn, once said that all their lives the children had heard rumors that their father would be killed by romantic rivals, as many a preaching Lothario has been. Predictably, when Aretha at the age of thirteen gave birth to her first child, the word went out that Franklin had fathered his own grandson. Among those who knew Frank as both co-workers in the vineyard and drinking buddies, men like J. Robert Bradley and Herbert Pickard, this was pure slander: "Frank loved those children unto death"; and Paul Owens, one of Aretha's early suitors, a mere sixteen years her senior, said Franklin "hated me," most likely because he knew that quartet singers were as casually promiscuous as he was.

Still, the ubiquity of the rumor obliged Nick Salvatore, Franklin's biographer, to confront it and plead, since there was no evidence, would the gossips finally shut up?

Aretha told her biographer David Ritz that the rumor was a canard, and that its source was John Hammond, the Vanderbilt heir who had produced her first album for Columbia. (Having worked with Hammond, I know that he could be unforgiving, and Aretha's decision to go with other producers greatly rankled him. He would also condemn Mahalia Jackson for her materialism, though only after her records for Columbia had stopped selling. He also once accused Sister Rosetta Tharpe of being "a terrible person." Her fault? Demanding a $400 advance in 1968 for a reissue of her appearance in the "Spirituals to Swing" concert he had produced in 1938. Hammond was far more protective of his socialite pals. When biographers revealed that Carl Van Vechten's celebration of Harlem culture was linked to his attendance at male brothels, Hammond grew livid: "Carl was my friend!" That kind of scandal was reserved for the 'hood and not the Four Hundred.)

Many gospel singers were born out of wedlock. Many fathers abandoned their families. The great Dorothy Love Coates never forgave her Baptist-preacher dad for leaving her mother, Lillar McGriff, and their six children. In her own composition "You've Been Good to Me," she sings the familiar lines "You've been a mother to me, / You've been a father to me," but then adds a killing "hmmm," as if to underline the role God was forced to play. Once, at the Apollo Theater, I saw Dot testify about her mother's lot, "raising six fatherless children." Afterward she introduced me to a short, sweet-looking man, a handsome Desmond Tutu. "Tony baby, come and meet my father, Reverend McGriff, and his wife." He must have heard her words about him.

C. L. Franklin's affair with Clara Ward was notorious for its physical violence. Many people have reported that Frank beat Clara in public. (Since Clara had this experience with other men, it might have been partly her own choice.) It was expected that rich women occasionally paid for their pleasure. In Gayle Wald's biography of Sister Rosetta Tharpe, an ex–Dixie Hummingbird boasts of being her gigolo and then, adding sanctimony to his lack of class, adds that he's now got the Holy Ghost. Rosetta's third husband, Russell Morrison, did very little but manage her career, and very poorly at that. Mahalia Jackson's last years were cursed by her acrimonious divorce from the younger, handsome, and notably unchurched Sigmund Galloway (who would die, anyway, shortly after she did, as would her first husband, the ex-bookie Ike Hockenhull). Yet, according to Willa Ward's autobiography, Frank remained at Clara's beck and call and was by her side during her last hours. The women who told Nick Salvatore that Frank really didn't like Clara, that it was Baptist love for Baptist sale, may have been simply jealous. After all, why shouldn't two geniuses have found each other?

The women in Aretha's gospel circles didn't treat each other very well. It was a world inhabited by "mothers against daughters, fathers against sons." Ever since Aimee Semple McPherson's mother, Minnie Kennedy, began managing her daughter's work for the Lord, it was traditional for parents to aggressively protect their anointed children from the world and its woes. Eventually Minnie and Aimee had a public and permanent split. When Aimee died in 1944, supposedly of an accidental overdose, she was speaking to neither her mother nor her daughter. (She was still a star evangelist, having briefly converted the ex–boxing champion Jack Johnson, much as, decades later, Bennie Hinn would leave Evander Holyfield slain in the Spirit. And then it turned out that the latter wasn't even sick; he had been misdiagnosed! Minnie would have chuckled over all that slaying in vain.)

Gertrude Ward was gospel's Minnie Kennedy. Rosetta Tharpe had begun traveling with her singing and ukulele-playing mother, Evangelist Katie Bell Nubin. But Mother Bell was the embodiment of sanctified behavior; even as Rosetta used to perform in low-cut gowns, the old lady would dress in unadorned, consecrated black. Madame Ward liked glamour. Just as Aimee Semple McPherson had dressed her "Angels" in frilly robes—"God means his people to be beautiful"—Madame Ward would reimagine the traditional choir robes of the black church. Admittedly, it was a homespun glamour; she designed her group's robes and sewed them herself. But they astonished gospel fans of the 1940s and 1950s, many of whom attended the Wards' programs, not simply because they were the best of all groups, but to view their outfits. By the late fifties, inspired now by Josephine Baker, she had her "girls" sport ponytails. Her final fashion statement was to appear, during her seventies, with a skunklike hairdo in which a white streak bisected her jet-black wig.

This was a decorative impulse shared by the men of that era who, like C. L. Franklin, sported processed hair, the result of extremely painful scalp treatments. (Years later, these men would joke that they had "cooked" off their hair, and that now, like their wives, they too had to wear wigs. If you'd ask them whether the baroque hairdo was actually theirs, the standard reply was, "Sure it's mine—I paid for it!") It is perhaps too easy to see the wigs and processes as a form of racial self-hatred . . . although the face lighteners might be another story. In one famous photo, Clara Ward can be seen kneeling at the Apollo Theater "singing out of her soul" with her face lightened to a Kabuki-like pallor.

The singers realized that wigs and processes didn't change their racial status. In fact, the styles were at best parodies of white fashion. Sallie Martin said of one pioneer cosmetician, "God gave Madame Walker a special formula—for *us*." Mahalia Jackson, a famous beautician in Chicago, sported an immense beehive that made her seem formidably tall. Clara Ward didn't have that kind of hair, but Marion Williams did, and it became enough of a fashion statement that Little Richard, who was already singing like Marion, employed the same beehive in his early publicity photos.

Publicity became something that gospel singers, having moved from amateur to professional status, craved. Getting into *Jet, Ebony,* and the *Pittsburgh Courier* became a big deal; when Clara Ward beat out Mahalia in a newspaper contest, fans joked that Madame Ward had bought the votes. By the mid-fifties, gospel singers and quartets were getting the full treatment from the show-business photographer James Kriegsmann. Today the photos look unnaturally studied, not to mention touched-up. The poses are as ingenuous as Hollywood shots of Judy Garland or

Mickey Rooney. That they completely contradicted the actual person-
alities was not an issue: the ideal was a kind of virginal glamour, without
fault or blemish.

Gertrude Murphy Ward, one of fourteen children, was born in Anderson, South Carolina, but moved to Philadelphia, where her daughters
Willa and Clara were born. During the early 1930s, she and her children became the East Coast exponents of the new gospel coming out
of Chicago, pioneered by the composer-pianist Thomas A. Dorsey and
his song seller Sallie Martin. Dorsey's other protégée, the singing pianist
Roberta Martin (no relation to Sallie), would found the Roberta Martin Singers, the first important gospel group. Among Dorsey's and the
Martins' first protégées were Clara Ward and Dinah Washington, who
began her career singing with Sallie, but preferred Roberta.

(The queen mothers could be intensely competitive. Alex Bradford
used to claim that if either Sallie Martin or Mahalia heard that one of
her tenants was seen shouting off the other's performances, she'd raise
his rent. In one Chicago legend, Mahalia: Sallie, and Roberta all sing at
a church program. Afterward, the promoter apologizes to Mahalia: "I'm
sorry. The offering was no good—we only raised two hundred dollars."
She replies, "That's all right, darlin'. Just give me one-fifty and give the
rest to the little singers." Upon which Roberta steps up: "B[for bitch],
who you calling a little singer?")

Madame Ward had a soft but moving voice and was a master of the
old Baptist hymn style, a style that Clara would perfect. In fact, despite
her years in the nightclubs, Clara told me, shortly before her death,
"that's all I like to sing, those old hymns." But the pioneer gospel life was
brutal. By the early 1940s Gertrude had suffered a nervous breakdown
(as had Dorsey and Sallie Martin) and had acquired a goiter, which
transformed her lilting mezzo into a gravelly screech. That voice became
the stuff of national parody, at least in the churches. But Madame Ward
made a point of narrating for the group, presenting her ruined voice as
a battle cry.

Willa remembers that one time while traveling in the South, the
women were stopped by a group of Klansmen, who began to threaten
them. Suddenly Gertrude assumed the role of a witch and started
calling—not on the Lord, as she famously commanded her audience,
but on Lucifer. Clara, Willa, Marion, and Henrietta Waddy all fell
to the ground, murmuring "Lucifer" in timid, tremulous voices while

Gertrude boomed to the heavens. The lads ran screaming through the woods.

On their Sundays, the Klansmen might well have been listening to the Grand Ole Opry, where they might have heard groups like the Blackwood Brothers and the Statesmen Quartet feature songs that had been introduced by the Ward Singers. Long before white rock-and-rollers started "covering" (or "copying") black artists, white religious groups had been practicing the art. The Jordanaires recorded the Soul Stirrers' arrangement of "Working on a Building" with their tenor Gordon Stoker making whoop notes like the Stirrers' peerless tenor, R. H. Harris; later they would back Elvis in his cover versions of the Swan Silvertones and the Harmonizing Four. But the Ward Singers proved most influential. At least eight of their songs were covered by white quartets, among them Marion Williams's torrid gospel blues "I'm Climbing Higher and Higher," with its Brewster lyric

*I'll bid farewell to this house built of clay
Then I'll go a-running up the milky white way.*

Another Ward Singers hit, "O My Lord What a Time," features a lead by the group sparkplug Henrietta Waddy, but is most notable for a series of high notes by Marion wherein she mimics the polyrhythms of a steel guitar. When the country tenors tried to sound like her, they were nowhere as successful as Little Richard or the drag queen Ruth Brown, but their very attempt demonstrated that Madame Ward's group had conquered the imaginations of black and white Christians throughout America.

Dorothy Love Coates once said, "You have to call Gertrude a god-sent Christian. Because to come out of nothing and make the Ward Singers, no education, nothing but mother wit, she gotta been anointed." She managed a great group, chaperoned female ensembles onto a gospel highway that previously had been restricted to male quartets, guided the youthful careers of Clara and Marion, two of gospel's greatest singers. But she was also the mother from hell.

She would live and die a businesswoman. The times demanded it—not merely the poverty in which they had all been raised but the exigencies of gospel touring, the constant arguments with crooked promoters. Women had to outsing the men and outhustle them too. Sallie Martin

The Ward Sisters (l. to r.) Gertrude Ward, Marion Williams, Henrietta Waddy; standing, Clara Ward, 1951: Aretha's greatest inspirations. Photograph from the author's collection

was an archcapitalist; her publishing firm, Martin & Morris, was notorious for swindling its composers. (Roberta Martin bought some gospel standards for less than fifty dollars; Marion Williams sold "We Shall Be Changed" to Clara Ward's publishing firm for twenty-five.) Mahalia Jackson had run a beauty shop for years, and it was hairdressing, not singing, that first delivered her. Indeed, if Clara Ward had had the business sense and thick skin of women like Sallie, Mahalia, and her mother, she would have been a stronger artist, and probably not have died at forty-eight.

Clara led a noisy private life—fancy parties, liquor, many men and many women. But Gertrude dominated her, enfolding her with an iron grip. Willa says, "Mama wouldn't let Clara breathe on her own." Possibly she could overlook the private shenanigans as long as she called the shots. Rough talk didn't frighten her. One time, supposedly, Mahalia, who as a good Baptist and New Orleans native knew how to curse, complained that Clara's mother just didn't know how to have fun: "Miss Ward think her pussy just for pissin'." Gertrude replied, all dignity, "Well, Ma-hay-lee-ah, I've birthed three children. You ain't had not none. So I guess I must know sumpin'."

The Ward Singers' biggest rival was a younger group of Philadelphians, the Famous Davis Sisters. When Thelma Davis died, Madame Ward turned her obituary into an apology. Contradicting any rumors started by the sisters' friends, she had never abandoned her "adopted" girls; they didn't tell about the many times she had paid their bills. Embarrassed by her mother's lack of tact, Clara was compelled to give the performance of her life: "The Day Is Past and Gone," in Gertrude's words, "sung as never before." Some years later, when Ruth Davis died, Clara and her mother showed up, both wearing hats one quarter their height and body weight. "Goodbye," Gertrude proclaimed, "to my daughter Ruth in the Lord." Once again Clara had to reach back for "The Day Is Past and Gone."

Funerals became the ground of reunion and reconciliation, with an occasional note of rivalry. In 1963, Dinah Washington died of an accidental overdose of sleeping pills. Despite a brilliant career, nine husbands, and quite as many wives, she had been an unhappy woman, her famous "evil" at least partially fueled by the fact that her evangelist mother disrespected her for leaving the church. Clara, who remembered a teenage Dinah singing "I'm Going On with the Spirit in Jesus' Name," traveled from Las Vegas to Chicago. Mahalia sang the painfully apt "Move On Up a Little Higher," and Clara grew distraught. Mahalia shouted the church, but *Jet* magazine showed Clara, and everyone joked that by Gertrude's lights her daughter had won this latest skirmish.

In 1972 Mahalia died. Gertrude and Clara showed up at the wake. First they sang a duet of "The Storm Is Passing Over," a song composed by C. A. Tindley, Philadelphia's greatest gospel composer and Thomas A. Dorsey's inspiration. (The duet would have carried old fans back to the days when the family group was known as "Gertrude Ward and Daughters.") Then Clara sang by herself, Tindley's "Beams of Heaven." It was another historic performance. She was moved to tears, and when the performance ended, she tossed her mink stole "like she was playing horseshoes." As if heaven-sent, the cape landed squarely on Mahalia's open casket.

At the funeral the next day Aretha, and not Clara, sang "Precious Lord," in a style much influenced by her mentor. (She had recorded the song at fourteen in her father's church. A few years earlier she had been electrified when Clara sang Dorsey's "Peace in the Valley" at her aunt's funeral and, there as well, tossed her mink coat at the coffin.) The atmosphere was very familiar; an elegant C. L. Franklin was photographed smiling as if the funeral were merely a gospel reunion. Clara and Gertrude Ward sat in the first row onstage. J. Robert Bradley, Frank's favorite hymn singer—and Mahalia's—sang his version of "I'll Fly Away."

As if it were New Bethel, and Bradley setting the church up for her father, Aretha followed right behind him, and her version of "Precious Lord" received an even more tumultuous reception. Once the women began to scream, Gertrude rose to her feet, encouraging her musical granddaughter. Her gesture translated into "The Ward Singers are still clinging." What Aretha felt is another story. In her autobiography she writes that Mahalia had sponsored her first concert in Chicago. Afterward the Queen of Gospel told her to tell Frank his daughter had torn up, and if Halie said so, it must be right. But she didn't pay the girl. While Aretha sang, did she also remember Mahalia's betrayal? (In private conversations with this writer, she has indicated that Mahalia had bequeathed her a lifetime legacy of ambivalence.)

Meanwhile, Sallie Martin, who despite a coarse, unattractive voice had been Dorsey's most famous interpreter, felt thoroughly neglected. The night before, a member of Mahalia's church had called her and invited her to speak at the service. "I'm sorry, darlin'," said Miss Martin, "I'm a singer, not a talker." "Well, Miss Martin, I'm just telling you like it was told to me." "And baby, I'm telling you like it *is*." I happened to walk into Chicago's Arie Crown Theater with her and, rather hypocritically, assumed a positive note. "Well, at least, we know Mahalia moved on up a little higher." A little thing like death could not diminish years of gospel rivalry: "We don't know that," said Sallie Martin.

Within a year Clara too was dead. She had suffered a series of strokes and had recovered enough to return home. Her mother commanded her back to work, though Clara said she didn't feel ready. One evening, she insisted that Clara sing "How I Got Over," her most famous rocker, and one later recorded by Aretha. That must have been exhausting enough. But Clara decided to sing a song for herself, C. A. Tindley's mournful "Stand by Me."

When I'm growing old and feeble, stand by me,
When I'm growing old and feeble, stand by me,
When my life becomes a burden
And I'm nearing chilly Jordan,
Thou who knowest all about me, stand by me.

According to Gertrude, Clara sang "as never before," rose from the piano, and then collapsed, the victim of a final stroke.

Clara's funeral gave Madame Ward one last chance to command the spotlight. She made that *two* chances, funerals being held in both Los Angeles and Philadelphia. In LA, she had a fan play a record of the group's greatest hit, "Surely God Is Able." Clara's twenty-six-year-old voice sang the first chorus, and then Marion Williams, Miss Ward's most famous singer, stepped out to finish the song, running down aisles as she had in her youth. Next, Miss Ward returned to Philadelphia, where during the funeral Aretha would sing "The Day Is Past and Gone," while Kitty Parham, an ex–Ward Singer, sang "We Shall Be Changed," the song that an unwitting Marion had given away years earlier. But this time Gertrude wasn't wholly satisfied. When a minister began to read a modern translation of the Bible, her King James upbringing rebelled. "What is this mess?" she complained. "Tell that fool my child's in the coffin. I want the *Holy* Bible."

She outlived Clara by almost a decade; no money having been saved, she lived off her husband's army pension. Toward the end Marion Williams volunteered to assist her. Marion had given Madame Ward her youth. It is universally conceded that for all Clara's great vocal gifts, Marion was the group's star. She had brought to their Baptist style her own background in the sanctified church and her love of male quartets. While Clara and Willa were northern girls—they had even studied at Philadelphia's top high school for girls until their mother removed them so they could tour with her—Marion was an "ol' barefoot girl come from Florida." The contrast between Clara's Baptist discipline and Marion's Spirit feel made them queens of the highway.

Jackie Verdell and the Davis Sisters (l. to r.) Alfreda Davis, Jackie Verdell, Ruth Davis (partially hidden, arm raised), 1957: an innovative stylist, singing with one of Aretha's favorite groups. Photograph by Lloyd Yearwood

But while "Surely God Is Able" was reportedly selling a million copies, Madame Ward was paying Marion a hundred dollars a week. In 1952 she quit and joined up with her old pal Sister Rosetta Tharpe. Rosetta stiffed her too. "I had to cry like a baby until Sister and her husband paid for my train fare home." (In what would seem a pattern, Marion sang Rosetta's last request, "Precious Lord," at *her* funeral.) She rejoined the Wards for another six years. In 1957, Marion earned the Wards another gold record with her virtuosic solo on "Packin' Up." More money for them, none for her. Even more insulting, she became pregnant in 1958, and Gertrude, whom she'd regarded as a second mother, was most unsympathetic. First she proposed that Marion get an abortion, and then asserted that the baby's father was really her own boyfriend.

Dependent on loans from Henrietta Waddy and a couple of old pals, Marion gave birth to a son and returned almost at once to the group.

By the summer of 1958 she and the four other nonfamily Ward Singers had left the group and formed their own, the Stars of Faith. Madame Ward, sounding like an aggrieved capitalist, told *Jet,* "It's a sitdown strike," and hired a whole new group. The Stars of Faith's first record was "Mean Old World," a gospel blues composed by Marion, with the lyric "Folks don't care how they treat you." Everyone understood that "folks" meant one woman and her daughter. Three months later she recorded another gospel blues, "The Lord Only Knows," with the words "I've been through some rough times since my childhood / Nobody know about." The authors of those rough times were never in doubt. Three years later she would sing "Packin' Up" and beckon her son onstage. There he'd hand her a pocketbook, emblematic of her leavetaking. Back then it all seemed like some good Gertrude Ward–sanctioned clowning. Now it seems like a feminist statement, her declaration that she was a "lone woman" with a child, just like most of the audience.

Years later, in 1978, Marion found herself singing in Los Angeles and showed up at Madame Ward's doorstep. For the next few days, she acted as maid and nurse. She also tried to avoid conversation, and would roam the cluttered hallways singing, praying, and speaking in tongues. After she returned to Philadelphia, Gertrude muttered about the tongues, "I taught that heifer ever'thing she know. I didn't teach her that."

Some fans confronted Marion in church. "Well, Mother Williams, I heard how good and kind you were to Miss Ward, and how you were just calling on all the Lord's many blessings." Marion got the reference. "Well, baby," she replied in a husky whisper, "you know Miss Ward, and how she get next to me. I knew I better pray without ceasing . . . or I'd lose what little salvation I got."

This is the world that raised Aretha, and the one she had to escape.

"THAT CHILD CAN SING ANYTHING AND MAKE IT SOUND LIKE GOSPEL"

It was a great education for Aretha, unobtainable in any conservatory, to watch men like Herbert Pickard and James Cleveland accompany her father as he led the congregational hymns or burst from preaching into a musical chant. Their piano chords orchestrated the ritual drama, frequently cued it, advising Frank to strike now, it's shouting time. She began to accompany him as well. She was often perceived as shy and withdrawn, undersocialized; J. Robert Bradley says, "I told Frank that's a troubled child." Women like Marion Williams and Frances Steadman of the Ward Singers became surrogate mothers, advising her in questions of personal etiquette.

The first time I saw her perform, at Washington Temple, she sang from the piano, rising only after her songs had ended, and then merely to shout, the musical and emotional completion of her songs. No matter what kind of instrumental sweetening turns up in her later recordings, her ear focuses primarily on her own piano chords.

She made her recording debut performing at one of her father's services, with an adolescent's timbre and a grandmother's authority, "Never Grow Old," a singularly apt prologue to a fifty-year career. Though it apparently was not a consideration, it was also a very poignant choice for a teenager; to paraphrase William Hazlitt, most young people do not think of growing old, much less dying. She had learned the song from a recording by Samuel "Billy" Kyles, accompanied by the Maceo Woods Singers of Chicago. Befitting her model, Aretha's phrasing is unusually direct, with very little of the melisma (what church ladies still called the "flowers and frills") that would later grace most of her gospel. Her melodic innovation—perhaps suggested by her father's chauffeur Singing Herbert Carson—occurred in the chorus:

We'll never grow old, never grow old,
In a land where we'll never grow old,
Never grow old, never grow old,
There's a land where we'll never grow old.

A rare photograph of Aretha (seated, center), circa 1955. She is listening to Sammie Bryant, the lead singer of her father's, C. L. Franklin's, touring ensemble, to the vocal accompaniment of the Famous Ward Singers. To her immediate right: Marion Williams, Kitty Parham, and Ethel Gilbert, with Aretha's role model Clara Ward at piano. Photograph from the author's collection

In the original, as performed by white country singers, no "old" is emphasized more than the others. Kyles gives it a much slower, more soulful reading, and he turns the "old" in the third line into a dramatic obbligato, "o-old," lyrically and melodically the song's high point. But Aretha repeats the word twice, each reiteration a step higher and more fervent: "Old . . . OLd . . . OLD," followed by a series of "never"s, emotional ad libs that signified her arrival as "a singer all to herself."

(In later years, Billy Kyles would become a pastor in Memphis, where he would be involved in the 1968 strike of the city's sanitation men. He spent the last hour of Dr. King's life with him and was on the balcony of the Lorraine Hotel when the great man was assassinated. A recent documentary about that last, fatal hour focused on Kyles and ended with his 1954 recording of "Never Grow Old," thereby turning the gospel song into a civil rights anthem, but also into a memorial to the visionary shot down in his youth.)

Aretha's next hit, "Precious Lord," was a precise echo—virtually a tribute record—of Clara Ward's version. And there too, the subject seemed peculiarly morbid for someone her age:

> *When my life is almost gone,*
> *At the river, Lord, I'll stand,*
> *Guide my feet, hold my hand.*

She works the phrase "At the river" to a degree that leads a woman to scream and fall out. Common to both songs are simple, nineteenth-century melodies and intimations of death. These recordings fixed her image as that amazing child who tears up her daddy's church.

With two hit records to her name, she joined her father's troupe on the gospel highway at the age of fifteen. When she dropped out of school in tenth grade, she had already given birth to two of her four sons. (She has never publicly identified the fathers of the first two boys.) She struck the older women on the circuit as bashful and awkward. Her talent was indisputable, but she seemed to lack the ego needed to compete with singers who believed that "if somebody don't shout, you ain't done nothing." Her first records were big hits, but in person she could disappoint; more often the show was stolen by C. L.'s other soloist, Miss Sammie Bryant, the dwarf with Goliath's voice and confidence. Aretha admits that she suffered stage fright: against such titans, what youngster would not? But that didn't prevent her from studying them, and although her glance was characteristically aslant, she didn't miss a thing.

Her earliest work was indebted to Clara Ward. As this fifteen-year-old wailed "Precious Lord," sounding uncannily like Clara, a member of New Bethel hollered, "Listen at her!" Over the next four years her style evolved, thanks to other artists she had encountered, particularly James Cleveland, the director of New Bethel's choir. He introduced her to some "deep piano chords," allowing her a vocal and harmonic freedom beyond Clara's ken. Aretha's ascendance came at the end of gospel's best period; the soloists, groups, and quartets all began to be upstaged by choir directors, with Cleveland leading the pack. Just as Aretha quit the field, it changed utterly. Ironically, by re-creating gospel as it was *before* she left it, she became the last custodian of the very music she had seemed to abandon.

Before she made her move, another prodigy had enjoyed a moment of fame. Cynthia Coleman (1934–1986) grew up in Newark, the niece of a famous local quartet, the Coleman Brothers. In her teens she began recording with a family group, the Colemanaires, and revealed a huge, rangy voice, and an ability to growl, moan, and twirl notes that was astounding for a young woman of that time; she had a particularly swift and graceful melisma, always rooted in bluesy moans. (She anticipated later singers like Mavis Staples and Laura Lee Rundless, though with far more volume and vocal control.) By 1955, under the name Ann Cole, she had begun recording pop and doo-wop tunes ("In the Chapel" and the first recorded version of "Got My Mojo Working"). Perhaps her voice was too large, her vibrato too fluttery (and not unlike Edith Piaf's), for though she was voted *Cash Box*'s Most Promising New Female R&B Vocalist, her career did not pan out. In 1962 she was involved in an auto accident, retired from the business, and spent the rest of her years in a wheelchair.

Rosetta Tharpe's old partner Marie Knight toiled for a modest ten years in the pop field, but she was never the hard, house-wrecking type of Ann Cole. Neither woman is well remembered, nor are such gifted church-trained singers as Lula Reed, Marie Adams, Shirley Gunter, and Wynona Carr. Better known are Savoy Records' biggest stars, Big Maybelle and Little Esther. Big Maybelle may have had the mightiest blues voice since Bessie Smith, and a style right out of the sanctified church. (After she left Savoy, the owner, Herman Lubinsky, decided that Marion Williams would be the next Maybelle. Between Lubinsky and Gertrude Ward, it's amazing that Marion got out alive.)

Like Aretha, Esther Phillips was a child star, who also recorded her first hit, a blues, at fourteen. She was an immensely appealing stylist, if not an original one; she was far more steeped in Dinah Washington than Aretha was in Clara Ward. (In the early 1970s, she recorded an album that alluded quite specifically to the years of drug addiction that would eventually kill her. Aretha was so impressed that she gave Esther her own Grammy, a gesture worthy of the queen she had become.) Musical history can be unfairly selective. Despite the work of her seniors, Aretha joins Ray Charles in myth as the first singer to unite gospel and blues. At least she had the pedigree.

In 1960, she signed with Columbia Records. Her style was set in place: Byzantine note bending; bold contrasts in dynamics, from brooding complaints to ecstatic shrieks; a meditative approach that obliged her to sing behind the beat; spontaneous asides; pauses within a syllable; a lyrical use of aspiration until breath itself could be musically notated. All that was *echt* gospel, as was a perception of everything nongospel as indiscriminately Other. Each attempt to mold her into a more conventional singer gave way to the inevitability of her gospel temper. Aretha's route had been prepared by two men, Ray Charles and Sam Cooke. But there was a difference. Charles was an R&B-jazz musician whose adaptation of gospel devices was both derivative and expedient. According to his musicians, he never improvised; once an arrangement was figured out, it was not to be toyed with.

This totally subverts the idea of Spirit feel. Marion Williams once said, "If you want somebody to repeat herself, I'm the world's worst." Of course, that made her one of the best. It also confirms that gospel is meant never to be the same, not if it's "anointed." Aretha's performances have often been criticized as erratic, undisciplined, free-form. Without excusing the less inspired moments, that's what makes her so quintessentially gospel.

The Soul Stirrers' affinity to doo-wop eased Cooke's crossover, as did Robert Anderson's example as a balladeer. His early hits studiously downplayed gospel fervor to the point where he resembled a slightly more animated Nat King Cole. (One time Herbert Pickard ran into his old friend and missed his famous mustache. "Pee Wee, I shaved it off. White folks don't like us to wear 'staches; it scares them.") Only at the end of his life did he begin singing as hard as his former colleague Julius Cheeks, the raucous model for Wilson Pickett, a man nobody would confuse with Sam. But that was a rare moment in a ghetto nightclub, and might have signified a voice on the verge of ruin. By their early thirties, Dinah Washington and Clara Ward (and, for that matter, Aretha) had lost their clear high notes; Sam may have replicated their plight. For the most part he's remembered for lightweight ditties and boyish charm.

Aretha, then, was really the first gospel star to switch fields without switching styles.

At her first session for Columbia, she performed a kittenish duet, "Love Is the Only Thing," with her boyfriend, Paul Owens of the Swan Silvertones. She sounds almost too cute, like a baby Dinah Washington, while Owens's moans suggest a form of gospel whimsy. Yet this probably signified her versatility, as did her inclusion in the session of both Judy Garland's "Over the Rainbow," with its salute to Hollywood, and "Today I Sing the Blues," which remains one of the profoundest performances of her career.

Though she is in her best voice, she downplays the virtuoso in favor of someone emotionally stricken. The song's first words, "Without a word of warning," convey an alarm that borders on terror. The next phrase, "The blues walked in this morning," introduced America to the subtleties of her style: the word "blues" is soft, minimally slurred, and sustained. Crucial phrases like "my lonely room" and "sad lonely feeling" are sung with a quiet intimacy. But when she distinguishes between a gentle "yesterday" when she sang a love song and a harsh "today" when she's singing the blues, by coloring the second "day," holding the word and using vibrato to italicize it, she makes the process from joy to melancholy audible. (Among her mentors, C. L. Franklin and Marion Williams made brilliant use of vocal color for dramatic purposes.) Of course the song has a wailing climax, but there is no sense of deliverance. The song conveys about as stark and unflinching a note of despair as any teenager ever sang.

"Today I Sing the Blues" set the matrix for Aretha's later masterpieces. For example, it predicts the mood and meter of classics like "I Never Loved a Man," "Good to Me," and "Going Down Slow." Her 2011 release, *A Woman Falling Out of Love,* zoomed in many directions, most of them unsatisfying. But her version of B. B. King's "Sweet Sixteen" (a blues first released in 1960, the year she left gospel) demonstrated her command of the idiom. Give her a long-meter moan or a slow blues, and she remained nonpareil among living singers.

In fact, she had inaugurated her career with a precise distinction between love songs—frivolous, unwitting, kids' stuff—and the blues. Is it overlistening to say that her stance was well deliberated? Of course she could sing the light stuff—"Rainbow" proved that. She could soothe and croon, be the singer preferred by those who like understatement. In class terms, she could be the subdued bourgeois, a veritable debutante, and not the closest thing to a welfare mother: a girl who knew about poverty only by hearsay, though she was surrounded by the poor. But by affirming blues *over* love songs as the more serious vehicle, she accomplished an amazing rhetorical sleight of hand. Blues became deep the way gospel was deep—and she could moan her heart out in either form.

Yet she was also capable of a playful wit. In an early session she demonstrated her piano chops on a Ray Charles blues, "Hard Times (No One Knows Better Than I"). She plays some respectable vamps—much like her singing, her early instrumental work set an extremely high standard for her. Then she starts ad-libbing, "They call it hard times, yeah yeah," and proceeds to scat, moan, and growl with the stamina of her mentors and a humor that's hers alone. It's as if she's defying everyone. Her last spoken words are "Ray Charles said it was hard times, but I feel all right." It helps to know that "feel all right" means getting happy. Except that there's nothing churchy about her exuberance. This is someone delighting in her own artistry.

A minor hit, "It Won't Be Long," demonstrated her ability to cruise both sides of the street. Accompanied by her own rocking piano, she delivered line readings ("He's a longtail rooster and I'm his hen") that staked her claim for sexual authority. And then she converted her anxiety into a double-time shout, giving anticipation a gospel urgency.

John Hammond was clever enough to hire Ray Bryant, the churchiest keyboard man to accompany Aretha until she would be teamed up with James Cleveland's protégé Billy Preston. It's doubtful that Hammond knew that Bryant's sister, Vera Eubanks, was at the time accompanying Mary Johnson Davis, the singer who had inspired both Clara Ward and Barbara Franklin. But it helps explain why his chords made Aretha feel at ease.

A very strong performance from her early sessions is Johnny McFarland's "Maybe I'm a Fool." Its lyric is a standard litany of self-abasement, sung to a tune that she converts into a sixteen-bar gospel blues. During the bridge, she notes that her friends tell her, "Aretha, why don't you find somebody new?" but she tells the doubters to get thee behind. Her voice breaks as she soars into the last chorus: "I said, I said" (sung with the deep breath of her preaching father) "if taking you back" (one of the all-time perfect blue notes) "would be foolish, then maybe" (another preacher rumble) "maybe I'm a fool."

Gospel's fans hailed this final chorus as her secular anointing. She knew she had gotten through, and closed with a series of jammed-together "yeah!"s—a gospel signal of uncontrollable excitement. Her aplomb undercut any trace of masochism: clearly, this woman's love was degrees more powerful than the bum who made her seem foolish. "Maybe I'm a Fool" exhibits Aretha at the top of her form. Only her deepest vocals on Atlantic can match the emotion displayed here, and they tend to be mixed so that the instrumental accompaniment almost drowns her out or renders her shrill, one of the constant dangers faced by a mezzo-soprano who lives for the top notes.

Even better is "Nobody Knows the Way I Feel This Morning," one of the last blues recorded by Dinah Washington. It is fascinating to compare the versions of Aretha, young, strong, with every note intact, and Dinah, her voice close to shot. Both are similarly extraordinary. Both play with the time, dividing a line into discrete but surprising units. For example, in her first verse, Aretha introduces one line with a choppy "let me tell you," then sings a long, wordy phrase with one breath, "that the graveyard would be the place where my man would lay this . . . ," takes a pause, and lets "morning" stand by itself. Her reading of the word "morning" resembles the "day"s in "Today I Sing the Blues," different every time. Dinah's "morning"s are just as surprising, as if each one reveals a deeper kind of self-knowledge. Her gospel idol Roberta Martin had been famous for demonstrating soulfulness by singing softly. None of her "morning"s are sung loud, but each one has a devastating impact.

Both women use the church's technique to convey worldly sentiments. In one verse, the singer is rendered so abject that she must pawn everything she owns. In a fabulous line, she contemplates "pawning myself but I felt kinda ashamed." Both women relish the sentiment, and even more the following verse, "Lord, I feel I could scream and cry." But while Dinah tries to control herself ("I'm too stout-hearted, I'd rather die"), Aretha wallows in her misery ("I'm just a little too cold-hearted . . . I'd, uh, I'd rather lay down right here and die").

"Scream and cry" is a gift to both singers. It allows Dinah to sound ugly, to employ a rasping tone she would never have allowed herself in her early days, not to mention hums, slurs, yodels, and emphatic "yeah yeah yeah"s. The same words allow Aretha one of the triumphs of her career. Even then, when her voice was at its loveliest, some people thought she screamed too much. But others were emancipated by the same screams: Lena Horne once said that there was a screaming Aretha hidden in most black women. Aretha loves the word "scream," at least partially because she loves the impact of an "eee." It dominates some of her favorite words to sing (or contemplate)—"evil," "Jesus," "freedom"—as well as supplying five of the spelled-out sounds of her biggest hit, "Respect."

So where Dinah announces the possibility, Aretha delivers the goods. She gets so caught up in the process that she cracks on the verse's last iteration of "scream and cry," a failure of the flesh that affirms the spirit; of course she keeps on singing. In the last verse when she contemplates "leaving," the notes are solid and shattering. "And I'm—and I'm—and I'm LEAVING HERE on a southbound train this morning." She clarifies her attention by ad-libbing, "I'm going all the way south," a line worthy of her father or the many quartet singers who loved to remind their audiences of their early days in Mississippi or South Carolina. In the last phrase, a final "Nobody knows the way I feel this morning," her voice breaks again, which inspires an intricately spun out "morning," deep in the Spirit, followed by two much quieter readings of the same word. She has flirted with hysteria in order to arrive at wisdom. No less than Dinah, she exudes authority. At last she had found a song big enough for her story, an event that would occur much less often after she became the Queen of Rock and Soul.

Everything Aretha sang in those early days reflected her gospel training, and there is more of the pure church singer in her records for Columbia than in anything that would follow, despite Jerry Wexler's famous comment that he had struck gold by returning her to church. If anything, her records of pop standards, even more than her blues, are saturated with all that she had learned by studying the greatest singers of gospel's golden age. She remained their daughter, never more true than when she echoed their voices in work they would never dare to sing.

By applying her ancestors' sensibility to some of the classic American songs, she virtually colonized American music for the gospel style. The union of white composers, all of them deeply influenced by African-American music, and the most brilliant black singer of her generation was magical, exemplary, one of the significant events in the history of popular music. These ballads let her assume different personae, engage different tones. From the stark dialectic of the gospel hymnodists, she advanced to the more nuanced world of the great pop lyricists. Their songs allowed her to be witty, whimsical, and wistful, a girl who might speculate about dying but also dream of life and love.

From singing the plaintive hymns of the eighteenth and nineteenth centuries, she moved to the greatest melodies of the twentieth. It was as if she had acquired a new sensibility. At fourteen, she imagined an afterlife where "we'll never grow old"; ten years later, she sang of a bitter earth, where "too soon we grow old." At fifteen, she was singing of a fountain filled with blood; three years later she was singing, "It ain't necessarily so."

Even if she had not been a vocal genius, this development would have been remarkable, simply because of her representative status. (Who could imagine the daughter of Billy Graham or Pat Robertson singing "I Want a Man"?) Precisely in the era of civil rights, the daughter of a progressive Baptist minister became a star. But besides her controversial role as Reverend Franklin's blues-singing daughter, she did happen to be exorbitantly gifted, as had long been affirmed by those who knew her best, the singers of Philadelphia, Chicago, and Detroit, who had inspired her until she began to outgrow them.

For these, her toughest critics, the early records have remained the ones to reckon with. And why not? They displayed her most creative ideas about singing, her singular adaptations of her idols Clara and Marion and of the Famous Davis Sisters, Ruth Davis (a squalling wonder, who counterintuitively worshipped the laid-back cadences of Little Jimmy Scott) and Jackie Verdell (the younger stylist closest to Aretha's heart). Not merely was she at her vocally brightest and most focused, she was also in possession of her best voice. With age, the extremely youthful mezzo-soprano would deepen, and inevitably coarsen. But in the early sixties, the voice was both childlike and womanly; and no note she desired was unavailable to her. So she could wail a G5 on the word "say" in "Say It Isn't So," Clara-style, and break your heart, and growl the same note in "That Lucky Old Sun," à la Marion, and tempt you to do the holy dance.

She wasn't only a gospel bird; she had listened well and deeply to other singers. Two in particular were influential: Little Jimmy Scott, to whose languid parlando she had been introduced by the Davis Sisters; and Billie Holiday. Billie was the least church-derived jazz singer, more Irish Catholic than black Baptist. But gospel singers loved her, particularly *Lady in Satin,* a huge hit during the months when Aretha plotted her move into the world (even if Aretha's version of "God Bless the Child" is most un-Billie-like!). Though Holiday and Franklin are seldom mentioned in the same breath, you can hear the traces throughout Aretha's early work, the whispered asides, the delicately playful approach to time and phrasing. The difference is that Aretha, the preacher's daughter, can overstate as well as understate, belt as well as croon. Billie was a consummate diseuse; Aretha was both that and a gospel shouter.

Her more surprising influence was a white singer, Judy Garland, whom she has sometimes called her second inspiration after Clara. This is not as strange as it sounds. We know that Billie learned from Mildred Bailey, that Ella Fitzgerald grew out of Connie Boswell. C. L. Franklin adored Al Jolson, blackface and all. Black audiences always listened to

Your Hit Parade on the radio; even the archetypal blues singer Robert Johnson sang his share of pop tunes. In retrospect, Aretha's love of Garland makes total sense. They were both wunderkinder, child stars imperiled by the danger of early fame. Garland offered the example of impeccable diction and a clear voice throbbing with trumpeted emotion. This probably explains why Aretha included "Over the Rainbow" in her first recording session as a pop singer, along with "Today I Sing the Blues." Her diction and phrasing are extremely, even excessively, formal until the last chorus, when she annexes Harold Arlen and E. Y. Harburg to the gospel hymnal, ad-libbing about "pretty little bluebirds." There's another wrinkle to the cultural pattern: Harburg's left-wing politics infuse the song's lyric. Aretha's imagining of something like the land where we'll never grow old is a place that was intended to be a workers' paradise.

In C. L. Franklin's favorite Broadway song, "Look to the Rainbow," Yip Harburg's lyric imagines a father promising his child, "There's an elegant legacy waiting for ye." Often when Aretha performed the song, she would sing her father's version, "an elegant legacy waiting for Ree." In gospel style, she had turned a musical number into a personal testimony.

This cultural interchange was once quite common. At that time, another Detroiter, Jackie Wilson, was selling his own transmutations of the gospel sound: "Lonely Teardrops," for instance, derived its hook from the Dixie Hummingbirds' "It Must Have Been the Lord"; and his sublime "Higher and Higher" (his live performance of the song is perhaps the finest soul clip on YouTube) is the equal of any of Aretha's most impassioned blends of church and state. But Wilson's real idol wasn't a quartet singer like the Hummingbirds' Ira Tucker. It was Al Jolson, whom he called "the one man I admire most in the business." In 1956, I heard Jackie at the Apollo Theater singing Jolson's "Sonny Boy," with the crystalline diction and effeminate headtones of an Irish tenor. In 1961 he recorded a whole album in homage to his idol. His love of Jolson may even have led him to convert to Judaism.

(Another parallel between Aretha and Jackie is their complicated devotion to a parent. In Jackie's case, it was his mother, a gospel powerhouse. In 1968, at the Apollo, on the last night, Jackie brought her out to perform. While he pirouetted around the stage, half-boxer, half–ballet dancer, Eliza Mae Wilson sang with the down-home volume of a Willie Mae Ford Smith: "You better stop doggin' my Jackie around. / Because if you don't stop, my Jackie will have to put you down." Her love was such that when she visited him after the heart attack that would leave him in a vegetative state for eight years, she collapsed and died. C. L. Franklin might well have preached a sermon about that, and included a version of the old song "Your Mother Loves Her Children All the Time.")

There were male singers in Aretha's ear as well. Sam Cooke's pop success had helped motivate her. But Sam and Lou Rawls (with whom years later, at the White House, she would sing Marion Williams's "Born to Sing the Gospel") both came out of the male quartet genre, in which the guitar overruled the piano. This may be one reason why they didn't do as well with the gorgeously chromatic melodies, all of them keyboard-generated, that Aretha embraced with aplomb.

Particularly in her recordings of pop standards, Aretha completed a circle. Irving Berlin composed "On Revival Day" for Al Jolson as early as 1913. He was also known for composing in one key, the blues-friendly F-sharp (the Davis Sisters' only key—like Berlin, their musician Curtis Dublin could play in no other). While composing *Porgy and Bess* George Gershwin drew heavily on the music of South Carolinian Gullah singers. Johnny Mercer, a proud son of the South, and Hoagy Carmichael, the lyricist and composer, respectively, of "Skylark" (a song inspired by Mercer's infatuation with Judy Garland), were so indebted to black music that they qualify as the blue-eyed soul singers of their day. The less familiar Meredith Willson had composed an inspirational standard, "May the Good Lord Bless and Keep You," that Aretha would have heard performed by the Harmonizing Four of Richmond, Virginia. Aretha turns Willson's "Are You Sure (You Better Think)," the first pop song on which she accompanied herself on piano, into a gospel romp, sung with the transparent intention of wrecking a church. (It also anticipates her thoroughly secular hit "Think.")

No lyric scared her. Ira Gershwin and Johnny Mercer specialized in wordsmanship, multiple rhymes demanding precise articulation. But Aretha grew up listening to Marion Williams sing "Surely God Is Able," a song composed by Reverend Brewster, a rhyming whiz himself. From Brewster's "Don't you know God is able, / Clouds may gather above you, so dark and sable," it's no leap to Ira Gershwin's rhyming of "li'ble" and "Bible" or Mercer's "my remark" and "Noah in the ark." Irving Berlin's vows of love were as exorbitant as any religious testimony: the hyperbole of "How Deep Is the Ocean" betrayed a secular visionary. How much of a rhetorical leap could that have been from Brewster's "He'll be a mother for the motherless, a father for the fatherless"?

The unfriendliest lyric was catnip. "Rock-a-Bye Your Baby with a Dixie Melody" has been called a racist song. No sweat. She sings, "Weep no more, my fair lady," letting you know that she's no country hick, she's seen Broadway. "Ol' black Joe" becomes "Little Joe," Uncle Tom turned into a do-right-man. (In later years, she would simply replace the noun "Dixie" with her own name: "Rock-a-bye your rock-a-bye baby with an Aretha melody.") "Swanee" was equally surmounted. Where the original sings, "My mammy's waiting for me, praying for me," she makes the easiest and most logical of adjustments, "My *people* are waiting for me, praying for me." Thus she turns a demeaning song into an interracial anthem of the South. These are not easy victories.

Her early work was dense with gospel allusions, a signal to her friends that she hadn't fundamentally changed: you could take the girl out of the church, but . . . Consider "What a Difference a Day Made," a song made famous by Dinah Washington. With a tyro's chutzpah, Aretha ignores her example. With her fifth word and sixth note, she introduces a bluesy slur on the words "day made" that makes the song her own. She follows this with a reading of the line "My yesterdays were blue, dear" in which she sings the word "blue" twice, each so suffused with blue tonality that it becomes un-bluesy, a reading of the word that evokes church more than club, simply because no blues singer untouched by gospel would color the blues in that way—or give the song's last words, "And the difference is you," the note of a moaned testimony. Aretha wasn't parodying gospel ecstasy, she was making a holy blues of . . . everything.

She had musical allies. In an early photo, she stands happily engrossed, her eyes stabbed shut, while four young women studiously regard the lyric sheet. These background singers include Cissy Houston (Whitney's mother), Dee Dee Warwick (Dionne's sister), Judy Clay (Cissy and Dee Dee's cousin), and Estelle Brown. Not merely were they all gospel singers, but Judy had established her name as Newark's answer to Dorothy Love, while Estelle's brother Eddie Brown had just begun to sing duets with Ruth Davis. In other words, the daughters of the Gospel Harmonettes and the Davis Sisters were singing background for little Miss Ward Singers. Deliberately or not, the five girls were taking their mothers' gospel sound one step higher.

But Aretha was conspicuously unlike America's most famous gospel singer, Mahalia Jackson, at that time one of Columbia Records' biggest artists. While Mahalia was notorious for her thick New Orleans accent and her rural malapropisms ("Paul and Silas" became "Paul and Sila"), Aretha's models, her father and Clara, were virtual elocutionists. Aretha delights in a finishing-school enunciation; unlike Mahalia, she has no trouble with "s," it becomes a sensuous delight, you await its reappearance. She can inhabit an unfamiliar word like "skylark" (not a common bird in Detroit) with sheerest joy in its sound. (Something similar occurs in Marlene Dietrich's magnificent "Lazy Afternoon," when she sings the words "a fat pink cloud" with so thick a German accent that the cloud becomes a sex toy.) Her pleasure in prosody accompanies a sly sense of humor. For example, in the shimmering "How Glad I Am," singing the line "My love has no bottom, my love has no top," the word "top" free-associates into "tip top"; in the house-wrecking "Trouble in Mind," she interjects a comedian's "say what?"

Her sense of time was comparable with the best in jazz (Billie Holiday) or gospel (Marion Williams). There are the virtuosic polyrhythms of "It Ain't Necessarily So," but there's also the more subtle play of "Say It Isn't So," where she sings behind and ahead of the beat, repeats the verb "say" various times and ways, all with the bald purpose of silencing the unspeakable with noisy sound: "say, sAY, SAY" (the "Never Grow Old" crescendo) that you're not saying anything at all. Aretha's early hymns had been sung without any beat—the songs commonly known as "long meter" or "no meter." They demanded an extreme attention to mood and harmony. Knowing how to make silence lucid would help her master the complex arrhythmic structure of "Only the Lonely" (without any of Frank Sinatra's wavering pitch).

Her harmonic sense was informed by piano technique. In 1968, she told an interviewer that she was not a jazz pianist, and that "passing chords" of the sort she'd learned in church gave her all the support she needed. Two musical triumphs predicated on harmonic and melodic development are Billy Strayhorn's "My Little Brown Book" and Berlin's "How Deep Is the Ocean." Strayhorn, like Aretha, was a precocious genius, raised on his grandmother's hymns. He composed the song when he was eighteen; she sang it when she was twenty. Her intimation of blue notes in words like "book" and "pages" flatters his gorgeous melody. Berlin's song was never so bluesy, its despair so immense. Robert Mersey's arrangement, filled with atonal dabs and smears, inspires one of her greatest performances. Her ear allows her one final moan that complements the orchestra: a similar conjunction occurs in her deftly harmonized reading of the syllable "ness" in "Try a Little Tenderness," the wit lying in her intimation of the several ways to please a lover.

There were many such coups in these early records. "Trouble in Mind" had been sung by everyone, including gospel singers like Sister Rosetta Tharpe and Marie Knight. But only Aretha turns it into a rocking testimony, a shout song of deliverance, the next-best thing to "How I Got Over." She's run her race, and outfoxed the wolves. Meanwhile, "That Lucky Old Sun" becomes pure gospel, the word "Lord" repeated so often that thoughts of pop are banished. When she sings "Show me the river," we are back in the world of "Precious Lord" ("At the river, Lord, I stand"). I'd even say that this is her most original gospel performance . . . precisely because she had no model, no Clara, Jackie, or Marion ringing in her ear. When she sings about working for her family, you remember that her grandmother, "Aunt Rachel," had been a sharecropper. When she sings about toiling for her kids, you think of her own two children.

With this song Aretha helped change gospel history. She had always acknowledged the influence of the great pianist-singer James Cleveland. But two years later Cleveland and his colleague Cassietta George would take her rendition and, copying every curlicue and cadence, transform it into "Walk Around Heaven All Day," one of the last hits of gospel's golden age. The daughter was now feeding her parents. After that, a whole generation of younger singers arrived, all of them singing like her, nursing each of her traits from the jazzy scat to the Olympian melisma. In reformulating gospel, she had given it a new life.

Forgetting the pioneer efforts of a Sister Rosetta Tharpe or Dinah Washington, gospel singers came to the conclusion that Aretha was inventing something new. Around 1964 I began hearing from gospel singers like Inez Andrews and Mavis Staples that they liked "soul . . . what Aretha Franklin's doing." That meant enjoying all the freedoms of gospel while singing better tunes and more interesting lyrics. Having it all: still wailing gospel but earning pop money. Changing almost nothing about your style but the message . . . and even that could be implied by the churchy runs and hymnal melisma.

This was just what enraged conservative critics. Rex Reed complained that "she's a worse ballad singer than Robert Goulet." He probably meant that she disregarded the legato line, pausing and breaking time, defiling the melody. In other words, the Clara Ward in her beat out the Judy Garland. She has always claimed to love strings, but it's a morganatic marriage. Remember when she sang "The Star-Spangled Banner" at a political convention and ad-libbed so loosely that she was still at "gleaming" when the orchestra hit "the rockets' red glare."

According to myth, Columbia, at one time, saw in Aretha a black Barbra Streisand, playing on her affection for Broadway pizzazz. (Its most unfortunate manifestation was the time she appeared as Josephine Baker, tossing lemons to the audience.) Her only top-forty single for the label was "Rock-a-Bye Your Baby with a Dixie Melody." But wasn't it precisely the mainstream clarity of her voice that let Aretha cross over where others had failed? Her light, girlish tone and crystalline diction were far more accessible to pop fans than the monolithic volume and down-home drawls, not to mention the wide-open vibrato, of earlier gospel women. In a word, she had a *modern* voice. (Can you imagine the teenagers of the world rocking to Big Maybelle?) The real problem may have been her ambivalence about performing. One record-company executive who saw her at the Village Gate in the early sixties recalls a demure youngster who delivered supper-club ballads with a lovely voice and impeccable time, and who seemed scared to death.

Columbia also tried to make R&B hits with Aretha. The attempts were not aesthetic failures, but they went nowhere commercially. Hits were what she wanted, and after her move to Atlantic in 1967, that's what she had in abundance. For a few years she could do no wrong. Her gospel artistry dignified rock and roll even as a generation of white fans began treating their heroes with a devotion bordering on sectarian fanaticism.

While the Beatles trafficked in gurus, Aretha excavated gospel roots, her Jesus against their Maharishi. Jerry Wexler, who produced her Atlantic albums, made sure that the arrangements were geared to her vocals, her piano and backup singers—initially her sisters, Erma and Carolyn. At sessions, she would first perform a series of scratch vocals with the band, do a penultimate instrumental, and then overdub what was to be a final vocal. Wexler remembers that Aretha would come up with astonishing inventions and then, to his horror, reject the take, only to top herself on the next one.

(She has expressed her irritation that she has never received a co-producer credit for her Atlantic hits. After all, the material was often composed by her and her husband of the time, Ted White, and the band charts were invariably based on her own piano arrangements. In other words, Jerry Wexler et al. may or may not have provided the atmospher-

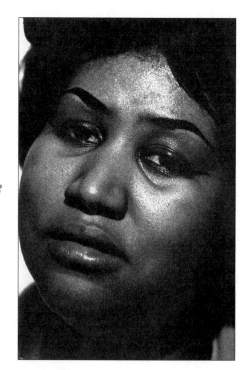

Aretha Franklin
Atlantic Records–era pictures, 1968
Photographs by Stephen Paley

ics, but the vision was always hers. This was even more true with her gospel album *Amazing Grace*. Wexler has famously rued his naming of "rhythm and blues": had he known better, he would have called the music formerly known as "race" rhythm and gospel. A nice homage, but he clearly had nothing to teach Aretha about church singing.)

While she had hits with laid-back ditties ("Spanish Harlem," "Day Dreaming"), she saved her best licks for songs in which she could work a synthesis of sexual and spiritual ardor. On "Son of a Preacher Man," she slows down the bridge to a meter punctuated by chords that any gospel fan would recognize as deeply hymnal, applied here to petting and necking. Rock critics, unfamiliar with that tradition, found Dusty Springfield's version more impassioned, but that only showed how little gospel they were prepared to receive.

In perhaps her best vocal, "Good to Me," she sails to the top of her register, violating meter, decorum, and bel canto as she implores some loving reciprocity as fervently as she might call on Jesus to make a way out of no way. In her best Atlantic album, *Spirit in the Dark* (1970), the gospel stands in bold relief. The title track is a blatant excuse to speed up the tempo and shout. (There's a clip of her in 1972, performing the song at the Montreux Jazz Festival, and dancing for almost five minutes, shouting as hard in Switzerland as at her daddy's church—insisting that she was anywhere, everywhere, his daughter.) "The Thrill Is Gone" begins with a brilliant improvisation: "The thrill is gone," she sings. "Oh, oh, oh, yeah, the thrill is gone all away, away from me"—and it's one soaring musical surprise after another, as the track evolves into the spiritual "Free at Last." Another song of emancipation, "Pullin'," builds to a series of pre-climaxes, never going over the top to a shouted release. Instead she bears down on the word "harder." The result is a gospel bolero that evades the money shot. It ends with the old church exclamation "Well!," signifying "Now, didn't I tell you?"

In the early seventies, she began to experiment with newer rhythms ("Rock Steady") and themes ("Young, Gifted and Black"). That second cut united her at last with a gospel accompanist, the organist Billy Preston, who had been playing for James Cleveland since he was fifteen. While Aretha had arranged the Nina Simone ballad to resemble a Ward Singers hymn, it was most likely Preston's church chords that led her to holler "Thank you, Jesus," and give a gospel identity to the proud young blacks with their "souls intact." (Just as her transcendent reading of "Freedom" in *Think* really defies the song's logic: she's not seeking liberation but a meeting of true minds. She makes the word her cue to shout, sounding as it does like "Jesus.") This tangle of emotions confused some, enchanted many more. She wanted the listener to do his own interpreting.

Besides the deeply sympathetic Preston, her other favorite accompanists included the saxophonist King Curtis; Bernard "Pretty" Purdie, who spent years as her drummer and band leader; and the vocalist–keyboard artist Donny Hathaway. With Hathaway's help, she proved that one could be both soulful and wistful. One of her loveliest performances, "All the King's Horses," is a valedictory to a failed relationship:

All the king's horses, all the king's men
Couldn't put our two hearts together again.

After the nursery-rhyme allusions and the requisite gospel shouting, she ends on a quiet, melancholy note, implying that just as in the nursery rhyme, a gospel catharsis won't change matters; this is one situation she can't sing herself out of.

(Aretha's love of nursery rhymes deserves special attention. Whether this was her introduction to the broader national culture, or whether she simply finds the rhymes familiar—the same way quartets will interpolate the verses of an old hymn like "A Charge to Keep I Have," not because it makes particular sense, but as a means of getting to the next chorus—she keeps quoting the songs of kindergarten. On occasion, she will recite the verses of, say, "Little Jack Horner," and make them sound like double entendres. Other times they sound like a church girl's attempt at something more universal: at least we have these references in common. Her occasional use of French and Spanish words, especially in her disco era, served the same function.)

She had become a huge star, and a contested figure. Was she the woman who had never loved a man with greater abnegation, or was she the wary protector of her money—and the respect it deserved? While there were rumors that her first husband, Ted White, whom she married in 1961, had mistreated her, he was the co-writer of her boldest assertions of autonomy, "Good to Me" and "Think." (He also wrote the lascivious gospel parody "Doctor Feelgood.") If her stormy marriage pained her, she was also disgusted by intrusive reporters and estranged friends who predicted that she was doomed to be another Billie Holiday. At once reclusive and assertive, Aretha wanted all the accoutrements of fame without the attendant notoriety; she was happy to be a star but refused to be an icon. Perhaps that is why she also remained aloof politically; when she appeared at civil rights rallies, it was to sing "Precious Lord"—she left the preaching to Dr. King and her father.

A series of public woes, particularly the end of her marriage to Ted White, led Mahalia Jackson to prophesy Aretha's return to church. As it happened, two weeks before Mahalia's death, that's where Aretha found herself, singing to an audience that included her father and Gertrude and Clara Ward. After romping through "How I Got Over" and Inez Andrews's "Mary Don't You Weep," she turned to the deep hymns "Amazing Grace" and "God Will Take Care of You," guided by her favorite accompanist, James Cleveland. Here was a marriage made in heaven, absolute proof that the best gospel musicians remain uniquely attuned to the singers they accompany. Cleveland's chords were as allusive as a C. L. Franklin sermon, each harmonic turn the equivalent of her daddy's moans. In particular, his shifts from major to minor, his bar-by-bar attention to meter, his pianistic filigrees, are all the accompaniment she or the choir need: the rhythm section is spunky enough (they were New York's top studio musicians) but their absence wouldn't mean a thing. James and Aretha are so aligned that during "Amazing Grace," he leaves the piano to cry—having just testified that twenty years earlier, when he was living in her daddy's parsonage, they had no idea that he would become the King of Gospel, and she, Aretha Franklin. He wept over the "many dangers" they had both overcome.

On the next night, after she sings a rocking version of her father's hit "Climbing Higher Mountains," James ad-libs a slow cadenza, his time sense easily as nuanced as hers, and his bluesy runs as thrilling. He then proceeds to sing an old congregational number, "He's All Right," the only song on either night that gets the people shouting. Yet he always acknowledges her as both "Queen of Music" and the star of the show.

Whenever she got caught up in the Spirit, he also knew what spoken interjection would fan the flame. At the end of a re-created "Never Grow Old" he expounds on the message of eternal youth. Aretha returns, moaning, "I'm so glad I've got religion, my soul is satisfied." The Southern California Choir answers her reiterated "soul." It's as if an army of Aretha's had convened, each as capable of flamboyant runs as C. L.'s daughter. Their massive vocalization, sung just as soul music was at its apogee, was a musical wink distinguishing the real from the "for real." You want soul? We've got *Soul*.

My favorite moment in the filmed version of the concert* occurs during the song, but it doesn't involve Aretha. She is seated at the piano, raining down sweat. Right opposite her, in the front row, are her father and Clara Ward, her musical mother. Clara looks totally absorbed, telepathically conveying something essential to her spiritual daughter. That look tells us more about the nature of her best singing than any record she would make after Marion Williams left her group. She is yanked out of the moment by a sudden commotion and leaps to her mother's rescue: Madame Ward is stomping and hollering, apparently out of control. It was an old saint's response, making threatening gestures, as if to say, "You better sing or I'mma hurt you." It was also her means of reminding the world that Aretha was really Little Clara. (I asked one Philadelphian how much was Spirit and how much self. "One thousand percent self," said the man, who hadn't been there but knew Gertrude Ward.)

—

After 1972, with a few exceptions (such as the mid-seventies rave-up "Mr. D. J." and the ballad "I'm Not Strong Enough to Love You Again"), the quality of her output declined. Well into her early thirties, she exploited a range that soared from a Mahalia low moan on "Precious Memories" to a Marion Williams high D on "Good to Me," covering a good three octaves. But as time decapitated her top notes, and soul music became passé, her career ground to a halt.

She cut some disco recordings, but while disco's alliance of divas and gay men replicated the emotional world of the gospel church, Aretha was unable to remake herself in the new commercial image, and she was superseded by other, less gifted singers. Indeed, she remained too much the descendant of "prayer warriors" like Aunt Rachel to qualify as a convincing dance-club queen. Her dress size alone made her the anti-Diana, and she ended the decade impersonating a waitress in the movie *The Blues Brothers,* blowing away the other performers in what must nevertheless have been an embarrassing Hattie McDaniel moment for someone with her love of glamour.

John Hammond once said that gospel singers have nine lives. Uplifted by their fans, even the most vocally damaged can revisit the old landmarks. In 1980, Aretha signed to Arista Records. Where once she offered

* Still unreleased as of 2011.

vocal beauty, now she employed growls and funny sounds à la Stevie Wonder. Her songs were catchy and inane tunes like "Jump to It," "Freeway of Love," and "Who's Zoomin' Who." She performed a duet with Annie Lennox, of the Eurythmics, on the 1985 feminist rocker "Sisters Are Doin It for Themselves," but the sentiment seemed disingenuous. (She has never talked about doing it without a man.) Surprisingly, the most soulful vocal she had delivered in years was on "I Knew You Were Waiting" (also 1985), another unlikely duet, this time with George Michael. The melody and lyrics ("I didn't falter") succeeded in arousing the ever-dormant Clara Ward in her.

And where was the church? During those years James Cleveland remained the King of Gospel; the top quartet, the Mighty Clouds of Joy, boasted a lead singer, Joe Ligon, who sounded just like Reverend Franklin. Mahalia was gone, as was Clara; but the greatest loss for Aretha occurred in 1979, when Reverend Franklin was shot and entered a five-year coma from which he never awoke. His funeral was the largest in Detroit history. During the next years Aretha lost her brother, Cecil; her sister, and musical alter ego, Carolyn; and her grandmother, Aunt Rachel. Many of her gay colleagues and fans succumbed to AIDS, including, in 1991, James Cleveland.

In 1986, Aretha recorded a second gospel album, *One Lord, One Faith, One Baptism,* for which she revived the Ward Singers' "Surely God Is Able" and "Packin' Up," sang duets with Joe Ligon, and called on Jesse Jackson to fill her father's role with an inspirational sermon. But as she made her commercial and gospel moves, a group of contemporary gospel singers had taken her mannerisms to their gaudiest extreme, busying the melismas, bullying the harmonies. Most of the early culprits were Detroiters. While Vanessa Bell Armstrong (once known as "Little Aretha") and Karen Clark Sheard might also acknowledge the influence of Stevie Wonder, Aretha inhabited their vocal cords. Where she has periodically scatted—an homage, perhaps, to Ella Fitzgerald—they turned scat into the new moan.

What I have dubbed "the Detroit disease" and "the gospel gargle" provide the basis of the *American Idol* style, the ululations that drive some listeners crazy. The critic Jody Rosen has tried to exonerate Aretha, writing that her melisma has nothing to do with this new excess. But, in fact, it's the basis. Not for the first time in popular art does very good seep into very bad. Young women attended to her every inflection. For years the pop charts were led by her acolytes—all of those Whitneys and

Mariahs—riffing on her runs as she had once moaned past her idols. In fact Carey acknowledged her debt to Aretha *and* the "Little Arethas," like Armstrong and Sheard.

Betraying her ignorance of Aretha's later work, an unfortunate *Washington Post* critic has compared Aretha's most rococo passages to the Christina Aguilera school of oversinging—as if she couldn't go over the top on her own! Her latest album includes a gospel song, "Faithful," featuring Karen Clark Sheard. More duel than duet, it drowns in its own convolutions. To a fan of the great tradition, it exemplifies the decadence of contemporary gospel. But today's gospel fans love the ornamentation; by outdoing a younger challenger, Aretha reminds them that she's still the author of their salvation.*

In her sixties, Aretha could seem both withdrawn and seething with plans and resolutions. Some were intellectual—bespeaking her love of high culture, from ballet to opera—and others, entrepreneurial. She once wanted to start a new label and produce records by other artists, including her sister Erma (who died in 2005) and her rapper son Kecalf (her child by Ken Cunningham, her former manager).

In 1998 she astonished the Grammy Awards by replacing Luciano Pavarotti and singing "Nessun dorma." The response was ecstatic: "She can sing anything!" Except for those who detected a musical version of the Emperor's New Clothes. She missed the final high note (during her salad days, it would have been a piece of cake). Instead she employed an old gospel trick, touching on—or, more accurately, intimating—the note, and then descending to a bluesy melisma so complicated that you forgot about what you *should* have heard. A classical-music fan wrote *The New York Times* decrying her "soar-till-you-crash mode," calling it more "colossal failure" than "noble effort." Fans didn't know the difference, and the aria remains in her repertory. She told the *Times* that she'd like to study music theory at Juilliard, an ambition C. L. Franklin would have applauded.

Meanwhile, Aretha watchers whiled away the hours gossiping about her romantic travails (her second marriage, to the actor Glynn Turman, ended in divorce) and her financial indiscretions. In 1992, the Internal Revenue Service sued her for payment of back taxes; and in 1995, Saks Fifth Avenue filed a lawsuit demanding six figures to settle her outstand-

---

*The circle has always been hers to complete and correct. Predictably, after Whitney Houston's death, the most eloquent tribute occurred during a concert of her godmother Aretha Franklin. In a moaned chant worthy of C. L. or Clara Ward, she saluted the star-crossed diva, while slyly quoting "When the Gates Swing Open," a gospel standard popularized by Inez Andrews fifty years ago.

ing debt at the department store. Her famous unwillingness to fly limited her ability to generate income from touring, and sheer economic necessity may have been her chief motivation in signing a reported $1.2 million book deal with Villard for the singularly unrevealing autobiography she wrote with David Ritz.

News reports tended to emphasize her profligate spending habits. In 1996 she traveled from Detroit to Toronto to see Diahann Carroll in a production of *Sunset Boulevard*. Arriving in Toronto during a cold spell, she bought a mink coat and two tickets for the show, one seat for herself and one for the coat. Each year brought new glimpses of someone marching to a drumbeat inaudible to everyone else, often including her own singers and musicians. (Of course, this could be seen as Spirit feel carried to its zenith. And a musician like her pianist Richard Gibbs, Inez Andrews's son, knows how to follow her, because the church prepared him for anything.) In the fall of 2009 she began a concert at Radio City Music Hall late and tried to assuage her public with the promise of five hundred White Tower burgers. When the food didn't show up, she shrugged: "It's the thought that counts." At an HBO special honoring the Rock and Roll Hall of Fame, she intermingled hits and show tunes. Liza Minnelli's "New York, New York" could be heard as a salvo against the assembled taste. At the least it confirmed that she wouldn't settle for being just a rocker—which probably was her point. Such tales are legion.

But she was also a matriarch who had incurred large, painful obligations, and these she has never shirked. The most loyal of daughters, she spent a fortune keeping her comatose father alive for the years between his shooting and his death. Clarence, her eldest son, is a paranoid schizophrenic who lives in an adult foster-care home. One news story told of a nurse demanding one hundred and fifty dollars an hour as compensation for acting as his companion; Aretha had offered fifty. The actual cost of her son's care must be a drain on her finances, even if she grossed a reported $3.8 million between 1990 and 1995. She also performed numerous benefit concerts. In April 1995, she raised nearly $2 million for New York's Sloan Hospital for Women. For the women she championed—impoverished, ill, frequently battered wives—melodrama was not an overstatement.

Pushing seventy, she occupied a unique position in pop music. The spotlight had dimmed for most of her contemporaries, and many of them were now dependent on infomercials and Las Vegas. But she still inspired much younger producers, like Narada Michael Walden, Kenneth "Babyface" Edmonds, and Sean "Puff Daddy" Combs. Very seldom has a black artist so identified with one style allied herself with so many others. (Imagine Louis Armstrong jamming with Cecil Taylor.) Since the disco era, she has often seemed either a chameleon or a hapless bystander at the mercy of her producer's whims.

Even so, her collaborators wouldn't all try so hard if it were not tacitly agreed that she was the last of the great ones. The question remains if her strengths apply to new notions of pop. It leaps off the screen in *Going Home,* a 1995 documentary film about her that was produced by Arista Records and broadcast on the Disney Channel. The film consists largely of MTV-style videos, interspersed with clips of her grandiose appearance at the 1993 Inaugural Ball (complete with Clara Ward ponytail and enough mink coat to enrage a nation of animal lovers) and a tantalizingly brief shot of her singing and dancing in church. But the film's best reason for being is a series of brief performances by Aretha at home. She is seated before her piano, demurely garbed in a simple blouse and tailored vest. Most important, the emphasis is on her music. Recalling her early days as a pop singer, she performs the first lines of "My Funny Valentine." She sings and plays like any standard-issue Sarah Vaughan devotee of the early sixties. Three lines into the song, she stops, poses grandly, and haughtily asks, "Where are the strings? Where are the French horns? Where are the cellos?" The great moment is her revision of Inez Andrews's "Mary Don't You Weep." As in most improvisatory art, it helps to know the original. In her 1958 recording, Andrews chant-sang a mighty sermon while her group, the Caravans, wailed the title line as an admonitory refrain. Aretha turns the group effort into a solo. Her piano chords duplicate the choral accompaniment in a graphic instance of what classical musicians call instrumental "voicings." She imposes one time signature on another, much as a gospel lead syncopates off her background. Interjecting runs that mediate between her father's moans and the "Detroit disease," she exhibits a mastery of each element of the gospel aesthetic: vocal color, rhythmic play, emotional intensity. In less than a minute, she convinces you that the best Aretha record would be a re-creation of 1950s gospel, preferably with nothing but her piano as support. No backup singers, no synthesizer players, and decidedly no rock guitarists need apply.

Yet who would buy such a record? Or produce it? And would Aretha, still looking for a hit, want to cut it? Once again, she posed an uncomfortable question. If your strong suit is outdated—the tessitura of your art no longer audible—what does it require to keep up with the times? Is the idea of a hip-hop earth mother worth entertaining?

If her voice on the soundtrack of *Waiting to Exhale* sounded muffled and sheathed, she was still the one entrusted with the album's only serious song, "It Hurts Like Hell." Once a diffident performer, she had become perversely defiant, daring the public to accept a series of performing selves, to watch her exchange bodies nearly as often as she does gowns. No longer shy, she started clowning like the Ward Singers of her youth. One of her favored ploys was to shake her head until her wig flew off, a sign that she was beyond happy. Of course, the hair revealed was thick and lustrous, worthy of a queen.

Manipulating her image proved the best way to control it. In late 1993 she appeared at a Kennedy Center Lifetime Achievement tribute to Marion Williams, re-created "Surely God Is Able," and hollered "Hallelujah!" The night before the concert, a dinner for the honorees took place at the State Department. Spotting Williams in the crowd, Aretha knelt before the half-blind singer and whispered in her ear, "Don't you know God is able," the first line of their favorite song. "Hi, baby," Marion said, recognizing the voice before the face. In her Arista promotional video, Aretha mentions hanging out with George Michael: "I think certain artists should talk to each other and communicate . . . just like van Gogh had . . . friends who were other great artists, painters like himself." The talk between Aretha and Marion was less abstruse. Teeming with implication, it involved the naming of old singers, most of them long gone, and their vocal specialties. Aretha was as modest and respectful as if she were still a child, asking polite questions of her idols.

In the spring of 1994, she gave a concert at the White House, an event she apparently regarded as her career's high point. Coming on like a Ella Fitzgerald wannabe, she advanced to the maudlin, the hoary, and the trifling: "Ol' Man River," "Drink to Me Only with Thine Eyes," and "Freeway of Love." Except that the show tune became a gospel tribute to her "Aunt" Rachel, replete with gorgeous intervals; the English ballad became the Ward Singers hymn "I Heard the Voice of Jesus Say," which shares its melody; and the finger popper became a spirited gospel anthem.

Several black politicians were in the audience, among them Jesse Jackson, seated a few feet away from President Clinton. A couple of years earlier, the rift between the two men had been symbolized by another singer, Sister Souljah. But Lady Soul had brought them both to her altar (or, as the hymn says, "humbly to their feet"). During "Freeway of Love," Reverend Jackson clapped rather awkwardly, each burst accompanied by a little jump from his seat. During the bridge of "Ol' Man River" Aretha sang about landing in jail. Mrs. Clinton shook her head with appropriate sadness while the president nodded in furious assent, as if convicted by a sentiment he had never heard before. He looked like any white blues lover trying to get with the program, but one doubted that he would take the words to heart and change his approach to penal incarceration or the death penalty. Just what were these listeners embracing as gospel truth?

History would assign her the role of the Last Woman Standing, the most full-throated witness of her parents' generation. She would outlive her father and her siblings, as well as all of her mentors. Mahalia dead at fifty-nine, her last years diminished by scandal; Clara dead at forty-eight, though she looked seventy. At sixty-five, Marion Williams received both the Kennedy Center award and the MacArthur "Genius" Award, and was dead within a year, that last burst of fame a poisonous chimera. Jackie Verdell died in obscurity at fifty-seven, having briefly survived the amputation of both legs. Even less remembered is Leila Royster, another Davis Sister, who shared the young Aretha's vocal range and tessitura. Indeed, her top notes were stronger and her moans more inspired. She was a protean performer, capable of outsinging a quartet on Sunday and delighting a tavern the next night, Baltimore's answer to Aretha. The reason nobody knows her is that a year after cutting some classic records with the Sisters, she would die, burned alive in a house fire.

These women remain Aretha's vocal models, their songs still deep in her repertory because she has never heard better. (This may explain her celebrated froideur toward younger artists. Having heard the best, why waste praise on lesser talents?) But singing for Jesus had not protected her saints: their message was good news; their experience, very bad times. Nor had sermons sheltered C. L. Franklin. Surveying their fates would make any singer wonder how she got over, and as Aretha says, "I'm sentimental, I don't forget." And so she became the last celebrated singer to keep their music alive. Who today sings like Clara, Jackie, Marion, Mahalia? Nobody but her.

In 2007 she would record her strongest work in years, a most gospelly duet with Mary J. Blige of "Never Gonna Lose My Faith." It would bring her back to the Grammy Awards, where she followed it with "The Old Landmark." A year later, emulating the many singers who have quit big labels to record for themselves, she released her first self-produced album, a collection of Christmas carols.

Of course she gospelized them. Appearing on *The View,* where her very grand muumuu startled the natives, she sang "Angels We Have Heard on High" and followed the word "glorious" with low-scooping, bluesy runs. This led her into "Respect," a song whose charms should have been long exhausted. She now included a mini-sermonette, in which she informs her boyfriend that her demands are modest. "I'm just a simple woman," she says, something that only a fool would believe. But the conclusion offered her a chance for some more moaning. Her eyes shut, she rambled so ecstatically that her background singers started lifting their hands; her singing had made them happy. Even telling off some trifling Romeo couldn't stop her from singing the gospel.

The middle-aged women, mostly white, in the audience screamed like bobby-soxers. She had become the greatest example of a woman singing to other women, with an authority that made vocal quality irrelevant. When you had a sister like that, you'd be a sniveling ingrate to grumble over misbegotten octaves. The wounded voice guaranteed her authenticity to women of her generation. (Thus, when asked about Jennifer Hudson, her comment "She has a good clear voice" could be heard as a put-down. Once she had owned the clearest voice in the land, but now a little living had changed all that.) The confessional stance predates Aretha, and goes back to the roots of black vaudeville, from Jackie "Moms" Mabley to Pearl Bailey, or much later, from Shirley Brown to Millie Jackson. Pearl's addresses to some unidentified "child" were always sister-to-sister. Esther Phillips once said, "I'm singing this song for all my lady friends in the house. I do most of my blues songs for the ladies, because we always have the blues, you see." (This is a great, if unwitting, riposte to all the white blues boys, who considered blues a manly art.)

Years before "Respect" or "Think," Aretha had been talking to her sisters. One of her early Columbia singles, "Can't You Just See Me," is a song of deliverance: she's loosed the man and let him go. The lyric reads, "Can't you just see me with my head in the air?" But she ad-libs, "Can't you just see me, girls . . . ?" This is *our* victory. She asserted a similar pride in her attempt at a disco anthem, "Ladies Only." "This is for ladies only" translates into something more intimate, "for the girls only. This is your night to shine." Of course the tempo picks up, from slow dance to church shout. In her vision the disco floor is a place where a girl can shout her freedom, act cosmopolitan one moment, country the next.

(Ergo, she follows a series of French phrases with the funky command, "Party down, *s'il vous plaît.*")

A male admirer guesses that Aretha's feminism has nothing to do with politics and everything to do with a woman reveling in her own experience. The beauty of her "Try a Little Tenderness" is the way she pleads for herself; even the harmonically advanced "ness" lets you know she's worth the trouble. Many times she has played her sex's ambassador, letting men know what ladies really want—whether it be respect, freedom, tenderness, or the simple chance to show out.

Her disciples have reformulated the message. Mary J. Blige offers herself as a guidance counselor: "Use my songs as remedies whenever you're feeling down or blue / I'll be there for you." The delightfully secular West Indian rapper Nicki Minaj announces herself as every woman's friend. "I'm fighting for the girls that never thought they could win . . . / I am here to reverse the curse they live in."

A proud grandmother, Aretha remained a natural woman. Thus her newest album would be called *A Woman Falling Out of Love.* Not since Mae West or Helen Trent—the radio-soap-opera heroine of her youth, who proved that romance could last well after thirty-five—has a prominent woman so insisted on remaining a romantic player; she could even imagine Halle Berry impersonating her in a biopic. Though increasingly few remembered the fact, she had once been a slim girl who had released photos of herself in a ballet tutu.

But then she was also promising to record an album of classical music, entering a field in later life that is usually barred to anyone starting out after twenty-five. The Church Lady stood revealed as She Who Must Be Obeyed. Academic categories have always been trifling concerns to the great gospel women: in 1961, Marion Williams rearranged the "Hallelujah" Chorus for a five-woman group. So why couldn't Aretha, nearing her eighth decade, threaten to study voice at Juilliard? Having inaugurated her career with "Never Grow Old," she continued to live by its principles.

HER DAUGHTERS

Some time in the early eighties, Aretha started combining gospel and secular material in her act. Such versatility had crucified Rosetta Tharpe. But at a Radio City Music Hall concert, she followed some risqué pop with a gospel version of "Precious Memories" that drove Bishop Paul Morton, whose church choir supported her, to an ecstasy that he couldn't contain. The poor man danced all over the stage. Later in the program she introduced Willa Ward, Frances Steadman, and Kitty Parham of her beloved Ward Singers, and even sang Marion Williams's specialty "Weeping May Endure for a Night."

Aretha could sing a blues one moment and gospel the next, spin on a dime from Foxy Grandma to Church Mother. (Among her more astonishing outfits—not an easy choice—was the robe with a cross, tailored to her width, on its back.) Thanks to her example, hip-hoppers began praising Jesus along with bling. Beyoncé, on the same Destiny's Child album, could sing "Bootylicious" and "Yes Jesus Loves Me." Cognitive dissonance fled. Oil and water jelled.

Loleatta Holloway, the anti–Shirley Caesar, rode this dialectic to delirious heights. In the last minute of her disco hit "Dreaming," she initiates a vamp around the phrase "I can stand up and tell everybody I've got him." Upon hearing her growl like a young Marion Williams, a gospel fan would just know the "him" had to be Jesus: who else could make a woman act so wild? Except Loleatta opts to holler and shout about her boyfriend (as Aretha will go from a "motherless child" and "pilgrim to sorrow" to a woman singing the blues, translating her moan for those unable to do it for themselves). In another hit, "Keep the Fire Burnin'," she starts to preach, advising her listeners to step out—not in the name of Jesus, but "in the name of love, in the name of money, in the name of everything you believe." You could write a thesis on those options. In her years with the Caravans, she might summon the saints to shout their praise, in the hope of "healing and deliverance," churchy euphemisms for both love and money.

The church took notice. Gospel singers may not be able to duplicate the feats of an Aretha or a Loleatta, although a singer like Ann Nesby can flit between the two fields. But now gospel women can discuss their experiences with unprecedented candor. Formerly a woman's complaints got no further than Dorothy Love's citation of a wayward father, or Dorothy Norwood's fable *A Denied Mother,* in which a man abandons his wife after she rescues their child from a fire and "wasn't beautiful anymore."

But now the testimonies advert to adultery and bisexuality; LaShun Pace dances across a stage because she didn't acquire HIV from her ex-husband (just as Donnie McClurkin shouts simply because he is no longer gay). The guru of such testifying is Bishop T. D. Jakes, the pastor of the Potter's House, a fifteen-thousand-member Apostolic church in Dallas. Bishop Jakes has become the most popular gospel preacher since C. L. Franklin, not with parable but with psychobabble. He has packed arenas coast-to-coast with his sermon "Woman, Thou Art Loosed." The thrust of his message is that a saint can be delivered from the scandal of her sexual past. Born again, she can become "Daddy's Little Girl." He may step down from the altar and walk up to some woman and address her with scriptural passages that he translates into a gloss on her particular condition ("Daughter, the Lord's got better things for you"). To an organ accompaniment straight out of radio soap opera, he will dismiss the emotions that he considers childish things. Fondling a doll that symbolizes all that, he whispers, "I love you, baby, but I'm going to have to kill you," and women weep profusely. His *explication du texte* can seem so personal that women collapse, slain in the Spirit. This is truly "a word from the Lord" meant for them alone.

Jakes's message is fraught with an implicit hatred of the body, unless lawfully wedded and "covered by the blood." If the womanizing C. L. Franklin had talked like Jakes, he would have been laughed out of Detroit.

The Christianizing of sexual liberation had begun years earlier among white evangelicals with Marabel Morgan's *The Total Woman*; their literature includes many books in which saved women are encouraged to move in a state of perpetual readiness, shaved, douched, and fragrant for their loving husbands. "Behold the Bridegroom Cometh" never seemed so real. This approach is intensely womanist and stridently antifeminist. It is also politically conservative, the love mantra of the religious right, and frequently invoked in the meetings of Women Aglow, a Pentecostal and charismatic group with chapters all over America.

C. L. Franklin and Martin Luther King, Baptists through-and-through, represent the alternative to all of that, to Women Aglow as much as to T. D. Jakes's right-wing politics. (The members of Women Aglow told one academic investigator that homosexuality was unknown in their ranks. But, then, the Soviet Union and China also claimed that they had wiped it out.)

And yet, when T. D. Jakes, a best-selling author, wrote *God's Leading Lady*, who topped the list? Not an evangelist; not his mother; not the Virgin Mary. It was Aretha Franklin. He remarked as particularly miraculous her performance as a mezzo-soprano of Pavarotti's tenor aria. That placed her higher than missionaries and saints. For Bishops Jakes and Morton, she remained Our Lady.

Jakes's most celebrated protégée is Prophetess Juanita Bynum. A Chicagoan, raised in a strict Pentecostal home, she dreamed of a career in show business, even playing the lead in her high school's production of *My Fair Lady*. She went through a series of low-paying jobs, and after a failed marriage she began to lead what she considered a promiscuous life. Until she turned up at one of Bishop Jakes's conventions and shouted the house with her sermon "No More Sheets." No more a wretch undone, she testified that she was now a complete and holy woman, delivered by Jesus from the hell of premarital sex.

The video of "No More Sheets" sold over a million copies and made her the biggest thing in black religion. Huge audiences, primarily of women, showed up to hear her prophetic messages about overcoming the flesh and getting rich in the process. These messages came at a cost; there were frequent calls for love offerings, and reminders that getting more meant giving more. And if the giving hurt, all the better: "No cross, no crown." She began making trips to Israel and returning with immense prayer shawls that had been multiply anointed; they could only be bought in patches. One time, on a Christian TV program, she asked the singer Candi Staton to cut a snippet for some donor, then snatched the scissors out of her hand. "You know that woman can't stand that much anointing!"

She would marry Bishop Thomas Weeks, another child of the sanctified church, in a wedding that reportedly cost $5 million; the video sold in the hundred thousands. The audiences of women grew even larger. Asserting her role as a prophet, she would drive the saints to super-high praise, women roaring louder than an arena of screaming sports fans. Then she would command them to sit down and be still. They did— until a minute later, when she had them back up shouting at full blast. They seemed less God's leading ladies than Juanita's marionettes, but she claimed scriptural authority: "The prophet is always in control."

Her husband began preaching similar messages of a new sexual life in Christ. In one sermon, "Cursing in the Bedroom," he insisted that the marriage bed could never be defiled. "You don't speak in tongues in the bedroom" (though many a saint, safe in her "secret closet," had done just that). He seemed to be saying that married love was so deeply spiritual that raunchy sex was the supreme anointing, the equivalent of an all-day Holy Ghost revival. While he spoke, one saint stood, transfixed by his word, beholding him in his power. It was his wife. Both of them looked deadly serious. This was sex as sacrament, as manifest prophecy.

Alas, the prophetess was myopic. In 2007 *The New York Times* published a front-page story about Bishop Weeks's arrest for publicly beating his wife. The scandal kept reverberating. Among the victims were the marriage, the husband's ministry, and very possibly the wife's. In a pathetic appearance she boasted that she had repented, although she admitted no sins, and that, renewed in her faith, she was entitled to "wear white" in God's presence, probably a sign of born-again virginity. Regrets or recriminations would only divert her from pursuing "my destiny," words that caused her to shed tears. Other women began crying over a "destiny" so humiliatingly deferred, their prophetess reduced to just another sister.

Prophetess Bynum's misadventures dramatize the new themes—and distractions—that swept through black churches in lieu of progressive politics. From the years of King and Franklin to those of Jakes and his equally reactionary brothers is a decline that can make one weep. The only solace is the voice that spanned and inspired both eras—Aretha Franklin's voice.

—

For years she denied there was anything wrong with that voice, or blamed the very audible damage on tobacco and the weather. (Was she hoarse performing "My Country 'Tis of Thee" at the Obama inauguration? "Mother Nature" had betrayed her. Just to outdo that lady, she proceeded to record an excessively gospelized version of the anthem, complete with more high F-sharps than she had sung in years, amid double-timed "[let freedom] ring"s from her chorale. By chance this faux shout was the only splurge of rhythmic energy on the album!) On various occasions, she has said that her voice didn't span three octaves but six; that she now sounded infinitely better than she had ten years ago (having quit smoking); and that 150 pounds was her best singing weight—upon which some of the gospel children started moaning, "The day is past and gone." And then, as if to spite all her enemies, she announced her plans to master opera.

On a vastly more public stage President Obama's inauguration replayed some of the same themes and conflicts Al Duckett had recognized that afternoon almost fifty years earlier, when he introduced

Aretha Franklin to the wider world. Now the reactionary figure, then represented by J. H. Jackson, was the obese homophobe Rick Warren, though when he saluted the work of men like Dr. King (and, implicitly, Reverend Franklin) and imagined that there would be "shouting in heaven," you knew that C. L.'s idioms still prevailed. And Warren was more than balanced by Reverend Joseph Lowery, who quite stole the show with his one-liners ("when the red man can get ahead, man") and quotes from the Negro National Anthem and C. A. Tindley's "Beams of Heaven." Rhetorically and politically he played the C. L. Franklin role.

In between, acting as the musical mediator, was Aretha. Her gospel arrangement of "My Country 'Tis of Thee" was not her finest hour vocally, but she nearly stole the show with her beribboned hat. It had been designed by a young Korean-American man, trained at Parsons but living in Detroit, whose main clientele was black church women. Seeing Aretha in her gone-to-meeting hat, one old-timer said, "That girl will live and die a Ward Singer."

The inauguration also led to a one-sided diva battle between Etta James and Beyoncé. Etta was furious that Beyoncé had serenaded the Obamas with "At Last," her most famous song. Both women had come out of the church. Etta grew up in St. Paul Baptist Church in Los Angeles, singing in a choir directed by J. Earle Hines, one of postwar gospel's first stars; and her vocal inspiration was Cora Martin, Sallie Martin's adopted daughter. (There's far more Cora in Etta's "At Last" than there is Etta in Beyoncé's.) Beyoncé had sung with the newer, contemporary stars like Kirk Franklin, had even boasted of speaking in tongues. But her voice was much clearer (if less multichromatic or stylistically assured) than the young Etta's. Indeed, her sweet-voiced, understated vocal recalled the Judy Garland side of Aretha.

Beyoncé had previously offended Aretha, a year earlier, during a Grammy Award presentation, when she introduced "the Queen of Soul, Tina Turner." That has been Aretha's title for years. As a girl in Nutbush, Tennessee, Tina had sung in a choir. She hadn't been overly stirred by the spiritual messages but was transfixed by the rhythms. The secret of her muscular dancing has always been the church shout: that's why she's always too athletic to be merely lewd. It's also why Mick Jagger could get away with his heavy-footed mimicry: Tina had turned dance into a sport available to male imitators, just as gospel men had long taken their physical cues from Mahalia or Marion. And just so, when Beyoncé started making her dance videos, male imitators—including

Justin Timberlake—intuited the androgynous note and danced along with her.

Tina Turner had traveled much further than Aretha. Now living in Europe, she was also a convert to Buddhism, albeit with a soulful caveat. She told *Jet* that she considered herself a "Baptist Buddhist." And when she appeared on *60 Minutes,* performing a chant, she sounded more sanctified than Baptist, her words so foreign and fluent that she seemed to be speaking in tongues.

Aretha, however, would never leave her daddy's church. The night before the inauguration, she gave a gospel concert at the Kennedy Center. Just to make things plain, she climaxed with "The Old Landmark." Just to make them real, she proceeded to shout across the stage—inaugurating the inauguration, so to speak, with a holy dance. For me, the great moment had occurred earlier, during "Precious Memories," which, as ever, allowed her to moan and slur to her Baptist heart's content. But this time, she ad-libbed a reference to "the days of Dr. King." The gospel sound was bearing a political witness. With a moan, she invoked a half-century of struggle. In the subsequent months, the inaugural euphoria would dissolve into the sourest national mood since 1968.

Further cause for Aretha Louise Franklin to sing the gospel.

Anyway, she had participated in a more stirring conjunction of gospel and politics. In 1990, after Nelson Mandela was released from prison, he made his first visit to the United States. When he reached Detroit, there was a huge gathering, presided over by Reverend Jesse Jackson. Of course Aretha appeared, this time with a Ward Singers ponytail, singing the group's biggest hit, "Surely God Is Able." She began at the piano, but rose to her feet in order to rock the house. Hand placed, Marion-like, on her left hip, she roared Reverend Brewster's words of encouragement: "Surely, surely," the word repeated a dozen times, "he's able to carry you through." "Take it back to Africa!" she advised the great man. For any lover of traditional gospel, this was a transcendent moment. Reverend Brewster's gospel message of freedom addressed to Nelson Mandela by African America's envoy to the home country. If only Brewster or Dr. King or C. L. Franklin could have seen that!

—

She remained an inescapable presence. In the spring of 2010, she boasted that she had lost twenty-three pounds, and tantalized with the prospect of a biographical film. Perhaps now all the stories withheld from David Ritz would be told. She also hinted that Denzel Washington would play the role of C. L. Franklin. Were the film to adhere even to Nick Salvatore's kindly biography, it would have to present her father's love of wine, women, and song. Would she allow that? The ever-surprising queen gave no clue.

In July she gave a concert at the Mann Center for the Performing Arts in Philadelphia, Clara Ward's hometown. Of course she sang "The Old Landmark" in honor of her idol. But before that, she had sung a few songs, accompanied by Condoleezza Rice, exhibiting a political sangfroid worthy of Barack Obama. But she assured reporters that she remained a true Democrat, lifting her arms as if giving a testimony. To prove it, she planned to appear at a surprise birthday party for the very troubled Congressman Charles Rangel. Only a bad fall prevented her appearance. This accident presaged more serious medical issues. She took a six-month leave of absence and underwent surgery in a Detroit hospital. Since both Carolyn and Erma had died of breast cancer, the fans became very alarmed; the diagnosis of pancreatic cancer broke many hearts. Ever the Church Lady, Aretha told them not to worry; she had an army of saints on her side, who could "sure 'nuff get a prayer through."

Reviewing the Philadelphia concert, a *New York Times* critic offered tentative approval for a Handel aria, but was spellbound by "Doctor Feelgood," a Ted White aria, in which she accompanied herself on piano. Over many years "Feelgood" had been subtly de-eroticized. At times she would speed up the song's tempo, "I've got a new friend, his name is Doctor Feelgood," to the same cadence as the gospel standard "Doctor Jesus." In 1990 she appended a gospel coda, filled with her daddy's moans. "Oh . . . Doctor Feee—eee-eelgood . . . yea-ea-eah . . . beginning to feel real good . . . sure 'nuff. Everyone ought to have one . . . sure 'nuff . . . Feel all right tonight . . . feel all right in my *body*." The audience took it very seriously: not a lewd holler in the house.

An even greater catharis occurs when she wails "Today I Sing the Blues," the oldest pop song in her repertory. In a Nashville concert last year, she sang with such intensity that women started screaming . . . something that happens very rarely these days, even in church. The song ended with a surplus of bluesy runs and moans, except that this was moaning out of C. L. Franklin. It was testimony time: "Something about it, makes me want to jump and shout . . . Say yeah . . . I feel all right tonight," the organ moaning along with her. "I don't know about you all . . . but I've come from a mighty long way . . . and I just want to say thank you." The "Jesus" was noisily implicit.

But something new was going on. In the past she would segue from a rocker to a gospel shout song. But now she went straight from the blues to the shout, as if there were no contradiction. The gospelized blues was not a metaphor, it was a spiritual devotion requiring a spiritual release. She had abolished the distinctions between gospel blues and bluesy gospel. She was also reasserting her oldest self. I remembered the Aretha I had heard at Washington Temple in 1959, who had sung a slow, sad song, proceeded to moan like Clara Ward and her father, and then leapt from the piano to cut her shout steps. Fifty years, and the essence of her performing self had barely changed.

She continued to be a presiding figure in gospel. The music has changed dramatically. You will now hear echoes of Prince and Michael Jackson, of university chorales and garage rock (electric guitar has replaced the Hammond organ as the vehicle of meditation). But as for "The Old Landmark"? It's been virtually forgotten. One old-time warrior complained, "I don't know what they're playing, and they don't know what I'm singing." You almost feel like Gertrude Ward demanding "the *holy* gospel" at her daughter's funeral. Even so, there remained a few male vocalists, like Joe Ligon and the Atlanta pastor Johnny L. Jones, who were still feeding off C. L. Franklin's scraps, singing and preaching with his mighty voice echoing in their ears. Vanessa Bell Armstrong recorded her biggest hit in years, a semi-gospel song called "Good News." Aretha had recorded the song five years earlier, ending the track with some hard-singing gospel ad libs. She still sounded better than her daughters. She was now truer to the tradition she had previously bowdlerized than any woman still performing, outside of Shirley—once "Baby Shirley," now "Mama Shirley"—Caesar.*

Within that tradition, a good singer need never lose her inspira-

---

*Among younger male singers, Reverend Timothy Flemming, the sixty-year-old pastor of Atlanta's Mount Carmel Missionary Baptist Church, has carried the sounds of Mahalia Jackson, Brother Joe May, and—particularly—Marion Williams into the twenty-first century. Younger women like Vicki Winans and Shun Pace have recorded convincing versions of old-timey gospel; both have the pitch and chops for inspired a cappella singing. But you sense that it's a stunt; they're impersonating their ancestors. Not surprisingly, some younger quartets—like the mixed-gender Ronica and the Mighty Blazing Thunders—seem more comfortable reimagining traditional Gospel. Among the few surviving veterans of the golden age, my particular favorites are two wondrously named Philadelphians, Romance Watson and Goldwire McLendon: check them out on YouTube.

tion. Madame Emily Bram, perhaps the strongest-voiced member of the Church of God in Christ, continued to sing with room-shaking power into her nineties; confined to a wheelchair, she could spin out more bluesy gospel than any American still alive. In Aretha's Detroit, Lois Russell, one of New Bethel's first members, continues to sing at one hundred—and do the books for her new church as well. (She was one of the quartet ladies who used to scare R. H. Harris, back in the day.)

In October 2010, almost forty years after Mahalia Jackson's funeral, Aretha returned to Chicago to say goodbye to another gospel queen, Albertina Walker. Although she was clearly not in the best health, she rose to sing. As if to summon Mahalia's going-home service, she sang "I'll Fly Away," in the arrangement that she had learned from J. Robert Bradley. She told the church that she could never forget her early years, listening to the Ward Singers or Albertina's group the Caravans.

There were unhappier echoes of Mahalia's funeral, with its recapitulation of old feuds and hostilities. Albertina Walker's nephew beat up her manager. Horrified by this turn, Shirley Caesar told the church, "We're gonna make sure these colored people treat Albertina's memory right . . . I will call the police on you in a minute." A reminder for Lady Soul that church was a great place to visit, but you wouldn't want to live there.

Was she aware that this might be her last concert? She gave no signs. If anything, she remained gospel's dutiful daughter. Spotting Delois Barrett Campbell in her wheelchair, she ran to console her as she wept over Albertina, whom she had known since the Caravans were simply the background group for her father's pal Robert Anderson. Back in Detroit, she asked Richard Gibbs to tell his mother, Inez Andrews, to FedEx her that rhinestone-studded black watch Inez had worn at the funeral.

And, ever ready to defy expectations, within a month of her surgery, she was granting interviews of a thoroughly secular nature. Her health was now "superb," she told Wendy Williams, and she was ready for action. She meant business, too. All of her postponed dates would be rescheduled. Notably absent were any shout-outs to Jesus or mentions of church. Instead she spoke of casino hotels and sunny beaches. Asked if she had any boyfriends, she declared, "I don't have boyfriends. I have *men*." Then she gave an impromptu salute to the scandal-plagued R. Kelly. His recent hit "When a Woman Loves" could have been recorded forty years ago: it is Percy Sledge redux, except for ladies. With his hyperfervent tenor he declares that a woman in love "for real" will take anything, everything, for her man's sake. You might say that notion subverted generations of "Respect" and "Think," that it was old-school masochism. But Lady Soul found the sentiment persuasive, and the singer hot. "If he isn't careful I might become a cougar."

As confirmation, in the penultimate song of her newest CD, "When 2 Become One," she sang:

I'm feeling you, when you're into me.

To paraphrase James Cleveland's first hit with the Caravans (the ur-source of Ray Charles's "This Little Girl of Mine"), what kind of woman was this? A holy woman? A natural woman? R. Kelly's woman? After fifty years, the answer remained the same: her own woman. Obviously she saw herself as sui generis. In a later interview, Wendy Williams asked her to name her successors. There were none. She could only imagine "Aretha, Aretha, and Aretha."

Therefore she exhibited no distress when a CBS interviewer solemnly inquired, "Aretha, how's your love life?" (How many sixty-nine-year-olds would allow such impudence?) As she had so many times, she continued to extol Sam Cooke as the last word in male pulchritude. Her memories of the quartet heroes of yore coalesced with her searing performance of B. B. King's "Sweet Sixteen," the blues of her youth. If she were a cougar, she kept her heart in the past.

When she appeared to be mortally ill, people stopped joking about her size, her outfits, her voice. But, having apparently recovered and lost ninety unwelcome pounds, she was once again fit to be patronized. In a review of her uneven new album, a Chicago critic wrote that she might be the Queen of Soul, but as for blues or jazz, she was "only a pawn": a comment of dumbfounding stupidity. *New York* magazine had fun mocking her recipe for peach salad.

Yet this made her seem even more the heroine of her own existential drama. What other female performer had so tantalized her audience with thoughts of mortality? Having departed the musical scene in Chicago, at Albertina's funeral, it was right that she re-emerge in the same place, giving a triumphant concert, accompanied expertly by Inez Andrews's son.

—

During Aretha's ordeal, her fans sustained themselves with her old records and, even more, the many YouTube clips, a large number provided by the Queen herself.

Some of the grandest were not even the biggest hits. From the sixties there was a charming duet of "Mockingbird" with the pianist Ray Johnson, in which she seems atypically relaxed and content, a happier girl than her Detroit friends would have remembered. A few years later she performs with Sammy Davis Jr. a jive interrogation of the word "soul." "Who's got soul?" he asks. "Ray Charles?" "He's got soul," she sings. "Mahalia?" "She's got soul." In perfect voice she segues into a hair-raising "Think." They end with a series of statements, moaned as if from the pulpit.

His preaching growls may be gifted, amorphous mimicry, but her Clara moans and Marion whoops, her Mahalia ebullience and Dinah cunning, have produced something epochal. She can define soul because she has become the word incarnate.

Almost forty years later, she sings a very moving "Amazing Grace" at the funeral of her friend Luther Vandross, whom she has graciously called "the premier vocalist of our time," adding in that cosmopolitan style of her late years, "He had savoir faire." She and he were oddly chosen prophets of love, both subject to huge shifts in weight, neither of them conventionally graceful: she, the preacher's daughter, who had made lovemaking a sacred act; he, the gay man, who had succeeded Reverend Al Green as America's proudest "baby maker." Aretha's tribute could also be heard as Lady Soul's reward to the gospel children, as if it was her grace that had delivered them.

She had a greater gift in store for them. On October 23, 2011, precisely a week after singing "Precious Lord" at the Martin Luther King Memorial in Washington D.C., she traveled to New York to perform at a same-sex wedding. As the grooms danced, she saluted them with Whitney Houston's (and Dolly Parton's) "I Will Always Love You," thereby reminding any haters that nobody could outsing the queen. Her appearance must have mortified the mega-pastors like T. D. Jakes, now forced to reconcile their Aretha-worship with her tacit embrace of gay rights: "God's Leading Lady," indeed. But elsewhere, the descendants of James Cleveland and Ruth Davis—and of her first promoter, the great Alfred

A. Duckett—were beaming. "Go ahead, girl," they must have hollered. *"Let Him use you."**

"Amazing Grace" itself had never seemed to fail her. During Luther Vandross's last illness, she had performed it for Oprah Winfrey, who was moved enough to start talking down-home church. "Girl, I hear you had a prayer vigil for Luther and were calling down *all* of Jesus' power." Aretha replied magnanimously, "The Lord is good," and then added, in a heretical non sequitur, "Girlfriend, that's some serious bling-bling you've got there." The day before her comeback concert, she performed the hymn at a mass tribute to Oprah held at Chicago's United Center. Winfrey's last shows had been filled with wrenching tales, a farewell to her audience of embattled women and gay people, the very groups that comprised Aretha's most devoted followers.

On May 18, 2011, the song was retrofitted to the occasion. Stedman Graham, Oprah's companion, looking every inch a superstar pastor from the C. L. Franklin days, surveyed his lady's journey. That "a colored girl from the backwoods of Mississippi" could have made it was living proof of "God's amazing grace." He had set the song up as well as the finest gospel narrator, Gertrude Ward, on a Spirit-filled day. And Aretha delivered, singing only one verse, replete with so many inspired turns (if someone else had worked the article "a" in "a wretch" so intricately, it hadn't been her) that it could only lead into a Reverend Franklin moan and a holy dance.

Having challenged Mother Nature, and declared herself the victor in high notes and sex appeal, she was now serenading the most famous woman in the world, giving her lyrical summation of a career no more astonishing than her own. She had all reason to shout the victory. There she was, singing hard gospel to an audience way beyond counting; ten thousand megachurches couldn't hold them. Her father's daughter. Safe thus far.

—

How did she get over? By dragging a lot of people along with her.

*Aretha was similarly bold after Whitney Houston's death. Perhaps to squelch the many rumors of lesbianism, the Houston family chose the church's arch-homophobes, from Donnie McClurkin to T. D. Jakes to Marvin Winans, to eulogize the singer. But the night before the funeral, during a concert at Radio City Music Hall, Aretha selected Bishop Carlton Pearson, the champion of an "inclusive" gay-embracing ministry, to perform a similar role. The message was probably inaudible to Middle America, but the children in their secret closet understood every word.

II. NOT QUITE AT HOME

SOMEBODY ELSE'S PARADISE

I'll do what I must if I'm bold in real time.
A refugee, I'll be paroled in real time.

AGHA SHAHID ALI

YESTERDAY'S HEROES

When Albert Einstein quipped that he had been exiled into paradise, he implied that the journey was provisional and the destination unreal. The contribution of Hitler's émigrés to American culture is immense, worth a book, worth many books. And given the quizzical, unsentimental tone of émigré culture, it has seemed a success story beyond their wildest dreams. If not always a paradise, America proved to be a homeland where they could both find sanctuary and exert unparalleled influence, where they could live what Thomas Mann's Joseph in Egypt knows as "the fat years."

Yet the years ended, and many of those reputations have suffered a major decline. This could be a function of publicity, the quicksilver superannuation of yesterday's heroes. The two most famous émigrés, Albert Einstein and Thomas Mann, both arrived in America knowing

Einstein would be severely attacked for his critiques of Israel.

that their reputations were not entirely safe. In 1930, a group of brilliant young physicists, most of whom would emigrate to America, composed a play, *Faust in Copenhagen,* with a lyric that blithely advised that a physicist was old at thirty and that Einstein was yesterday's news, scientifically speaking. Even earlier, in 1913, D. H. Lawrence had reviewed a translation of *Death in Venice* and sneered, "Thomas Mann is old, and we are young." But I think how the refugees are now regarded has more to do with the political and cultural changes of recent years, some of which they had anticipated. Precisely now, long after most of them have died, the same kinds of enemies remain to challenge them as historical figures.

In other words, and no refugee could ever doubt this, there were no happy endings. When I reviewed the current status of figures once considered exemplary, it appeared that each one of them—Arendt, Brecht, Adorno, Mann—was contested, scandalous: to use Arendt's term, more pariah than icon.

Only a few years ago, that was not the case. With advocates like W. H. Auden, Mary McCarthy, and Robert Lowell, with forums like *The New Yorker,* Hannah Arendt reigned as a magisterial figure. Her benign, benevolent view of American politics as a fortress of law and reason against the hysterical tendencies of European fascism was a huge tribute; a circuitous route had brought her to centrist politics. Unlike Einstein or Mann, she flattered Americans with her notion of a meta-ideological politics, one that led her to value states' rights so greatly that she found it difficult to legally indict segregation, a position that won favorable notice in *Commentary.* But when she returned to the themes and tone—particularly the stinging, take-no-prisoners tone—of her great collection *The Jew as Pariah,* as she did in her riveting study of Eichmann, Americans had trouble reading her. *Eichmann in Jerusalem* was a book most intimately addressed to her generation. In the book's most haunting passage, she describes herself seated in the courtroom, surrounded by other German Jewish refugees, all of whom had long reached their own conclusions, and certainly didn't need her exegesis. This not always modest woman acknowledged them as her only peers.

The response to *Eichmann*—violent is not an exaggeration; one refugee said, "I thought they would kill her"—has never lightened. But she has been challenged elsewhere. Her generalizations about totalitarianism have been condemned as too exclusively focused on European treatment of Europeans, although, to be fair, she often alluded to the excesses of imperialism. Her emphasis on terror as an ineluctable tactic remains her most compelling argument. Except that her conclusion that ultimately it doesn't work has been unhappily disproved many times; because she was fearless, she assumed that everyone else was. In that sphere, Thomas Mann had anticipated her, when in *The Magic Mountain* Naphta, the Jewish-Jesuit-Communist-Fascist, spells out the need to instill fear in the masses. Mann paid special attention to the sexual frisson of terror, as would Kafka, though with her disdain for psychoanalysis this was not an interesting question for Arendt.

Precisely because she abhorred a politics overrun by emotion, a frenzy of needs she caustically described as "the cares of the household," Arendt has become a less useful guide to politics. In 2011, with Michele Bachmann summoning her forces with appeals that would strike Europeans as irrational, if not deranged, Arendt's idealization of a political arena where such matters are beneath consideration seems ungrounded in reality. Even if politics had not been swamped by publicity, the Web has swallowed the town meeting. Her vision can appear charming, quaint, and implausible.

And while her generalizations and conclusions have been questioned, Arendt has been subjected to the kind of attention she always dismissed as kitsch, and other émigrés called *schmus* and *quatsch*. After her death, Mary McCarthy wrote a short, sweet memoir about her friend. I can remember one fan objecting to McCarthy's revelation that she had caught Hannah sneaking a midnight meal of anchovy paste on toast—anchovies, a special Jaecke taste.* Far more intimate details have since been vouchsafed about her affair with her teacher Martin Heidegger and about her marriages. In 1945 Arendt wrote that Heidegger was both a neo-Nazi and "a philosopher of absolute egoism." A year later she reignited their friendship with a letter in which she called herself "the girl from abroad," as if she were a soubrette in a Franz Lehár operetta. In a review of their correspondence, James Miller compared the couple with Heloise and Abelard, a far cry from Rosa Luxemburg and Karl Liebknecht: Arendt would have been appalled.

She also played a historic role that she could not have predicted, but that evolved ineluctably from her identity as a German Jewish refugee. In time it became clear that the attacks on her were the first salvos of the neoconservative movement. With the exception of the émigré scholar Walter Laqueur, most of her biggest enemies were American Jews of Eastern European origin. Many of these were the first members of their family to leap from ghetto to academy, and it's fair to say that they observed the cultured German Jews with suspicion, if not contempt. The foolish battles between West and East once raged hot. At their most banal they could be reduced to the Westies' contempt for "those filthy Eastern Jews" (a contempt that sadly both Arendt and Gershom Scholem would demonstrate when they spoke of the unwashed and superstitious Israelis who had fled not, say, from Germany or Austria, but from Romania or Egypt—or, worse, America) and the Ostis' (Eastern Europeans) hate-filled remark that "the German Jews were worse than the Germans." Irving Howe once admitted to me his antipathy for the bourgeois milieu of German Jewry. In a famous meeting, Howe's ad feminem attacks provoked Alfred Kazin to tell him, Irving, cool it, or, more precisely, "This disgraceful piling-on has got to stop."

Not that Arendt had not played her own intramural games. She advised against the academic publication of Raul Hilberg's monumental *The Destruction of the European Jews,* the major source of most of her

---

*By legend, "Jaecke" was the 1930s name Palestinian settlers gave to the German-Jewish émigrés, to connote their extreme formality—they wore their jackets and ties in the noonday sun. (My émigré father wore them to Jones Beach!)

research, simply because she disagreed with his thesis that the Holocaust was deeply rooted in centuries of anti-Semitism. She thought it was a unique product of totalitarianism. Likewise, while she stressed the role of her contemporaries the European Judenräte, who had been forced to engage with the Nazis, Hilberg discovered far earlier instances of Jews collaborating with the authorities in order to save themselves. Arendt also may have employed Hilberg to smear Leo Baeck, chief rabbi of Berlin, whom she described as "in the eyes of both Jews and Gentiles . . . the 'Jewish Führer'": in fact, Hilberg ascribed the remark to one man alone, Eichmann's assistant. (She dropped the gratuitous insult in later editions of the book.) Meanwhile, Hilberg, a Viennese émigré twenty years her junior, would also be attacked for years as a "self-hating Jew" because he despised the right-wing takeover of Zionist politics.

Arendt was particularly drawn to a certain group of free-floating, nonacademic intellectuals whom she called "men in dark times." She characterized Hitler's victim as "the superfluous man," as if he were a figure imagined by Franz Kafka or Walter Benjamin. But, in all fairness, her early writings about these men had made her name in Jewish circles, as well as keeping their names alive when they were not yet the figures who would bestride their age.

Ironically, her pedantic insistence on Hilberg's conceptual failure may be linked to her most grievous error about Eichmann. He was not simply an affectless technocrat, exemplifying the banality of contemporary life—in other words, a product of something new under the sun, twentieth-century totalitarianism. The most recent documentation reveals that he was a driven anti-Semite, as mired in his bigotry as a Martin Luther or a Richard Wagner. While living in Argentina, he was interviewed by the Dutch-born escaped war criminal Willem Sassen, a hyper-Nazi who had shocked even the Germans, and was now hoping to inaugurate a Fourth Reich. Speaking to the converted, Eichmann declared but one regret, that he had not killed more Jews. Arendt hardly exonerates Eichmann—she dispatches him to his death simply because he would not let others live. But wedded to her procrustean categories, she made him less of a monster. A humbler attitude toward Raul Hilberg might have pre-empted her enemies salivating over any sign of rhetorical weakness on her part. The problem might simply have to do with popular journalism. She had been known as the first lady of Jewish letters, a prolific contributor to the German-Jewish weekly *Aufbau,* long before Mary McCarthy impressed on her a *New Yorker* state of mind.

The rage at Arendt comprehended years of irritation with German Jewry, and its gratuitous signs of cultural superiority, each one a rankling offense to fellows whose grandparents had not read Heine or Schiller, who might not have read at all. They had forgotten that Arendt grieved most for the little people, "the Hänschen Cohns," who had died in hugely greater numbers than the intellectuals and scholars, most of whom had managed to escape. Since most of Arendt's critics—Podhoretz et al.—were themselves cultural snobs of the first order, their attacks on the Jaecke queen betrayed a provincial form of bad faith.

What the *Commentary* critics particularly hated was Arendt's hard-won objectivity; sentimentally, they asked, couldn't she display a little bit of affection for her people? Why did she have to be so insufferably German? The alternative they always invoked was Gershom Scholem, and his legendary encounter with Arendt when he accused her of lacking a fundamental, heart's-truth love of the Jewish people. I don't love them, she replied famously, I'm simply one of them, and that's enduring and unconditional. Einstein concurred: he refused to grant Jews any moral superiority; they had escaped being tyrants simply because they had lacked the chance. Neither Arendt nor Einstein was disowning their Jewish identity—how in the world could they? But their objectivity led them both to criticize Zionist activities in Israel; the moment Arendt started referring to the Jews as "them," not "us," was pivotal.

What her American enemies didn't realize—not that it would have assuaged them—was that self-critique was the house specialty of German and Austrian Jews. During the 1920s they read with great enthusiasm Karl Kraus, the Viennese essayist who so deplored the excesses of the Jewish bourgeoisie that he reconverted from Catholicism back to Judaism after the Christians started acting like Jews (his example was the flamboyant passion plays directed by Max Reinhardt). Kraus caricatured his fellow Jews as cultural arrivistes, Molière's bourgeois gentlemen, barely a generation out of the shtetl. But German Jews had long made comedy of the passage to high culture. In one joke, a Jew visits a museum and, seeing a painting titled *Mandelbaum at the Riviera*, ponders whether it's a still life (*Mandelbaum* means "almond tree") or a portrait. In another, a Jew attends a concert and observes his neighbor swaying in a kind of trance. *Sind Sie musikalisch?* he asks. "No. I'm Izzy Kalisch. My brother Mosie Kalisch is in the balcony. Hi, Mosie!"

You could tell such jokes and be furious at Israel's policy toward the Palestinians or, forty years later, totally disagree with the neocons' position on Iraq. To those neocons, it was all of a piece; and so when Norman Podhoretz penned his j'accuse, it definitely included left-wing Jews among the culprits. Arendt had chosen to be tough on her own—even to questioning why more Jews hadn't fought back, a position that was certainly not unique to her, and that was often used as a justification for Israeli hawks.

She had long harbored suspicions about her fellow thinkers. In 1964, she told a German scholar that after Hitler's accession to power, intellectuals had been the first to jump ship. And so she decided that she could never work with such people. She would change her mind, and spend years dazzling and dismaying readers with her vast generalizations, at least some of them damaged by what she graciously acknowledged as her "usual exaggeration." Those who loved her short essays might groan over her larger, more speculative readings of history and philosophy. She would reply that they had expressed the same temperament, generalizations and all. She might also have detected a sexist animus, a rebellion against the house mother. But, instinctively antifeminist, she refused that argument.

Her insistence on truth telling made her generations of enemies. As recently as 2009 a young neolib, Jacob Heilbrunn, couldn't resist slapping her down for her scholarship, though his prime source was Walter Laqueur's forty-year-old attack. That same year an overwrought Ron Rosenbaum would attempt to turn the author of *The Jew as Pariah* into a closet anti-Semite. It appeared that whenever American Jews spoke up against Israeli policies, they were exhibiting the vile self-hatred of Hannah Arendt. (And she was very far from the boldest critic. German-speaking Israelis like Yeshayahu Leibowitz or Amos Elon composed truly fierce attacks on Zionist policy—Leibowitz, for example, decried a "Judeo-Nazi" mind-set. Even more devastating was the observation of Arthur Goldreich, a South African émigré who had mentored Nelson Mandela in the early years of the South African movement. He spent his last years in Tel Aviv, declaring Israel an apartheid state. I will return to this issue later.) She could have taken such knocks, and defended herself brilliantly. But though her position evolved with blinding clarity from her experiences and her reading of history, it allows her enemies to accuse her of the very *trahison des clercs* she spent a lifetime exposing.

On the level of melodrama, which her critics have employed to bury her, the piquant aspects of her romance with the Nazi-loving Heidegger are modest in comparison with the histories of two Hollywood beauties. Hedy Lamarr's first husband was Fritz Mandl, a right-wing Austrian Jew, who succeeded in buying up most of the prints of her notorious first film, *Ecstasy,* in which his thrillingly beautiful wife revealed her breasts to the camera and mimed the cinema's first orgasm. Like later Jewish masters of the universe, he didn't mind cultivating his enemies, namely Austrian fascists, inviting them to splendid dinners which, of course, his trophy wife attended. She would leave him, and ultimately arrive in Hollywood. Though known as "the most beautiful woman in movies," she never became a star of the first order, precisely because she was too much a Viennese Jew, which is to say that audiences found her cold and severe—and, in fact, only the émigré director Edgar G. Ulmer would reveal a warmer temperament in the little-known movie *The Strange Woman.* In 1940 she starred with Clark Gable in *Comrade X,* a piece of post-*Ninotchka* fluff about an American's affair with a Communist apparatchik ("You're prettier than Karl Marx," he tells her), who says, at one point, that she comes "from what used to be Austria."

But during this time—the period of the Hitler-Stalin pact, when most of left-wing Hollywood was fulsomely pacifist—Hedy Lamarr was doing something remarkable. She had become friendly with the composer George Antheil; and drawing on her own knowledge of science as well as the information she had gleaned from her husband's Nazi guests, she and Antheil invented a code they named "frequency hopping" that they hoped would unlock the mysteries of torpedo technology and could be used in fighting Hitler—a battle that she, unlike almost everyone in show business except for Noël Coward, saw as inevitable. This idea of defeating your enemy by diverting him was worthy of a spy film; that its creator happened to be the most beautiful woman in Hollywood would have been beyond anybody's imagination in those benighted days. Though the military declined to employ it, frequency hopping later became a basis of cell-phone technology. According to Lamarr's son, she has become an idol of teenage girl scientists, who wouldn't remember her as a movie star. Her more celebrated contribution to the war effort was the seven million dollars she raised at one event, selling her kisses for twenty-five thousand a pop. But she will most likely be remembered more for her smarts than her beauty.

From her daughter Maria Riva's biography, it's clear that Marlene Dietrich managed her career with the single-minded obsession of a (pre-Depression) CEO. Had she stayed in Germany, she could have become its virtual queen. Her refusal was a greater sacrifice than is usually recognized—especially because her best work as a singer was always reserved for the Berlin songs of her youth. In 2005 her daughter and grandson revealed that even the aged Dietrich retained her political savvy. They report monthly phone bills of three thousand dollars, and long, passionate calls to Ronald Reagan (who would have countenanced her advice because she was Dietrich) and Mikhail Gorbachev (the same). An old movie star who refused to allow herself to be photographed in her dotage, she now commanded her authority in a political realm. Similarly, Lilli Palmer, once promoted as a new Ingrid Bergman, was too intellectual and feisty, too much a product of haut-Berlin Jewry, to become a glamour girl. Instead she became the host of television's first highbrow program, *Omnibus,* and eventually a critically acclaimed novelist. Lamarr, Dietrich, and Palmer have nothing in common with Arendt except for being much smarter than anybody expected them to be.

During Bertolt Brecht's brief American sojourn, he was often asked to spell his name: "And oh, once that name was considered great." Only after his return to Europe did he assume such authority that the adjective "Brechtian" is almost as common as "Kafkaesque." While he was here, he left us some sharp, waspish comments about Hollywood, along with hilarious descriptions of the Frankfurt School metaphysicians, and some truly vicious dismissals of Thomas Mann. Perhaps because Mann had introduced Brecht to American readers of *The Dial* as a homosexual playwright, Brecht composed obscene ditties, ostensibly by Mann, about the joys of backroom sex. Brecht's American career ends with his amazing appearance before a congressional committee, when he manages to elude the hell-hounds by claiming that the words printed under his name are not actually his—perhaps the first time that mistranslation worked in a writer's favor.

He escaped in 1948, but historical criticism has caught up with him. His defenses of Stalinism (among them such winners as his remark in 1940 that "we"—the Soviet Union being Hitler's ally at the time—will soon own Paris; that "we" have no way of knowing anything outside of the Party—which, of course, he never joined—or that the Soviet invaders of postwar Europe have been exemplary in their restraint and decorum) have prompted writers like John Lukacs to speak of the "Brecht vomitorium." His cryptic remark, apropos the German Communists' battles with disgruntled laborers that perhaps "the government [should] dissolve the people and elect another," reveals someone lacking in what Germans call *Zivilcourage*. But since he would die soon after, there's no telling where his anger might have led him. (In addition, Eric Bentley says that during his last year, Brecht sought a return to the Lutheran Church, covering his bets, as it were, which a streetwise Berliner always knows to do.) There was also a clumsily mounted attack on his authority as a playwright in which John Fuegi listed all of his offenses from stinking hygiene to stinking ethics, baldly accusing him of plagiarism— namely, a heavy, unacknowledged debt to the many friends and lovers whose research had informed his plays.

Yet Brecht defies such criticism. This is the era of sampling, when the "geniuses" of rap and electronica swipe recorded snippets in aural collages released under the master thief's name. It's still their vision, and similarly, Brecht remains the author, the singularity of his vision undiminished. To paraphrase Huysmans, details could be left to the servants. Indeed the wily, abominable Brecht's career prompts the speculation that dialectics means never having to say you're sorry. His most surprising legacy may be his influence on Bob Dylan, who says that "The Ballad of Pirate Jenny" inspired the form and rhetorical expanse of his own digressive ballads. (Brecht, the poet who advises lovers, "In me you have a man you cannot trust," can be detected in the fellow who sings them away with "It Ain't Me Babe.")

Late in his life, Brecht traveled to Paris. He delighted, as always, in the idea of good food. Ogling a sliver of cheese, he told a friend that he'd like to transport it to the lobby of his theater in Berlin—then he'd show those Germans what culture really is. Surveying his generation's lifetime of disappointments, he once again defined matters. In a very late poem, "Things Change," he recalled:

> *I've been old, and sometimes young,*
> *Old in the morning, and young at night,*
> *I've been a child recalling sad times,*
> *And a graybeard without memory.*

Switching to the singsong rhythms of a popular tune, he adds:

> *Was sad, when I was young,*
> *Am sad, now that I'm old.*

So, when can I be happy?
It had better be soon.

Ah, but in that "So," with its Berliner shrug, there is the great achieve-ment of émigré tone—the gallows humor that turns all surprises, even death, into components of a comedy that is simply too political for pathos.

Brecht's death at fifty-nine allowed him to miss the further degenera-tion of the East German system. (Stephen Parker, a British scholar, has recently surmised that the playwright's early death was actually hastened by the Stasi, who may have withheld a 1951 X-ray that demonstrated the damage to his heart of a childhood bout of rheumatic fever. But would knowing this have led Bert Brecht to drop his cigar?) Less fortunate was his old friend the composer Hanns Eisler, whose songs of freedom had once been left-wing anthems. Shortly after Brecht's death a drunken Eisler was reported wandering through West Berlin, complaining of life in the East. In fact, unlike Brecht, Eisler was never an uninflected Stalinist. In 1940, even while Brecht was rejoicing that "we" would soon control Paris, Eisler complained that Stalin was as bad as Hitler. After emigrating to America, Eisler was quite content, working in Hollywood, composing occasionally for the movies, and collaborating on a book about film scoring with Theodor Adorno.

His luck went bad in a most public and melodramatic fashion. In 1948 the postwar attack on Communists began with a congressional investi-gation of reds in Hollywood, and it started with Ruth Fischer, Hanns's sister, testifying against him and particularly his brother, Gerhart, another émigré and a leading figure in the Communist Party. After Ger-hart's happy departure (the New York *Daily News*'s headline was "Red Sails in the Sunset"), an unhappy Hanns joined him. But he despaired that his beloved America had turned on him, and saw it correctly as a sign of further horrors to come.

The families of illustrious émigrés were often fractured. Ludwig Wittgenstein's brother, Paul, didn't forgive his sisters for their desperate dealings with Hitler (who bought their disingenuous argument that they were not really Jews but "mischlings," because of a purported adultery committed by their grandmother), and chose to end communication with Ludwig, who had not even been involved. After Thomas Mann's death, his surviving five children fought over his legacy: the right-wing

Golo and the left-wing Erika wouldn't speak to each other, and having survived his siblings, father, and uncle Heinrich, Golo would extract his revenge by attacking their politics when they couldn't reply.

But that was quite tame compared to the Eislers' public spats. Ruth Fischer seemed the most disloyal of sisters, particularly in the McCarthy era. But with the years, her story grows more complex. She had once been "Red Ruth," the first member of Vienna's Communist Party, and the most obvious heir to Rosa Luxemburg. She came to despise Stalinism, particularly after a period of living in the Soviet Union. But her perspective remained leftist, and most probably—as the Stalinists would contend—Trotskyist. She had seen many of her comrades killed by the Stalinists, including, very likely, her second husband. During World War II, she distinguished herself as a social worker who, according to the émigré historian Henry (né Heinz) Pachter, helped many other refugees. She would also show up at public meetings handing out printed warnings against her brothers. She gave public notice that if anything happened to her, the Communists would be to blame. Like her brothers, she too would return to Europe, where she continued to see herself as a left-winger. She wrote a new book praising Khrushchev's reversal of Stalin's most egregious programs. She even managed to see her nephew, Hanns's son. You could argue her case—after all, many family members have disowned their relatives' crimes. Unfortunately, she is most remembered as someone who finked on her brothers, and thereby ushered in McCarthyism.

The ironies of Eisler's case didn't stop there. At first, after his return to the East, he was a star and a hero. He chose to compose an opera based on Goethe's *Faust,* which, in keeping with his progressive agenda, became a musical dramatization of class conflicts. But the apparatchiks turned out to be, if not philistines, very culturally conservative. They were horrified that the great German epic should be reduced to agitprop, an argument that would have to strike Eisler as baffling. Or, worse, that even the reds were German before they were anything else. During this time Thomas Mann was receiving similar attacks—from the right—for his (to their eyes) misuse of Goethe in his great novel *Doctor Faustus.* Whether East or West, the rulers of Germany would not let the national legacy be tampered with. Now, whether Brecht would have risked as much as Eisler is open to question. He didn't, and the Communists kept his name alive. The Berliner Ensemble ultimately became one of East Germany's few attractions.

Brecht remains, with Beckett (whom Theodor Adorno was among the first to recognize), the great figure of twentieth-century theater. Whether Adorno will survive as triumphantly as Brecht is less clear. For years, his thoroughgoing contempt for every aspect of commercial culture made him appear the most formidable of critics. But his stance appears increasingly irrelevant. Just as Arendt's dismissal of quotidian concerns does not illuminate American politics in the Tea Party era, so Adorno's contempt for soap operas—one of his earliest American jobs was a thematic analysis of radio serials—doesn't explain why the melodramatic overkill of the television miniseries *Holocaust* brought the awful story to public attention as no previous vehicle had succeeded in doing.

Even Adorno's defenders deplore his attacks on American jazz—e.g., his caricature of Louis Armstrong as a castrato. I used to think Adorno hadn't heard the real thing in Germany, though Brian Morton has now shown that the level of journeyman jazz professionals was quite high, and was even unsuccessfully deployed by Nazi propagandists. Adorno shared his distaste for jazz with his colleague Hanns Eisler, with whom he wrote *Composing for the Films*. In 1940, Eisler attended New York's Café Society with an American friend to hear the great boogie-woogie pianist Meade Lux Lewis. He was unimpressed, complaining loudly during the set that there was no harmonic development, it was all a matter of three chords—the 1-4-5 that later informed rhythm and blues and early rock and roll. If your reference is Wagner, even if he's the composer you love to hate, 1-4-5 will provide a very spare diet. (American music, particularly African-American, is more indebted to Italian opera, with its elaborate ornamentation. Our music is expansive precisely where the German music Adorno loves is discreet.) As it was, Eisler's music would resonate in early Dylan (e.g., "The Times They Are a-Changin'"), and has been performed by Sting—not perhaps what he would have predicted during his unhappy nights at Café Society.

Adorno could survive the incapacity to enjoy blue notes. Far more questionable was his approach to academic music, famously represented by his well-vocalized preference for Schoenberg over Stravinsky—that is, until Schoenberg himself became "ossified." (Schoenberg—another California émigré, his son a judge in the O. J. Simpson trial—once remarked that he never considered Adorno his ally.) But as Charles Rosen has shown, Adorno's aesthetic criteria spilled over into the baldest chauvinism, as when he accused Stravinsky of a characteristically

Slavic "infantilism." For Stravinsky's heavy emphasis on rhythm, color, and orchestral texture—the metrical surprises that are not unlike jazz, though immensely more complex (in the 1940s he even composed a concerto for Woody Herman), has proved more durable than the musical expositions Adorno preferred.

But recently we have received a great surprise in the form of two letters written in the spring of 1942. In the first, Adorno, now residing in Los Angeles, informs Kurt Weill of Brecht's "paradox" of a suggestion that in order to revive *The Threepenny Opera* it should be transformed into a Negro musical, even if "African-American reactions could never be completely grasped by us." From Teddy Wiesengrund, this is an astonishingly populist note. Weill responded a week later, beginning his note with "please allow me to write in English. It is easier for me and I like it better." He doesn't buy the idea. Broadway has become "next to Russia, the most interesting theater center in the world." He is startled by such brazen tactics, especially from one "who was always a defender of musical integrity." Then, in an even more surprising twist, Weill remarks that "jazz-variation" has been "mastered to much greater perfection by white musicians and arrangers than by Negroes"—namely, among others, by Weill himself. Who could these arrangers be? Jerry Gray? Artie Shaw? Rather than Duke Ellington or Billy Strayhorn? This letter challenges many of our received opinions.

(Another posthumous surprise was the evidence that Fritz Lang had suppressed Brecht's allusions to the war on Jewry in the film *Hangmen Also Die,* Brecht's only Hollywood screen credit. It would have been the first cinematic acknowledgment of the Holocaust. That it should have been devised by the fellow-traveling Brecht is a small shock; but downright mind-boggling is that the censorship would have been dictated by Lang, who had been born a Jew, raised a Catholic, and whose former wife Thea von Harbou had remained in Germany, an ardent Nazi. No doubt even more unforeseen denouements lie in somebody's archive, though few remain to care about them.)

Adorno once compared himself to the smallest child in a classroom filled with bullies. He ended his life in a similar position. Consider the grotesque circumstances of his last days. He had returned to Germany, where he became the pre-eminent intellectual figure; during the 1960s, the critique identified with the Frankfurt School—Adorno, and especially his colleagues Max Horkheimer and Herbert Marcuse—was taken up by the New Left. But Adorno was dismayed by the German students' atttempt to turn a very subtle and refined epistemology into a political agenda. He refused to make the next step, and with a humorless stubbornness that seems *echt Deutsch*, the students became outraged. In particular German students identified with Iranian students attacking their shah. Adorno wouldn't join the chorus—perhaps because he saw that the ayatollah would be far worse than the shah. A group of young women confronted him and revealed their breasts. This was a Walpurgisnacht worthy of *The Magic Mountain*. The Valkyries thought they were compelling Adorno to see the full implications of his argument, that sexual freedom and political freedom were indivisible, and that he had better get with the program. Adorno, who reportedly was as diffident in private as he was caustic in print, was mortified. After writing Beckett that it was an unpleasant experience being branded a "reactionary"— especially, he might have added, by the children of Nazis—he fled the campus and joined his wife on a trip to Switzerland. Here, despite the advice of his doctor, he chose to go mountain climbing, and was dead within two days, aged sixty-five.

"AMERICA, YOU HAVE IT BETTER"

Very few of the émigré writers made their mark in America, which may be why Thomas Mann had to write so many prefaces to introduce them. Ten years ago you could have picked up a signed first edition of Hermann Broch's *The Death of Virgil* for fifteen dollars. That book appeared shortly after Mann's novel *Joseph the Provider* had sold a million copies through the Book-of-the-Month Club.

While other writers languished in obscurity, the 1940s were Mann's golden period in America. Though he had first attacked the Nazis, particularly excoriating their anti-Semitism, in 1923—and indeed would introduce Hitler to the same *Dial* readers he informed about the young playwright Brecht—Mann had been all-too-still between 1933 and 1936, encouraged perhaps by his radical brother, Heinrich, and Jewish publisher Gottfried Bermann Fischer, but silent nonetheless. In the years after, he became Hitler's most outspoken critic. In 1938, after his flight to America, his extended essay *The Coming Victory of Democracy* outsold his latest Joseph installment. He was a welcome guest at the White House, so enamoured of President Roosevelt that he incorporated him into the middle-aged hero of *Joseph the Provider.* Wartime was terrifying but also a period of absolute moral clarity. He was so well assimilated that in an astonishing photo from 1945, he can be observed chatting with Eddie Cantor and Will Rogers Jr.

But by 1950 everything had changed. His defense of Hanns Eisler against the congressional investigators led to a prophetic condemnation of the American right, who immediately pounced on him as a fellow traveler. Now he knew terror of a less edifying sort: he intended to flee his quondam paradise, reduced as it was to a "soulless soil." The death of his brother, Heinrich, and the suicide of his son Klaus occurred during this period. And perhaps most alarming of all was the collapse of his public. He complained that his royalties had fallen to the low two figures. When the Harvard professor Harry Levin changed the title of his famous course "Proust, Joyce, and Mann" to "Proust, Joyce, and Kafka," Mann knew exactly what that signified. Among the many firsts in his career, he may have been the earliest to see that an academic demotion could doom a writer's reputation.

Two of Mann's greatest novels, *Doctor Faustus* and the alternately riotous and melancholy *Confessions of Felix Krull,* were composed in America. Yet the one work that survives in America is *Death in Venice.* From an unparalleled role as "the world's greatest novelist" and "one of FDR's wise men," he has been reduced to the author of one, admittedly perfect, novella. A few years ago it was honored as the greatest gay novel of all time. I happened to be one of the judges of that contest. But my own recommendations for later and happier works (including those composed in America) were ignored: Mann would be recognized only as the creator of Gustav von Aschenbach, and not of Felix Krull or Joseph or even his consummately reimagined Goethe.

Aschenbach has haunted American writers, both gay (Susan Sontag, Harold Brodkey, James Lord) and not (Philip Roth). Roth, for example, may have written dismissals of gay playwrights that were baldly homophobic (e.g., attacking Edward Albee's "ghastly pansy rhetoric and repartee"). Yet, according to the émigré scholar Edgar Rosenberg, Thomas Mann is the writer he most often cites. A Mannian sensibility saturates his late novel *The Human Stain,* both in its explicit references to Aschenbach and Tadziu and in sentences that read like Mann's diary jottings about young men. "That's what it's like to be an old man. To be like that ugly girl"—the wallflower languishing in her corner—"because she is never chosen." Or, most Mannian of all, "Who can grasp at thirty-two that at seventy-one it's exactly the same?" The Thomas Mann who conceived Aschenbach when he wasn't even thirty-five could have done that.* In fact, his greatest contribution to American letters has been the imagining of an old man in love.

This was an ironic, and perhaps not dissatisfying, development. For if there was one thing Mann loved about America, it was its homosexuality. It can fairly be said to have rejuvenated him. He never had the image of a young man. Recall that famously snide review of *Death in Venice* in which D. H. Lawrence wrote, "But Thomas Mann is old—and we are young." (He had confused Mann's age, thirty-eight—thirteen years his senior—with that of Gustav von Aschenbach, the story's fated hero. Perhaps not coincidentally, he had recently finished his own homoerotic tale, *The Prussian Officer*.) Within a few years, Lawrence had composed his *Studies in Classic American Literature*, in which he surveyed a canon presided over by Walt Whitman, the prophet of a universal "sympathy," a mode of "feeling with people as they feel with themselves," in which Lawrence delighted. But it would be only a few years later that Thomas Mann would use the same Walt Whitman in a quixotic attempt to defeat Adolf Hitler. Mann understood German history as one long queer epic—from Frederick the Great to Goethe, Wagner, and Nietzsche—but one fatally damaged by its love of militarism: the same kind of sadomasochistic Prussian officers that Lawrence had imagined. So he offered young Germany the spectacle of Whitman's "Calamus" poems, a homoerotic idyll in which democracy triumphed with the promise of a new lover/brother waiting around each urban corner. Naturally, this rhetorical conceit was not persuasive; and years later, at the advice of his American patron Agnes Meyer, he removed the queerest passages from an English translation.

During Mann's years in exile, he kept returning to his enduring subject of thwarted desire, an impossible *Sehnsucht* that could inspire a lifetime career but never be enacted. Even his attack on Hitler in 1936

---

* Of course William Butler Yeats discerned the old man's plight long before Roth. His very late poem "Politics" begins with a magisterial quotation, "In our time the destiny of man presents its meaning in political terms," and then reveals the speaker as not quite up to the age's demands. He wants to pursue deep thoughts, but he spies a lovely girl, and what he really thinks is "O that I were young again / And held her in my arms." By chance, the opening quotation comes from Thomas Mann himself, who, in his seventies, would have totally endorsed Yeats's sentiment, except that the entrancing youth would have been a boy.

had a homosexual subtext. Despite his Jewish wife and half-Jewish children, Mann was careful not to claim any of the Jews' pathos for himself. Instead he summoned his idol August von Platen, Germany's best-known gay poet, citing him as a cusp figure, permanently homeless, despised by both right and left. While living in Pacific Palisades, Thomas and Katia welcomed many of their children's gay friends, men like Auden and Christopher Isherwood (who quite liked the old man, and compared him to "a well-behaved English governess," much as Rabindranath Tagore had impressed Mann in 1921 as "a refined old English lady").

During the 1940s, he was electrified by the works of gay American writers. But, unlike Whitman's shaded double entendres, these were modern, comparatively emancipated, and extremely graphic. He was overwhelmed by Gore Vidal's *The City and the Pillar,* particularly the idyllic love scenes of the hero and his boyhood pal ("The loveplay between Jim and Bob is glorious"). In his diary, he mentions that he didn't care at all for the gay bar scenes and wonders, disingenuously, how one could actually make love to a man. (Before leaving Germany, Mann and his daughter Erika had burned his youthful diaries. Since those that escaped the flames reveal his fundamental love of men—with barely a gesture toward women, and that usually as a spillover of his gay lust—one may wonder about that putative lack of actual experience. Especially because he turns the great love of his youth, Paul Ehrenberg, into Rudi Schwerdtfeger, the male vamp who sleeps with *Doctor Faustus*'s hero, Adrian Leverkühn.) Such scruples were absent from his reception of a story mailed to him by Donald Windham. He praised the ways this "surprising little story poeticizes with serene composure the naivete of the flesh and its warmth." It's worth noting that the love scenes between two men could have been written by Dennis Cooper.

In a typically quiet way, he allowed himself a modest breakthrough. It coincided with his recognition that perhaps his monumental novels were no longer suited to the times, or at least to his deepest self. He had been at his best as a short-story writer; on that both his wife, Katia, and his enemy Bertolt Brecht would agree. And in 1954 he wrote that his new model was a miniaturist, Anton Chekhov, who had convinced him that "genius can be bounded in a nutshell and yet embrace the whole fullness of life by virtue of a brevity and terseness deserving of the highest admiration." He told Alfred A. Knopf that he resented comparisons of his grandly composed sentences with "the overcrowded, overburdened,

Thomas Mann (top left): from the 1920s until his death in 1955, Mann was enthralled by American writers like Walt Whitman, Herman Melville, and Gore Vidal.

dragging and thoroughly opaque periods" of Willian Faulkner; his, by comparison, were "graceful toe-dancing."

This relaxation of style and subject coincided with the major development of his later years. In 1950, shortly after his son Klaus's suicide, he traveled with his wife and daughter Erika to St. Moritz. There, at one of the palatial resort hotels, he fell in love with a young Bavarian waiter, Franzl Westermann. Of course the poor fellow had no idea of Mann's adoration. Mann would not have had it otherwise—he kept his passion and his erotic fantasies for his journal—describing one morning's masturbation as a final "kiss" to all the boys and men he had secretly loved. His wife and daughter perceived everything and, with great kindness, made it possible for him to return to St. Moritz and some more glimpses of his beloved.

All this would become clear with the publication of Mann's diaries—as would the immense ramifications for his own writing. Previously, with the rare exception of Leverkühn's unpleasant night with Schwerdtfeger, or astonishingly bold revelations of a father's—Jacob's—love for his seventeen-year-old son, Joseph, he had allowed only his women to adore men, converting his journal notes into their heterosexual fantasies—e.g., Mut's delirious love of the male nymph Joseph. (In this he resembled another great novelist, Stefan Zweig, whose novella *Letter from an Unknown Woman* inspired the most glorious of émigré films—Max Ophuls's cinematic dramatization, in which the heroine pursues her lover with glances as heartbreaking as any imagined by the two suppressed homosexuals Mann and Zweig.) But finally, inspired by Franzl, Mann revealed himself.

In *Confessions of Felix Krull: Confidence Man,* Mann comes out in two guises. The hero sleeps with a woman novelist, Diane Philibert, aka Madame Houpflé, who confesses that the adult world of fame and position is a chimera: "I live in my so-called perversion . . . in the love of my life that lies at the bottom of everything I am . . . I live in my love for all of you, you, you image of desire, whose beauty I kiss in complete abnegation of spirit." As for grown-up life? "It's a matter of indifference to me—this whole world of men and women and marriage." Matters don't end there. Felix is later wooed by a fifty-year-old Scot, Lord Strathbogie, a figure who resembles Thomas Mann in form and spirit, with "eyes" that "seemed to meet one as though with a great effort of self-discipline."

He continued to reveal himself in small works. In the novella *The Black Swan,* he imagines a middle-aged woman who falls deliriously in love with a young American tennis player, Ken Keaton (Mann's version of Vidal's Jim and Bob). Just as Mann felt himself bodily renewed by Franzl, at least to the extent that he could still masturbate, Rosalie Tommler finds herself bleeding and is convinced that Ken has made her young again. In fact, it's the sign of cancer. A sick joke, to some readers: an objection that Mann even incorporates in the story. Yet he lets her die happy, convinced that nature ne'er betrayed a heart that loved. Desire, in the form of a young American, has given her a life-in-death.

The very last thing Mann composed was a tribute to Herman Melville's *Billy Budd,* another short work that trumps the idea of masterpiece. He called it "the most beautiful story in the world." In a final act of erotic sympathy, Mann stated his preference for the American sailor over Shakespeare's Desdemona. Quoting from Melville's text, he evoked the crew who all loved their Billy. His Whitmanesque vision did not fail him. "Ah, could I have composed that!" he wrote modestly, an astonishing echo of Goethe's famous words "America—you have it better." What's more, he wrote these words after the nation had effectively turned its back on him. J. Edgar Hoover's secret service considered him a subversive; his books had stopped selling; the academic caravan had moved on to Franz Kafka; newspaper hacks were patronizing him: in a 1958 review of a film version, Bosley Crowther of *The New York Times* called the wonderful *Felix Krull* "pathetically weak." There was no longer any "commercial advantage" (a term he ascribed to Goethe) in praising the country. Still, he died deeply in love with at least some portion of America. It was not the land of his dreams, but no other had come closer to realizing them.

(It should be added that while Franzl Westermann enjoyed the notoriety of Mann's diaries—often announcing, "I am Felix Krull"—he didn't enjoy the novel partially inspired by him. But his wife did—a Mannian turn of events. In addition, she was a Berliner, and Mann had always insisted that they alone knew how to read. And in naming those inspired by Mann, another woman proved a particularly good student. Marguerite Yourcenar, the French-Belgian novelist, wrote *Hadrian's Memoirs,* a book he greatly admired for its tactful treatment of the emperor's love for a young Roman. In her late seventies, Yourcenar, previously a lesbian, became infatuated with Jerry Wilson, an American tennis player living in Paris. She became so entangled in his fantasies that she occasionally disguised herself as an old man, pursuing him through the cruising grounds of Notre Dame. She was re-enacting Aschenbach and Strathbogie, proving herself a bolder Thomas Mann than he ever dared to be.)

———

A bitterer tale of exile could be told about his oldest son, Klaus, whose story is actually more representative and even exemplary. He may not have been much of a novelist, but as a cultural arbiter he had few peers. Consider that his short-lived publication the New York–based journal *Decision* was among the first to publish the most interesting young American writers of his day—Carson McCullers, Eudora Welty, Paul Bowles (Klaus and his sister Erika introduced Bowles to his wife, Jane), and Paul Goodman. He stands tallest as one of the century's heroes of journalism. Not only did he edit *Die Sammlung,* the first anti-Nazi journal, but he edited the fiercely antifascist *Decision* during the period between 1939 and 1941 when much of the American left had followed the Stalinists into a rapprochement with Hitler. Despite bouts of alcoholism and drug addiction, Klaus never quit the battlefield.

What enemies he collected in Germany and America! Hitler burned his books and J. Edgar Hoover investigated his sex life. Poor Klaus could be forgiven if he took politics personally. Gustaf Gründgens, Germany's leading actor, was Erika's first husband and one of Klaus's first lovers. After Hitler became Gründgens's protector, the Mann family speculated that there was a sexual connection between the two. We all know about *Mephisto,* Klaus's roman à clef about Gründgens. I did not know that in 1941, Gründgens appeared in a movie about Johann Sebastian Bach's untalented son Friedemann, a wan film whose raison d'être seems to be making sport of the failed scions of great men. Take that, you miserable Kläuschen! This must have been a gift to Gründgens: by then Thomas was Hitler's number-one enemy, and Klaus, just another émigré has-been.

Despite copious evidence of his "deviance," Klaus managed to enlist in the U.S. Army, the happiest event of his life. After the war's end, as a correspondent for *Stars and Stripes,* he was the first to interview Winifred Wagner at Bayreuth, and observe, "There is only one self-confessed Nazi left in Germany and she is an Englishwoman." She remembered him too, but as a refugee who insisted on speaking English with an atrocious German accent. Not long after, Klaus attended the triumphant postwar return to the stage of his former brother-in-law. He was the only one not to join the standing ovation.

By then Klaus was running out of allies. Even his gay friends made fun of him. Glenway Wescott called him a "tragic twerp" (a remark I regret quoting in my biography of Thomas Mann), and his brother-in-law W. H. Auden was merciless behind his back. (Auden also used to bring his tricks to the Mann home and enjoy them in Thomas's bed. Had he read Mann's self-revelatory diaries, he might not have been so disrespectful. Given his own strictures against the transatlantic "homintern," he might have complimented Mann for living a closeted life.) But Klaus's importance supersedes his lack of literary talent, especially because he, like so many other émigrés—and not only émigrés—could not do his best work in hard times.

Instead Klaus's example counts because he was such a prophetic critic. I especially value his observation that the Pentecostal faith healer Aimee Semple McPherson was a terrifying figure precisely because she had the best mike technique of anyone outside of Adolf Hitler. Klaus saw the connection between right-wing evangelism and fascism long before Pat Robertson and Sarah Palin started haunting the sleep of liberal Americans. He's also a plausible symbol of the émigrés' gay sensibility. Consider to what an extent the refugees were responsible for granting lesbians and gay men the dignity of simple recognition. Of course, even as *Death in Venice* was being taught as pure myth and symbol, generations of gay men knew how to read it.

But there was also a daring political aspect to the émigrés' gay witness. Erika and Klaus Mann became the stars of several cliques, émigré (Janet Flanner wrote in 1940 that refugees had to be vetted by the siblings) and American. During the early 1940s, their house in Brooklyn—also occupied by their quietly gay brother Golo and a group of largely gay Americans, including Paul and Jane Bowles—became a symbol of bohemian culture. However, precisely because the Manns were so identified with their opposition to Hitler, they made the two positions—anti-Nazi and openly gay—coterminous. In 1934 Klaus had decried the vulgar Stalinist argument connecting fascism and homosexuality. He turned the argument on its head, making antifascism the homosexual position. (Reasonably, considering that Hitler might well have killed him as a queer as well as the son of a Jewish mother. Coincidentally, Klaus's secretary

Richard Plant would later become the historian of the pink triangle, the insignia worn by Hitler's gay prisoners.) Other antifascist groups might not have been so forthright. But Klaus and Erika were; and given their fame at the moment, that was sufficient.

As could be expected, gay émigrés were particularly influential in show business. Rudi Gernreich, a teenage refugee from Vienna, would become the designer of the topless bathing suit and—far more important—the guru of unisexual fashion. Androgyny is as much an émigré contribution as the Frankfurt School's critique or Billy Wilder's comedy. The lesbian or bisexual woman is impossible to imagine without the émigrés. Indeed, the unspoken assumption for years was that continental women knew all sides of love. Here the models were Greta Garbo, especially as she was reimagined by her scribe, scenarist, and possible lover, the émigré Salka Viertel (whose husband, Berthold Viertel, would be immortalized in *Prater Violet,* a novel by the Mann family friend Christopher Isherwood) and—pre-eminently—Marlene Dietrich.

Whether Dietrich had many female lovers or not, she was brilliantly calculating in her actions. Starting in Berlin, where she had a popular hit singing "Me and My Best Girlfriend," she played someone too sexual to be confined (dramatizing the credo associated with Errol Flynn—"What, give up an entire sex?"). Long before Madonna or Patti LaBelle she figured out that gay men would be her most loyal audience. According to her daughter, she would whimsically imagine her own funeral. She forecast troops of soldiers and fans, Germans and Americans. And finally, the largest number of them all—the gay men of all nations.

Dietrich's voice alone made her an androgynous figure, the voice that Ernest Hemingway said could break your heart. With the years her chirpy alto had dropped to a baritonal register. She became a brilliant stylist, the mistress of sprechstimme. Her tone could be alternately insinuating, bawdy, and languid; nobody else could make inertia so alluring, as in her classic performance of "The Laziest Gal in Town." Yet she could revive the old songs of Berlin and move the most cynical émigré. Closing a set with "Das Lied ist aus," a sentimental ballad made famous by Richard Tauber (the opera-and-operetta tenor whose head tones could make refugees weep), she did what the greatest singers do, make kitsch transcendent. Frank O'Hara writes that during the 1950s, the two voices gay men loved most were those of Billie Holiday and Marlene Dietrich. William Burroughs, of all people, recorded a song in her style. She was, universally, the favorite chantoosie of the boys in the backroom.

There's a link between Dietrich and the Mann siblings, through their uncle Heinrich, from whose novel *Professor Unrat* Dietrich's signature film, *The Blue Angel,* was adapted. Heinrich's life in America was unhappy, marked by years of failure in Hollywood, financial dependence on his brother, and his awful marriage to Nelly Kröger, a much younger woman, who committed suicide a few years before his death at seventy-eight. He died on the eve of his return to East Germany, where he might finally have regained his fame as the bolder Mann brother, or at least the more prematurely antifascist. Like Walter Benjamin's suicide—which might have been averted if he'd waited a couple of days—Heinrich's death was a particularly nasty trick of fate.

PROPHETS WITHOUT HONOR

You might think that if the writers suffer, language itself is largely to blame. But scientists, speaking the neutral lingua franca of their disciplines, had their own horror stories. Einstein's outspoken politics earned him numerous enemies. They helped produce the notion that the century's greatest genius had lost his senses in his dream of a super-theory. Thus it's a more than slightly political vindication that the latest wonders of string theory pay homage to the questions Einstein posed, and rely on a union of algebra and physics that was his preferred method. As early as 1929, young scientists like Wolfgang Pauli had joked to his face that he was outdated; at Princeton Americans like Freeman Dyson said, "Young people saw these old men making fools of themselves." Another person might say, "Who's a fool now?" Except that he seemed congenitally impervious to his critics. In 1915, he's almost there: "Sometimes when you're indifferent to the feelings of your dear fellow humans—but you are never as indifferent to them as they deserve." He was so poorly treated at the Institute of Advanced Studies that in 1949 he wrote his old friend Max Born, "I am generally regarded as a sort of petrified object. I find this role not too distasteful," since he took neither himself nor anyone else "seriously." A few years later, he wrote that "Go to hell" had become not merely a figure of speech but his modus vivendi.

Émigrés were among the most active anti-nuclear scientists. Many lived well into their nineties, like Victor Weisskopf, a Manhattan Project physicist who died in 2002, aged ninety-three. Eleven years earlier, after justifying Hiroshima, he said of Nagasaki, "the second bomb I don't hesitate to call a crime." Using the idiom of Freud, he described the cold war as "a collective mental disease of mankind." Émigré scientists in other eras could be equally severe on the very disciplines in which they had previously triumphed. In 1965 Joseph Weizenbaum, a Berliner who fled as a teenager and had studied at Wayne State University in Detroit (not all émigrés zoomed through the Ivy League), invented a conversational computer program and, with an émigré's humor, named it Eliza, after the heroine of *My Fair Lady.*

To extend the literary analogy, he was also something of a Frankenstein, unleashing an artificial intelligence that he came to loathe. In 1976 he published *Computer Power and Human Reason: From Judgment to Calculation,* in which he foresaw the computer as a potential weapon of right-wing governments. He had helped dream up a monster and was now historically obliged to fight it. This argument proved so appealing to German students that in 1996, at the age of seventy-three, he returned to live in Berlin. On a similar note, the émigré Frank Milan Berger, the inventor of Miltown, was also a believer in universal health care. He came to hate the sales tactics of the large pharmaceutical firms and how they misrepresented his product. He was one of the first to deplore the ways they exploited their customers' vulnerabilities. Like Weizenbaum or Weisskopf, he saw the full implications of his invention, ethical and political, and felt obliged to address them. This imperative may not be unique to émigré scientists, but it recurs often enough to demand attention. Some historian of science will ultimately determine whether they were tougher on themselves than were their American-born colleagues.

One of the most remarkable figures of the scientific emigration, Erwin Chargaff, died in 2002 at ninety-six. We know of the refugees' contribution to nuclear physics. Less known is Chargaff's contribution to DNA research—he discovered consistencies in the balances of the base ratios among the four chemical units of DNA that are now known as Chargaff's Rules. Though he had many students, he acknowledged only one teacher, Karl Kraus. Events would cause him to draw on the satirist's withering irony. James Watson and Francis Crick, who had underwhelmed him on their first encounter, would run with his theories and receive the glory for discoveries he had anticipated. Rather than see this as a natural development of scientific inquiry, Chargaff made fun of their success. When DNA specialists became alarmed by the potential for its misuse, he wrote, "That was probably the first time in history that the incendiaries formed their own fire brigades." Chargaff turned on the Anglo-American scientific establishment. By 1974, relations were so unfriendly that he was locked out of his office at Columbia. When colleagues later apologized for this scandalous treatment, Chargaff was unappeased. He severed ties with Columbia and requested that upon his death, "I . . . not be remembered by the university."

In 1975 the great scientist wrote, "I have not fitted well into the country and society in which I had to live, into the language in which I had to converse: yes, even into the century in which I was born." That is the true voice of the exile in paradise. Hear it echoed in Hannah Arendt: "So you ask me where I am. I am nowhere. I am really not in the mainstream of present or any other political thought. But not because I want to be so original—it so happens that I somehow don't fit." Or in Eric Hobsbawm, perhaps the most successful living historian, whose recent memoir reveals that his glory days as a young Berlin Communist have never been recaptured: I am "someone who does not wholly belong to where he finds himself, whether as an Englishman among the Central Europeans, a continental immigrant in Britain, a Jew everywhere—even, indeed particularly, in Israel—an anti-specialist in a world of specialists, a polyglot cosmopolitan, an intellectual whose political and academic work was devoted to the nonintellectual, even, for much of my life, an anomaly among communists, themselves a minority . . ." Or in 2007, shortly before his death, by Raul Hilberg: "I don't feel part of anything. I don't feel part of the university I've been a part of for decades. I don't feel part of Burlington [Vermont], where I've spent all my years since 1956. I think some of us are just destined to be alone." The fate of some exiles is to be not quite at home anywhere.

Note how frequently émigré scientists embed their critique of American politics in their own experiences. The scientist Gunther Stent called his memoir *Nazis, Women and Molecular Biology: Memoirs of a Lucky Self-Hater,* a whimsical reference to his youthful dreams of joining the group that would never have him as a member. (The overloaded title exhibits the density of German-inflected refugee humor.) Jay Katz fled Germany as a teenager and ultimately became a physician and medical professor at Yale Law School. He brought an émigré sensibility to the nexus of politics, medicine, and ethics. In 1972 he was appointed to a panel investigating the Tuskegee syphilis study. He found the report insufficiently stark: he issued a statement that the poor black men had been "exploited, manipulated and deceived." Twenty-four years later he would condemn the Food and Drug Administration for reversing a principle, dating back from the Nuremberg Code of 1946, that forbade medical research being conducted without the patients' consent.

———

Among the émigré specialties, the one that has suffered most would have to be psychoanalysis. Other forms of treatment, particularly the use of psychotropic drugs, have proved more effective, at least temporarily, and the Freudian enterprise has been devastatingly deconstructed by writers like Colin McGinn and Frederick Crews. But other, even less scientifically grounded therapies have survived nicely. I think the declining fortunes of psychoanalysis are inherently cultural. Not merely all that was lost in translation: for example, the replacement of literary language with scientistic—remember that Mann rather impishly proposed Freud for the Nobel Prize in literature and not medicine—the "it" with the "id." More than that was the problem of tone. This struck me when I read J. Allan Hobson's critique of psychoanalysis as "a strange way of caring for people."

Many Americans considered the shrink tone the distilled vinegar of human communication, a cold, hard manner frequently associated with the Jaeckes. The superficial lack of warmth or compassion bled into a ritual and, if you will, ceremonial sangfroid—a dry-eyed embrace for a weepy culture. But just think if the psychoanalytic persona had been Molly Goldberg or even Woody Allen rather than Bruno Bettelheim or Portnoy's doctor barking in broken English, "Ve vill now to begin!"

In Vienna Karl Kraus had complained that after taking over the press and the economy, the Jews were now colonizing the subconscious: was there no place they wouldn't invade? Once again he forgot Jewish humor and humanity, namely its show business. For while psychoanalysis became yesterday's news, the power of movies to shape and alter consciousness never stopped. But, remarkably, it was accompanied by something critics of popular kitsch (including, for example, Hans Hofmann, whose student Clement Greenberg could find remnants of kitsch in every art form outside of abstract expressionism, and sometimes even there) had not predicted. Popular culture has made possible the educated fan. Fans now have become expert in their own responses, diagnosing the curve and swerve as if they were undergoing therapy. A self-regarding fan is not a complete fool. Not to mention that the tropes of psychoanalysis were beautifully suited to popular culture.

So, after surveying so many declines in critical fortune, we can also find areas where the émigrés continue to surprise and delight. Most of these are associated with popular culture. The émigré contribution to movies has endured with recent, barely postmodernist homages to Fritz Lang and Douglas Sirk. Billy Wilder died in 2002 at ninety-five. By then his famous motto "What would Lubitsch do?" had been reformulated to "What would Wilder do?" by his troubadour the director/critic Cameron Crowe. What he would have liked to do is keep making movies; the guru's role was not a happy fit.

Perhaps the greatest émigré contribution to Americans' pursuit of happiness was nonverbal. Consider how many images of pulchritude were provided by designers like John Weitz or Rudi Gernreich. In 2003 Helmut Newton donated hundreds of photos to a museum in his native Berlin. His exploitation of political imagery for baldly commercial, not to mention sexual, purposes has alarmed many conservative moralists—see the 2003 condemnation by *The New York Times*'s David Brooks—but it can also be read as a photographic version of the *Berliner Schnauze,* a devastating riposte to the Nazis' aesthetic. To my mind, one of the greatest tales of an exile in paradise stars another Berlin Jew. Bruno Bernard Sommerfeld was born in 1911. At twenty-three he earned a doctorate from Kiel University, where he had studied both criminal law and theater. Exile brought him to California, where he became Bernard of Hollywood, master of the pinup. His images of Marilyn Monroe and Jayne Mansfield invaded more dreams than the Frankfurt schoolmasters could ever penetrate. What makes his story exemplary is its end. After Monroe's suicide, he left Hollywood and returned to Berlin, where, at age fifty-one, he began the world again as a photojournalist. When Hannah Arendt attended Eichmann's trial, she could have rubbed shoulders with Bernard of Hollywood, covering the event for *Der Spiegel*.

The great émigré directors—Max Ophuls, Fritz Lang, even Billy Wilder—all have a knack for cinematic details so grippingly realistic that their films have become historical documents (not to mention chapters in the evolution of American taste). But that didn't let reality off the hook; émigrés were obliged to question that too. As somebody joked, dialectics were an émigré's second nature. This discomfited their American colleagues, the ability to take everything most seriously and yet not quite seriously, in the manner of Berliners, who used to boast, "We say no to everything." Many years ago I attended a seminar at New York's Lincoln Center entitled "Documentary Film: Fact or Fiction." There were two speakers, the American Albert Maysles and the Frenchman Marcel Ophuls (*The Sorrow and the Pity*), son of my favorite of the émigré directors, Max Ophuls. Maysles spoke first. He considered the topic a waste of time; everyone knew that a documentarian's role was truth telling. By definition he couldn't lie, and the question didn't really exist. With the suave delivery of a continental charmer, Ophuls disputed him. "The answer is obvious, I'm afraid. Of course, it's fiction." I felt he had much the better argument, that the mere arrangement of data on so immense a scale demanded a quality of artifice. Despite his best attentions the documentarian could only produce his own vision of events, and that would always be incomplete, biased, and personal.

He could have quoted Adorno's objection to making art out of the Holocaust: "Through aesthetic principles or stylization, the unimaginable ordeal" was domesticated, robbed of its full sting, and therefore an immense injustice perpetrated against the victims. His conclusion was that poetry couldn't be written after Auschwitz, though history could. Hannah Arendt would have replied that until poets distill the historical moment, it remains shrouded in darkness. Ophuls, practicing deconstruction before the fact, went beyond both Arendt and Adorno by arguing that no investigation would be fully adequate to its occasion—implying that, at more than four hours, *The Sorrow and the Pity* was nowhere long enough to discover why so many Frenchmen had collaborated with the Nazis. While he spoke, Maysles looked as if he had been personally violated. Of course, he should have seen that as an émigré, even more as his father's son, Ophuls was not being reductive. An artful fiction would always hold more truth, even of a documentary nature, than any other form. Having been the subjects and objects of so many conflicting stories, most émigrés would have agreed.

———

One of the least told and most gratifying tales of emigration involves African-Americans. The mistreatment of black people was a well-known topic in European leftist circles, one reason that this country was viewed with suspicion. In Kafka's novel *Amerika (The Man Who Disappeared)*, once the hero, Karl, has reached the paradise of polymorphous pleasure known as the Nature Theater of Oklahoma, he is asked for his name, and identifies himself as "Negro," thereby declaring his anonymity and insignificance. But this is a poetic conceit. A more pointedly social, and typically prophetic, observation was made by Joseph Roth in *The Wandering Jews.* He writes that a Jew in New York has been finally and ironically emancipated "because they have people who are more Jewish than the Jews, which is to say the Negroes. Of course Jews are still Jews. But here, significantly, they are first and foremost whites. For the first time, a Jew's race is actually to his advantage."

Roth's words illuminate Simone Weil's Christianity. During her brief time in New York, the frail scholar's only joy was her visits to the gospel churches of Harlem. Here she would have found an alternative to whatever she despised in Europe, expressed with an earthy humanity that could seduce her out of her senses. She would also have heard reiterations of Old Testament themes in the songs and sermons, as if American blacks were the most Jewish of Jews. She might also have heard a story I heard several times, many years later, at Manhattan's Congregation Habonim and Brooklyn's Washington Temple Church of God in Christ. In order to still universal criticism, the authorities in Germany / Mississippi find the only contented Jew / Negro left in the land. After much coaching, the fellow is instructed to give the radio audience a word or two. "One word, dearest commandant / boss?" "Two if you'd like, Ikey / Tom." And in both stories, the fellow utters the same word: "Help. Help!"

Albert Einstein was a prominent advocate of civil rights. A personal friend of Paul Robeson, and a man who had opened his home to Marian Anderson on several occasions, he was predictably outspoken. In 1946, he addressed the historically black Lincoln University and said, "The separation [of races] is not a disease of colored people. It is a disease of white people. I do not intend to be quiet about it." This made right-wingers hate him even more, and Republican congressmen would shortly call for his investigation. He didn't mind.

Other émigrés played an active role in the promotion of African-American culture. Many émigré scholars, finding no work in the major universities, wound up teaching in small black colleges, a story well told in Gabrielle Simon Edgecomb's *From Swastika to Jim Crow: Refugee Scholars at Black Colleges.* (Edgecomb is the cousin of Klaus Mann's secretary Richard Plant.) Émigré composers were inspired by African-American music, in bold violation of Adorno's strictures. Kurt Weill liked to compose art music for black voices, splitting the difference between academy and folk song much as he saturated his musical theater with echoes of Lutheran chorales and Tin Pan Alley. Stefan Wolpe discovered a way of leavening the airless practices of serialism by incorporating the spontaneity of jazz improvisation (supposedly Charlie Parker came close to studying with him). Eric Hobsbawm moonlighted for years as the jazz critic Francis Newton, named after Frankie Newton, the only Communist jazz musician of note. During his exile in London, the great drama critic Alfred Kerr (longtime nemesis of both Mann and Brecht) became entranced with black religious singing. At the age of seventy-four, upon hearing the Four Harmony Kings, he declared them superior to any of Milan's opera stars: "Never have I heard greater male voices."

The most resonant appreciation of black music came from two ex-Berliners, Alfred Lion and Francis Wolff, who ran Blue Note, the premier jazz label. I am especially fond of the publisher Julian Aberbach, a Viennese Jew, who directed the famous Aberbach Gallery after he had made his fortune with Hill and Range Music (I detect in the name the émigrés' love of American idioms). The Aberbachs owned the publishing rights to the songs of many country stars, most particularly those of Elvis Presley. But it means more to me that when they represented black gospel composers like Thomas A. Dorsey and Roberta Martin, instead of splitting the earnings fifty-fifty, they gave these "mom and pop" entrepreneurs an unprecedented seventy-five percent.

One of the longest interactions occurred between Marian Anderson and her accompanist of twenty-five years, Franz Rupp. A refugee from Hitler, married to a Jewish woman, Rupp was a nonpareil accompanist, commanding a rhythmic and harmonic authority that played to all of Anderson's strengths. Her favorite genres were lieder and spirituals. Having accompanied Fritz Kreisler and the great baritone Heinrich Schlusnus, Rupp was a master of lieder, and Anderson's willing acolyte in spirituals. Together they recorded several masterpieces. In Schubert's "Erlkönig," while Rupp duplicates the galloping horses, Anderson mimics four characters—the narrator, the anguished father, the frightened child, and the fairy king, whose hypnotic, lilting tones culminate in a fierce cackle. Mortality registers another voice in "Death and the Maiden"—low, resigned, and terminally seductive. The marriage of Eros and Thanatos became a Rupp/Anderson specialty. She graced her spirituals with a similar range of vocal colors, thereby treating anonymous black lyricists as the peers of Goethe and Schiller. For example, on April 11, 1945, she recorded Schumann's "Silent Tears," basking in its sumptuous harmonies. The next day she recorded the spiritual "Hold On," infusing the lyrics with a blues tonality that would do any gospel singer proud. In both, Rupp's accompaniment was impeccable, sympathetic, and idiomatically correct.

During the Second World War, Anderson and Rupp toured the country. They were a charming duo, he a stalwart five feet three, she a regal five feet nine. It was his habit to close each concert by kissing her hand, a gesture both ardent and, given the difference in their sizes, good-humored. When managers of auditoriums in the South protested, Rupp would reply, "It's your hall but our program." Many nights, as they strolled off, the audience, so lately enthralled by their musicianship, burst into catcalls. But their collaboration had a bittersweet aspect. Anderson did not make her debut at the Metropolitan Opera until she was well past her vocal prime, and Rupp's obligations to her prevented the cultivation of his own career as a soloist.

The émigré identification with black culture survives in new ways and other lands. Pieter-Dirk Uys is a great star in South Africa, where his impersonation of an Afrikaner grande dame has made him "the most famous white woman in South Africa." For years Uys devoted most of his time to combating the Thabo Mbeki government's criminal neglect of AIDS treatment. He calls the result "genocide" and makes pointed comparisons between the world's failure to protect the Jews under Hitler and its disregard of AIDS victims in Africa. He justifies his anger—which has made him persona non grata within the African National Congress, of which he is a member—by reminding critics that his mother was a Jewish refugee from Berlin. She lived the life so he could tell the story.

"THE REICHSTAG IS BURNING IN MY SKULL"

Increasingly, the task of defending the émigrés' ideals has fallen to the next generation. Which ideals is another question.

I have spoken mostly about refugees who would be identified as liberal, if not Marxist. But consider the cases of some notable conservatives. After 1989, the decline of the left was accompanied by the spectacular rise of Leo Strauss, whose disciples ranged from his student Allan Bloom (the most famous scourge of Marcusean youth culture) to the Kristols, Irving and William, Robert Bork, Justice Antonin Scalia, and Paul D. Wolfowitz. Not unlike Walter Benjamin, Strauss developed strategies of reading esoterically, finding the moral and intellectual essence invisible to the uninitiated. But where Benjamin sought elegies for the dead and even tactics of resistance to avenge their murders, Strauss was untroubled by history's losers. He despised the Enlightenment for introducing a pragmatic, mechanistic approach that had led, or so he believed, directly to the gas chambers, and, even more, for supplanting traditional religion, the only proven means of keeping the mob in check. One product of the Strauss ascendancy was an affiliation between Jews and the religious right, as evident in the full-page expressions of gratitude to Pat Robertson, the Pentecostal mentor of Liberia's Charles Taylor, and Guatemala's Efraín Ríos-Montt, but also a fervent supporter of Israel's Likud administration.

You can imagine the responses of Einstein or Mann to such an alliance. But apparently Strauss's own daughter objects to the neoconservative misuse of her father's work. In June 2003 Jenny Strauss Clay wrote, "I do not recognize the Leo Strauss presented" as the éminence grise of the war on Iraq. Instead he was "a small, unprepossessing and, truth be told, ugly man"—daughters can be a father's worst critic—"with none of the charisma that one associates with 'great teachers.'" He was not an archconservative, she says; his heroes were Churchill and Lincoln. He simply "despised utopianism—in our time, Nazism and Communism." He was not an observant Jew, not a Jewish chauvinist, "but he loved the Jewish people and he saw the establishment of Israel as essential to their survival." (She might have added that he agreed with Einstein that Jews should never return to Germany.) She also believes that his greatest contribution was not political but pedagogical. "I personally think my father's redisovery of the art of writing for different kinds of readers will be his most lasting legacy," as if he were a genteel forerunner, not of Richard Perle, but of Derrida. In her eyes, Leo Strauss is yet another émigré betrayed in paradise.

Henry Kissinger found his mentor in a German-born, anti-Nazi conservative, Fritz Kraemer, who loved the Hohenzollerns almost as much as Joseph Roth loved the Hapsburgs. Parenthetically, I've always suspected the editor Max Frankel's rage at Kissinger was provoked by his belief that one Washington Heights refugee boy would not mislead another.

Somehow Kissinger's survival is inseparable from his refugee status. It's true that he helped prolong the war in Vietnam even while knowing that it was already lost; likewise he endorsed the Iraqi misadventure. Yet he seems to have dodged the bullets that shot down, at least figuratively, Nixon and George W. Bush. That's because he's identified not with any ideology but with realpolitik, itself a German word. He continues to talk in his ponderous, sepulchral way, but as somebody said of a politician's piety, "At least he seems insincere." In a refugee oldie-but-goodie fable, somebody interviews Kissinger's brother and marvels at his lack of a German accent. "That's because I'm the brother who played baseball," goes one version. In another, he replies, "I'm the brother who listens."

At least once Kissinger tried to claim the pathos of the émigré intellectual. At the funeral of another mentor, the political scientist Hans Morgenthau, he acknowledged that they had profoundly disagreed over the Vietnam War. (For Morgenthau this was a particularly disillusioning moment: according to another friend, Noam Chomsky, he felt that America's "transcendent ideals" were the country's "reality," even if those ideals were barely given lip service.) While, unlike Morgenthau, Kissinger exhibited no remorse or melancholy, he suggested that they were comparable in their singularity. "But we were both, in a way, lonely among our associates." After the war, they may have reconciled, but Kissinger had the grace to add, "I do not wish to burden Hans's memory with the army of my critics."

It should also be noted that for every refugee who hated Kissinger, there was another who viewed him with pride. The annual fête of the Leo Baeck Society, an organization devoted to the commemoration of German Jewish culture, will often be addressed by Kissinger himself, along with representatives of the German government, a perfect instance of the various establishments dining *ensemble*. Years ago a Leo Baeck librarian professed astonishment when I observed that many émigrés despised Kissinger: "But why?" he wondered. "Because he married a shiksa?" Indeed, it is one of the ironies of emigration that German Jewish refugees have become the models of their native culture, as if Thomas Mann's famous comment "Where I am is Germany" had become a chorus. Younger Germans adore the old Jaeckes, largely because they speak the language and transmit the culture of their parents without sharing in the national guilt. Similarly, in this country, distinguished old African-Americans, war veterans or baseball players, have become the last American gentlemen, exemplifying styles of courtesy and social grace that might seem condescending or arrogant in those, literally, to the manor born.

Just as Kissinger incarnates the statesman as immoralist, there continue to be émigré voices decrying his position. In October 2007, a group of émigrés, all in their eighties like Kissinger, spoke up against the Bush-Cheney policies on interrogation of prisoners. In 1945, as young refugees from Hitler, they had interviewed his generals. But they had not disgraced themselves, not even then. "During the many interrogations, I never laid hands on anyone," said eighty-seven-year-old George Frenkel. "I'm proud to say I never compromised my humanity." Instead of physical torture, he pursued "a battle of the wits." Henry Kolm, ninety, added that "we got more information out of a German general with a game of chess or Ping-Pong than they do today with their torture." Hearing such testimonies, you understand the old joke that Jews have always made the best Germans.

Neoconservatives still depict radical critics of Israel as "self-hating," even "anti-Semitic." The alternative conservatives always invoke is Gershom Scholem and his legendary encounter with Hannah Arendt when he accused her of lacking a fundamental love of the Jewish people. Yet even Scholem would fail to meet the standards of Cynthia Ozick or Norman Podhoretz. According to Amos Elon, Scholem detested the post-1967 "triumphalism," the factitious use of scripture to justify settlement of the occupied territories. For all his celebration of Jewish mysticism, he was too much the well-bred Berlin aesthete to get messy with the stuff, and the presence of Israeli holy rollers particularly offended the old secularist. Elon remembers Scholem's anger when his cosmopolitan Jerusalem neighborhood was invaded by American Orthodox families, "each with numerous small children." Brooklyn was crowding out the Old Jerusalem. "At one moment the eighty-two-year-old Scholem leaned out of the opened window, made a half-circle with his arm, and cried, 'Look. They are all around.'" This sounds the true Jaecke note, and I believe Elon's account completely.

Scholem's impact would extend to matters the neocons would consider totally unkosher. His protégé the American religious historian Morton Smith is identified with the argument that the apocryphal Gospel of Mark, in which Jesus and his disciples lead what appears to be an emancipated and very gay life (six days after a young man is raised from the dead, he spends a night with Jesus, who instructs him in the mysteries of "the Kingdom of God"—a queer version of D. H. Lawrence's *The Man Who Died*), is the real deal. This might please some Jews contemptuous of their Christian allies, but it would rob Israel of its most devoted evangelical supporters.

Refusing most consolations, the émigrés seemed to have little taste for religion and its joys. For many years Einstein was represented as essentially devout, as demonstrated by his famous remark that God didn't play dice with the universe. Even if this only implied a pantheistic faith, it was seen as large enough. But in 2008, a letter composed in 1954 surfaced. A year before his death, Einstein wrote the philosopher Eric Gutkind, "The word God is for me nothing more than the expression and product of human weaknesses, the Bible, a collection of honorable but still primitive legends, which are nevertheless pretty childish." Anticipating those who would recruit him as a believer in spite of himself, he added, "No interpretation, no matter how subtle, can (for me) change this." Further offending the Jewish nationalists who would claim him, he observed, "For me the Jewish religion like all other religions is an incarnation of the most childish superstitions. And the Jewish people to whom I gladly belong and with whose mentality I have a deep affinity have no different quality for me than all other people." It's true that they've been spared the "cancers" of history by their "lack of power. Otherwise I cannot see anything 'chosen' about them." This is a franker and deeper confession of identity than Hannah Arendt's short-tempered reply that she didn't love her fellow Jews, she simply was Jewish.

As early as 1929 Einstein had warned Chaim Weizmann that if the Zionists won at the expense of the Palestinians, "we would have learned absolutely nothing" from history. Later, when invited to become the president of Israel, he warned its people that he was absolutely not the voice they'd want to hear. The Jewish establishment could find little use for this Einstein.

Even more discomfiting to them would be the voice of Konrad Kellen, who argued, with the unimpeachable authority of someone whose father had been killed by the Nazis, that the Jews should finally shut up about the Holocaust. A native of Berlin, Kellen emigrated to New York and became a friend of Klaus Mann, who recommended him to be his father's secretary, a job the young man (whose good looks charmed Thomas) held between 1939 and 1943, before entering the U.S. Army. In some ways he can be seen as the son Thomas never had, Klaus being too unbalanced and Golo too right wing. "Konni" observed Mann closely, saw in him a supremely gifted noticer and listener who was also cold and formal, particularly with his brother, Heinrich, whom he would address as if they were sharing a podium. In Konni, Mann found a disciplined employee, a superb reader, and, most surprisingly, a political disciple.

(Apropos sons, here is one real and one figurative. Stefan Brecht died in 2009 at eighty-four, twenty-five years older than his father Bertolt had been when he died. Unlike his proudly anti-academic father, he had earned a Ph.D. in philosophy from Harvard, and had done research in Hegel and Marx, displaying an interest in theory that would have confounded old BB. He became a scholar of the avant-garde and was particularly interested in queer theater. Quite a different slant from his dad, but they seemed to share an émigré's disposition. When he died, his family informed *The New York Times* that he had been "a prickly man, quick to argue," perhaps not the first thing relatives would put in an obituary. The Berlin-born Thomas Franck, who also died in 2009, at the age of seventy-seven, might be seen as a figurative brother of Klaus Mann, sharing his politics and sexuality. He was eulogized as "the leading American scholar of international law," a theme dear to the hearts of both Mann and Einstein, and one of special relevance during the years when the Bush-Cheney administration turned their backs on the world's opinion. Also, a year before his death, he married his longtime male partner. If Klaus has found a second life as an avatar of gay rights, Thomas Franck was his beneficiary.)

After the war Kellen pursued a good, conventional American career. He married an American woman and began working as a political consultant for Radio Free Europe, the Hudson Institute, then directed by Herman Kahn, and the Rand Corporation, all three of them center-right organizations: he gave the appearance of someone closer to Golo than to Klaus or Erika, at least in his politics. In 1962 he exhibited some independence by defending *Eichmann in Jerusalem,* at least partially; there was "considerable worthwhile matter in it" despite its "numerous grievous shortcomings": "Let us not lose our heads. Hannah Arendt is not the enemy." (It may not be unrelated that in 1972 he became one of the first men to compose a feminist manifesto, *The Coming Age of Woman Power.*) The enemies he pounced on were those conducting the Vietnam War. Because of his extreme sensitivity to propaganda—the "Siamese twin of modern technology"—he concluded that attempts to win over the Vietcong simply demonstrated "our obtuseness in matters of psychological warfare." He became one of the earliest establishment figures to call for a swift withdrawal, most dramatically in a 1969 letter he co-signed with four Rand colleagues, including Daniel Ellsberg.

Kellen's specialty was terrorism: one of his last books to be published by Rand was his 1979 *Terrorists—What Are They Like?* This task obliged him to interview the members of the Baader-Meinhof Gang; something like the refugee soldiers interviewing Nazi generals in 1945, he spoke the members' language and was able to make them talk. Indeed, with him as an interlocutor, they wouldn't shut up. He considered right-wing terrorists a constant and potentially fatal threat, and was quite willing to deny them their civil liberties. Ultimately he wished to expand sedition laws until the extreme right wing was outlawed. Alas, a similar program was adopted by the Bush regime, except the terrorists targeted by Cheney, Libby, and Yoo were not right-wingers. But Kellen didn't buy their argument; his enemies remained right-wing fascists. About George W. Bush he exhibited a withering contempt, writing in 2003, when he was ninety, that the president had "mastered the art of saying nothing . . . platitudes of emptiness."

This attention to language and its misuses was a noble homage to Thomas Mann himself. During the years of Kellen's employment Mann wrote a few political addresses, and many letters, most of them high-minded agitprop (calling in 1941 for President Roosevelt to exhibit a saving "nobility of spirit") that frequently embarrassed him. But his important work was the Joseph tetrology, which is a huge novel about storytelling. Throughout the four novels the narrator considers and reconsiders his craft. Can a modern writer make these old bones live? How do we tell or not tell those we love—our parents, our children, our fellow citizens—what they don't want to hear? In what narrative form do we reveal or conceal ourselves? How much can we elaborate on a text until it becomes entirely our own? And do the gods of storytelling reward us for our dreams and lies, by illuminating those old tales, and not merely renewing them but making them our stories as well? (In his last volume Mann congratulates himself to the point of saying that every listener has become mesmerized by his words.)

In 1992 Kellen wrote an astonishing essay, "Must Jews Tell Their Story? A Dissident View." Twenty years later many liberal Jews had come to deplore the tendentious use of the Holocaust by right-wing American Jews and Israelis. A point was reached when daily film critics pleaded for an end to Holocaust films with their facile pathos and barely hidden propaganda. But Kellen's piece appeared when the only support he could find would come from other émigrés. (I often heard my parents say "Enough," or, more impiously, the Passover chant "Dayenu.") Kellen was in no way an apologist for the Germans. Instead he argued powerfully that they had gotten away with their murders: "The non-Jewish world forgave the Shoah without batting an eye." If it were politically or strategically useful, if it would "revive the economy" and "prevent Communism," then the West would employ Hitler's industrialists and scientists and not shed a tear. His anger spills over: "Americans, British, French, everybody—were so easy to forget and forgive that Nazism was buried before even the Jewish dead had been buried."

Kellen saw an immediate danger in the reiteration of Holocaust lore. "If there's a chance of it happening again, it can even be provoked by the insistence of Jews on telling their story." Already, by his death in 2007, the line between attacking Israel and the hoariest of anti-Semitisms, replete with citations of the Elders of Zion (the protocols that confirmed Kellen's sense of propaganda as the quintessential evil of modernity), had been breached. Now the story was held against those who lived it; Israelis, and their supporters, were the new fascists.

Kellen knew, Thomas Mann knew, Einstein knew, a generation of unheralded refugees knew that a storyteller must know when to stop.

—

In 2003 an event occurred that sounds almost apocryphal. The Anti-Defamation League chose to honor Prime Minister Silvio Berlusconi of Italy with its Distinguished Service Award, primarily for his defense of the Sharon government, but also for his support of "a beleaguered American president." Shortly before the award, Berlusconi told an interviewer that Mussolini was no Saddam; he had no blood on his hands, nobody had died. This amazing comment provoked an immediate response from Franco Modigliani, the Nobel-winning economist, who had continued to teach at MIT well into his eighties. In a letter to *The New York Times*, Modigliani cited the thousands of Jews and radicals murdered by the Italian Fascists. Two nights later he died in his sleep at the age of eighty-five. On May 13, 2004, just as the scandal of what the president called "Abu Gurrab" had broken, 240,000 pages of government documents were declassified, revealing what refugees like Klaus Mann had always suspected: that during the cold war the FBI and

CIA had employed Nazi war criminals, including at least five associates of Adolf Eichmann, in both the U.S. and West Germany.

This story would continue on December 11, 2010, when new documents revealed that American counterintelligence had employed even more Nazis, some of them in Germany, where attempts at sabotaging the East German Communists were known as "Project Happiness" (that sounds like something Brecht made up). Political activists, many of them Jewish, continued to be spied on by these former Nazis, a perverse tribute to their professional skills. This news confirmed the postwar fears of some émigrés on the left. But fewer of those people remained, and the story did not stir much interest.

There was always some new evidence that the émigrés were not entirely wrong when they kept an empty suitcase handy.

The conductor Lorin Maazel, himself a French Jewish refugee, once met the avant-garde composer Karlheinz Stockhausen in Cologne, Germany. There Stockhausen blamed his career's shortfall on "the sentimental weakness of German Jewish immigrants" for the music of the Berlin concert halls. Someone has said that all the classical-music stations of old-time radio had thrived on the support of those émigrés. Going well past Theodor Adorno, Stockhausen called this benign form of nostalgia an "obscene love," and chose a devilish way to punish it. He invited Maazel to hear one of his works, and when the conductor put his ear to the speaker, "A tremendous blast came out of it which almost destroyed my eardrums, which he knew perfectly well would happen . . . Total monster." To paraphrase the movie star, "They hate us, they really hate us."

I know of so many similar tales—e.g., the famous woman doctor who, shortly before her death, summoned her daughter to her bed and said, "The Reichstag is burning. It's burning in my skull." All the stories remind us that the past never releases us. Or, in the idiom of Billy Wilder, you can't beat the house—the house always wins.

That once was common knowledge. During the 1950s, a story circulated in émigré circles. Two refugees are sailing on the Atlantic, one toward Europe, the other toward America. As their boats pass each other, the two old friends burst out simultaneously: "Are you nuts?" I can imagine Bert Brecht saying, *"Mensch,* you might as well laugh . . . because if you started to cry, you would never stop."

THE EMPEROR OF AMBIVALENCE

The hottest literary evening of a frigid New York winter took place recently at the city's Goethe House. It was a salute to Joseph Roth and a confirmation that he is now recognized as one of the twentieth century's great writers. It was not always thus for this author, a Galician Jew who became the Hapsburg monarchy's most symphonic troubadour, a blazing radical, *der rote Roth,* who venerated the piety of shtetl Jews and peasant Catholics, the highest-paid journalist in Berlin's golden 1920s, who died when he was forty-five in Paris, an impoverished alcoholic with barely a rumpled suit to his name.

But thanks greatly to Michael Hofmann's luminous translations, which capture the incomparable verve and energy of Roth's supremely musical prose, many of Roth's novels, stories, and essays are now available in English. The response has been stunning: Nadine Gordimer, for example, finds him an even more comprehensive novelist than Thomas Mann, with a greater range of inquiry and tone, and she may be right. Roth composes the most pleasing prose imaginable, but he can also trouble your mind and break your heart. Unlike any other great European modernist—Proust, Kafka, Mann, Musil—he can write with equivalent authority about high culture and low, country and city, dumb smart boys and preternaturally wise fools.

Because his best-known novels, particularly his masterpiece, *The Radetzky March,* celebrate a bygone era, Roth is sometimes called—though respectfully—a nineteenth-century author, willfully nonmodernist. Actually, he is definitively modern, since he writes always from the current moment's perspective, while saturating that moment with a past terminated barely a second ago and a future that promises further cycles of loss: "Every new development constitutes a mysterious circle, in which the beginning and end touch and become identical." He describes this aesthetic stance as "the hard and proud melancholy of a solitary who wanders on the fringes of pleasures, follies and sorrows."

A photograph of Roth reveals a man peculiarly of his times: with his little head, his large eyes, his Nolde-like slashes of eyebrow, he could have been sent over from Central Casting as a model of the exiled intellectual, too wily to be dumbfounded, too stunned to be blasé. Despite his short life (1894–1939), he was the most peripatetic of émigré writers. Born in Galicia, he served in the Austro-Hungarian Army during World War I. Afterward he worked as a journalist, first in Vienna, then in Berlin. An early and ardent radical, Roth championed the new objectivity, with its conviction that technological breakthroughs would facilitate political liberation. In 1926, he visited the Soviet Union. He returned totally disabused of his radical confidence, and announced as much in his novel *Flight Without End* (1927). Never again would his work exhibit a unity of experimental style and radical perspective.

Even so, Roth's greatest strength is his prose, a uniquely modern idiom. Its secret is, in his words, the application to "minutiae" of "the dialectical intelligence of the Jews." Where he differs from his great contemporary Rilke—and Hofmann is splendid in finding parallels—is in his recoil from that greatest of Rilkean dangers, a diaphanous whimsy. (Similarly, he can outdo Brecht, as he distinguishes two whores, "Bavarian Annie" and "Silesian Annie," without acquiring Brecht's worst trait, the hectoring snarl.) The constant joy of a Roth reader is his ceaselessly inventive power of description, enlivened always by that dialectical intelligence. He is the prose equivalent of a great jazz improviser, finding new resources in the familiar.

Dickens seemed to require a defenseless child to set his pen on fire, Mann a troubled relationship between two men. Many things stimulate Roth, but he is most transcendent when something—inanimate objects not excluded—allows him to distill vast implications in a pithy formulation. A small detail is all he needs: "the diminutive of the parts is more important than the monumentality of the whole." His rhetorical triumph, for which he frequently congratulated himself, was to be simultaneously breezy and profound; his ambition was to describe things better than anyone before or after by concentrating a universe of implications in the most abbreviated of commentary. At times, his rat-a-tat lyricism can remind you of a standup comedian on an inspired roll. But it can also achieve a biblical eloquence, as when he hears in the grunts and half-sentences of the poor "the sorrow of an entire world" and sees in "a silently bent head . . . the misery of all time" or views a line of mourners "slowly being pushed along by silence."

The empathetic range is apparent in his famous discussion of shtetl Jews. Only James Baldwin has matched his vision of the fundamentalist's world. Indeed, Roth's details—the confidence of "God's Jews" that they alone have a pipeline to the deity; their musical service, a compound of Bible and folklore; their flamboyant ritual with its culmination in a physical release that borders on the erotic; the cultlike worship of charismatic, faith-healing "wonder rabbis"; the pleasure in the rebbetzin's fine clothes because of what they "represent"—could serve, with minimal changes, as a guide to the African-American church. Roth's sympathetic embrace of traditional culture was one reason he bitterly opposed Zionism. As early as 1927, he compared the Arab residents of Palestine to Jews fighting against the imposition of Anglo-American civilization, whose representatives were Jewish settlers engaged in "national rebirth" whom he bluntly compared to Crusaders.

At the Goethe House conference, Cynthia Ozick raged against this anti-Zionism. "He saw," she said, her voice rising with vexation, "but he was not a seer." Some might argue he saw all too clearly. (And it must be added that, at least in Europe, he despised the capitulation of Jews, most particularly German Jews, their quixotic attempts to survive by getting by. Long before Hannah Arendt spoke her piece about the Jewish leaders' collaborations with Nazis, he deplored the existence of *Kulturbünde,* the separate-but-unequal cultural societies enforced by the Nazis.) Either way, his sympathy for the Arabs was a corollary of that for the shtetl Jews.

But, as he says, history has driven most Jews from the shtetl, and the literary payoff has been epochal: "The great gain to German literature from Jewish writers is the theme of the city." Roth is at his best strolling through a city, even though—if not precisely because—he doesn't much like the place. Writing about Berlin enables him to imagine towns he's never visited. "It's as though I'd been to New York, having sampled the bitterness of the metropolis, because most major discoveries can be made very locally, either at home or a few streets away." *What I Saw: Reports from Berlin, 1920–1933* contains some of his most delightful prose and some of his most perspicacious. Though the essays are shorter than his best stories, much less his novels, nothing is missed. The interaction between his unique voice and an immense range of subjects provides all the drama anyone needs. These are not personal essays in the traditional sense. But if, as Oscar Wilde says, criticism is the most refined form of autobiography, then these essays are shot through with Roth's personality. (Of course, so are the novels, in which, if one wanted, one could use the fact that he never knew his father, who died in an insane asylum, to explain his devotion to the soil, which signified a fatherland, which meant a father: Emperor Franz Joseph.) From the subjects chosen to the virtuosic play of that dialectical intelligence to the minutest of grammatical details, the essays reveal him whole. In his fine introduction to Roth's short study *The Wandering Jews,* Hofmann is surprised that Roth never identifies himself as a Jew. I would reply that he carries throughout the implicit burden of speaking for them all. In his role as gadfly, he was the Wandering Jew incarnate.

Roth may have questioned urban civilization, but he was not immune to its charms. He regarded the fans of popular music and of sports as little short of insane, yet he too could succumb and reach the point where "my knees fell to their knees." He can sing the splendor of skyscrapers, turning an engineering feat into a new kind of metaphysics, a benign version of Fritz Lang's *Metropolis,* and find in the noise of machines a "completely new language, a means of communication as universal as German," a prelude to "a beautiful and audible future music," a kind of Rilkean spell. He captures the manic-depressive rhythms and ritualized etiquette of sports fans and then jolts the crowd by having a practical housewife remove her family's lunch from its newspaper wrapping, thereby wafting a perfume of "cheese and politics" over the "dust storm of ecstasy." Who before had compared a Turkish bath to Dante's Inferno? Or tracked popular culture by going from the swankest nightclub to the lowest joint, observing the aging dancers and musicians who move ever downward as their bodies widen and their lips fail?

But paradoxically this master observer feared the power of images. In 1927 he decried "an inhuman, technically accomplished future whose symbols are the airplane and the football and not the hammer and sickle." The only antidote was a language informed by thought and feeling. Even in his last, demoralized years, he could write, "Action stands roughly in the same relation to words, as the two-dimensional shadow in the cinema to the three-dimensional living man."

The most powerful essay in *What I Saw,* and the longest, is "The Auto-da-Fé of the Mind," written in September 1933 for a small Jewish magazine in Paris, to which he had moved a few years earlier. The only indictments of Hitler that match Roth's eloquence are those Mann composed in the mid-1930s, at far less risk and exceedingly late in the day. When he finally spoke out, he made the Rothian point that German culture would be unthinkably dry without its Jewish element.

Roth saw the situation more clearly than Mann, and earlier. In his devastating essay, he surveys a world in which paradox and irony have ceased to be Rothian tropes but have become the plain truth. Gentile writers, like Mann, might compromise with the Nazis, but Jews, defeated on every other front, would be spared that indignity. His tone ranges from a bleak lucidity to a universal jeremiad. Nobody has proven worthy. He condemns the Jews for not being Jewish enough (by their susceptibility to the "journalistic clichés" and "failed European ideology" of political nationalism, namely Zionism), Christians for not being Christian enough (for not seeing that anti-Semitism was, by definition, an attack on Jesus), Germans for not being German enough (for failing to see that Jewish writers had sung their culture alive), and professors for not being scholarly enough (for not remaining absent-minded oafs but instead broadcasting "the philological equivalent of poison gas"—with one phrase, replacing the image of Emil Jannings in *The Blue Angel* with that of Martin Heidegger).

The only honorable exception was the Jewish writer. And he then proceeds to a thrilling roll call of those who have been hounded out of Germany. He knows that many of these men (there is only one woman, Elsa Lasker-Schüler) hated each other as literary rivals, and not a few recoiled from their quarter- (Rilke) or half- (Klaus Mann) Jewish identity. Some composed tragic epics; others, boulevard comedies; one, Hugo von Hofmannsthal, was "the classical heir to the Catholic treasures of old Austria." No matter; they were all now, in their enemies' eyes, "shtetl yids." And even the assaults of literary critics now became a thinly disguised form of anti-Semitism. A writer—and he could only be describing himself—was dismissed as a "superficial scribbler" when he displayed "charm and lightness of touch." Only at this moment does he bring himself into the picture. His cry is greatly more eloquent and disturbing than Mann's because it speaks for so many besides himself. And how much more provocative than "Where I am is Germany" is Roth's contention that the only German culture that ever existed was the one that Jews had imagined.

—

In one of literature's saddest ironies, three years earlier Roth had published a novel in which the tragic circumstances of emigration were forecast, and even—albeit unconvincingly—transcended. *Job: The Story of a Simple Man,* a short novel that reads like an extended parable, contains some of his most sublime prose. It is the story of Mendel Singer, an impoverished Hebrew teacher living in a forsaken outpost, and his wife and children, particularly an invalid son, Menuchim, who is either autistic or retarded, and a vivacious daughter, Miriam, who suffers from a psychosexual disorder like the one that felled Roth's wife, the beautiful and doomed Friederike (Friedl) Reichler. The novella was something of a hit in America, where it appeared in a wretched translation by Dorothy Thompson (who would later prove one of the German Jews' earliest advocates). Fortunately, a new translation by Ross Benjamin captures the varied delights of Roth's prose style, his ceaselessly inventive syntax and range of metaphor. *Job,* thanks to Benjamin, is revealed as a short and nearly perfect work, bliss to read even as it terrifies you.

The Singers lead lives of unrelieved poverty, whether in their village or in New York. Yet Roth's eye remains attuned to wonder. Sentence after sentence is filled with astonishing details. Roth implies that someone with Mendel's eye can find visionary delight in the barest of surroundings. He always enjoyed varying the sentence structure, complicating the grammar to reflect a sudden alteration of consciousness. Only he can make the humblest of abodes seem charged with hallucinatory splendor. And none of his contemporaries and peers—not Mann, Kafka, or Musil—has his gift of inhabiting the humblest lives and granting them unimpeachable authority. For example, the wordless Menuchim dominates each of his scenes, as if he were trumpeting his plight. In Katherine Anne Porter's great story "He," a poor woman raises her retarded son until she is forced to send him to a nursing home. As she leaves him, he utters the most woebegone sounds, and her heart stops, suddenly imagining a felt life that may have existed all these years without a single utterance from his lips. Roth doesn't wait for a last-minute surprise; we always feel that Menuchim is a breathing, perceiving character. In the midst of showing us the precisest details of the Singers' life, he can also intimate the inaudible and invisible.

Mendel's existence is baldly Job-like. He must abandon Menuchim and say goodbye to a son now serving in the Russian army. Giving up Menuchim nearly destroys his wife, Deborah; learning that her other son has died serving with the American army kills her. Shortly afterward, Miriam goes mad. (Both mother and daughter are depicted with great sympathy, albeit as fundamentally instinctual creatures, Deborah with an animal-like devotion to her family, Miriam with a raging libido that may seem perilously close to a caricature of nymphomania.) Having lost almost everything, Mendel begins to identify himself with Job.

Roth was occasionally and quirkily pious. He shows Mendel and his friends to be Jewish holy rollers, shivering ecstatically as they read the Torah or cry the songs of Zion. Like Deborah, who seeks out a wonder rabbi in hopes that he will heal Menuchim, Roth brought his sick wife to a similar faith healer. (Can you even imagine a Mann or a Kafka doing that?) Yet *Job* becomes a masterpiece of apostasy. Outside of the biblical Job or Milton's Satan, nobody has ever raged more eloquently against the sadistic master of the universe. "It's over, over, over for Mendel Singer! He has no son, he has no daughter, he has no wife, he has no money, he has no house, he has no God! It's over, over, over for Mendel Singer!"

The biblical Job revealed a masochistic devotion to the author of his grief. "Yea though he slay me, yet shall I serve him!" The Bible commands all believers to cultivate the gifts of patience. "They that wait upon the Lord shall renew their strength. They shall mount up on wings like an eagle!" The Jobian Mendel has lost those gifts. When his friends ask what can relieve his sorrows, he replies, "I want to burn God."

This is the most staggering moment in all of Roth, not least because we know the fates of all the Mendels and, for that matter, all the Friedl Roths. Even more than Kafka's, Roth's work seems to contain the moments that he came close to predicting.

And yet he blinked. There is a happy ending for Mendel. He hears a phonograph recording (and, of course, Roth writes about the charms of this newfangled technology as well as Mann when he has Hans Castorp listen to records of Wagner) and, as the Bible says, recovers his joy. The singer turns out to be Menuchim himself, who appears, an international star, ready to pay all of his father's bills and return Miriam to Europe (!), where she is sure to regain her sanity (!!!). Quite literally, he has become a deus ex machina. Roth admitted that he could only have composed these preposterous, if moving, events in a drunken stupor. But that was increasingly his state of being. And even this turn of events, so insanely arbitrary, does not remove the novel's sense of doom. In A. A. Milne's poem "King John's Christmas," the hero has only one desire, a big red India-rubber ball, clearly a cipher for all the friendship and affection he has spent his life without. Comes the holiday, and Father Christmas has denied him yet again; we share his palpable grief. But then, purely by accident, such a ball bounces through his window. Milne may have intended this as a sign of the world's gratuitous wonders. But like Mendel's good fortune, it leaves one unconvinced. If your own hope is a lucky break, then shame on you. Shame, too, on poor Mendel. And Roth's irrepressible ambivalence colors even our last glimpses of the poor man.

Two years after *Job,* Roth published his most famous novel, *The Radetzky March.* In countless ways, from subject to tone, from cadence to scope, it differs from his journalism. What makes it uniquely Rothean is the merger of sensation and thought, the ways it ponders deeply the apparently lightweight actions of figures too small for history, unless it is the profounder history that remains Roth's specialty. Even allowing that, the book reveals his immense versatility: it's as if a rapper had reincarnated himself as a Wagnerian tenor or a cantor—all of them roles Roth was suited to play.

The Radetzky March is as singular today as when it was first published in 1932: a passionate homage to the Hapsburg monarchy composed by a Galician Jew. The current revival of interest in Austrian émigré writers has led to new editions of work by Robert Musil, Hermann Broch, and Stefan Zweig. Roth is not like any of them; in fact, he is so willfully perverse that he frequently contradicts his own idiosyncratic self. But for two reasons he may be more accessible to modern readers. For one thing, his style is a model of German prose emancipated from the ponderous abstractions and discursive interludes that American readers consider—not always fairly—insurmountable obstacles. Roth is a master of imagery: his characters live in images while those of Broch or Musil dwell largely in thought.

In contrast to the Marxist Brecht or the philo-democratic Mann, he evolved an unlikely amalgam of Trotskyism, philo-Catholicism, and nostalgia for the Hapsburg monarchy. Other lapsed Marxists have wound up in strange places; Roth's distinction is that he seemed to believe several contradictory things at once. *The Radetzky March* may be his masterpiece because the myth he discovers is embracing enough to console its previously inconsolable author. (He needed help—as he writes about his hero, "He was like a man who had lost not only his home but also his homesickness for it.") From the initial description of the "safety" soldiers feel in their lieutenant's presence, Roth is in pursuit of protection. Using unconventional means, he finds it in the reactionary myths of Austro-Catholicism—presided over by a universal father, Emperor Franz Joseph, aka the King of Jerusalem.

Roth likes his characters to be naive, if not dumb, the better to bombard their thoughtless minds with images. Like Tolstoy, he swoons before displays of peasant piety; he determines to find the simple and true in what most of his peers would consider extreme banality. A typical Roth joke is to make his characters' salvation coincident with the redemption of clichés. One example: his hero, Lieutenant Carl Joseph von Trotta, falls into debt, and his valet offers him his life savings. Carl Joseph is embarrassed by the action, particularly because it seems so *kitschig*: that's the way servants act in novels. Roth makes one of his rare narrative intrusions to scold the lieutenant: he knows little about life, so he doesn't know how much truth resides in "bad books." Roth's coup is to write a good book that ought to have been a bad one.

The Radetzky March, in keeping with the Strauss composition of that name, celebrates three generations of Austro-Hungarian patriots in the half-century leading up to World War I. The first Lieutenant Trotta is a former peasant who enters the military. He becomes "the hero of Solferino" when, quite by accident, he takes a bullet that might have killed Emperor Franz Joseph. His unwitting sacrifice earns him a baronetcy. (He has enough integrity, however, to object loudly—all the way to the emperor himself—when school texts endow him with foresight. At once, Roth is having it both ways: ridiculing the phony heroism manufactured in books while applauding Trotta's act precisely for being mindless and contingent.) Trotta's son, known by his title of District Commander, and his grandson Carl Joseph, a professional soldier, spend their lives basking in Trotta's fame but aware that they are not up to his standard of devotion or courage.

Carl Joseph is bivouacked with troops at the outposts of the empire, first in Moravia, then on the Polish border with Russia. His life is tedious and his consciousness limited: as his mistress observes, he is an unhappy man whose grief has not taught him a thing. Yet this dummkopf is capable of feeling an abundance of sensations. Roth's gift for sensuous description, free of commentary or inflection, allows the reader to share a soldier's pleasure: the heft of swords, the gleam of helmets, the smell of new wool, the womblike snugness of a well-lit barracks. From solitary bliss, Carl Joseph moves to fellow feeling for his comrades. His best friend is an intellectual Jew, Dr. Max Demant (he too regrets the distance from his peasant grandfather). With typical thoughtlessness, Carl Joseph precipitates a duel that will involve Demant, a man totally unequipped for such contests. While both men recognize Trotta's folly, they still enjoy walking together—"both would have liked to continue forever along the road." Only by embracing the morally clumsy Carl Joseph is Demant able to regain the spirit of his ancestors: "Pity overwhelmed the doctor's heart and love's thousand flickering tongues sprang up in him." A continuum from sensuous detail to redemptive epiphany is Roth's signature.

History catches up with the Trottas, and the novel's last pages are filled with astonishing events. Roth provides an imperial benediction as the emperor appears and turns out to be the physical twin of the District Commander. He is at once the father of all his peoples—Roth emphasizes the devotion of his Jewish subjects—and a compassionate ironist, aware that his empire will terminate with his life. (The superior ironist, Roth understands that the empire really dies with the Trottas.) When his son gets badly in debt, the District Commander learns how hard it is to be both helpless and dignified: the insight drives him crazy, and with insane gumption he beseeches the emperor to rescue Carl Joseph. Likewise, after supervising the massacre of a band of striking workers, Carl Joseph suffers a breakdown and retires from the army. He becomes an estate manager, living among the peasants, sharing their religious faith. Recommissioned, he proceeds to act as heroically and mindlessly as a figure out of Christian fable. Coming across three hanging corpses—two of them swing around the third "like dumb clappers in a soundless bell"—he cuts the bodies down and buries them in a churchyard. Later, when his troops demand water in the midst of battle, he goes to a well where, to the inaudible strains of the Radetzky March, he is shot down by a sniper. This is not the heroism of professional soldiers, but it is rooted in the simple decencies of everyday people.

Carl Joseph's sacrifice recalls an earlier moment when "in the space of a single swift second the facility of seeing the images descended upon him, so that, exalted, he saw the ages roll toward each other like two rocks, and he himself . . . was crushed between them." Characteristically, Roth merges fatal prophecy, spiritual fulfillment, and sensuous perception. Like a caterpillar, Carl Joseph dies into himself. The historical boulders that crushed Carl Joseph did in his creator as well, and one cannot read *The Radetzky March* without seeing it as a product of the terrible events that Roth lived through. Its numerous stylistic beauties cannot disguise the desperation of his myth.

—

Roth spent his last years living in shabby Paris hotels. Seated in a café, addressing a round of absinthes, he became the unofficial arbiter of the émigré experience in France. For him it had become a game that wound down somewhere, sometime. "I tell you one loses home after home. Here I sit, wandering, footsore, heart-weary, dry-eyed. Misery huddles beside me and keeps getting gentler and bigger. Pain stands still, grows vast and kindly, terror roars and can no longer terrify. And that precisely is the dismal part." Apparently cried out, he seemed beyond tears. (But he remained susceptible. After learning of the suicide in New York of his friend Ernst Toller, he mourned in a two-week drunk that would kill him.) The Kafkaesque image of a terror grown vast and kindly expanded to encompass a world in which danger was protean and commonplace, and evil ubiquitous to the point of banality. Even in his decline, Roth's vision remained impeccable. And, apparently, so were his manners. Soma Morgenstern, another great Austro-Hungarian writer, stopped in the hotel en route between Berlin and New York. His son, Dan, then ten years old, remembers Roth as unusually kind, and concerned with the ways he occupied himself. Roth might have seen his generation as lost, but he held out hope for the next one. (Dan Morgenstern would become one of America's most famous jazz critics.)

Walter Mehring reports that Roth's funeral was a predictably confused event. Eulogies were offered by a Catholic priest who had converted from Judaism and by an emissary of the deposed Austrian monarchy. Then a left-wing exile convoked a minyan to say kaddish.

—

I love Roth the novelist. But forgive me if I prefer the journalist. Perhaps because, outside of gospel music and John Milton, I have a limited patience for the religious vision, even one as beautifully qualified as that of *The Radetzky March*. Also, I dream of urban vistas, not rural ones. And I want Joseph Roth as my walking buddy through the modern city.

In the last pages of *Job,* the hero moves from his basement cell on the Lower East Side to a Broadway hotel. "There he saw for the first time the American night from up close, the reddened sky, the flaming, sparkling, dripping, glowing, red, blue, green, silver, golden letters, pictures and signs. He heard the noisy song of America, the honking, the tooting, the roaring, the singing, the screeching, the creaking, the whistling and the howling." After pages of drab, colorless, impoverished life, where the sounds range among fearful whispers and noisy prayer, suddenly we are within the land of the living. This shimmering world, filled with color and blazing sound, reads like a Technicolor deliverance after a submersion in starkest black-and-white. This is my preferred Roth. Of course, because of his inbred ambivalence, and because we know what happened next, hotels are not simply a form of paradise. We think of the seedy hotels where he spent his last years. We think of the glamorous New York Hotel Mayflower, a close proximation of the hotel Mendel beholds, where Ernst Toller committed suicide—the same Toller who found in *Job* "the discipline and rigor of German classicism"—the event that triggered Roth's own death. No place guaranteed redemption; shtetl or hotel, they'd get you anywhere.

All that's left is the telling. People of letters will treasure Roth because in the face of all contenders—politics, popular music, the heart with its voluminous unreason—he gave final say to the word. Knowing more deeply than any of the century's other great writers that language, too, wouldn't save him.

III. THE FANS
WHO KNEW
TOO MUCH

BRAVE TOMORROWS FOR
BACHELOR'S CHILDREN

The term "soap opera" is so common an indictment that one forgets its recent origin. Barely eighty years ago a bold, indeed revolutionary, kind of storytelling made its debut on local radio stations. Because its audience was largely female and working-class, it became a laughingstock. Not until rock and roll "ruined" popular music was a form of popular culture condemned so thoroughly. This reception was as biased and uninformed as the early attacks on Little Richard and Fats Domino. For, in truth, the soaps were a fascinating phenomenon, a means of enlightenment and acculturation that went far beyond melodrama, deep into the perverse and surreal, pushing narrative to its formal limits.

At the very least, they domesticated Freud, making sibling rivalry, transference, Oedipus and Electra complexes the stuff of daily life. Even now, when reality television has virtually buried the soaps, reducing their daily number to four, everyone understands that the term means either a reduction of life to its most passionate excesses or a grudging admission that life can never outpace those excesses. As Irna Phillips, the presiding figure in soap history, once informed the critics of the Frankfurt School, "Life is a daytime serial, escape it if you can."

If you want a further justification for studying this most despised of forms, consider the émigré director Douglas Sirk's fascination with melodrama, "those strange stories in which the bizarre, the impossible, the accidental and the odd were boldly embraced to expose a force that lay underneath." He would make great art of soapy novels like Lloyd C. Douglas's *Magnificent Obsession* or Fannie Hurst's *Imitation of Life.* Radio soaps and Sirk movies can be seen as raw and cooked versions of melodrama, with the proviso that the raw can be almost as nourishing.

The genre appealed to the least respected members of society, house-wives and maids, "vulgar people," the sick and shut-in, single people sequestered in their small rooms. Blacks were among the biggest fans: one gospel singer, Bessie Griffin, called Ma Perkins "my company keeper," while another, Alex Bradford, saw Helen Trent as a real woman: "I've been listening to her for years." This kind of cross-racial identity was possible because even though the serials were not racially enlightened, they did propose a world in which everyone suffered alike and together. Ma Perkins became "America's mother of the airwaves," and that meant everyone's. There must have been enough of Ma's children for soaps to command huge audiences (an estimated twenty million listeners a day) and profits for the sponsors, agencies, and a few lucky writers and actors. In 1932, there were five; in 1942, fifty; in 1952, thirty-five; and in 1962, none, the genre having left radio for the daytime hours of television.

In a patriarchal era, the soaps were feminist no matter the intentions of their creators. While the authors insisted that their values were tra-ditional and, indeed, conservative, their critics saw them as secret sabo-teurs of traditional marriage. The superwomen were castrating wives, and their husbands demonstrably emasculated. This in particular may have explained the serials' great appeal to gay men. Boys who identified more with Helen Trent, dress designer to the stars, than with private eye Dick Tracy; the stay-at-home kids who didn't recognize themselves in Jack Armstrong, the All-American Boy. Soaps became the one form uniquely geared to society's outsiders and pariahs, "losers for losers."

But they were also bound up with a classic American narrative, the story of making something out of nothing. From the start soaps' heroes and heroines were strivers, most of them poor, and many of them minor-ities. The early genius was Henry Selinger, a Chicago radio executive and former violinist, who dreamed up *Sam 'n' Henry*, which developed into *Amos 'n' Andy* in 1928. (The creator-actors were both white.) Broad-cast for fifteen minutes, five nights a week, the serial became a national sensation. By 1929 Madame Queen's breach-of-promise suit against the hapless Andy had listeners transfixed; it was claimed that one could move from house to house and not miss a beat of the show—everybody was tuned in. It was usually seen as a comic serial, and its characters, notably the affably corrupt George "Kingfish" Stevens, as stereotypes, its dialect (Andy's "I'se regusted") a racist insult. Of course there was more at stake. Amos's language was as low-keyed and all-American as Andy's was minstrel-like. And in later sequences, the serial dealt with issues of race prejudice and police brutality.

By 1929, a haute bourgeoise named Gertrude Berg and a Brooklyn College dropout named Himan Brown had created a Jewish version, *The Rise of the Goldbergs.* Brown, still a teenager, would part company with Berg and shortly supervise New York's first radio soap, *Marie, the Little French Princess,* before creating series like *Inner Sanctum* and *Grand Central Station.* Gertrude Berg, now sole owner of *The Goldbergs,* would run the show as it moved from ethnic comedy to nightly serial to—after 1936—daily soap, in which Molly Goldberg's yiddishkeit would be a light unto the nations for her gentile neighbors in a small New England town.

Probably the first daytime soap opera premiered in early 1930 as a local show on Cincinnati's WLW. *The Life of Mary Sothern* contained many of the soap tropes. Its heroine, a former movie star, had returned to her small town with two babies, perhaps born out of wedlock. The series ran locally for a few months. It would be picked up for runs of two or three years several times (1934, 1943, 1950). By 1955, Australian radio was broadcasting decades-old scripts with local actors. The show's author was one Don Becker, a man with a dry sense of humor. In 1928 he had begun a weekly skit about the crazed employees of a Lavender Network. The play on "lavender" goes with his naming of Mary Sothern's archenemies, the wicked Mr. and Mrs. Proust, a surname almost unknown in 1930s America. Becker's pioneer role has gone unsung. But in 1938 he and Carl Bixby conceived *Life Can Be Beautiful,* one of the classic soaps. Its leading characters were Papa David Solomon, the nominally Jewish but Christlike and sexually neutered owner of a Lower East Side bookstore, and his adopted daughter, ChiChi. Becker liked to begin each broadcast with Bartlett's Familiar Quotations. He was obviously in love with the serial form, in all its sententious glory. When not writing as many as four serials a day, he found time to compose the musical themes and, merely for sport, turn two thousand Chinese legends into mini-soaps. In 1940 he created *The Light of the World,* a serialization of the Bible; the first day's episode ended with a cliffhanger about Eve, trying to make a life for her family in a friendless, new space eons removed from the small town called Paradise.

Nineteen thirty also saw the appearance of the two most important figures in soap history, Irna Phillips and Frank Hummert. Their backgrounds were as dissimilar as would be their creations or their politics. Hummert was the product of upper-class Anglo-Catholicism. He was the leading advertising copywriter of his day. During the "Great War" he had dreamed up the slogans for Liberty Loans ("Bonds or Bondage"), and he had later conceived a campaign for Kotex, a product whose function could not be named. (Remember the similarly ethereal "Use Modess . . . because"?) Perhaps his greatest coup as a storytelling salesman would be twinning Edna Wallace Hopper, a cosmetics firm devoted to recapturing the beauty of youth, with Helen Trent, a serial heroine pledged to finding love "at thirty-five . . . and even after."

But Hummert's rhetorical efforts were also politically tinged. Himan Brown claims that Hummert ghost-wrote some of Franklin Delano Roosevelt's speeches; and his language betrays the same Thoreauvian cadences as "nothing to fear but fear itself." For example, Helen Trent "throws herself against the rocks of despair, fights back bravely, successfully"—a Thoreauvian adverb—"to prove in her own daily life what so many women long to prove." Hummert would later admit that "we write successful stories about unsuccessful people." Yet his series were also brazenly populist tales in which the poor always outwitted the rich, as well as displaying a finer sense of ethics.

Hummert had two allies. Anne Ashenhurst, his assistant, was a patrician graduate of Baltimore's Goucher College who had worked as a reporter in Paris. After Hummert's first wife died, he and Anne were married. Soon after, he left the ad agency, Blackett-Sample-Hummert, to found Air Features, a company that produced over thirty daytime serials, all ostensibly "based on [a] radio play by Frank and Anne Hummert, and produced under their supervision."

There never were any radio plays, and for the first few years the serials were mostly dreamed up by Robert Andrews, a Chicago reporter of legendary stamina and virtuosity. By 1930, the twenty-seven-year-old had already written a series of city novels about career girls and their misadventures; scholars have found the novels' journalistic details intriguing. In 1931 Andrews turned one of his potboilers, *The Stolen Husband,* into a short-lived radio serial. Anne Hummert encouraged him to create *Bill the Barber,* later known as *Just Plain Bill* (and briefly as *Just Plain Bill and Nancy*). The first episode flitted between comedy and melodrama. Bill the Barber is first seen making sport of his enemy, the town con man. Then, like a figure in a vaudeville sketch, he starts to play the harmonica. Andrews and Hummert were obviously hoping to attract the audience of Jimmie Rodgers, the country singer known as the Blue Yodeler. But the episode ends with a shock. Bill receives a letter and faints. It announces a visit from Nancy, the daughter he hasn't seen since her mother died in childbirth and he allowed her to be raised by her snooty grandmother. It was a classic Hummert note, combining doubts about class status with the rawest forms of pathos.

Ultimately Nancy would find in Daddy Bill the parent of her dreams, and for over twenty years the two of them and her lawyer husband, Kerry Donovan, would remain the show's leading characters, never changing, never growing, always threatened, never harmed (though Nancy did lose her first child, named after her mother, Nellie). A more checkered career would confront the Hummerts' next creation, Helen Trent. In the first chapter of her romance, Helen is divorced by her wicked husband, Martin Trent (the storyline echoed *The Stolen Husband*). She is accompanied in court by an elderly Greek chorus, her lawyer and her aged roommate, Agatha Anthony. But she is surprisingly blasé, and dismisses their attention. She's too blasted by events, immune to consolation or hope. The chapter ends, "Romance? No romance for Helen. Not now."

But what a difference two weeks made! By then Martin had come back, pleading for a reconciliation, and she had acquired two new suitors. For the four years Andrews wrote her story, she was an independent woman, trying on careers from secretary to undercover agent to nightclub singer to Broadway dress designer; along the way she acquired even more suitors, who tended to marry other women or die young. In 1937 Andrews's successor, the novelist Mary Watkins Reeves, would move Helen to Hollywood, where she became the Edith Head of soapland, and meet her most enduring Romeo, the lawyer Gil Whitney. Their romance lasted nineteen years, until the last writer, Margo Brooks, began to suspect Gil's sexuality. But just to prove that reality had not destroyed the fantasy, she allowed Helen's next suitor, Paul, to propose in 1958, "We can still have a life, Helen. I'm thirty-eight, you're thirty-five." Twenty-five years and she hadn't aged a day.

Between 1932 and 1936 Robert Andrews served as the Hummerts' writer. From minimal notes he dreamed up *Five-Star Jones*, about a crack reporter and his pregnant wife; *Rich Man's Darling*, about the Cinderella mating of a girl reporter and an elderly millionaire; and *Backstage Wife*, the famous tale of Mary Noble, the Iowa stenographer married to

Larry Noble, "dream sweetheart of a million other women." The Hummerts' series were shameless revisions of the characters and themes of late-Victorian fiction. In 1935 Andrews turned the novel and movie *Mrs. Wiggs of the Cabbage Patch* into a soap devoid of Alice Hegan Rice's humor. A year later he began *David Harum,* a sequel to the Will Rogers movie, in which the kindly philosopher talked to his horse for a few episodes before becoming just another Just Plain Bill.

The Hummerts' most successful adaptations would appear in 1937. *Our Gal Sunday* was based on a 1904 play in which a youthful Ethel Barrymore had starred as a Colorado foundling seduced by an English playboy. In the Hummerts' version, the evil Sir Arthur would be succeeded by his brother, Lord Henry Brinthrope; and for twenty-two years, to the folkloric theme of "Red River Valley," Sunday would try to find happiness married to "England's richest and handsomest nobleman," one superlative alone being an insufficient obstacle.

Later that year the Hummerts turned *Stella Dallas* into one of their most successful soap operas. The first episodes were even true to the novel's tone. A pregnant Laurel receives a set of baby clothes in such shockingly bad taste that they could only have come from her mother. It is by such means that the two are reunited. After that, rather than withdrawing from her daughter's life, Stella became more invasive than Molly Goldberg. But the series retained a class bias. For many years she contended with two wealthy enemies, Lolly Baby's mother-in-law, "imperious Louise Grosvenor," and "insane Ada Dexter," who had the fancy that Laurel would marry her son, a dream that continued even after the poor boy died.

This may have been the Hummerts' most inspired device. Their heroes tended to be mindless twits, men clearly unworthy of the heroines who loved them, despite their bouts of irrational jealousy and feckless behavior. So the heroines lived most passionately in what academics call a homosocial world. Suitors came and went, but a heroine's rivals were Best Enemies Forever. Helen Trent endured a good fifteen importunate lovers during the decade when her every step was trailed by her two greatest enemies, Cynthia Swanson and Daisy Parker. Though both women had a case, having seen their men fall for Helen and die, the causes were buried in the past. Just being Helen Trent was sufficient reason for a bad woman to hate her.

Instead these women—like similar harpies on *Our Gal Sunday* and *Young Widder Brown*—lived to torment Helen. They began their days

Mother love and sacrifice: Stella Dallas (Anne Elstner) and her daughter, Laurel "Lolly Baby" Grosvenor (Vivian Smolen), emoting in the 1940s

gossiping about her and plotting her public disgrace, preferably in some daily tabloid's headlines. Since all the actresses had full-bodied contraltos, pitched to the key of an American Garbo or Dietrich, there was a doubtlessly unwitting element of lesbian tension. A Hummert fan always knew that the greatest danger lurked among women; they were the sharpest and the deadliest. The English play *The Killing of Sister George* portrays the events after a beloved character is killed off a radio soap. The confrontations between the soap stars and their simpering young girlfriends was an inspired coda to the tensions exploited so profitably by Frank and Anne Hummert.

Class tensions also darkened the existence of Young Widder Brown, the widowed mother of "two fatherless children," whose seventeen-year romance with Dr. Anthony Loring ended more happily than the saga of Helen Trent and Gil Whitney. But Anthony's sister Victoria thought Ellen was too low-rent for her elegant brother. The serial's first episode underlines Ellen's poverty. Her son Mark wants to join the YMCA, but where can she find the two dollars it will take, especially when her late husband's mother considers her unrefined?

The famous knock against soaps, that nothing ever happened, didn't fit the Hummerts' serials. Reading the daily plot summaries provided by men known as script editors to the so-called dialogue writers (many of whom came up with their own plots, not the hugest challenge), you will find so many incidents that you can only wonder at the ability to tell so much and achieve so little. Usually, after three months, there would be a new storyline with absolutely no connection to the previous one. That somebody had stood trial for murder in September was forgotten in November.

While the shows often featured homespun types, friends and relatives who offered the kind of wisdom city slickers could never acquire, the Hummerts insisted on being formally correct. Our Gal Sunday may have been raised by two miners, but she spoke the Queen's English. Stella Dallas might utter an occasional "ain't," but Anne Elstner, who played her for the series' entire run, had a contralto so emulsified that it seemed little short of Shakespearean (perhaps the reason that Cole Porter loved the show). Whether it was the Hummerts' own upper-class background, or some unwavering commitment to prewar standards, their actors sounded like voices of a very distant past.

It's hard to imagine that in 1939 America, with blues, jazz, and even gospel saturating the networks, you could still hear the Hummerts' *Orphans of Divorce,* in which the leading actress, "the divinely gifted Margaret Anglin," spoke an English almost too refined for Our Gal Sunday. Listening to old Hummert shows allows for a dip in camp's purest streams—those grand nineteenth-century voices reciting hollow 1940s dialogue, always with the utmost seriousness. And then there were the unwittingly hilarious announcements. *Helen Trent* and *Our Gal Sunday* have lived in radio history. But how about *"Amanda of Honeymoon Hill,* laid in a section of America few people know," or *"John's Other Wife,* the story of modern marriage," or, my favorite, *"Second Husband,* starring Helen Menken"?

The Hummerts can also claim credit for putting the opera in soap opera. At precisely the same time that he introduced the early serials, Frank Hummert conceived a series of programs devoted to light opera and semiclassical music. The first and most famous was the deliciously titled *American Album of Familiar Melodies* ("Malodies" in the Bob and Ray version). He brought the same sensibility to daytime radio. His first soaps opened with songs. *Just Plain Bill,* in honor of the Barber's humble background, featured a triple-threat musician who played guitar and harmonica and also whistled "Polly Wolly Doodle." The more upscale

Helen Trent opened with a Sigmund Romberg baritone singing "Just a Little Love, a Little Kiss." (Later the show was accompanied by a singing guitarist, who would hum the plaintive melody of "Juanita," a tune ultimately credited to Handel.) *Stella Dallas* initially began with a quartet of classically trained vocalists precisely enunciating "Memories." Later, an organ played the hymnlike "How Can I Leave You?" For *Young Widder Brown* there was the iconically morbid "In the Gloaming."

Mrs. Hummert specialized in selecting theme songs and leitmotifs that reflected her stories and characters. In so doing she exhibited more wit than the shows ever betrayed. For *Mr. Keen, Tracer of Lost Persons,* she chose Noël Coward's "Someday I'll Find You." For *Mary Noble, Backstage Wife,* "The Rose of Tralee." For backwoods *Amanda of Honeymoon Hill,* "When the Saints Go Marching In." For the very rare comic serial, *Lorenzo Jones,* the story of a hapless inventor, she picked "Funiculì, Funiculà." To highlight the hero's zany character, she selected "I'm Forever Blowing Bubbles." In 1952, the Hummerts turned Lorenzo's story into a melodrama. He became a man suffering from amnesia, who couldn't recognize his beloved wife, Belle. For this turn Mrs. Hummert chose "When I Grow Too Old to Dream (I'll Have You to Remember)." But by then it was an archaic gesture, Victor Herbert in a doo-wop era. Their most ingenuous selection may have been "I'll Take You Home Again, Kathleen" for the homeless *Nona from Nowhere*—though no selection was more comic than the one Bess Flynn chose for *Bachelor's Children:* "Ah, Sweet Mystery of Life (At Last I've Found You)," played on a music box.

Other soap authors chose as carefully. *Hilltop House,* which depicted life in an orphanage, was introduced by Brahms's "Lullaby." *Mary Marlin,* most haunting of the soaps, would be identified with Debussy's "Clair de Lune." Characters in the early soaps would break out in song, particularly Bill the Barber and Eileen Moran, the musical daughter in *Today's Children.* To extend the operatic, the Hummert actors' speech often bordered on sprechstimme and parlando, especially when accompanied by a plangent Hammond organ. Outside of gospel music the Hammond organ achieved its melodramatic fulfillment in those old soaps. For many older listeners the instrument will always evoke the afternoon melodramas of their youth, an association it took years of jazz and soul to live down.

In a typical season the Hummerts gave employment to hundreds of actors as well as a good dozen dialogue writers. Mrs. Hummert claimed that her husband preferred to hire women because their dialogue was less "arch." Actually, the first Hummert writers were all male: Robert Andrews, Julian Funt (who initiated *John's Other Wife* and later became the unchallenged master of soap psychoses), Lawrence Hammond (who initiated *Young Widder Brown*), and John DeWitt (*Our Gal Sunday*). But by the mid-1940s, most of the dialogue writers were women. Helen Walpole would write *Stella Dallas* for fourteen years, the same span for which Jean Carroll wrote *Our Gal Sunday*. The Hummerts didn't pay top dollar, but their employees liked them. They cooperated with the unions, and made sure that their better writers handled two or three shows at a time.

They were also politically honorable. During the 1950s, when the blacklist ravaged daytime radio (Julian Funt lost his job writing *Young Doctor Malone* because one of his plays had starred Uta Hagen—and that play flopped!), the Hummerts ignored the boycott. Anne Elstner, a zealous anticommunist, used to shout down the lefties, but Anne Hummert saw to it that they kept their jobs. This could have been predicted, for during World War II the Hummerts had been downright radical in their promotion of Roosevelt's policies. For example, Our Gal Sunday helped exonerate a French émigré who had killed her Nazi husband. Stella Dallas's ex-husband's second wife, Helen, suspected adultery; so, in an amazing revision of *Lysistrata,* Stella took her female co-workers in the factory that Stephen owned (forget the issues of nepotism) on strike, in which they threatened to withhold their conjugal affections until their demands were met.

Black characters usually figured in menial roles. In Robert Andrews's very successful *Betty and Bob* (1932), the story of a secretary who marries her wealthy boss, Nancy Reagan's mother, Edith Davis, played both the nasty mother-in-law and the "colored girl," charmingly named Gardenia. Even the famously sophisticated Elaine Sterne Carrington teamed Joan Davis, the heroine of *When a Girl Marries,* with a devoted maid, Lily, whose overbearing tributes to "Miss Joan honey" will shock a modern listener. But during the war years the Hummerts insisted on presenting their black characters as model soldiers and citizens. If their parents talked a quaint dialect, the children spoke like Stella's Laurel or Our Gal Sunday.

Best of all, in 1942, when Sunday went into labor, it was her friend Susie Robinson who attended her. A few years after Butterfly McQueen and Miz Scarlet, the Hummerts presented a black woman expert in birthing babies.

Let's go back to 1930, when Irna Phillips explored the road not taken by the Hummerts, thereby becoming the most significant and controversial figure in soap history. Henry Selinger had decided that ethnic comedy/drama could be transferred to the daytime. He created a serial about an Irish widow, Mother Moynihan, her daughter, and a female boarder. Prophetically he called it *Painted Dreams,* a title he drew from a surrealist manifesto. From *Painted Dreams* stem the many abstract titles that manage to be both ominous and pointless: *Today's Children, This Day Is Ours, Brave Tomorrow, Thanks for Tomorrow, Right to Happiness, The Road of Life, Against the Storm, Follow the Moon, Thunder Over Paradise, This Life Is Mine,* and the oxymoronic *Bachelor's Children* (suggested by a folk idiom about the importance of mothers; the series initially told about a bachelor who receives guardianship of an army buddy's daughters, one of whom he later marries).

Irna Phillips, mid-1940s. The daytime serial's unwed mother helped domesticate Freud for the masses.

To play the roles he hired two Chicago theatrical wannabes, Irene Wicker and Erna Phillips (who doubled as the matriarch and her tenant), both of them approaching thirty, both gifted with great faces for radio and versatile voices. After a numerologist advised them to change the spelling of their names, Ireene Wicker and Irna Phillips acquired a renewed confidence. Ireene became known as "the lady with a thousand voices," and Irna billed herself as "the female Amos 'n' Andy." In her case that meant blackface once removed: a Jewish girl with strong Semitic features (a Margaret Hamilton of the shtetl) who specialized in Irish roles, although she admitted that her sisters thought she sounded Hungarian.

According to Les White, a writer and psychologist who has thoroughly examined her secretive career, Irna spent a joyless youth. She was the daughter of an East European Jewish father, a former street peddler, and a German Jewish mother who recited passages from Goethe and Heine. The father died young, and the mother, a caustic, "stoic" woman, having already given birth to nine children, four of whom had died, didn't have much affection to spare her tenth. In her unpublished memoir Irna's self-hatred and alienation are transparent. She liked her brothers, was forever at war with her sisters, admitted to thinking she was an interloper in the Phillips family. School was no better. She had no friends, and was never asked to join anything. In her own words, she was a "colorless wallflower," "an ugly duckling."

College was only marginally better. She had dreams of becoming an actress, and wisecracked herself into a Jewish sorority. But rejection and humiliation continued to be her lot. Her teachers said she had the talent but not the looks; a married doctor abandoned her, according to White, "pregnant and with syphilis, a botched back-alley abortion rendered her sterile." Her sisters and sisters-in-law exhibited no sympathy, treating her like a fallen woman. She buried herself in courses in education and psychology and determined that "sublimation" would be her fate.

After a few years of teaching, she became friendly with the homely but vivacious Ireene and her husband, a handsome writer named Walter Wicker. In 1930 Ireene dreamed up *Judy and Jane,* which she alternated writing, first with Irna, then with Walter. In 1932, after the radio station WGN refused to grant Irna ownership of *Painted Dreams,* which in fact she had not created, she conceived her first serial, *Today's Children,* in which she now played Mother Moran and her boarder, Kay Norton, while Ireene played Eileen Moran, the singing daughter, and Walter played Kay's suitor, Bill Crane, while sharing the writing credit with Irna. Perhaps in honor of Henry Selinger, the classical violinist, Irna selected as a theme song "Tales from the Vienna Woods."

She told the press that she and Wicker divided the insights of their respective sexes. It is hard to determine his contribution, possibly excepting some melodramatic sequences involving Ma Moran's son Terry's forays into local politics. But the Irnaisms were noteworthy. During her first months in radio she had been presented as an elecutionist, reading in lilting tones from Shakespeare and Byron. She also broadcast *Thought for a Day,* a series of familiar quotations and dime-store philosophy. Both prepared her for the serials to come. Ma Moran was the block philosopher, and General Mills, the show's sponsor, regularly offered transcripts of her golden rules. Irna liked being didactic, an echo of the not unhappy years she had spent teaching. In her best-known creation, *The Guiding Light,* a nondenominational minister, Dr. John Ruthledge, spread his sententious wisdom throughout the community. For years he debated the cynical Ellis Smith, nicknamed Mr. Nobody from Nowhere, who expected the worst in humanity while Dr. Ruthledge acknowledged only the best.

But the real Irna Phillips drew from her varied and emphatic neuroses. Not only did she play Ma Moran, the mother of today's children, she also played Kay Norton, who spent years trying to track down her real mother, and who often lamented that having already been rejected by her parents, she would never earn a man's love. During those years Irna was still living at home, supposedly sleeping in the same bed as her mother, while carrying on with numerous men, including her pal Ireene's husband, Walter. This situation might have contributed to the show's ambivalence about working women. Ma Moran's other daughter, Fran, dreamed of a life as an artist, encouraged by Bertha Manners, a feminist and careerist who disdained romance and had no time for her own mother. In a highly dramatic sequence, Bertha's mother died, and she nearly lost her mind. Fran, terrified about her own mom, rushed home to find the gray-haired madonna faithfully seated by the fire. Irna had figured out how to capitalize on a daughter's ambivalence.

And that was only the start. Her serials would involve less action than, say, the Hummerts'. But the psychological complexity was unprecedented. In 1937 *The Guiding Light* introduced Dr. Ruthledge; his daughter, Mary; and his ward, Ned Holden, another character haunted by his obscure origins. He would discover his parents only after his mother had killed his father in order to prevent his learning that they were both ex-convicts. Ned proceeded to leave town and return married to a déclassé nightclub singer (who, years later, would marry Mr. Nobody from Nowhere, now revealed as the heir to the town's biggest fortune). Meanwhile, Irna came close to outing herself in the character of Rose Kransky, a Jewish girl with a lovable widowed mother. Rose had an adulterous affair with a married man, gave the child a name by mock-marrying Mr. Nobody from Nowhere, then lost the child in an accident, upon which she became the governess of the children of a Jewish couple.

The wife was insane, which didn't stop Rose from falling in love with the husband. Subtitling the serial "My Baby and I," Irna began to focus on Claire Marshall, who adopts a small boy, and then unwittingly marries his father. Phillips herself had adopted a baby boy in 1941 and a girl two years later. Eventually Claire would adopt a girl, too. When a *Variety* critic wrote that this storyline was preposterous, Irna replied, "I am a proud spinster who adopted two children in their infancy and there is nothing dubious about such a setup."

A few months after introducing *The Guiding Light* Irna conceived *The Road of Life*, one of the first serials to focus on hospital life. To a tune from Tchaikovsky's *Pathétique* Symphony (pathos announcing bathos) the announcer would blast, "Surgery Calling Dr. Brent." The story dealt with the medical adventures of Dr. Jim Brent and his romance and later marriage to Carol Evans. She initially married Jim's best friend, but that was tame Irna. The real Phillips emerged in 1938 when in a blaze of sibling rivalry Jim's brother shot him in the hand, rendering him at least occupationally impotent. He wound up recuperating on a farm, where he befriended a widow and her small son, Butch. Somehow Butch would do what Irna may have dreamed of, killing his mother, albeit accidentally, and standing trial for matricide.

Meanwhile, Jim's professional nemesis, Dr. Reginald Parsons, had ruined the life of his best friend, a nurse named Helen Gowan. They married and divorced, just before Parsons kidnapped their baby son and left him with his friends the Stephensons. As folks did in Irna's soaps, Helen eventually married Mr. Stephenson and lived happily until he died and the boy refused to acknowledge her. The miserable Helen conducted long, bitter conversations with Dr. Brent, recapitulating the philosophical debates between Dr. Ruthledge and Ellis Smith. "We are flies in the hands of the gods!" she would cry, an unusually agnostic note from Irna, who professed herself the strongest defender of all social institutions. Sounding like an eighteenth-century Man of Feeling, Dr. Brent tried to console her.

In her memoir Irna says she always saw herself as the scribe of unwed motherhood. She had never been ashamed of illegitimacy, and regretted that she punished some of her heroines by killing off their children, or marrying them to the men who had initially betrayed them. "I lacked the courage of my convictions," she says. Indeed, she was so committed to the notion that she misremembered Helen Gowan as an unwed mother, mistaking her baffled intention for the creative deed.

Irna's mother died, and claiming that she'd lost the inspiration for

Mother Moran, Irna replaced *Today's Children* with *Woman in White*. Karen Adams, the eponymous heroine, was a nurse, with two siblings, a student nurse named Betty and a writer named John. Betty's boyfriends kept falling for Karen, a kind of sibling rivalry that would become an Irna specialty. But familial disloyalty reached its peak when Karen married Dr. Kirk Harding at the same time that John married Kirk's receptionist, Janet Munson. Janet had Kirk's baby but said it was John's. This would become the hoariest of soap clichés, but it appeared first in this 1940 serial. Ultimately, Janet would redeem herself by saving her son's life in an epidemic, and die after acquiring his infection. (A similar act of sacrifice killed off Rose Kransky's rival in *The Guiding Light*.)

For ultimate morbidity, Irna outdid herself with the 1939 creation *Right to Happiness*. Originally the series' focus was to have been on Rose Kransky, her mother, and her brother. But within a day it had switched to Rose's boss, Doris Cameron. Doris's husband was dying in another state while she was pursuing an (apparently sexless) affair with Bill Walker and trying to raise her headstrong daughter, Carolyn. Somehow the teenage Carolyn and Bill met and fell in love. By now Mr. Cameron had died, and Doris presumed that she and Bill would marry. Upon learning that she had stolen her mother's lover, Carolyn attempted suicide. In order to save her daughter's life Doris became Stella Dallas and pretended that she and Bill had not been intimate. Bill and Carolyn married. The focus shifted now to Doris's niece Louise, the daughter of a cursed marriage which ended when her father killed both her mother and himself. (Irna's parents were usually not the best advertisement for marriage.) All this within three months!

By the end of the year Louise had become engaged to Lyle, a man she didn't love but presumed to be dying. Just when she fell in love with someone healthy, the patient recovered. Meanwhile, Carolyn had fallen in love with Dwight, a younger man and one of Bill's employees. Revealing a vindictive streak (she was known to dispatch characters over the perceived slights of her actors), Irna killed off Lyle. Fate remained the boss, even as the boss determined her actors' fate.

A year later Carolyn had divorced Bill and married Dwight, who proceeded to leave her after Bill revealed her betrayal of her mother and then join the army. Half-mad, Carolyn threatened Bill with a gun. In the ensuing struggle he was killed, and Carolyn stood trial for his murder. During this period she gave birth in prison. After a four-month trial, she was found innocent, only to face a custody battle with Dwight's parents.

She won the case a few days before learning that Dwight had been killed in battle.

Irna was at the top of her profession. By 1942 a production house she ran with Carl Wester was turning out five serials, four of them ranking within the Nielsen Top Ten. But she had a knack for extracting defeat from the jaws of victory. Academic critics, led by the émigrés Theodor Adorno and Herta Herzfeld, had begun analyzing daytime serials as banal and intrinsically corrupt. In 1942 Dr. Louis I. Berg, who would later become famous for his attacks on comic strips, took on daytime radio, and found Irna's *Woman in White* and *Right to Happiness* the worst of the bunch. Listening to them filled him with anxiety and despair; he could only imagine their dire impact on all those women listening at home. The year ended with Procter & Gamble canceling *Woman in White* and Irna selling them *Right to Happiness.*

Her successor, John M. Young, had begun his soap career ghost-writing *Woman in White.* And though he ran *Right to Happiness* until it died in 1960, he always felt overshadowed by his predecessor. His storylines simply lacked her oomph. In 1947 he turned for assistance to Max Wylie, a versatile writer whose work ranged from literary adaptations to juicing up failing soaps. Wylie wrote Young, "Johnny, we're going to outdo Irna." In one storyline Carolyn's latest suitor, a lawyer named Miles Nelson, defended a woman accused of murdering her husband, only to learn that she was . . . but you all know the drill.

The attacks distressed Irna. She felt that her critics were impatient and inattentive; they didn't stay with her, and thereby missed all the subtleties that soap fans lived for. She also resented the government's demand that she dramatize wartime situations. The domestic life still counted, she insisted, so you men leave me space to tell my kind of stories. Whether out of obstinacy or a kind of literary daring, she dreamed up a new soap called *Lonely Women* and quickly retitled it *Today's Children.* The core family, the Schultzes, was German-American, a startling choice for a Jewish author in 1942. When questioned Irna replied that most German Americans were fine patriots. True perhaps, but she confounded expectations when she had Bertha Schultz fall in love with Keith Armour, an honorable (if misguided) Nazi pilot. Bertha married Keith secretly, annulled the marriage when she learned of his Nazi sympathies, moved out of state to have her baby (as Irna had done when she was pregnant), and subsequently miscarried. She later would fall in love with an army veteran who had masqueraded as her long-lost brother: all the titillations of incest without the actual deed.

What the critics should have seen was that Irna was the most emphatically Freudian writer in popular culture. Despite the ministers of *The Guiding Light,* her view was more fatalistic than pious—she admitted to believing in nothing and, while remaining a famous hypochondriac, considered death a mere detail, refusing to attend the funerals of her siblings. Her characters specialized in long monologues, though they never reached the otherworldly heights Jane Crusinberry achieved in her stunningly surreal *Mary Marlin.* But Irna thrived on the analytic perspective. In 1942 she introduced a character known simply as The Past, who showed up on several shows as a grudging reminder that Carolyn or Bertha was not being fully honest with herself. "I know all this because I am The Past": a line that usually announced a short solo on the Hammond organ, a breathing place for the heroines and the listeners to meditate on truth and lies.

A year later, the Schultz family began to encounter a quizzical character named Doubt, though whether Doubt and The Past ever ambushed anyone together is uncertain. In 1944 Irna revived *Woman in White,* but in a peremptory gesture she killed off Karen Adams and refocused the series on her protégée Eileen Holmes. Eileen's nursing supervisor, Helen Bradley, was an ambiguous figure, waxing either too warm or too cold. It would take all of four years for Eileen to learn what everyone else knew, and you did too: that Helen was her mother. The series also teamed Irna with perhaps her most skilled ghost writer, Herb Futran, who took the series over in 1947 and would later ghost-write *The Guiding Light* in its ripest years.

Futran toyed with Irna's sententious manner, her need to emphasize and reiterate, and found a grammatical correlative. His dialogue prefigures Samuel Beckett's, another writer whose characters and language remain vexed by doubt and the past. Thus, in 1947, Eileen informs Helen that she is about to have a baby. Her mother thinks (of course to herself), "A baby. Eileen, my daughter. My daughter Eileen. Can I tell her? My daughter Eileen. Tell her that I am her mother? Her mother, but can I tell her? Tell her now that she is going to become a mother? My daughter—tell her? Can I tell her?" Keep on like this, and you could drag a storyline out well past its shelf life.

Irna's monologues, especially when scripted by Herb Futran, became the aural equivalent of close-ups. In later years, when she reigned as the queen of daytime television, her serials, like *As the World Turns,* were dismissed as diffuse and old-fashioned; by then out-of-wedlock children were a dime a dozen. But her emphasis on pregnant stares and troubled pauses created a distinctive soap rhythm, yielding a deep sense of intimacy; for those enthralled, the characters became living presences. It was the method, the Irna Phillips rhythm, that hypnotized. It couldn't have been the banal dialogue—unless the very repetitions guaranteed the realism. She always understood that halting exposition reflected a psyche in crisis.

By 1946 Irna once again supervised four serials, still co-produced with Carl Wester. She even moved to Hollywood, along with her two adopted children, and began to imagine a career in movies. But after an NBC employee named Emmons Carlson proved in court that he had helped create *The Guiding Light,* Irna was forced to pay him a fortune and end the series. Wester—a figure even more right-wing than Irna (she simply deplored unions, unlike most of the other important soap authors, many of whom became leading figures in the Radio Writers Guild) and so conservative that he ran Douglas MacArthur's 1944 campaign for president (given the times, a most reactionary gesture)—ended their business relations. By mid-1947 she had lost all her shows.

Then a Procter & Gamble executive purchased a new series, also called *The Guiding Light* but with a new locale and cast of characters, excepting the single mother Claire and her second husband, Dr. McNeil, both of whom would disappear within months. The series began with an "Episode One"—therefore the television series that expired in 2009 was "only" sixty-two, not seventy-two, years old. For the first time, Irna announced herself. The series now began, "Duz presents *The Guiding Light,* created by Irna Phillips." Take that, Emmons and Carl—this is *my Guiding Light.*

The early days of the series amped up the morbidity that had darkened the first months of *Right to Happiness.* Ray Brandon, a new character also nicknamed Mr. Nobody from Nowhere, was released from prison after serving a bum rap and losing his wife, Julie, who had divorced him, remarried, and was now the mother of two children. Naturally their son would fall in love with the daughter of the man who had framed Ray. But Irna saved her worst punishment for Julie. In a terrible car crash Julie lost both her children, and her husband became a hopeless cripple.

He would die in due time, and Ray would have to defend his ex-wife in a murder trial; the series never made her innocence clear.

With a cavalier neglect of her original scheme, Irna eventually dropped Ray and his new wife, Charlotte, and focused her attention on another German-American family, the Bauers. She may have meant to convey a Jewish element, since her mother's maiden name had been Buxbaum, and the role of Papa Bauer would be played for years by an Austrian Jewish refugee, Theo Goetz. In *Lonely Women* Bertha's sister Maggie had masqueraded as Marilyn Larimore. Similarly Meta Bauer called herself Jan Carter, and had an affair with a rich man, Ted White, who dropped her upon discovering that she was not his kind of WASP.

In rapid order Meta became pregnant and had a baby adopted by Ray and Charlotte Brandon, and Ted returned, offering marriage if their son, Chuckie, was included in the package. Meta's dying mother begged Ray to defend her daughter, even though it meant giving back the son he had grown to love. But Ted turned out to be a brutish father. Within six months Chuckie had grown five years. Ted thought the boy was unmanly and sent him to boxing camp, where he would die in the ring. Mad with grief, Meta killed Ted, stood trial for murder, and was acquitted thanks to the detective work of reporter Joe Roberts, whom she subsequently married. Joe's daughter, Kathy, opposed the marriage, left home, married Bob Lang, who was killed, then married Dick Grant, had Bob's baby, a girl named Robin, said it was Dick's . . . Perhaps the only important addendum is that Irna would eventually kill off both Kathy and, some years later, Robin.

In retrospect Irna Phillips conceived and mastered a form in which the most baroque stresses of psychological conflict became routine. The self was battered by dangers external and internal. Anybody, particularly a relative, could be not what she claimed, could be a threat to your home and your safety. But you couldn't depend very much on yourself. Irna liked her characters ambiguous and ambivalent, the better for doubt and the past to gobble them up. Her career ended ingloriously after she had returned to her most famous television series, *As the World Turns*. She was fired in 1972, kicked out probably with glee after the many years of Napoleonic bullying. But she went out with some punch. In her last, perhaps most bizarre, storyline, one of the series' ingenues, Amanda Holmes, found herself threatened by an older woman who had fallen for her boyfriend. Events reached a point where she was forced to kill her rival in self-defense, only to learn that, yes, inevitably, her rival, her enemy, her victim, was her mother. Irna may have found herself impersonating both Ma Moran and Kay as she murdered their granddaughters.

Or, as her memoir suggests, the matricide may have been even more perverse. Irna admits that her adopted children came to hate her. Though she had adopted them, they had never adopted her. In the most passionate sections of her book she says that there is no worse fate than that of the single, adoptive mother. She had made a terrible decision, nearly ruining three lives, theirs and her own. One time she had overheard her daughter, Katherine, say that if she ever met her real mother—the mother who had abandoned her to being Irna Phillips's daughter—she would kill her. So, in having Amanda kill her mother, Irna was punishing Katherine's mother, and, inevitably, herself. She was assuredly no Shakespeare, but these were the actions of a female Lear.

Irna often threatened to write her memoir and title it, shades of James Brown, *It's a Man's World and It Ought to Be.* In the early 1940s, she told reporters that "I'd give it all up if the right man came around." Instead, as a woman fated to be forever alone, she called it *All My Worlds.* Having no religious feelings, she let her two children be baptized in the faiths of their real parents. Most of her close friends remained Jewish, and she claims that only in her later years did she experience anti-Semitism. Forgetting completely about Molly Goldberg, she boasted that the Kranskys were the first Jews on daytime radio. Her many enemies, adopting her Yiddishisms, called her a kvetch and a yente, and that was when they were kind. But outside of Sigmund Freud or Philip Roth, has anyone else grown so famous (much less rich) off the meshugas of a Jewish family?

During her fat years, this tiny woman got her kicks bullying the men from the networks and the agencies. When they accused her characters of immorality, she grew livid, the unwed mother defending herself. In the 1945 season of *Woman in White,* she conceived Martha Hanley, a spinster aunt who had raised her widowed brother-in-law's children and now became pathologically jealous of his new wife, Helen (who happened to have a secret child of her own). "I want to steal your happiness," Martha told Helen. Implausible, hollered the agency. "Now you're really going to get it," said Irna, explaining that in midlife, the sense of chances lost could drive the gentlest of persons mad.

While the official line is that she celebrated the great American family, she thrived by displaying its fractures. After all, hers was the proud perspective of someone who didn't fit anywhere, the stray whom nobody loved. In her last years, after a near-fatal heart attack, she grew so depressed that she entered analysis. Her unfinished memoir shows her at the verge of realizing just how anomalous, if not subversive, was her personal slant.

None of this bespeaks feminism; she was too much a loner to affiliate with any group. Nor did she see herself as an artist. Part psychologist, part dialogue writer, part mechanic was her own assessment. Whatever art there was resided in her uncanny timing. She boasted that one plot sequence in *As the World Turns* took about twenty years to work itself out. (Of course it involved an illegitimate child discovering his real mother.) In her vision, the daytime serial became the dramatic equivalent of a five-day-a-week psychoanalysis, marked by the same meandering small talk and the same world-shattering epiphanies. She had effectively trained her audience to view life as a daytime serial. Has any woman asserted herself to that extent, and won?

—

Irna and the Hummerts were the most successful soap practitioners. But others fared almost as well. The best-known promoted themselves as writers first, not originators or "plottists"; they tended to be more intellectual and nursed highbrow dreams, seeing themselves as moral educators, echoing Thomas Mann's claim "I have shown them how to live." Elaine Sterne Carrington, a popular magazine writer, specialized in dramas about middle-class life. *Pepper Young's Family,* her biggest hit, ran for twenty-three years, thus making her the writer with the longest pedigree (followed by Irving Vendig's twenty years with *Judy and Jane,* John M. Young's eighteen with *Right to Happiness,* and Orin Tovrov's seventeen with *Ma Perkins*). The Young family included the parents, Sam and Mary; their children, Pepper and Peggy; and their children's mates, along with family friends and . . . notably, employees. Their maid, Hattie, and Mr. Young's secretary, Sadie, achieved the status of second-line heroines. Mrs. Carrington moved in sophisticated circles, spending much of her time in Bridgehampton, Long Island. But though she was considered the class act in daytime—and was a beloved member of the Radio Writers Guild, where she was known as "the Member in Mink"—her serials were melodramatic in the extreme. Particularly *When a Girl Marries* ("a story of young married life, dedicated to everyone who has ever been in love"), which was actually written by a Broadway playwright and actor named LeRoy Bailey. Its heroine, Joan Davis, was married to a lawyer, Harry Davis, who kept falling for secretaries named Betty. When the first one died, after saving the life of the Davises' young son, he hired her cousin, also named Betty. And so, for half the serial's run, Joan fought off the Betties. After that, Harry's only option was to wander off, a victim of amnesia. Mrs. Carrington's third soap, *Rosemary* (which originally opened with the promise that "Rosemary is every woman; Rosemary is *you*"), cut to the chase. The heroine spent years loving and then marrying a man suffering from amnesia. Naturally, he turned out to have been previously married.

Other women had their specialties. Addy Richton and her life partner, Lynne Stone, were considered experts in child rearing. A very bright woman, who eventually became a psychologist, Richton dismissed the incidental melodrama in *Hilltop House* or *This Life Is Mine* (in an interview she even forgot that she had killed off some of her heroes) by saying that "I only wanted to help women raise their children." Gertrude Berg played Molly Goldberg so well that the melodrama, never very pronounced, tended to seem incidental; the show's point was Molly's loving malapropisms. Her finest hour may have been when she domesticated the Nazi threat by having a stone thrown through an open window while the Goldbergs were celebrating Passover.

Myrtle Vail, a failed vaudevillian, wrote and starred in *Myrt and Marge,* the story of two chorus girls. Marge was played by her daughter, Donna Damerel. Vail was enough of a trouper to keep the story going after Damerel died in childbirth. Her serial originally ran in the evening opposite *Amos 'n' Andy* and could be seen as its womanly alternative. The show was filled with local color, shot through with campy elements. Gay men became some of its biggest fans; Truman Capote used to call his literary pals "Myrt." And just as other soaps offered broad caricatures of blacks, Jews, and the Irish, *Myrt and Marge* had radio's first gay character, a stereotypical queen named Clarence K. Tiffingtuffer (who pronounced his name with a studied lisp). This caused enough of a sensation for the actor Ray Hedge to declare in a fan magazine, "I Am Not a Lavender Boy" (though his obituary in the 1990s would refer to a male companion).

The supreme anti-Irna, her greatest rival, was Jane Crusinberry. A former singer and musician who had lived in Europe, she had little experience as a writer, and none in radio. But during the Depression, a job was a job, and hers would be creating *The Story of Mary Marlin*. The serial began in Chicago, featuring many of the same actors employed by Irna and the Hummerts, in 1935. But its quality was immediately apparent, and by 1936 its ratings were higher than *Today's Children*'s or *Just Plain Bill*'s.

Originally it told of a small-town housewife married to an ambitious lawyer, Joe Marlin, who had just gotten his secretary pregnant. While introducing a townsful of oddball characters—patently Dickensian figures, including a local scribe, Jonathan, who commented on the action as if he were imagining it—Crusinberry also began trafficking in moral and psychic exotica. Mary, briefly separated from her husband, started flirting with industrialists and explorers. This allowed Crusinberry to introduce folkloric legends, exposing Mary Marlin to mind-sets ages and cultures removed from the Cedar Springs, Iowa, of 1935.

Mary reconciled with Joe, bore him a son, and joined him in Washington after he was elected to the Senate. This was a bolder move than Our Gal Sunday's marriage into British royalty. And Mary didn't remain just a senator's wife. Joe's plane was shot down somewhere over China, and he went missing for six years, a victim of amnesia. During this time Mary took his place, becoming Senator Mary Marlin and, after flirting with President Rufus Kane (a former labor leader), nearly became the First Lady.

Crusinberry made high drama out of Washington politics, even though the ad agencies warned her against any serious critique, most particularly anything smacking of racial conflict. She did not patronize her public. Where Irna Phillips's padres quoted from the Bible and Edgar Guest, Mary Marlin quoted Rilke and Walt Whitman. Crusinberry was brilliant at evoking an oneiric state, suggested by the show's theme music, "Clair de lune." Mary would dream of Joe; Joe would dream of some unknown woman summoning him across the Continental Divide.

But Crusinberry's unique trait was, in a word, spiritualism. As a girl she had played piano during seances, and her imagination was charged with otherworldly elements. Thus, President Kane's mother held long dialogues with her dead husband, as did Joe Marlin's Chinese guide with the late missionary who had taught him English. A French maid would chat with Marie Antoinette. Birds talked to dogs. Indeed, when Axel Gruenberg, the show's director, queried the author about one such dialogue, she replied that she had just visited Grant Park and the birds had given her their word. She thought nothing of depositing Joe Marlin in some polar clime, due north of the Gates of Heaven. Every storyline, even battle scenes during World War II, alluded to something surreal or supernatural. Where Irna Phillips might be accused of a pop-gospel Freudianism, Jane Crusinberry was baldly Jungian.

She was a strict boss, advising her sponsor that not a word of her script could be changed, "because only I know how the story will develop." Even so, she took vacations when ghost writers assumed her place. Not that she relinquished any ownership: the announcement "written by Jane Crusinberry" changed during the summer into the even grander "by Jane Crusinberry," as if her spirit ruled even in her hand's absence. Among her protégées was Sandra Michael, a young Danish-American who had briefly worked for Irna Phillips. In 1939 Michael created *Against the Storm*, the most literate and politically outspoken serial yet imagined. (The combination of left-wing perspective and serial hijinks was curiously similar to what Garry Trudeau would achieve with *Doonesbury*.)

Though the show included sequences that read like superior Irna Phillips, Michael was more interested in current events. For over a year she shifted focus between the American characters and Europeans fighting against Hitler. There were no surrealistic ploys; the conflict played as realistically as in the best of nighttime radio. In 1942 *Against the Storm* became the only radio soap to win a Peabody Award. Irna was appalled; this was not her vision of the daytime serial. But the more graphic Michael's scripts, the lower the ratings. By the end of 1942 the show was canceled, and Irna was frankly delighted.

Sandra and her brother Peter Michael did write two more superior dramas, *Lone Journey* and *The Open Door*. But their literate dialogue and sophisticated politics sailed above their audience's heads. On one episode of *The Open Door*, Sandra Michael deplored the positions of a then-famous right-wing author named Rupert Hughes. It figures that, four years later, Irna's former partner Carl Wester would produce a new soap, *The Story of Holly Sloan*, based on one of Hughes's novels. (About that time, having won the rights to *Today's Children* from Irna, he replaced her with a Catholic propagandist and changed the theme song to "The Lord's Prayer.") In 1946, Sandra and Peter had a character in *Lone Journey* observe, "Negro blood is just the same as ours." This was remarkably daring for its day, and, of course, it was stricken from the script. Sandra told the *Afro-American*, "My brother and I have gotten beat about the head so many times, we're used to it." Two years later the serial was canceled. In 1949, *Against the Storm* returned to the air for a few months. This time the Michaels made soap opera out of McCarthyism: the serial's hero, a college professor, was fighting against a premature retirement being forced on him because of his fervent support of academic freedom. Very high stuff indeed, and the ratings were worse than in 1942.

Sandra was defeated, but Crusinberry remained to challenge Irna's authority. *Mary Marlin* began to suffer in the ratings. Perhaps the public was tired of waiting for Joe Marlin's return; more likely the show suffered from being moved from NBC, where it ran at 3 p.m., to CBS, where it ran at the same time and had to compete with *Life Can Be Beautiful.* During the mid-1940s, Irna's quartet of soaps was scheduled at an unfortunate hour, from 2 to 3 p.m., and forced to run against competing soaps. The ratings were respectable but nothing like her earlier days, when she'd enjoyed the best hours, right after lunch time, and gone up against low-rated competition.

Somehow Irna became an adviser to the agency producing Crusinberry's creation. She proposed that Mary Marlin stop being a world traveler and political animal. "Let's go back to the plain Mary Marlin—the plain, average, everyday woman in a small town who loves her husband—a story that in many ways served as a mirror for a daytime audience in which their own lives were reflected . . . Money, position, prestige should be out the window. The only security, the only reality, a family unit." But Mary Marlin had never been "plain" or "average," and there was no back then when her life was "everyday."

Within months the show was canceled, and the weird splendor of *Mary Marlin* wouldn't recur until David Lynch's *Twin Peaks* or the wilder HBO serials of the 1990s. The show lasted long enough to commemorate the death of Franklin Delano Roosevelt in 1945. CBS informed Mrs. Crusinberry that the actress Joan Blaine had read "When Lilacs Last in the Door-yard Bloom'd" brilliantly even as Mary Marlin drifted into the inaudible ether. Crusinberry's big, bold vision of soap opera ended on that patronizing note.

—

After Jane Crusinberry quit the field, Irna had one more decade of radio left. *The Guiding Light* ended its radio run in mid-1956; for another six months she plotted *Young Doctor Malone.* After she left, the dialogue writer David Lesan became the show runner. But he remained spellbound by her narrative panache and would end his days writing dialogue for her TV soaps. Irna's rivals included Mona Kent, another midwesterner who had begun her career as an actress, and who shared Carl Wester's right-wing politics. (Many years later she would become Jack Kerouac's landlady and cosset his final, reactionary years.)

But her dialogue was more sprightly than Irna's, particularly in her most famous serial, *Portia Faces Life*, the story of a lady lawyer, "dedicated to all the brave women of America." Kent's most daring ploy occurred in 1944, when Portia's husband returned from the army. Actually he was a Nazi in disguise, an "imposter"—a word and concept so alarming that at least one young listener warned her mother that "Daddy isn't Daddy. He's an . . . imposter." Just to prove that women weren't uniquely imperceptive, five years later, in *Road of Life*, Dr. Jim Brent didn't recognize that his wife, Carol, was another imposter. (In 1951 Mona Kent wrote the scripts of a revived *Mary Marlin*. This time Mary's rival for Joe's affections was a Eurasian Communist. But the series didn't last long, Mona Kent being no better a Jane Crusinberry than Irna Phillips had been.)

Irna's main competition came from male writers, men who specialized in their own kinds of baroque storytelling, but with more wit and sensibility. Charles Gussman, a former sportswriter, found himself writing two of Irna's creations, *Right to Happiness* and *Road of Life*, and outdoing her many audacities. "She accused me of stealing storylines that she had planned to use. I told her that I didn't need any help."

Bored by the colorless Dr. Brent, he gave pride of place to Sybil Overton, a "bitch-goddess" (his words), who was alternately Jim's friend, would-be lover, patient, and nemesis, but always the most interesting character study in daytime radio. Gussman had once worked as a dialogue writer for Anne Hummert. Though he disrespected her storylines, he applauded her behavior during the red scare. He too would hire blacklisted actors and ghost writers. So while he considered Irna the bane of his days (likening her to Ilse Koch!), he refused to condemn Mrs. Hummert. He was generally considered the most imaginative soap writer. Thomas Mann was his idol; *The Magic Mountain*, his "dream book"—some actors even nicknamed him "Hans Castorp." For a few years Gussman matched Irna's success as a TV scribe. But his heart wasn't in it. In 1963 he lost hope after coming up with the title *Days of Our Lives*. "It didn't mean anything . . . and the bosses loved it."

A more successful career in television was enjoyed by Irving Vendig, who had spent two decades writing *Judy and Jane,* the serial devised by Irna and the Wickers. His breakthrough moment was the creation of a monstrous, unnatural mother, Jane's daughter-in-law Pam. Her type would recur throughout his years writing *Search for Tomorrow* and *The Edge of Night.* His heroines were almost as contrary as Irna's, while he could spin romance into murder mystery, a knack he had acquired writing the radio version of *Perry Mason.*

Irna had mastered one kind of soap. But there were realms of psychological complexity she had not explored, particularly those dealing with male sexuality. After Jane Crusinberry, her most interesting rivals would be men who introduced a frankly gay, or at least gay-friendly, sensibility. Julian Funt, who began his career as a journalist writing about Sigmund Freud, had long specialized in medical soaps. A month after Irna created the young doctors of *Road of Life,* Funt (and Himan Brown) created *Joyce Jordan, Girl Intern,* who would ultimately graduate into *Joyce Jordan, M. D.* But Funt's greatest hit was *Big Sister,* a series that had specialized in morbid sexual titillation long before he assumed control in 1940. In 1937 nurse Ruth Evans finds herself in love with Dr. John Wayne, a man with an insane wife, Norma. In an unwittingly hilarious sequence, Norma has the couple kidnapped and forces them to strip to their underclothes, thereby making them appear adulterers caught in the act. But the two are so true blue and humorless that only the low-minded are fooled.

By 1940 Ruth and John had finally wed. Funt imagined a new set of predicaments, sending John off to war, where he was lost in action, allowing Ruth to begin a sexless affair with another doctor, Reed Bannister. John returned from the war, devastated into professional, and presumably marital, impotence by the prospect of his handsome and gifted rival. Funt had begun writing plays about tormented gay men, melodramas that combined analytic jargon with the cadences of soap opera. Critics like Philip Wylie (Max Wylie's brother) and James Thurber were perplexed by Dr. John Wayne's weaknesses. As they saw it, Ruth had effectively castrated him. He became the model of all the men oppressed by their women. This was glib at best, and more likely, at least in Wylie's case, misogynistic. A man beholden to his wife's good graces had to be pussy-whipped. The soap operas were really about the end of American manhood.

They missed a more intriguing element. John was fixated on Reed's erotic power and quiet authority; in his presence he found himself reduced to a womanly kind of hysteria. Meanwhile, he spent years contending with an old army buddy whose only aim in life was to "destroy your happiness." (Recall how in *Woman in White,* Eileen's mother married a doctor whose sister-in-law, formerly queen of the house, also vowed to "steal your happiness.") But Martha Hanley's jealousy was more conventional. John's enemy was obviously infatuated with him. His object wasn't the seduction of Ruth but the breakdown of John, an altogether queerer desire.

Gay themes were also apparent in the various serials penned by Frank Provo and John Pickard, two actors who had met while performing in radio soap operas. Provo was a Californian; Pickard, a native of Australia, where he had written some of that nation's earliest radio scripts. Pickard especially was even more precocious than Robert Andrews. While the latter had mastered the newspaper serial by his early twenties, Pickard wrote his first radio drama in 1927, when he was seventeen, and within the next few years had acted in radio productions of Shakespeare, Galsworthy, Ibsen, and Shaw. During his last months in Australia, he played d'Artagnan in *The Three Musketeers* and adapted the American serial *One Man's Family* for local audiences, perhaps the first migration of American soaps to foreign shores. (Coincidentally, his future partner Provo was at the same time starring as the doomed first husband of Claudia Barbour, *One Man's Family*'s ingenue heroine.) Not surprisingly, Provo and, even more, Pickard were drawn to political themes. They created *Young Doctor Malone* in 1939. By 1942 Jerry Malone was serving in Europe, frequently captured and missing for periods long enough for his wife, Anne, to flirt with sensitive, artistic types as well as wounded pilots. These storylines allowed Provo and Pickard to hire many of their friends, gay and émigré actors.

In 1947 they created the equally successful *Wendy Warren and the News,* a serial that began with news bulletins delivered by Douglas Edwards, a real newscaster, followed by "news reports from the women's world," offered by the girl reporter. After that Wendy would leave the radio station and enter her fictitious world. She married Gil Kendall, whose mother believed that a postwar wife's place was in the home. It was implicitly feminist for the writers to insist that Wendy have a professional life, especially after women had been copiously advised to let men have all the good jobs.

After that marriage failed, Wendy found herself involved with a Middle European adventurer named Anton. Provo and Pickard imagined a cold-war sequence involving spies and, possibly, traitors. But they were bitterly opposed to the blacklists and red scare; like Gussman, they hired the unemployable. Pickard even published an attack on McCarthyism as strong and eloquent as anything penned by Arthur Miller. So they did something remarkable, confusing the world of spies with a gay underworld (thereby, perhaps, turning Joseph McCarthy and J. Edgar Hoover on their heads). In one episode Anton accompanies Wendy to the theater and introduces her to a sub-rosa network. "At times, I shall point out to you certain people . . . people important to the movements we are fighting. Do you understand?" "Yes." "When I do, I shall use a sort of code. Instead of telling you, uh, 'There goes Madam X, a spy working against our government,' which sounds ridiculously melodramatic, I shall simply say, 'There is one of those *interesting* people.'" And for the next few minutes, he spots a man here, a woman there, each "one of those *interesting* people."

It's heady enough to read the auto-critique "ridiculously melodramatic" in a soap script. But using a codified "interesting" that locks so directly into the various codes of queerness was inspired. (After retiring from radio and television, Provo and Pickard became the heads of the drama division of Simon's Rock College, where they produced plays in which the gay subtext manifests itself variously—e.g., a study of the intrigues of an all-girl boarding school keeps breaking for dance sequences with undressed young men.) Wendy's next husband, Mark Douglas, was a more extreme version of Dr. John Wayne. He kept falling under the unnamed power of men, who knew secrets about his past life. Eventually these would all be explained. But for months Wendy would have to contend, not with the usual form of soap rival, another woman, but with men whose hold on her husband she had no means of engaging. After Mark died, she fell in love with her editor. They were about to be married when he discovered an unknown son from a brief, youthful marriage. The boy wooed his father with a passion that bordered on the erotic . . . if one were disposed to hear things that way—as Provo and Pickard were.

But Irna's ultimate rival in those last days was a man who shared her background and some of her past. Orin Tovrov was a native Chicagoan who had been a precocious, left-wing playwright; he was also a major figure in the Radio Writers Guild, Irna's bête noire. His *New*

York Times obituary mentions that he was the guild's first president and had organized the first strike in broadcasting in the late 1930s. Like Irna, he was a Jew who applied his talents to gentile drama. He was most identified with *Ma Perkins,* a series he began writing in late 1938, and continued to write except for a four-year break during World War II—when Henry Selinger, the creator of *Amos 'n' Andy* and Irna's first serial, *Painted Dreams,* replaced him. *Ma Perkins* had begun as melodrama in the Hummert vein; Robert Andrews was its first writer. Ma was surrounded by a noble son, John; an ingenue daughter, Faye; a fickle daughter, Evey; and a scamp of a son-in-law, Willy Fitz. Ma's business partner and dearest friend was a Bill-the-Barber type, as wise and as sexless, named Shuffle Shober. (By the time *Ma Perkins* ended in 1960, soap operas had long banished characters with such ridiculous vaudevillian names.)

Under Tovrov, *Ma Perkins* became the obverse of everything Irna Phillips believed. His characters, too, spoke extra-slowly, and spent most of their time examining and re-examining their responses to the crises of the day. But these crises were seldom very dramatic, or their outcomes very compelling (especially after Faye finally settled down with her second husband, a playwright named Tom Wells, who was clearly Tovrov's stand-in). Instead, the action was interaction. Each broadcast would end with the blandest of teases: "Well, Ma gives her opinion . . . tomorrow" or "Shuffle disagrees with Evey . . . tomorrow."

Tovrov prided himself on a precisely limned universe, each detail calibrated to reflect the psyches of a small group of people, lovingly familiar to an audience that cared deeply about their every response. He told Charles Gussman that his characters resembled the members of a string quartet, a comparison Gussman found overwrought and pompous. After *Ma Perkins* ended her twenty-seven-year-run, Tovrov began writing TV soaps. He teamed up with David Lesan to write a serial that they failed to sell; their common mastery was yesterday's news. He wrote Lesan that he had always been a modest writer, specializing in a quiet drama, and these were not quiet times. This was not quite the revelation he thought it to be. Years earlier Lesan advised radio networks that Tovrov's shows were muted affairs and very . . . *slow.* In his prime Tovrov had staked his claims with a passive-aggressive kind of authority. *Ma Perkins* carried such an expensive nut—both Tovrov and the lead, Virginia Payne, earned a thousand dollars a week—that there was no budget for a larger cast or more expansive storylines. Still, the program remained the highest-rated of all soaps. Tovrov had reason to gloat.

In 1948 he created *The Brighter Day*, a serial that recalled Irna Phillips both in its storyline and in its abstract title. She responded immediately. This was one soap she really liked, and she tended not to like most things: a trip to New York that year allowed her to visit Broadway, where she was unimpressed by Arthur Miller and Tennessee Williams, but thoroughly enjoyed Giraudoux's *Madwoman of Chaillot*, her "kind of show."

The Brighter Day resembled a left-wing version of the old *Guiding Light*. Once again there was a pastor, Reverend Dennis, contending with a cynical naysayer, a journalist named Clint Sebastian. Much was made of the minister's poverty—a salary of $1,800 a year to support himself and five children. Sounding like a recent viewer of *The Best Years of Our Lives*, Sebastian cites the war veterans who can't afford a college education. He also scoffs at the "pulpit pounders," an obvious reference to the evangelical preachers then cluttering the radio dial. This was strong talk for its day, bordering on the impious. But just to reassure Procter & Gamble—and Irna—Tovrov has Clint say, "I'm not a radical but an idealist." And the episode ends with the narrator regarding the humble chapel and feeling "the presence of our Lord." In such ways the Jewish Phillips and Tovrov promoted a social gospel, virtually free of theological implications.

In his gentle, meandering way, Tovrov steered the serial through two comparatively uneventful years. But in late 1950, Irna snatched it from him: where his services had gone unannounced, the program now began, "*The Brighter Day*, written by Irna Phillips." The differences in tone and tempo were stark. Irna, unwittingly agreeing with his self-assessment, said Tovrov wrote great characters but didn't have a clue about plotting. Within a few months Reverend Dennis's flighty daughter, Althea, had become a Korean War widow, giving birth after she learned of her husband's death, and his responsible daughter, Liz, had fallen in love with a man slowly going blind.

During the 1950s, radio kept losing ground to television. The most important soap writers, led by Irna, transferred their attentions to the newer medium. *The Guiding Light* and *The Brighter Day* made successful transitions, unlike *Road of Life*, *Portia Faces Life* (retitled by Charles Gussman *The Inner Flame*), and *Young Doctor Malone*. Though soaps continued to dominate the airwaves—as late as 1957, twenty serials were still being aired daily—everyone understood that the form was dying. Broadcast time was sold in small segments, and the numerous commercials cut into the actual drama. Where once Ma Perkins was known as "Oxydol's Own Ma Perkins," now she was any sponsor's mother-for-hire.

The writers grew desperate. Even the Hummerts decided to experiment. They had lost all their evening programs, the musicals and mysteries. Perhaps this is why their dialogue writers now received directions from "Frank and Anne Hummert": during the 1940s, when they were producing fifteen shows a week, the soap directives were attributed to Mrs. Hummert alone. Their tone changed too, evidence of Frank's impatience. In one note he warned his writers that their critics might have a case: something needed to be happening all the time. Margo Brooks responded by upending Helen Trent as the world knew her. After dropping Gil Whitney, she started to go out with politicians and beatniks. (In the most unlikely line ever aired on a Hummert soap, a young artist wooed Helen by offering her the prospect of reading Nietzsche while listening to Stravinsky.) Jean Carroll decided to bring back Lord Arthur Brinthrope, the knave who had seduced Our Gal Sunday in that serial's first weeks. Demonstrating a Jesuitical attention to texts, Hummert cited the original play, and said that she was betraying its premises! Then, somewhat in the Irna Phillips manner, Carroll decided to make Lord Henry pathologically jealous of his brother. Hummert wrote a bemused letter: "Agreed, Lord Henry is not a mental case!"

Until then Carroll had known how to cover herself. The Hummerts required her to submit storylines every three months. These invariably ended with a promise of emotion, nothing but emotion—the word kept recurring. She understood that the genre had no other point. Not education or acculturation, not exposing the working class to their bosses. No, the Hummerts simply wanted to hit their audiences where they lived. For fourteen years Carroll had been their best student.

On other serials, logic and continuity were often sacrificed to advance a juicier storyline. In *Road of Life,* Dr. Jim Brent had adopted Butch McEwan, the boy who had killed his mother in 1939, but by the mid-fifties Butch had become his brother. Irna Phillips had no respect for chronology. While adult characters aged at a normal clip, children might grow up within a few years. So a parent in her mid-thirties might have a son in his late twenties. If time's passage could be so arbitrarily manipulated, it was nothing to get rid of beloved characters. So it was that virtually every non-Hummert serial in the 1950s involved the death of the leading character's mate. Dr. Jim Brent and Dr. Jerry Malone lost their wives; and the heroines of *Wendy Warren, Nora Drake, The Guiding Light, Right to Happiness, Hilltop House,* and *Pepper Young's Family,* their husbands. There were even attempts to complicate the characters. Many good but weak men turned bad before the writers dispatched them. Despite having killed one husband and married three others, Carolyn of *Right to Happiness* had been insufferably noble and humorless. But for the serial's last years she became a possessive mother who, like some villainess in an old Hummert soap, tried to wreck her son's romance with a poor girl.

The writing became more sophisticated. Provo and Pickard continued to compose their knowing dialogue; Charles Gussman surrounded his bitch-goddess, Sybil, with similarly ambiguous men: her last husband appeared to have killed his former wife, the serial ending before his innocence could be determined. A previous husband, Randy Ogden, had gone to his doom wracked by fear. When Dr. Brent assured him that what loomed ahead was simply "another form of darkness," Randy replied, "It's not our kind of darkness." (The actor Alan Hewitt told Gussman that was the best line he had ever recited—but were there any listeners left to appreciate it?) Going for broke, the last soap writers imagined a radio version of film noir, a specialty entertainment for listeners who valued all the particular qualities of a radio drama.

Meanwhile, the daddy of soap writers, Robert Andrews, now calling himself Robert Hardy Andrews, had established himself as Hollywood's most indefatigable hack: his screen work ranged from *Bataan* to *I Married a Communist,* from *The Cross of Lorraine* to *Girls Town.* During the mid-fifties, while his soap-writing comrades were trying to revitalize the idiom, he was applying his particular talents to a life of the Buddha. He began a screenplay, *The Wayfarer,* that was never produced, though Christopher Isherwood contemplated doing it his way, after Andrews's plans went to nought. Of course, the spiritual practice of meditation would have made an inspired theme for an inventor of the daytime serial. From Ma Perkins and Helen Trent (along with Little Orphan Annie and Jack Armstrong, heroes of his kiddy soaps) to Gautama Buddha, Andrews's career suggested that a soap writer could aim very high . . . unlike Irna Phillips, who never needed much more than a parsonage, a doctor's office, and, as the soul singer Bill Withers might say, some local unwed mothers.

The male writers enjoyed a spirit of qualified camaraderie. After Julian

Funt was blacklisted, his former ghost writer David Lesan abandoned him for Irna Phillips; but as soon as Procter & Gamble fired her, he was back working with Funt. The latter had created *This Is Nora Drake* (a story "seen through the window of a woman's heart") about a big-city nurse. He turned it over to Milton Lewis, with whom he had written a Broadway play (inspired by the life of Nijinsky, with a musical score composed by Paul Bowles!) in 1946. When Lewis developed Lou Gehrig's disease, Funt's *Big Sister* co-author Robert Newman took over the scripting of *Nora Drake* and let the dying Lewis retain all of his salary.

Irna remained the object of the male writers' envy and disdain. In her memoir, she depicts a very small circle of family members (most of whom she disliked), ghost writers, and her house musician, an organist named Bernice Yanacek. (Even there she got as good as she gave; in her memoir she "rues" bringing the Hammond organ to soap operas. She gave the soaps their tone and their sound and still wasn't happy.) She didn't socialize with the other writers, and declared that she never even met Frank and Anne Hummert.

The ending was swift and unkind. Vivian Smolen, the actress who had played Our Gal Sunday for fifteen years, learned that she was out of a job by reading it in *The New York Times*; CBS hadn't bothered to inform her. In 1960, when the last radio network serial ended, the vacuum was briefly filled with parody. Comedians Bob and Ray continued to perform "Mary Backstage, Noble Wife" and "Amanda of Mental Therapy." Leon Janney, the veteran actor who had played Helen Trent's last suitor, imagined a final week in which everyone from Ma Perkins to Gil Whitney died a violent death. A few months later, Virginia Payne—Ma Perkins—and the actresses who had played her daughters recorded a commercial that made radio's Mother of the Air a cackling harridan.

A decade earlier, after Irna Phillips moved *The Guiding Light* from Hollywood to New York, her disgruntled actors had imagined a wickeder pastiche. It began with an announcer promising "*The Guiding Light*...created by Irna... Phillips?" Meta Bauer was overheard trying to guess when her fatherless child had been conceived. "February? I was drunk all of February. March? March, I went with girls." A fake commercial advertised Duz as a douche nonpareil.

But these jokes were bitter. All those radio veterans with their average faces and godlike voices had no career options. "What will become of my actors?" said Anne Hummert. Television was kinder to the writers, at least until the mid-sixties. But then they too were seen as dated. Frank Provo and John Pickard conceived several series; none of them sold. Irna Phillips lasted the longest. But by 1972 the producers of *As the World Turns* were only too glad to fire her; by then, a new, hipper generation had arrived. Today, even as the television soaps face their own inevitable demise, the most rococo plots still sound like warmed-up Irna. On *The Young and the Restless,* tycoon Victor Newman has been married nine times, three of them to a former stripper named Nicki.

But Irna's couples had begun remarrying sixty years before the Newmans. Victor's semen has been twice stolen from a sperm bank, though only one thief managed to impregnate herself. That's bad sci-fi and inferior Irna. In its last years, *As the World Turns* included a gay romance between two male ingenues. She used to make fun of "pansy" disc jockeys even though, to modern ears, her actors sound most epicene (just like pre-1950 crooners, Frank Sinatra only butching up his act after his voice dropped). Who can doubt that she would have known what to do? When one of the gay boys was shot by his lover's stepfather, the deed seemed purest Irna Phillips.

For many years, even as she was backstabbing her rivals and brutalizing her employees, she realized that they were not her enemies. She wasn't bothered by amiable chatterers like Kate Smith and Mary Margaret McBride, the Oprahs of their time. But she was terrified by programs like *Queen for a Day.* "We of the daytime serial," she would announce, having earned the right to an imperial "we," had fought against everything they represent. Those programs always ended with poor, desperate people weeping as the fans pondered their fates. Like Pentecostals stricken by the Holy Ghost, the women would contort in anguish. In 1934 Wyllis Cooper wrote a withering review of one of Irna's early serials, *Song of the City*: "It panders to the crude emotions of the shopgirl type of listener . . . It will sell cheap products to vulgar people." (Within a year he was writing *Betty and Bob.*) Irna subjected the sob-sister quiz shows to a rage even more vitriolic. She happened to be right, and if soaps die victims to Oprah and Ellen, at least they weren't killed by *Queen for a Day.*

At their zenith, radio serials commanded a daily audience of twenty million people (far greater than TV serials do today, even with an exponentially larger population). Yet writers and actors who had infiltrated the fantasy lives of those millions would nearly all be forgotten. Anne Hummert died a wealthy widow of ninety-one. I happened to read a paid obituary in *The New York Times,* but when I visited the funeral parlor, there were no fellow mourners. She once had been the most powerful figure in radio, and nobody remembered.

Other writers suffered ends as grim as anything they had imagined. Max Wylie often had ridiculed the melodramatic excesses. His daughter Janice was raped and murdered, and the anguished father would kill himself. Howard Teichmann succeeded Irna as head writer of *Road of Life* and would later become the rare soap writer to succeed on Broadway (*The Solid Gold Cadillac*). But after he died of Lou Gehrig's disease, his widow told their daughter, "I used to say the soaps were nothing like life. And now I say they're just like life." The witty Charles Gussman spent his last years in a dilapidated farmhouse. His daughter, Brooke Gruenberg, who managed the family as if she were one of his heroines, informed me, "You are looking at four generations living under medication." In his last ordeal she sat at his bedside: "You can't leave me. You haven't given me your final word." He thought for a moment. "And now . . . for a word from our sponsor," he said, and breathed his last.

In 1972, after Irna Phillips had lost everything, she joined her old pal Ireene Wicker in a salute to old-time radio. Wicker had become famous as "the Singing Lady" before being blacklisted, and Irna was definitely not among the writers who had defied that list. But Ireene was now a wealthy widow, Armand Hammer's sister-in-law, and she could overlook Irna's politics. They were simply delighted to remember when they had begun the world and changed the culture. Irna remained in Chicago. Though she had made many fortunes—grossing $250,000 a year when $5,000 was middle-class—she was no longer rich.

Les White thinks her financial investors may have avenged themselves on the impossible Irna by losing her money. She was reduced to having her brother, a postman, negotiate the sales to Procter & Gamble of her biggest hits, *As the World Turns* and *Another World.* Together they earned her less than the seven-figure fee that good union man Orin Tovrov received for his serial *The Doctors,* a considerably less valuable title. Like one of her unlucky heroines, she couldn't catch a break. At sixty-seven. she admitted that the "competition" was "much tougher" than when she had started out. In other words, the writers today cared about all those pesky things she had considered pretentious—style, pacing, irony. So, in 1972, aged seventy-one, she decided to switch careers and become a saleslady at one of Marshall Field's most exclusive emporiums, dying a few months after—a death her niece, the postman's daughter, suspects was suicide. Her memoir alone would be dispositive evidence. Rose Kransky had ended as Thackeray's Becky Sharp or Balzac's Cousin Bette.

The radio serial format survived in other countries. Well into the 1970s the scripts of American serials like *Portia Faces Life* continued to be broadcast in South Africa and Australia. Meanwhile, some Americans believed that the singular pleasures could be revived for a new audience. In 1975 WOR, a New York radio station, introduced four serials. Among them was a dramatization of Thackeray's *Vanity Fair,* adapted by Nancy Moore, who had written for everything from the Hummerts' *Backstage Wife* to *The Edge of Night.* For many reasons hers was an inspired choice; Victorian novelists with their huge casts of characters and convoluted storylines had predicted the later genre. Thackeray's Becky Sharp seemed just right for a newly liberated soap form, closer to the Rachels and Lisas of daytime television than to the goody-two-shoes of radio.

After months *Vanity Fair* reached perhaps Thackeray's most glorious moment. For many years the exemplary George Dobbins has devoted himself to the fatuous Amelia Sedley. Becky happens to overhear his latest proposal and concludes that her dear friend is a silly goose, rejecting someone who is so vastly her superior.

"Ah!" she thinks, "if I could have had such a husband as that—a man with a heart and brains too! I would not have minded his large feet." Irna Phillips couldn't have said it better.

—

Her eighty-year reign ended on September 17, 2010, with the last chapter of *As the World Turns.* Dozens of actors were left bereft, though they were not as pitiful as the radio soap actors, who tended not to be as photogenic. (The actress who played Helen Trent ended her days running a bookstore and auditioning for summer-stock theater.) Though the writing was vastly superior to anything composed by Irna, the serial dynamic hadn't changed greatly. Shades of *Road of Life,* circa 1942, doctors were still fighting each other for the control of their hospitals. In 1944, Irna sent the heroines of three soaps, *The Guiding Light, Lonely Women,* and *Road of Life,* to Reno . . . only to have all of them remarry their ex-husbands within a year. *As the World Turns* ended with a few predictable remarriages. Just to be different, it also included the revelation that the father of a baby was really . . . his mother's husband! (Fidelity had become far more perverse than its opposite.) One of the gay characters had left his boyfriend for a young doctor, who was killed in an automobile accident. Before he died, he willed his body to the grandson of his greatest rival. In the last episode, his lover donned a stethoscope in order to hear the doctor's still-living heart.

Irna might never have predicted that, but it could not have transpired without her, the daytime serial's unwed mother.

THE MALE SOPRANO

We love him because he defies nature. Because manhood roars in a bass-baritone, and the Adam's apple is supposed to swallow the pure, high voice of babes. Yet male voices are always leaping octaves. Rebel yells, farmboy hollers, broken-voiced shrieks, dog-whistle laughs sound virile enough to their listeners. For most of their teen years, some boys can squeal as high and loud as before their voices changed. And an artfully cultivated falsetto, crooned by an Al Green or a Bee Gee, has become a vocalized foreplay. That women swoon to such voices has long been apparent, just as men consider Lauren Bacall's the archetypal bedroom voice. Both sexes are enthralled to hear their natural pitches claimed by a foreign power.

Yet there are some men who dream of notes far higher than Smokey Robinson's or David Daniels's. They dream of soaring higher than Maria Callas, higher than Mariah Carey. They don't imagine themselves women; they call themselves male sopranos. Their quixotic attempt, rarely lovely but often thrilling, makes distinctions of gender and culture, biology and physiology, problematic in the extreme. For what so boldly confesses male inadequacy as the need to reclaim the birthright of a boy or a woman?

The soprano voice has never been exclusively female. During the age of the castrato, throat and chest combined, so that a capon's range would have a bulldog's volume. Sopranists (the classical term for male sopranos) have limited themselves to an archaic repertoire: the baroque and early classical eras, when roles were composed for their range. But outside of classical music more casual attitudes prevailed. To many unsophisticated listeners, the whole apparatus of classical singing is thoroughly artificial, the soprano being only the most extreme version. Thus, the soul singer Wilson Pickett could insist that his falsetto shriek was an "opera note"— it was a soprano high C—and a YouTube clown will summon up "my opera voice," one three octaves above that with which he speaks.

In the nineteenth century an American man could hear falsetto coming from all directions, from the touring opera companies that provided a national entertainment as well as from blacks and Indians. By the early twentieth century, ballad singing had become the province of sweet-voiced high tenors. John McCormack had the most memorable head tones; later singers, like Donald Novis or Cliff "Ukulele Ike" Edwards, couldn't match his technique, and their top notes were lighter, with more of a feminine sweetness. Extreme ranges were cultivated. One of the earliest record stars was Charles Kellogg, a naturalist on the order of John Muir who cultivated the vocal range of some American Indians, one that allowed him to sing bird songs with an open throat, granting him supposedly a ten-octave range. The biggest star in vaudeville was a female impersonator who packed them in with his F above high C. Alas, we're not informed whether that was an F5, which would have made him a Beach Boy, or an F6, which would have made him a Queen of the Night.

In all these instances, the sound was identified as genteel and consoling—a lover's cry, not a bully's taunt. Perhaps because of the prevalence of castrato singers in the Catholic Church, or perhaps because the notes seemed otherworldly and desexualized (a bewhiskered man with a female voice), the sound also became identified as "angelic." This may have been an echo of the angels' androgyny or a forecast of a heaven where neither men nor women exist. The angelic sound, then, was not sexual—except when it was. One of the purest male sopranos was Frank Colman, an Englishman who recorded during the early 1930s (under the name "Frank Ivallo" he can be seen on YouTube). He recorded a couple of love songs. But he also recorded songs in which he impersonated an orphan singing, "Keep a place in heaven for me, Mother dear."

Colman's career was short-lived; some YouTube viewers have deduced from his long arms and late-adolescent face that he was genetically damaged, perhaps an endocrinological castrato. (If so, he was a master of rolling with the punches.) He was not a big star, and the high-tenor

crooners of the 1930s—Frank Parker, Kenny Sargent, Dennis Day—
sang a good octave beneath him. Their voices were notably high, and
this allowed radio comedians to tease them about their delayed adolescence or, once in a blue moon, about their lavender tendencies.

But falsetto was embraced most completely in black music. Moans
and hollers were often pitched in yodel terrritory. Alfred Lewis in 1930
reaches notes almost as high as Frank Colman's, but he combines them
with his harmonica playing so that harp and voice complete each other's
lines. Clearly, falsetto was sent out to astonish and delight; it required
agility and singing sense. While an occasional entertainer like Cab Calloway, "Mr. Hi-De-Ho," might send out a chilling note, the sound became
a convention of church singing, probably because it has always been so
adventurous, if not theatrical. Perhaps the first male gospel soloist—he
recorded a year before the spectacular guitar evangelist Blind Willie
Johnson—was a tenor formidably named Homer Quincy Smith. His
intonation is almost academic except that his falsetto soars well beyond
that of an Irish tenor into the range of a mezzo-soprano. His singing of
spirituals like "I Want Jesus to Walk with Me" is expressive and stark,
enough so to fascinate obscurantist folkies, who have discovered him in
a CD anthology called *American Primitive.* Yet his technique was sophisticated in the extreme—among other details, he's the first gospel singer
I've heard to employ the bluesy melisma later perfected by Mahalia Jackson. His falsetto gifts later earned him a spot in the Southernaires, a
vastly influential male quartet with their own weekly radio program.
With that quartet, he would inspire the falsetto specialist Billy Williams
(an early star of Sid Caesar's *Your Show of Shows*), who would in turn
inspire gospel-quartet stars like Ira Tucker and Claude Jeter. Since Al
Green claims Jeter as his inspiration, you can draw a clear line from the
so-called primitive Smith to the insidiously calculated Al Green. (To
complicate the appelation "primitive," Smith was the nephew of W. C.
Handy, the blues popularizer disdained by country-blues fans.)

Homer Quincy Smith probably had his own models, men who
employed a semi-operatic falsetto to raise church members from
their seats and out of their pews. Certainly, high notes have become
a time-honored way of wrecking a church—and after rock and roll
secularized gospel, a proven way of getting pop fans to shriek, half in
mimetic response, half in mindless bliss. But high notes have often made
strong men weak. According to David Huron, a professor of music and
cognitive science at Ohio State University, "When singers sing high and

loud, the brain releases the hormones epinephrine and norepinephrine, causing a general increase in psychological arousal—higher heart rate, faster respiration, increased perspiration and greater attentiveness." This illuminates the ways church members fall out and rockers mosh—and also why Lord Byron and Walt Whitman were both known to faint during the solos of their favorite sopranos. (In the nineteenth century, audience members often fainted. Charles Dickens observed after one of his readings drove an actor to tears, "Now do you know what it's like to have power?")

Though Homer Smith's falsetto is redolent of female sopranos and Irish tenors, his descendants command a technique that is as high but neither Irish nor womanish. Claude Jeter, my nominee for the Father of Falsetto, once told me, "Nobody ever said I sing like a lady. They say I sing like a cat." Counterintuitively, the quartet falsettists assumed a super-virile posture, and thrilled their female fans with the stunt. As one quartet veteran told me, when the women heard those notes, "they had fits," and the fits were physical versions of the double entendre.

More interesting would be the gospel-singing men who drew their inspiration from women. With them, the male soprano became a pioneer, the avatar of rock, and a singular cultural figure. And perhaps only then did the male soprano shoot for the moon and land on the stars.

"I LOVE YOU, HONEY, BECAUSE YOU MADE ME A STAR!"

A gospel soprano can evoke an opera singer's trill and a field worker's holler. She also wields a penetrating vibrato, huger and more quivering than would be acceptable on a concert stage—just one of many ways the church tweaks and confounds the expectations of white America. The vocal sound has often been dismissed by classical critics, who have missed the peculiarity of this hybrid. For just as the concert spirituals arranged in the mid–nineteenth century bore traces of Schubert and Schumann, so even more did the hymns and anthems sung in black churches. Therefore, when a Roland Hayes or a Marian Anderson moved from spirituals to lieder, they were exploring harmonic and melodic patterns for which they had been well prepared.

But what distinguished most black concert recitalists, particularly when they ended a recital with a series of spirituals, was their deployment of folkloric conventions, blue notes and slurs, the art lying in the rapprochement between technique and authenticity. (The concert singer Florence Quivar manages this particularly well.) Untrained singers—and most gospel singers cannot even read music—have often attempted feats that concert singers wouldn't risk, except in private and for fun. A gospel soprano may sing an octave higher than the high F of Mozart's Queen of the Night. She may hold a note for twenty seconds, color it red, white, and blue. A price will be paid. DeLois Barrett Campbell once lamented that years of singing had left her with a "librato." But this inspired neologism is the story of every singer's life. At least the gospel singer has earned her vocal scars.

Arguably nowhere outside of opera is the soprano voice so dramatic and expressive an instrument as in gospel. And just as opera fans, at least since Walt Whitman, have hollered, wept, and fainted over their heroines' high notes, gospel has made the soprano sound a singular call to worship. In gospel, a slurred, wordless moan can be as devastating as a sermon. A high soprano note can have the same effect, somehow merging the abstract instrumental quality and an unuttered, but fully understood, emotional content.

It's all in the timing. The first significant gospel soprano was Mary Johnson Davis (1899–1982), a Pittsburgh native who toured America during the early years of gospel's golden age. She was among the first to apply the freer, more improvisatory gospel technique to traditional hymns. Marion Williams, who first heard Davis when she was a girl in Miami, remembered, "Mary Johnson Davis would sing any hymn out of the Baptist hymnal, and tear up worse than anyone you ever saw."

Clara Ward, one of Davis's accompanists, would later front the most important gospel group, the Famous Ward Singers. The group's star would be that same Marion Williams. But while Marion had obviously learned from Davis, she brought in qualities all her own. Initially she was famous for her floating high notes. And yet, from the start, she found means of gospelizing the operatic. She usually applied a growled "yessir" to the coloratura-pitched "wow" (most likely the source of James Brown's scream). And if that weren't country enough, she would simultaneously turn to her side, singing in another direction, a down-home gesture that conveyed transcendence: hey, saints, this one's for me. Her notes were bold and varied, sometimes sustained to virtuosic lengths, other times stuttering like a Rosetta Tharpe guitar solo. She'd hit a falsetto note, then top it with one sung in her natural voice. And typically, she'd hit a note with her hand on her hip, a gesture that was either triumphantly confident or bawdily flirtatious; within the complexity of her persona, the tension between vulgar and transcendent was a given. Dorothy Love Coates observed that "Marion's the onliest one who can make her notes soulful."

Marion did what no other female soprano had done before. But that was largely because her inspirations were not always female. Gospel soprano takes androgyny for granted. Marion was a virile soprano, deploying her instrument with the confidence of a male preacher, beating him at his game by adding her notes to his growls. She admitted that male quartets had inspired her perhaps more than Rosetta Tharpe or Mary Johnson Davis. In later years she developed a contralto register, more foreboding if less acoustically brilliant than her soprano. (Around the house she would imitate the bass singers of various quartets; and frequently she would invite the men in the audience to sing with her: "Come on, fellas, you know you've got the prettiest voices.")

By the mid-1950s, the two male stars of gospel and R&B were both indebted to Marion's technique and showmanship. Alex Bradford, a huge-voiced baritone, was the most flamboyant soloist of that era, the self-proclaimed "Singing Rage of the Gospel Age." Marion showed him many things: how to holler and Suzy-Q, how to be flamboyant and sanctified (admittedly he had a host of effeminate male preachers to advance that education). After years of battling each other at venues like the Apollo Theater, they became the co-stars of *Black Nativity,* the first gospel musical. Many a night Bradford would echo Marion's high notes. (The A6s of his youth had dropped an octave, and they were more advanced countertenor than sure-'nuff soprano, but they were still his pride and joy.)

In this dizzying round of women and men doing each other, if Marion was a virile soprano, Bradford was a womanly baritone—albeit in a tradition where women sang as hard as men, and where Bradford himself had a neck as wide as a stevedore's or mill worker's, the jobs of his youth. In *Black Nativity* Marion sang a deeply bluesy "No Room at the Hotel," ending with the words "no room" sung in her lowest register. But since her voice was still comparatively high-pitched, the low notes were a breathy whisper, a falsetto bass. Some years later Bradford sang the same song and ended it with similar whispers, even though he should have had no problem negotiating the notes. Figuratively and sonically, this was a man's version of a woman's cross-dressing.

In 1993, shortly before her death, Marion was a recipient of the Kennedy Center Honors. Among those saluting their mentor, including Aretha Franklin, was an ebullient Little Richard. "I love you, honey," he yelled out to Marion, "because YOU made me a star! Because YOU gave me my note." She had given him more than the falsetto shriek that became his vocal signature, the note that changed everything and made him "the architect of rock and roll."

What Richard did with Marion's note was make a soprano intrinsic to rock-and-roll excitement. (Outside of the modest phenomenon of Duke Ellington's "Creole Love Song," with Adelaide Hall's version of a black concert singer's soprano gone bluesy, such high vocalism had not been associated with fun and games in popular music.) But though Richard made high notes part of rock, he himself—perhaps deliberately—desexualized them. Not a very convincing heterosexual, he displayed a delight in his high C's, his face glowing as he trilled, that was too narcisstic to be flirtatious.

Instead he made Marion's whoop a mark of rock-and-roll bravado. Richard gave birth to many sons; Otis Redding and James Brown always claimed that he was their major influence. Both men would have detected the Marion contained in Richard. But her name was most likely unknown to the many white rockers who would proudly scream in the years ahead. Mitch Ryder admitted where he got his sound, and by the 1960s, when they would jam together, Little Richard would let him provide the "screams." In a series of records he made after leaving the Detroit Wheels, Ryder revealed an impressive technique. His notes were nowhere as full-bodied as Alex Bradford's, but he could twirl and finagle them with obbligatos that frequently soared past soprano high C.

Inspired by Mitch Ryder, the young Bruce Springsteen would scream even higher, the notes more constricted and whistle-like. Few of Richard's acolytes attempted to make their tones as round and feminine as his. But they all delighted in their virtuosity. Steve Tyler had been screeching athletically for decades when he recorded a song that took him to a resounding E above soprano high C. In their day singers from Del Shannon to Bobby Hatfield of the Righteous Brothers to Rod Stewart to Alvin Lee of Ten Years After have all managed small but precise high C's and D's. (Some Rolling Stones high notes have been attributed to Billy Preston, the great gospel organist and soul singer, rather than Mick Jagger.)

A more legit-sounding male soprano would occasionally appear in rock and roll; and invariably he too had a gospel pedigree. By far the most gifted was gospel's greatest male soprano, Carl Hall. Though Carl often claimed that Marion was his biggest influence, his soprano idol was another Philadelphian, Carrie Williams (no relation to Marion). Short and cute, with a manner as flirtatious as Marion's, Carrie was raised in the extremely devout church founded by Daddy Grace, in which members frequently express their devotion with hours of athletic dancing in the Spirit.

True to her upbringing, Carrie could dance quicker than anyone else. But her notes contradicted her sanctified persona; they were huge and operatic, bordering on a parody of Wagnerian style. At one recording session, the engineers had to place her in another room because she drowned everyone out—this despite the fact that gospel sopranos usually have smaller voices and less volume than the contraltos, heavy famously drowning out light.

Carrie's coloratura was too legit to win gospel fans, too gospelly eccentric to figure in classical music. In her later years, surviving off disability insurance, she still made her mark by turning up at gospel concerts, getting conspicuously happy, and screaming not like an ecstatic saint but like a failed opera singer. On YouTube you can hear Marion Williams and her church choir perform "Heaven Belongs to You": in the last minute, Marion starts ad-libbing a solo passage, and suddenly Carrie screams out, her voice from the congregation almost drowning out Marion at the mike.

In 1954 Carrie's high notes would be re-created by Hall, the seventeen-year-old lead singer of Raymond Rasberry's group. Rasberry had worked with Clara Ward, and imagined a male version of the Ward Singers, with men singing as high as Marion or Carrie. Carl was willing: "Carrie was short and funny-looking and hit crazy notes. And I was short and funny and decided I'd hit me a few." The notes were remarkable, topping out at E-flat above soprano high C. Other men have gone higher, but none have sounded clearer or more forceful. Carl's other voices included a smooth and consoling lyric baritone and a screeching countertenor. Not content to growl like Marion, he decided to squall like Ruth Davis, another Philadelphia singer, whose group, the Davis Sisters, were the Wards' biggest rivals. But if Marion was a virile soprano, Ruth

Davis was virtually a male quartet singer in (unconvincing) drag. In other words, even when Carl was singing like a fellow, he was really doing a woman's work. Meanwhile, he made high singing seem an act of hard labor. While Marion supported her notes with a hand on her hip, Carl's torso would contort as if he were pulling magic up from his diaphragm.

After finishing his military service—and it was a treat to see him at the Apollo Theater wearing his soldier's uniform and singing his immense high C's, the male soprano as warrior—Carl became a pop singer. I first heard him performing in a Broadway musical, *Inner City*, where he made his entrance hollering the urban curses "Shit, motherfucker." Hearing this quintessential gospel voice in full power, singing those words as if he were praising Jesus, left me breathless. After the show, I introduced myself, and he confessed, "I'd still be in the vineyard but I've got me a wife and kid to support."

Carl's pop career never took off. He was versatile enough to improvise with jazz saxophonist Albert Ayler, sing exhaustingly fervent soul ballads like "You Don't Know Nothing About Love," and perform comic roles—for example, playing the eponymous figure in *The Wiz*. But mostly he became a background singer for numerous less gifted artists. "Who are those girls singing so hard behind" whoever? I'd ask. "I'm the girls," he'd reply. Actually, by his mid-twenties, he had quit hitting super-high notes, at least in his new metier. "My wife says I sing too hard," he'd say. But even without the soprano notes, his voice was perhaps too stridently unmasculine to be commercial. I've heard very few pop singers whose falsetto approached the quality of Carl Hall's. The best black exemplars—Joe Hinton, an ex-gospel-quartet singer; Dee Clark; and the inspired, protean Jackie Wilson—have all died. David Lasley, a big fan of the Rasberry Singers, resembles Carl in having spent more time singing background than recording under his own name. Turley Richards, a blind blue-eyed soul singer from West Virginia, had a much larger and purer sound than, say, Mitch Ryder or Bobby Hatfield. (Actually, Jimmy Walker, formerly of the Knickerbockers, who briefly recorded with Hatfield after Bill Medley left the Righteous Brothers to pursue a solo career, had a firmer, more shocking top than Hatfield.) Turley's record of a gospel song, "I Heard the Voice of Jesus Say," ends with three impressive soprano high D's, not merely notes but sung words ("Jesus," two times, and "plea"). Another blind singer, Tom Sullivan, had some of Turley's quality. It will be noted that these men are not household names.

By the early 1990s one male soprano would achieve, albeit briefly, superstardom. His name is Edson Cordeiro, and sadly, he came to my attention exactly the same week that I attended Carl Hall's funeral. (He had been a chain smoker for years; it's a wonder that he retained any soprano at all.) Cordeiro, a Brazilian boy, grew up in a *favela* and quit school before he was thirteen. Even he had a gospel background, having been raised in a Pentecostal church with a black pastor. A reckless, feckless singer, not unlike the wild American Mike Patton, Edson determined to sing anything in any voice, drawing on a range of over four octaves.

He had a strong, rangy baritone. But he only parked his clothes there. Instead, on his first albums, he chose to mimic women, ranging from Adelaide Hall ("Creole Love Song") to Aretha Franklin and the Brazilian jazz star Elis Regina. But his dream was to sing like Kiri Te Kanawa. His first and biggest hit was an in-your-face rock arrangement (originally conceived by Dollie de Luxe) of "(I Can't Get No) Satisfaction" and the Queen of the Night's second aria from Mozart's *Magic Flute*. Bending gender and genre, the recording opens with a rock combo backing a deep-voiced contralto, Cássia Eller, who sings the Rolling Stones' song. Then an orchestra intrudes, and Cordeiro sings the coloratura portion, complete with the two high F's. In the video both the female baritone and the male soprano look like street fighters.

In later years Cordeiro would prove a very campy performer, especially after he outed himself. But he initially presented himself as more Prince than Michael Jackson; like Prince and Carl Hall, he's a short man. In early videos he can be seen soaring to a high G, one note above the Queen of the Night, and making a muscle. See, he implies, only a tough guy would dare to do this! He would also surround himself with a chorus of female sopranos, none of them very gifted; amid their untrained but authentically high voices, his studied coloratura seemed the more artful.

(Claude Morrison, one of the founding members of the Canadian a cappella group the Nylons, seconds the emotion. In the early days he'd toss off high D's all night long; and once in an interview, he proceeded to sing a couple of songs, words and all, in the passage between soprano high C and the B-flat above that. After leaving me astonished, he joked, "I always say it takes balls to sing like this." On this affirmative note, consider Jacek Laszczkowski, a Polish film actor who has performed as both a tenor and a male soprano. He makes a striking impression with his trimmed beard and scalloped whiskers. In one film clip, he performs a winsome aria while the camera shows him engaged in karate with four other men. The film is entitled "The Voice from Heaven," implying that angels are both androgynous and athletic. Considering that they're supposed to be God's soldiers, why not?)

Cordeiro's notes are more high than astounding. Past a reasonable high C, they have the same thin sound as, say, Mitch Ryder's. But somehow his appealing delivery made him one of Brazil's biggest stars; he was dubbed "the new Yma Sumac." Recently he has started recording as a classical countertenor, and his top notes have dropped even as his mezzo has expanded. His most recent YouTube clips show him performing with a German jazz trio. He seems not to have recorded in Brazil for several years. Perhaps the novelty wore off. But the fact that somewhere in the world a male soprano could become a national figure is illuminating all the same. (The Romanian Mihai Trăistariu, advertised as "the male Mariah Carey," is another rare superstar of the stratosphere.)

Recently a young singer named Vitas has become famous in both Russia and China with his bastardized opera. Video clips show glamorous young women accompanying him on the violin as he flirts with the camera and delivers a modest countertenor and some ambulance-siren D6's. His version of *Lucia di Lammermoor*'s mad scene is a disheartening window into Russian kitsch. Yet millions of YouTubers find his shrieks electrifying. After his tour of China young men in Thailand and Korea began posting clips of their sixth-octave notes. As if to slay the Russian bear, a young Pole named Micah Young took his biggest hit an octave higher, landing on a piercing C-sharp 7. Take that, you Russkies—this time Poland wins.

A brief taste of stardom was enjoyed by Greg Pritchard, a rookie countertenor who kicked "Nessun dorma" up an octave to the amazement of Simon Cowell and the other judges of *Britain's Got Talent*. (Cowell compared his mezzo-soprano to a dog meowing.) As almost everyone acknowledged, Pritchard deserved an A for fortitude. The thousands of YouTube responses betrayed a total ignorance of his kind of voice. Those who loved him thought he was one in a million. Those who didn't used the all-purpose dismissal "gay." An occasional countertenor or male soprano posted his simple gratitude. Pritchard's ballsiness had redeemed them all; he had become their saint. His rocker's hairdo and working-class speaking voice made him accessible. Women wanted to woo and/or mother him; disgruntled fellows called him a fag. It was a dynamic familiar to all the gospel men who had spent their youths mocking Marion Williams. (And just as they demanded comparison with gospel women and not male quartets, Pritchard immediately became the most visible challenger to Susan Boyle. As in gospel, it took a male soprano to give the fat lady a run for her coda.)

Programs patterned on *American Idol* provided an international welcome for other ambitious falsettos. In Hungary a slight, balding fellow named André Vásáry was favored for several weeks, culminating his run with a timid interpretation of the Queen of the Night aria. He had the range: one of his popular recordings included a whistle-noted C7, but a whistle-noted F6 deflated the Queen's complaint. A brief international star was another self-proclaimed "male soprano." In April 2010 Lin Yu Chun, a twenty-four-year-old shop worker, charmed the audience of a Taiwanese *Idol* with his pitch-perfect version of a Whitney Houston hit, "I Will Always Love You." With her top notes Houston had channeled her mother, Cissy Houston, at one time the top gospel soprano of Newark, New Jersey. So, decades after the boys of gospel started mimicking their idols, a Taiwanese was replicating the process. Because Lin Yu Chun's falsetto was housed in a chunky, not conventionally attractive body, he was briefly hailed as another Susan Boyle. Within the week that he garnered over six million YouTube views, his distinction was not merely his womanish voice. It was also his lack of physical charisma; he was nicknamed "Little Fatty." A man could get away with high notes provided he was not sexually challenging. To be unkind, all manner of vocal freedoms could be allowed the unattractive. Like Susan Boyle, Lin Yu Chun represented a wallflower's partial, lonely triumph.

If viewers from Great Britain to Hungary to Taiwan could fall in love with unthreatening, high-voiced males, why didn't Carl Hall become an international star? After his funeral, one of his admirers offered an explanation. "When you sing so hard and high and pure and effeminine, they won't accept you." The church might embrace that inspired chiasmus, "pure and effeminine." But, elsewhere, men outsinging women was a deal breaker. As the hymn said, the world was not their home; they were only passing through.

DRAG QUEENS, OPERA QUEENS, AND SCHOLARS

Something about this cultural moment has liberated high-voiced men. For just as rock and roll seemed to grant male singers a whole new octave (mostly false, but sometimes architectonally high, as in the heavy-metal acolytes of Rob Halford, singing chest notes way above tenor high C), so classical music proved friendlier than it had for two hundred years. Not since the reign of the castrati have so many fifth-octave male singers made names for themselves.

I'd like to think that hearing long-haired rockers sing in feminine registers made it possible for men dressed formally in tux and tails to do the same. I'm old enough to remember when high falsetto was considered funny (or scary, or both). Perhaps the voice has to stop sounding freaky before it can be valued for its particular charms.

That's why high falsetto works so well in gospel; it's not questioned. The motto is "We're coming to you in our own way," and you better not turn us aside. Thus it has always startled me that so many wannabe classical sopranists feel compelled to appear in drag. Alex Bradford was heroically campy, but he didn't perform in women's clothes; Carl Hall sang in mufti. But some years ago New Yorkers were introduced to La Gran Scena, a company of male falsettists, all of them in costume. Led by the scholar and vocal coach Ira Siff (masquerading as Madame Vera Galupe-Borszkh, a superannuated diva, many a season past her prime), the men impressed as precise and devoted fans. Audiences familiar with the styles parodied were ecstatic. They laughed in affectionate recognition of their idols at their most stylized. But this was the mockery of the already converted; they laughed at the excesses but were prepared to swoon whenever someone executed them properly. As mimics always know, it's much easier capturing a great artist on a bad day; with talent, you can evoke their foibles. Duplicating their strengths is another question. And elaborating on their genius seems impossible. So to this listener, not invested in a replay of over-the-top diva mannerisms, the comedy was minimal. And very few of the voices exhibited the quality now common among a new generation of countertenors. Why, I wondered, does a soprano range have to be a joke? The gospel men didn't think it was.

For the most part, classical music has limited the male soprano to baroque operas or female impersonation. If Edson Cordeiro was the rare male-soprano superstar, one of the few musical-comedy vehicles for sopranists has been the role of Mary Sunshine in *Chicago*. This sob sister of tabloid journalism is really a man, as the audience ultimately learns—but not before she sings "A Little Bit of Good," a delicious parody of Victor Herbert or Sigmund Romberg. The actors tend to be identified in *Playbill* by initials only, from the original, M. O'Haughey, to the very impressive J. London, whose B-flats are captured on YouTube, and R. Lowe, current star of the New York production. Both London and Lowe have some of the power and color, though not the soul, of a Carl Hall.

The sopranists I've interviewed tend to be bright, serious men. Clearly, super-high singing has not wrecked their brain cells. Some years ago I spoke to Anthony Roth Costanzo, then a high-school senior at New York's High School of Performing Arts, who had made a notable debut in the movie *A Soldier's Daughter Never Cries*. He was joined by his mother, a college professor of psychology, and they spoke of his ventures in highly intellectual terms. Endearingly, after performing the cadenza from Leonard Bernstein's "Glitter and Be Gay," he did an acceptable Aretha Franklin and, at his mother's request, a deep-baritone version of "You'd Be So Nice to Come Home To." It writes itself that seeing the diminutive Costanzo (looking barely past the years of boy sopranohood) sing like a world-wearied traveler was more startling than his high F's. He would receive early admission to Princeton, from which he graduated magna cum laude. His senior thesis took the form of a musical drama, composed, directed, and choreographed by members of the faculty, that centered on a castrato (not, thankfully, one in drag). Clearly many of Costanzo's professors found his venture enthralling. Even at their most whimsical, academics tend to be deadly serious (this can make their humor peculiarly stuffy). Costanzo couldn't have gotten out of Princeton if his teachers hadn't respected what he was doing. In 2009 he would win a $15,000 vocal scholarship from the Metropolitan Opera. In 2010 he made a sensational appearance at Lincoln Center performing as a countertenor in Ligeti's *Le Grand Macabre*. Notably, three other men in the cast—including the virtuosic high tenor Peter Tantsits—stretched their voices way into the fifth octave. As I heard them, I found myself thinking that Carl Hall had been born way too soon.

Following the success of bravura countertenors like David Daniels, a few sopranists have moved out of the baroque ghetto. But they find themselves hapless Cassandras, offering a voice without a home. In Europe the scholarly Greek Aris Christofellis has retired; apparently his investigations of the soprano register were primarily academic, and he didn't much enjoy performing. His sound was thin, accurate, and almost free of vibrato; his performing style, severe and humorless. The American Michael Maniaci is perhaps the most acclaimed sopranist. But in one interview, he broke down in tears over the unsympathetic reception he and his brothers continue to receive. A way out may be to blur the distinctions between countertenors and sopranists, thereby bringing the multi-octave panache of a Cecilia Bartoli to their métier. The dapper Australian countertenor David Hansen has interpolated a soprano high C in the final cadenza of the aria "Vivi, tiranno" from Handel's *Rodelinda*. But the note is gone in a second, more an intimation than a realization.

The biggest and most opulent sound I've heard comes from Robert Crowe, a native of Kentucky, currently living in Germany. He classifies his voice as a spinto rather than a lyric, and his tones are large and heroic, reminding me of the thrilling heights reached by Carl Hall. He is not offended by the comparison, having studied at a college in Mississippi where gospel was required. In his youth he enjoyed singing in local churches. He noticed that the more evangelical the congregation, whether black or white Pentecostal, the more easily they took to his sound. They didn't hear gender bending, they heard an "anointed" voice.

Crowe makes a suggestion I find most sympathetic. He sees a through line that begins with the melisma of the castrato arias, the spellbinding twists and twirls between octaves that supposedly required the range and flexibility only available to an altered male or a woman. He follows the note bending from baroque opera to the ornamented congregational singing of Renaissance England (which used to drive Shakespeare crazy). That ornamentation is retained by English settlers in America and absorbed by Negro slaves. In turn they make the ornamentation their own by imbuing it with a special, blue-noted tonality that, of course, will permeate the spiritual, blues, gospel, and jazz.

Learning this provided a eureka moment. Of course gospel soprano had often been regarded as operatic, even though most of the singers couldn't read music. The trick was to sound legit, or semi-legit, without sacrificing the spirit. But notes with soul is a dream shared by Robert Crowe (he likes to sing the plaintive "O Death, spare me over 'til another year"). His analysis makes the most convoluted gospel run seem not an affectation (as many folklorists have argued) but historically grounded. In his recordings of Monteverdi's "Exulta filia" or Carissimi's "Salve, puellule," his sound is otherworldly, eerily alluring. The improvised melisma is dizzily byzantine, cued by harpsichords that are dense with grace notes and arpeggios. The distance from Monteverdi to modern gospel does not seem that long a stretch. (The countertenor Philippe Jaroussky concurs with Crowe: "Who are we to know that Monteverdi wasn't playing blue notes?")

Crowe leaps at the chance to improvise. "I improvise constantly, especially cadenzas, which I never write down. This drives musically unsure conductors insane. Good ones are delighted by it. In a long run of performances, I try to sing different ornaments every night." His sensibility differs markedly from gospel singers' in one place, the recording studio. "During recordings, I try to sing the same ornaments each time," though he regrets the loss of spontaneity.

Crowe addresses the biggest problems facing a male soprano. It's not a freak voice; composers once employed it regularly. Therefore he has a surfeit of possible roles: "heroes and lovers, tyrants and freaks—and occasionally over-the-top women." But reclaiming his right to sing them has not been easy. "The feminist movement that is now making itself felt in opera is replacing theatrical verisimilitude with the arguably easier-on-the-ears voices of women." His voice happens to be more conventionally pleasing than some of his brothers', and his rugged appearance (one German critic thought he resembled David Beckham) makes him a plausible leading man.

But it's also a big voice, deployed with the volume of a Wagnerian baritone. This alarmed some countertenors and female sopranos, whose exquisite roulades are decibels lower. Who wants to be drowned out by a male Joan Sutherland? For that matter, what woman likes to hear her natural voice amplified and superseded by a male's? One time Carl Hall showed up at a Marion Williams concert, and she invited him to sing. After he had finished with his five high C's and two E-flats, she observed, "Mr. Carl Hall. You never could beat him for those top notes." But she was unusually generous . . . and confident.

Then there are the problems all sopranos face. Crowe says that even the castrati tended to lose their high C's after forty, and where is a soprano without his/her top notes? (What a big price for a few years of coloratura! What an afterlife for a voiceless castrato!) Some men can make whistle notes throughout their lives: eighty-year-old Buck Henry burst into A6 squeals on a recent episode of *30 Rock*; and in *Victor Victoria,* Robert Preston parodied his beloved Julie Andrews's high note by squealing it an octave higher. But a trained sopranist will have integrated his chest and head voices and lost his darling little whistle notes in the process. "Only when I have a cold, when the larynx gets all messed up," can Crowe recapture those piercing, tiny notes. Think about it, gentlemen: how often when we're tired or sick or drunk do those sounds escape us? For most of us, it's a humiliating loss of manhood's authority; we are back in adolescence, at the mercy of our hormones. But for a few, it's a return of childhood's vocal freedom, a loss they continue to regret.

At least Crowe and Maniaci have found roles commensurate with their gifts. Ryan Lowe has a lovely voice (on his Web site, he sings a poignant "Songs My Mother Taught Me," an occasion worthy of attention from music critics, cultural historians, and cut-rate Freudians), but he supports himself with the drag role of Mary Sunshine in *Chicago.* At a recent AIDS benefit concert, he dressed in street clothes and played one chorus boy smitten with another, singing Maria and Anita's duet, "A Boy Like That" / "I Have a Love," from *West Side Story.* He performed with dignity and wit, and included a ravishing note that prompted the same kind of ecstatic and knowing applause Carl Hall might have earned in church. But, in the end, it was a camp moment, even if performed by an exceptional vocalist.

Crowe, Lowe, and Maniaci are serious and relatively fortunate artists. On another level reside men who are equally serious about their tessitura but not quite as accomplished. Some have posted YouTube clips in a valiant attempt to find an audience that has eluded them for most of their lives. They are a quietly heroic band, attempting feats once thought impossible. At this moment YouTube features a video clip of Edson Cordeiro singing the high-note portion of the Queen of the Night's second aria. But at least two men can be seen performing the entire aria in the original key. A middle-aged Argentine named Ghio Nannini is most enterprising for a man of his age, his runs strong and well supported. A young Italian countertenor named Francesco Divito seems to have just discovered his coloratura, and his sound is almost babyish. A sixteen-year-old Asian who doesn't identify himself is even more impressive. But the teen years seem to afford some singers a window of opportunity to extend their boy soprano. (One New Yorker has posted himself singing the "Doll's Song" from *The Tales of Hoffmann* with an interpolated high G.) An Australian schoolteacher named Adam Lopez lifts the Mozart passage a whole octave, landing on F7; and a wistful-looking young man has uploaded a clip titled "The Chinese first tenor sing the coloratura": his tenor is more of a wimpy falsetto, and the A7 on which he "resolves" the passage is the vocalized essence of chalk scratching. But the four corners of the earth seem populated by young men singing this demanding aria, all with a reasonable degree of accuracy. Humanity continues to surprise. And how many others have the potential?

A poignant case is that of Don Tatro, a San Franciscan who worked for eighteen years as an airline steward, a most damaging vocation for any singer, much less a lyric soprano. At fifty-three he regards his career as "shoulda, woulda, coulda. I was always tired and dehydrated." In recent years he has suffered further health problems. Still, he's soldiered on, and up to his late forties was tossing out abundant high F's. He has the vibrato of a black gospel singer, a liability in classical music. But when I played him for gospel musicians, they were enthralled. Joseph Jennings, the former musical director of the male a cappella group Chanticleer, agrees that the young Tatro had a most agile coloratura. But his daddy wasn't rich, and he missed out on the years of professional training. I take his situation as symptomatic. There must be countless Tatros, gifted with a talent that nobody knows how to exploit as something more than a novelty.

Some of them have been inspired by Tatro himself, whom they found—where else?—on YouTube. He has posted his version of "A Little Bit of Good," where just to spite all the countertenors who stick to the B-flat as composed, he appends a chilling E-flat 6. The note went viral. In Vienna, a student of musical theater named Marco Maurer was inspired to sing the song, and conclude with a lovely D6; he maintains a soprano resonance throughout, unlike most of the American Mary Sunshines, who throw in some notes for comic relief. Maurer's natural voice is a countertenor, and his pop voice sounds like a high-pitched heavy-metal singer's. Robert Crowe believes that most whistle-noters lose their top by their early twenties; Maurer, in his mid-twenties, may prove otherwise. Tatro also inspired a seventeen-year-old high-school student named Joey Saffren, who posted the aria, landing on a blustering California boy's C-sharp 6. But just to prove the ubiquity of male coloratura, Joey has also mimicked the Four Seasons' Frankie Valli and the Beach Boys. In one clip, he sings the theremin portion of "Good Vibrations," a feat he learned from Tim Waurick, the most virtuosic tenor in the specialized realm of college harmony groups.

Joe Jennings has tried to liberate all the high-singing men. He was raised in Augusta, Georgia, and grew up playing in gospel churches. Until his late teens he too could reach high F. Carl Hall remains his favorite male soprano, even more than the university-trained altos and sopranos who have sung with Chanticleer down through the years. While he has encouraged the men of Chanticleer to sing some gospel (I wrote the liner notes for one of their collections), he considers such experiments a jeu d'esprit. (He calls his gospel screamers "the eenas": "It takes a big man to be an eena.") For the rest of the time, his arrangements are disciplined, complex, and strictly adhere to all the classical conventions. Aretha Franklin's version of "Nessun dorma," with a failed high note converted into a melismatic rescue job, would not be tolerated in Jennings's scheme.

Even so, he has made Chanticleer the leading classical chorale precisely by exploring the multioctave range from bass to high soprano. (Though only Randall K. Wong, another high-voiced intellectual, gave them a full four octaves with his C's, D's, and an occasional E.) The men have also experimented with Tuvan throat singing, which has allowed them to soar off the piano, the basses and baritones proving even more agile than their higher-pitched colleagues.

Jennings insists that the male soprano is both natural and common: in his church days he heard too many people who sang any part, high or low, without giving it a second thought. His arrangements have allowed classically trained singers to claim the same freedoms. The male soprano becomes his avatar of liberation. His coup is fundamentally rhetorical; a male soprano is no less male because he's sprung a whole new octave.

An even more audacious claim was made by the vocal coach Alfred Wolfsohn, a German Jewish émigré who fled to London during the late 1930s. Wolfsohn contended that everyone had a limitless voice, the lows of a deep basso, the highs of a newborn baby. His students included young and old, male and female. His most famous acolyte, Roy Hart, caused a sensation in the London theater with his varied attempts at song, speech, and sprechstimme, stretching over five or more octaves. He liked to mimic a violin, a pitch that seemed to deny not merely his age and gender but even his species. (At least Charles Kellogg, the bird-singer, drew his inspirations from nature.) After Wolfsohn's death, his method became the foundation of a therapeutic approach not unlike Eli Siegel's Aesthetic Realism. Hart, too, claimed that freeing the voice would turn gay men straight. This was perhaps the only time that singing high became prima facie evidence of heterosexuality.

FIVE, SIX, SEVEN OCTAVES: WHO'S COUNTING?

Not everyone might agree, but all of these men, whether gospel, rock, or classical, aspire to something beautiful, pleasing, or at least expressive. As a result, they all top out in Queen of the Night country, high F being reckoned the highest note that doesn't ravage an ear. But high F is where some other guys just get started.

Once again their model tends to be a woman: Mariah Carey, the best-known exponent of F7's and G7's. (Minnie Riperton and Rachelle Ferrell also made careers of their notes, and improvised more freely than Carey, though they lacked her physical beauty and repertoire of hits.) But even here the androgynous stands revealed. When Carey first started singing, she was known as "the female Michael Bolton" (which makes the male Mariahs only semi-drag acts) because Bolton was noted for thin, whistle-like notes that reached to C7. These notes were arduously sung extensions of his ability to laugh up there. (The soul singer David Ruffin and the gospel singer Jessy Dixon also converted their laughter into high notes.)

If you go by YouTube, the world is filled with Mariah fans, men who live to mimic her. They post their clips from Germany, Thailand, Brazil, Germany, Sweden, and—with surprising frequency—the Philippines: even in thrash metal a shrieked B6 has been recorded by the Filipino-American Mark Osegueda of the band Dead Angel.

The hyper-male world of metal, thrash or death, has proved friendly to freakish high notes. A Canadian heavy-metal singer who calls himself Lord Castrato has the F7's to prove it. A startling number of rock vocalists have squealed out the occasional B6 or C7—among them singers as well known as David Lee Roth and Metallica's James Hetfield or as obscure as Ville Valo, Mike Soliz, Eric Knutson, Rody Walker, and Jeff Martin. (Diligent fans have posted each note of their vocal range, no belch or bleat going unmeasured.) There's a rush of liberation in hearing these voices zoom from grunts and growls to the shrieks of a teenage girl, as if rock has abolished all the barriers of age, race, and sex.

Another kind of vocalism is represented by Von Lee Smith, a short young southerner who sings as high and as fervently as grand divas of Broadway soul like Jennifer Holliday and Patti LaBelle. He can also whistle-note up to the seventh octave.

The interesting distinction is that the heavy-metalers don't aim to be pretty or to sustain melodic lines. Smith does—perhaps because in his fantasy life he hears voices, while the rockers hear guitars.

Some of the most skilled experimentalists display truly androgynous voices, capable of sounding like the lowest man and highest woman. A few of them are openly gay, but do not perform in drag or sing exclusively in a soprano voice, as does the amusing Varla Jean Merman, who has combined Lady Gaga and Mozart (with an F-sharp, a half-step higher than other Queens of the Night). The Eve Harrington of the group is a Filipino college student named Alei. He declares himself Mariah's truest fan, and then proceeds to sing notes a step higher and a second longer, even outmelismatizing her—not an easy task. As menopause threatens her trademarked whistle, the diva must face the Aleis of many nations, ready to replace her, if only in their dreams.

Less stratospheric but far more agile is the gifted soul singer Trey Lorenz, who has frequently duetted with Carey, most dramatically at the funeral of Michael Jackson (where she uttered an inauthentic and wildly inappropriate "Thank you, Jesus!"—a salutation forbidden to Jehovah's Witnesses, like the Jackson family). His melisma is remarkably delicate in the era of gospel gargling, a multioctave pleasure. But he has suffered the ignominious fate of all the male singers exploring a style identified with women.

There are hundreds of whistlers on YouTube. But the champ has to be Adam Lopez, who has entered *Guinness World Records* with his C-sharp 8. Actually he has recorded a E8. It's a petite tone; you expected volume? To paraphrase Dr. Johnson, the amazement is that it's done at all. Lopez says that he acquired the notion when he was in the conservatory. A soprano boasted that her gifts would always outshine his. So he proceeded to beat her in a competition. After that there was no containing him. Edson Cordeiro, when asked why he dared to go so high, answered, "Nobody told me to stop." Lopez was surrounded by academically trained nay sayers. He defied them by recording a version of "Nessun dorma" that sails off the piano. He, too, has re-created the

Queen of the Night. But his version of Mozart includes the bass parts and an upward transposition of the Queen's notes; his arrangement covers five octaves. He can accompany himself on keyboard and has enough confidence to improvise crazily, if not inaudibly, high notes in almost any context, from pop to "popera" to Latin.

He has made an impression; the *Guinness* clip has been downloaded over a million times, and he has acquired a squad of wannabes—he addresses them as "fellow whistlers"—including Sebastian Vilas, an Argentinian soft rocker who tosses out B7's with abandon. But so far pop stardom has eluded them. Lately a young Italian named Nicola Sedda has astonished fans with his ability to belt out notes in the seventh octave. On his Web site he has also posted a vocal exercise that supposedly reaches past the ninth octave.

A reckless Irish tenor named Michael "Mick" Kennedy does that with alacrity. Employing a technique he calls "microbreathing," he dives lower and soars higher than the piano. He also sings in a legit style, downloading opera arias along with exercises in which he sounds like a reincarnation of Charles Kellogg, the bird-singer. I can't imagine another singer with classical aspirations delighting in so many freaky sounds. But I assume this self-styled vocal coach has a sense of humor. Why else perform "Times Is Hard (Please Don't Burn Our Shithouse Down)," in which he sings seven—or is it seventeen?—different voices? His intolerable singing rather moves me. It's as if every vocal ambition known to man or beast has snuggled into his hapless throat.

Three singers have escaped the fringes where Nicola Sedda and Lord Castrato still dwell. The first was Demetrio Stratos, a Greek singer whose early work bore the traces of Tom Jones and David Bowie. He wound up fronting Area, an Italian prog-rock band. But he was also something of a visionary. After hearing his baby daughter make vocal sounds with a freedom and ease that she would never regain, he concluded that "a child loses the sound in order to organize his words," the aural correlative to Wordsworth's credo that heaven lies about us in our infancy. "Voice in today's music," he said, "is a transmission channel that does not transmit anything." In order to be most expressive, he had to abandon language and leap far beyond the prison cell of his woefully delimited vocal range. Rock quickly lost its charms; by the mid-1970s as he entered his own thirties, he was splitting his time between Area, wherein his vocals grew increasingly wordless, and the New York scene of John Cage. To recapture the freedoms of his baby daughter, he began experimenting with octave leaps and vocal distortion. Throat singing came to inform his technique. He began hitting small, extremely high notes that, Tuvan-style, seemed to open up into little conversations among themselves. At times there seemed to be a quartet of noisemakers snuggled in his throat.

He was also politically engaged, an unabashed socialist and sympathetic to movements of social liberation. Going beyond Alfred Wolfsohn, Stratos considered his vocalism a revolutionary tactic, since it was bourgeois society that had enfeebled those vocal cords. In 1979, as he seemed poised to be the left's prog-rock troubadour, he was stricken with cancer. A benefit concert in Milan drew over a hundred thousand fans, but it occurred a day after he had died in New York, where he had hoped to find a cure.

He was a big, fine-looking man, with a manner so charismatic that his fans of the seventies can still be moved to tears over his loss. Just as myth has Robert Johnson selling his soul to the devil, a story spread that Stratos's vocal experiments had killed him, not the cancer. His agenda was similar to the male sopranos', if not even bolder. They may try to sound like boys or women, but he wanted to recapture the octave range of early childhood. (Recently Claudio Milano, a neo-operatic vocalist, has revived some of his multioctave experiments.)

Blixa Bargeld, a Berlin actor, writer, guitarist, and vocalist, adapted his name from that of a German Dada artist, Johannes Theodor Baargeld. Fourteen years younger than Stratos, he joined an industrial-rock band, Einstürzende Neubauten, in which scrap metal and electronics usually stood in for acoustic instruments. These unnatural noises provided a cushion for his gloomy caterwauling. Frequently, after convincing you that he had a four-note range, he would soar three octaves into a series of garbled yelps and whistle notes. His fans said this eerily unmusical tessitura was the sound of postmodern culture; a death rattle granted a temporary reprieve. Actually, he phrased in a loping, deep-voiced, and *echt Deutsch* style that recalls Marlene Dietrich, reincarnated as—among his various rock personae—either an androgynous war orphan (he was born fourteen years after the war ended) or a jaunty, 1920s boulevardier. Even the fusion of cackle and whistle note seems a German thing to do, a vocal extension of Grimm fairy tales. These days, much stouter than the rock-and-roll wraith, he is primarily a theater artist.

Stratos's sole heir is the voraciously eclectic Mike Patton. Easily the most ambitious rock vocalist, he has tried everything from death metal to Italian pop (and even light opera, managing to produce a high C of sorts), from Chet Baker to Tom Jones to Spike Jones. Bored by a stint with the band Faith No More (where he impressed some listeners with his parody of Lionel Richie), he began making home recordings of mouth noises, ranging from grunts to shrieks, cooled by an occasional whistle, but in total as unlyrical a project as ever dared call itself *Adult Themes for Voice.*

A bookish kid, the son of a schoolteacher, Patton made his debut with a high-school band, Mr. Bungle, with whom he cut work far bolder and more avant-garde than the pop of Faith No More. The early albums were also filled with fabulously infantile and jejune songs like "Squeeze Me Macaroni," "The Girls of Porn," and "Bloody Mary" (a mournful ballad about menstruation). From his earliest recordings he had been playing with vocal sounds. But he grew conspicuously more adventurous after discovering Demetrio Stratos, Diamanda Galas, and John Zorn. Zorn and Patton began performing duets in which the saxophonist scrambles between octaves and Patton tries to match him, the horn's immense, bull-headed A6's challenged by the voice's tapered squeaks. About this time, fans rewarded his audacity by calling him the man with eight octaves.

By the late nineties, he had quit both Mr. Bungle and Faith No More for a series of new bands, each one with a discrete scope and slant. Some fans were infuriated by the avant-garde experimentation. Pop ballad singing was out; double-entendre lyrics disappeared, though Patton allowed his old fans a small relief with his frequent and noisy cursing. In a series of concerts with Zorn's small ensembles, some of them recorded and all of them posted on YouTube, within minutes Patton has growled, yowled, belched, gargled, flossed, whispered, shrieked, knuckled his teeth, and slapped his lips. His gestures will be as anarchic as his vocal sounds. Carl Hall accompanied his notes with gestures indicating physical labor, but Patton has been known to flop like a fish out of water, or pummel both cheeks, pushing sounds out of his mouth as if they were vomit. In one clip he makes two long, piercing shrieks. To assign them a pitch (even though Zorn boasts that the music cannot be notated), he's exhaled two A6's. Then he spits, loudly, and shrieks again—the same A6. That can't be easy. (The clip must have its appeal: it has received six hundred thousand hits on YouTube.)

Can Patton's shrieks be called singing? When his fans worry that he's straining his voice, he answers that the throat is a muscle, implying that he's a world-class athlete. He admits that he doesn't make his sounds "in a classical manner." Even the most amateurish whistle notes on YouTube have more body and tune. But not soul: Patton is obviously dedicated to exploring whatever gifts his throat will bestow.

If you have the stamina, compare a YouTube clip of Mike Patton with one of a young Austrian named Piet Arion singing a five-octave version of "The Long and Winding Road." One wants to abuse the ears; the other to seduce them. In keeping with their different aims, where Patton follows his super-note with a percussive spit, Arion holds his B-flat 6 for ten seconds and then blows his auditor a kiss. Two instances of vocal chutzpah with completely different grounds for their ambition.

Patton's "hideous, horrible sounds" (his term) will open your ears to the weird ululations that a surprising number of men have mastered. Actors and, especially, comedians like to make dog-whistle notes. In the film *American Splendor,* playing the cartoonist Harvey Pekar, who becomes deathly ill after his wife leaves him, Paul Giamatti starts wheezing out words that float around C7. Stephen Colbert has also made funny, exceedingly high sounds, usually for some comic purpose. In the series *30 Rock* Jack McBrayer plays a provincial naif whose usual response to the incongruous is a Mike Patton–like shriek. Catch how many comedians have laughs that break way above their speaking voice, and notice how lovingly they sustain them. Having discovered that the croak is brother to the squeak, they make their throats serve their comedy.

The sounds are not pleasing. But they are high—easily as high, if not as opulent, as those of most male sopranos. And the real shock is that male fans glory in those high notes. Mike Patton's shrieks thrill his fans. Somehow he has made womanly pitches ugly, nasty, and indisputably male. Nobody ever comments that his C7s are "gay, gay, too gay" (while they would abandon a Von Lee Smith in a moment), perhaps because they're embedded between strong-man growls and baby squeals—for him, too, the ultimate freedom is not female but infantile. So far he hasn't published manifestos like Stratos or Bargeld, though he clearly shares their ideology.

Trailing Patton as he ages are scores of young men, death-metal vocalists who have begun to cultivate the art of "pig squealing" and "inward screaming." One amateur has posted instructions on YouTube, and over half a million viewers have checked him out. Whatever vocal manipulation allows the Filipino drag queen and the Canadian pig squealer to hit that same C7, they share nothing else, temperamental or aesthetic, in common. Except they both come most fully alive when they succeed in abolishing the most audible distinction between sexes and, yes, species. To their millions of admirers, their sounds are musical—who wants tunes? who needs lyrics?—and they are heroes.

—

The male soprano intrigues more than it satisfies. I still haven't found singers like Carl Hall or Alex Bradford, and don't expect that even the most dulcet-toned of Joe Jennings's flock will replace Victoria de los Angeles or Dame Janet Baker. But the high singer has provided some unforgettable tableaux, scenes in which the voice has illuminated the forms of sexuality that, almost by definition, he renders suspect.

A blatant enactment is that Brazilian video in which the butch contralto Cássia Eller duels with the pugilistic coloratura Edson Cordeiro. But I prefer the unideological moments. In her early days touring the gospel highway, Mahalia Jackson would sing duets with her pianist James Lee, also known as gospel's first male soprano; in truth he was a countertenor, but the harmonies remained unprecedented, as if Mahalia required a man's ecstatic shrieks to confirm her womanly power.

Once, during a Spirit-filled moment at the Apollo Theater, Professor Herman Stevens invited two of gospel's greatest women, Inez Andrews and Ruth Davis, to join him in song. He turned to the right and Ruth squalled until grown men trembled. He turned to the left and Inez hollered so loud that grown men trembled some more. Then, whether high in his Spirit or challenged by theirs, he sang a startling pure whistle note, jumped off the stage, and ran all around the Apollo.

In a recent music clip Jack McBrayer plays a mailman. When a door opens and he beholds Mariah Carey, he can only utter a dog-whistle note. She looks bemused—not that he's mocking her but that he's wasting her time. But he is simply offering his queen the only devotion he can imagine: no greater flattery than imitation.

In James Ivory's movie *A Soldier's Daughter Never Cries,* the youthful heroine, Channe (Leelee Sobieski), befriends an eccentric schoolmate (Anthony Roth Costanzo) with the suspect name Francis, whom she first observes singing a Mozart aria to the smirking amusement of the other boys. Though Ivory saw himself in Francis's inchoate striving, he's too smart to assign Francis a sexuality. Once Channe starts falling for the opposite sex, virile lads win her fancy, thereby breaking Francis's heart. But until she moves into adult heterosexuality they are inseparable.

At one point the two start running, overflowing with adolescent zeal. Channe shrieks like a happy kid. Francis answers her with beautifully rounded notes, as high as and higher than hers. She's a screamer, he's a soprano. Her nature inspires his artifice. But his falsetto is as true as his love for her, impossibly pure and, under the circumstances, totally authentic. Whatever or whomever he salutes, the male soprano lifts his voice to praise. What a guy am I! he says, with all the voice in the world.

THE CURSE OF SURVIVAL

Whose blues is it anyway? On his first trip to the Mississippi Delta, Elijah Wald, the critic and blues musician, found himself performing a Robert Johnson song at the Mount Zion Missionary Baptist Church. He reckoned that the members wouldn't care for the old blues sound, much less have heard of his idol. But he didn't expect their response: unmitigated glee. Taking for granted the musical strategies that Wald had spent years mastering, they attended instead to Johnson's hilarious double entendres in "Terraplane Blues."

> *Motor's in a bad condition,*
> *You gotta have these batteries charged,*
> *But I'm cryin', please,*
> *Please don't do me wrong.*
> *Who been drivin' my Terraplane now for you*
> *Since I've been gone?*

Instead of a blasted prophet, they heard a vivacious entertainer. Where Wald gleaned tragedy, they spied fun.

In *Escaping the Delta* Wald places Johnson in his proper context, allowing us to hear him as he would have been heard in 1936. More bravely, he confronts the generations of white blues boys (most of them boys, most of them white, including everyone from Eric Clapton to the street-corner slide guitarist) who commandeered and reconfigured the blues. In the process, they upturned hierarchies and banished to invisibility artists they deemed frivolous, artists who had frequently been the African-American audience's favorites. In their place, the new fans anointed singers like Johnson, who would come to personify the blues, with millions of albums sold and even a postage stamp bearing his image. The blues audience of his time barely knew him. The pop audience today hardly knows anyone else.

Josh White, the original soul man and matinee idol of the country blues, mid-1950s

A professional musician and the author of *Josh White: Society Blues,* Wald wrote this book largely because a "more polished, professional approach has been disrespected by generations of blues writers in search of wild Delta primitivism." Yet he shares these writers' enthusiasm, and his book also challenges himself: how could he have missed so much splendor? In transforming "a music notable for its professionalism and humor" into an existential lament, had the blues fans gotten everything wrong? Were they guilty, terrible to admit, of provincial bad taste?

Wald's view of American culture is therapeutically revisionist. He celebrates a time before there were categories, when sounds had yet to be codified, when everybody heard everything. Did you know, for instance, that country fiddling was largely based on jigs and reels mastered in slavery (and originally associated with the Irish, who, like their musical fellow travelers the Jews, were not considered much whiter than slaves)? Or that B. B. King loved hillbilly star Jimmie Rodgers, while Muddy Waters grew up listening to Gene Autry?

That's not all Wald presents. Did you also know that Robert Johnson, when not dodging hellhounds, liked to sing "Yes Sir, That's My

Robert Johnson, circa 1935

Baby"? That a decade before Elvis crash-landed on all the charts, Louis Jordan's jump blues were number one on the country Hit Parade? Or that Johnny Shines, Johnson's singing partner, boasted of their skill at playing "the better type of stuff"?

The first blues recording, one learns, was made by a white man; the first Queen of the Blues was a white woman. In the 1920s, the earliest black blues stars were robust divas who had apprenticed in vaudeville or the circus. Country blues, the sound identified with Johnson and with Wald's favorite, Skip James, was recorded later and never matched the popularity of the other forms. Nobody is quite willing to say which came first, country blues or city blues. Simply because guitar (country) blues sounds more primitive doesn't mean that it preceded city blues, which employed instruments like piano, cornet, and saxophone. My own guess is that the development of country blues in the 1930s parallels what was going on in black churches, where old forms of religious music were updated to conform to new aesthetic demands. Except that in the case of country blues, the updated form actually involved a return to the roots of holler and moan.

Though blues scholars have canonized the field holler, I'm not sure of its influence. It wasn't widely sung, even in the workplace, and the example cited by Wald, a 1947 jailhouse lament by a man named Tangle Eye, is a secular adaptation of the old hymn "I Wonder Will We Ever Meet Again," sung with the byzantine melisma universally identified with a church moan. That moan usually takes the form of a hum, though it can also be an "ooh," "ah," "oh," or "hey," and it can be expressed in guttural tones or high falsetto. When slurred moans are introduced into spoken and sung words, the result is a hallowing of language, a transcendent state. As with the donning of a scarf or a yarmulke, everything becomes solemn, sacred.

Country blues shares gospel's habits of rhythm, harmony, and verbal repetition. In both forms, rhetoric aspires to seduce as well as persuade. That's why, in both forms, verses are interchangeable, and straight story-telling is disregarded in favor of the moment's prompting, a cascade of epiphanies—not all of them related, but all performed with the same intensity. When a great singer slur-moans her words, harmony is infused with emotion. No other sound so simple and ubiquitous can also be so deeply, immediately serious. Robert Johnson takes this for granted, which is why his best performances were extended moans.

Little is known about Johnson, and Wald spends few pages on his biography. He was born in any of the five years from 1907 to 1911, most likely in Hazelhurst, Mississippi, and he died, perhaps murdered by a cuckolded husband, in August 1938. We know that he was raised in the church, that his idol was an ex–shouting preacher named Son House, that he had a lazy eye, and that, according to Shines, he had "sharp, slender fingers that fluttered like a trapped bird." We are fascinated to learn that Shines and Johnson traveled far from Mississippi—to Canada, where they sang in a gospel quartet, and to New York, where they sang in the streets. We seem to know that Johnson was admired but not revered, a good sport and a loner, a ladies' man and a mama's boy; that he could move a crowd to tears but could not dazzle them with "clown-ing" shenanigans (play guitar with his teeth or between his legs). That he invented almost nothing.

Wald has produced, for the Yazoo label, a musical anthology called *The Roots of Robert Johnson*. Even more than his own analyses, this album demonstrates that Johnson was a blues chameleon who mixed and matched the sounds of all the then-current stars. These included men like Peetie Wheatstraw (a pianist-singer whose vocals were dense with yodels and metrical variety), Kokomo Arnold (a virtuoso slide guitarist whose slashing baritone could soar to a mezzo-soprano high), Leroy Carr (a pianist whose vocals linked Louis Armstrong's audacity to a Bing Crosby croon, and whose intonation would be echoed by R. H. Harris, Sam Cooke's gospel mentor), and Son House (whose huge voice sounds newly sprung from the church: after singing the line "Lord have mercy on my wicked soul" twice, he replaces the anticipated third line—the traditional B to his AA—with a wordless moan). They're all unmistakably present, Johnson was that shameless.

But why not? Like any folk singer, Johnson claimed a right to every offshoot of his idiom. And he had confidence born of good guitar technique—distinguished by his pioneering use of the bass shuffle, later intrinsic to rock and roll—and a magnificent voice. For blues fans, as Wald constantly reminds us, singing and not instrumentation has always been the focus of attention. Johnson had many registers: he could sing first tenor without too much strain, drop to a well-supported baritone, growl like a preacher, sail into falsetto, employ comical voices when performing vaudeville hokum, and manage to sing lead or background parts so distinctly that you might imagine two men standing at the microphone.

Wald knows that by contextualizing Johnson, he risks demystifying—even demoting—him. So be it. If we end up valuing Johnson less, we acquire a greater purchase on musical history.

Take one of his most famous songs, "Come On in My Kitchen." The melody had been popularized a few years earlier by the Mississippi Sheiks in "Sitting on Top of the World." On this astonishing record, a beautiful fiddle sound straddles the territory between country music and blues, looking back to a tradition of black string band music and forward to Nashville's signature yoking of blue notes and hymns. The vocal and the instrumental are both plushly legato and ironically deadpan, since each verse depicts someone at the bottom of a pit insisting that he's "sitting on top of the world." The melody was next employed by Tampa Red, the most influential of all slide guitarists, in "Things 'Bout Comin' My Way," another lyrical instance of whistling past a graveyard:

When I was sick down on my bed,
My friends forgot me, thought I was dead.

Red's pianist was "Georgia Tom," who soon quit the blues field to become Thomas A. Dorsey, the father of modern gospel music, in which his streamlined blues-based ballads found immediate acceptance. By then, the blues ballad was a Tin Pan Alley staple: Irving Berlin composed more than a few.

Johnson's "Come On in My Kitchen" is a much deeper performance, perhaps his finest. It is also his most churchy. He begins the recording with two moaned lines and then sings, "You better come on in my kitchen / Because it's going to be raining outdoors." He employs a growling tone that immediately, almost shockingly, mimics the gospel singer Blind Willie Johnson. The preaching tactics could be a light-voiced attempt to duplicate Son House's huge sound, but I think the echo of Blind Willie is deliberate. Johnny Shines says that "Come On in My Kitchen" could move grown men and women to tears, as any passionate, gospel-rooted performance ought. Wald notes that the verses are fungible and generic. I notice that the penultimate verse invokes a woman in trouble, abandoned by her friends, and that the last verse summons a vision of universal storm. Johnson recorded a second take of the song, and though not as intense a meditation, it ends with a verse about a motherless child. These were the customary themes of Baptist sermons, invariably the notes that got closest to the people. Johnson's kitchen becomes a sanctuary, the ark of safety in a desperate season. Two other Johnson masterpieces, "Walking Blues" and "Preaching the Blues," both previously recorded by Son House, use the same vocal devices. This leads me to propose that rather than selling out to the devil, House and Johnson were extending the varieties of worship in moaned form, enacting the parable of the Prodigal Son without any sacrilegious motives.

Johnson died in 1938. His records had been minor regional hits and were soon forgotten. Wald isn't even convinced that he would have stuck with his original sound: with his shuffling rhythms, he might have become another T-Bone Walker; with his merging of ballad, gospel moan, and blues, he might have become the original Ray Charles. Either way, by 1941 the era of acoustic singer-guitarists had drawn to a close. Wald lists the selections found on jukeboxes located on a huge Mississippi plantation. There's virtually nothing close to "down home." The most popular blues was "Going to Chicago" by the Count Basie band featuring Jimmy Rushing. There were several swing bands performing blues tunes. The singer-guitarist represented most often was gospel star Sister Rosetta Tharpe, with a terrific version of "Stand by Me," a Thomas A. Dorsey gospel blues.

White fans may be shocked by this transfer of loyalties. But since I like many of the selections and especially admire the Rosetta Tharpe number, I would argue that Mississippians had proved themselves quite as hip as audiences anywhere, town or city. The program they got with happened to be a great one; it was one of pop music's finest hours.

For the next twenty years, blues remained central to black music, whether it was called "race," "rhythm and blues," or "soul." Wald surveys the many talents who updated the form, thrilling their audiences only to be dismissed as too "light," too "popular," too "commercial" by white blues fans. He then does something very interesting as he traces the development of these fans' tastes to three WASP socialites, Carl Van Vechten, John Hammond, and Alan Lomax, who were drawn to black music for vastly different reasons. Van Vechten may have had the purest aesthetic and the most visceral agenda: his love of the form coincided with his attraction to black men. Lomax was the academic savant and the political maven. But Hammond, the legendary record producer, would be the most linked with Johnson, because he had invited him to perform at the epochal concert "From Spirituals to Swing," not realizing that the singer had died, and because Johnson's records would be reissued under his auspices in 1961. Like many a committed fan, Hammond was fiercely arbitrary. His insistence on the comparative purity of one talent over another—and it was usually a battle—was incorrigible. Count Basie's band made the cut, and Duke Ellington's mostly did not. (Hammond loathed the musical ambitions of arrangers like Fletcher Henderson, since he thought the blues provided inspiration enough.)

These men set the tone for later white fans. But even at their most egregious, none of them made the kind of mistakes Wald proceeds to catalog. Time and again, the guys who share his "tastes and predilections" got things backward. They ranked the guitar well above the piano, although, with its shimmering overtones, that instrument has liberated the most inspired blues, jazz, and gospel vocalists. Even their guitar hero Muddy Waters, interviewed in 1941, cited as his favorite artists the singer-pianists Walter Davis and Fats Waller, while observing that black music's superiority to white lay in its "harmony in the blues line," by which he meant voice and piano. (Judging by his long association with Otis Spann, Waters's appreciation for the piano sound did not diminish.) The new fans trumped the old standards. Where once the singer had been the star, now it was the accompanist. Singing itself was demoted; huge, opulent voices were dismissed as "ornate," "pretentious," or, in a recent vile idiom, "gay." Authenticity, "realness," was all. Artistic compromise, particularly if it involved a showmanly pandering to the crowd, was beneath contempt. The judgments have been merciless.

Women suffered the most, all the more because until Johnson, Bessie Smith and Ma Rainey had been the most famous blues singers. On a few recordings, Johnson scaled the expressive heights, as did Skip James once or twice (though it's hard to imagine his wispy wail ever scoring with black listeners, who never exhibited a taste for the ineffable). But I am far more moved by, say, Smith's 1926 recording of "Gin House Blues." When she sings

> *It takes a good smart woman these days*
> *To hold her man*
> *When these gals have got so many different ways*

the moaned slur she imposes on "hold" conveys a power and melancholy that make most bluesmen sound like babes in the wood. In my experience (I started attending the Apollo Theater when I was in junior high school over fifty years ago), the blues singers the people talked back to most were Dinah Washington and Big Maybelle.

Wald reminds us of the huge investment that fans of the last fifty years have placed in whatever—music, films, comics, sports—cuts to their marrow. The evolution of taste has become an index of the psyche. You can dispute folks' politics or theology and still drink with them. But say, for example, as our finest composer-critic, Ned Rorem, recently did, that Bob Dylan's music is "worthless," and, well, you're on your own.

Inevitably history continues to be rewritten. Robert Christgau, the veteran rock critic, recently drew a parallel between Elvis Presley and Sam Cooke, ignoring the difference in age between the two or the fact that Elvis pretty much invented his style on the spot while Cooke arrived on the pop scene the acknowledged master—albeit in gospel—of his. Christgau also observed that Elvis had many male acolytes, while Cooke was simply a "heartthrob." Indeed he was that, but he was also the biggest influence on his genre: all the soul men tried to sing like him.

Out of such blithe error and dialectical conceit flows the received wisdom. That is, until an Elijah Wald simply looks at the music on its own terms, judging it by its own criteria. Against the charms of postmodern bricolage, he offers the superior rewards of close listening. In the context of most writing about popular music, *Escaping the Delta* is more than a tonic. It's champagne, Muddy Waters's favorite drink.

—

When Elijah Wald first mentioned Josh White to his parents, their memories clashed. His father recalled an earthy laborer, sweating soulfully; his mother, a sleek entertainer who changed his silk shirt twice during a performance. The greatest strength of Wald's *Josh White: Society Blues* is its recognition that this division was intrinsic to White's career and that its balance of folk art and show business was singular, inspired, and even heroic.

White was a cusp artist who consolidated his style as country blues was winding down and gospel music was revving up. He was born on February 11, 1914, in Greenville, South Carolina, the son of a laundress and a tailor who served as a part-time preacher in a Methodist church. Much of his childhood was ill-starred. His father was beaten so badly by the police that he ended his days in a mental institution, and his mother could barely support White and his six siblings. He went on the road at the age of eight, guiding blind itinerant singer-guitarists, banging the tambourine, witnessing two lynchings, shivering and starving but sending home good money.

His precocious talent made a way for him. He was handsome and popular, and the beneficiary of a childhood as artistically fruitful as it was otherwise barren. The main reason was his mother's participation in a sanctified church, one of the small Pentecostal congregations where song and dance comprised most of the service. The harmonic and melodic demands of religious music were far more expansive than blues, and mastering them enabled White to much later "adapt his style to jazz, pop, and European folk melodies." (A similar education led classical vocalists like Marian Anderson to progress from spirituals to lieder.)

Blue notes came originally out of church moans and slurs, and a gospel singer could apply them whenever, wherever. Blues itself might not even be the best vehicle, but White knew that blue tonality was his ace. In 1950, while allowing that white men could play jazz and blues, he added, "Negro musicians manage to get those in-between tones, that sort of strained intonation, better than any white musician can." It was the closest he ever came to a racial challenge.

His recording career began at eighteen. Wald allows that these early blues exhibit a callow facility but insists that the great work lay years ahead. I disagree. From the beginning, White's style was fully achieved and strikingly new, at least for blues. Greenville was the home of the Dixie Hummingbirds, later to become a world-famous gospel quartet; and White is more properly measured, not against Blind Lemon Jefferson and Blind Willie Johnson, but against the Hummingbirds and its lead singer, Ira Tucker, or the group's bass singer in 1939, Claude Jeter, who later cultivated a slinky falsetto that would be shamelessly echoed by Al Green. Within a few measures of his first record, "Black and Evil Blues," White leaps into falsetto. A few takes later, his voice drops an octave into a growling bass, part Louis Armstrong, part storefront preacher. Within the first session, he covers almost three octaves. His first instrument had been the tambourine, and he clearly loved percussive, rapid-fire syllables, occasionally singing such lines a cappella because his fingers weren't quick enough.

In 1927, Blind Willie Johnson had recorded the first gospel blues (a minor-key version of the sixteen-bar form), "Motherless Children," in which his guitar, standing in for the congregation, frequently completed his thoughts in sustained wordless moans. Similarly, White's use of "passing chords" to bind the melodic units derived from melisma, the extravagantly configured runs of a lined-out hymn. Having learned from quartets to sing different vocal parts, White played his guitar high and low—indeed, several keys lower than Blind Willie, as if voice and guitar obeyed the same impulse. He seldom belted, preferring a dry, laconic style (not the obvious choice of a young virtuoso), and his reading of songs like "Things 'Bout Comin' My Way" exhibited an introspective authority that could not be faked unless he was more of an actor at eighteen than he would be in his fifties.

Even better than his blues, which he recorded under the names Joshua White and Pinewood Tom, were the gospel recordings attributed to "Joshua White (the Singing Christian)." In his early masterpiece, "There's a Man Going Around Takin' Names," a song he recorded many times but never with the same intensity as the first version, an ad-lib spirit allows him all kinds of sanctified freedom ("Lord, Lord, Lord, takin' names") and a blood-curdling conclusion ("He's writing left and right / Among the colored and the white").

Pace Wald, the young White was a trailblazer in blues and gospel: his "In the Evening" anticipated Robert Johnson's phrasing by two years, and in August 1935 he became only the third artist to record one of the new songs known as "gospel," composed by the man who named the genre, Thomas A. Dorsey. In "How About You," White sings out as if in church, his guitar deliriously breaking time, grabbed by the Holy Ghost.

Most remarkable about White's early records is their juxtaposition of secular, sacred, and (latently) political. On one session, supported by Walter Roland's churchily florid piano, he veered from "Sissy Man Blues" and "Homeless and Hungry Blues" to biblically derived gospel songs, all of them brilliant performances. Another recording, "Prodigal Son," a deathbed confession to a brokenhearted mother, was released under Pinewood Tom's name but would have wrecked any church with its terrifying vision of the wages of sin. In later years, White's repertory would encompass more sophisticated lyrics, but none richer in thematic terms.

By the mid-1930s, he had moved to New York, where, at nineteen, he married Carol Carr, an unglamorous, practical woman, the well-chosen wife of a sensationally handsome man, cocksure and gregarious to a fault. A crippling hand injury nearly ended his career, and he spent the next years doing manual labor to support Carol and their kids. But by 1939, through a series of fortuitous connections well traced by Wald, he had entered a whole new world, that of folk music. Though his chops had been compromised (his high notes shot along with his speedy arpeggios), he adopted a style that retained his best qualities: when he sang "Strange Fruit," his version was far more churchy than Billie Holiday's, stressing words like "blood" in a way that interrupted the legato flow to great expressive purpose and adding moaned vocals that duplicated his passing chords. He was also singing lyrics that were defiantly political.

White was embraced by the musical left, black and white. Black progressives had argued throughout the 1930s about the political implications of folklore. Richard Wright declared that blues were the new spirituals, their visionary leaps more than compensating for the forays into violence and mindless sex (similar apologies have been mounted for rap). As White replaced his more evangelical spirituals with freedom songs, he sounded like a working-class radical, a figure black progressives had despaired of finding. The white left was even more gratified to claim White. He may have briefly joined the Communist Party, perhaps because its civil rights positions were unimpeachable, at least before World War II, when the party opposed labor strikes and civil rights protests as diversions from the effort to defeat Hitler and save Stalin.

On the strength of albums produced by John Hammond, he made many new fans. In 1941, two years after the Daughters of the American Revolution refused to let Anderson perform in Constitution Hall, an act that prompted a mass protest led by Eleanor Roosevelt, FDR's inaugural gala, held at Constitution Hall, would include White and the Golden Gate Jubilee Quartet along with Charlie Chaplin, Ethel Barrymore, and Mickey Rooney, and the Daughters did not object.

But despite his new public, the former star of "race records"—the term used at the time for rhythm and blues—had lost his old one. He griped that black bobby-soxers only wanted to hear double-entendre blues like "Jelly Jelly" and lacked the patience for deeper, more political anthems. But you can't blame them. In 1940 White's vocal support had come from quartets such as the Golden Gates and the Carolinians, featuring Bayard Rustin's tenor. With the Carolinians, White had romped through "King Jesus Knows I'm Coming," a rearrangement of a song Mahalia Jackson had recorded three years earlier. But by 1944, his vocal accompaniment came from the dreary Almanac Singers in a lumbering Popular Front rewrite of the spiritual "Hold On," which offered godspeed to FDR, Churchill, Chiang Kai-shek, and Stalin (what a quartet—and who sang lead?). How could such music inspire black audiences when they could fly with the Dixie Hummingbirds?

Moreover, "Jelly Jelly" was his signature. For, as Wald stresses, White was a surpassingly sexual performer. Traces of his multioctave range now informed a variety of liquid gobbles and ecstatic squeaks that left nothing to a woman's imagination. As he had introduced blue notes to polite society, he now became the first soul man, a muscular athlete supremely comfortable in his gleaming skin. No black man had displayed himself so confidently before a white audience (the light-skinned, wavy-haired Cab Calloway represented something more stylized and frenetic). Josh White Jr., a star in his own right, marvels at his father's audacity: "It's lucky he didn't get killed for it." You get a sense of White's magnetism from a DVD, *Josh White: Free and Equal Blues,* which includes performances made almost twenty years after his prime. As women always noted, when he tunes his guitar, he's actually flexing his muscles. His carriage is at once dignified and tantalizing. During "Jelly Jelly" his shoulders rock sinuously while he strokes and pounds his guitar, more love object than musical tool. At forty-eight, he makes rockers such as Elvis and Mick Jagger seem gauche and unseasoned.

White's persona seduced his listeners, female and male alike. He despised anything that smacked of the stereotype: in 1939, he deplored the use of "nigger" in Broadway lyrics. In 1951, he demanded the excision of blackface Al Jolson routines in a London musical. All showman, he reckoned himself an "actor," not a "clown," his brutally dismissive term for older artists such as Lead Belly. It signifies that his pupils included women like the singers Libby Holman and Eartha Kitt (both may have been his lovers; the army was very large). He showed them how to flirt and not pander, and they showed him that one could be provocative and enigmatic, tease and give nothing away.

The 1940s were White's glory days. He had a near–pop hit, "One Meat Ball," packed the best clubs, and appeared in a movie with Randolph Scott. He popularized what he considered the anti–"Strange Fruit," "The House I Live In," an inspirational anthem that he sang without any blue notes, as if to extend its democratic embrace. (Frank Sinatra was equally known for the song; comparing the two versions reveals Sinatra to be more formal and derivatively bel canto. White's later version of "One for My Baby" also benefits by comparison with Sinatra.)

But the good times ended with the McCarthy era. In an attempt to win the support of the publication *Red Channels* and thereby escape a blacklist that might—and would eventually—stymie his career, he met with right-wing journalists and even volunteered to testify before Senator Joseph McCarthy's House Un-American Activities Committee. He named no names, distancing himself only from Paul Robeson's putative declaration that no Negro would fight against the Soviet Union (Robeson had in fact been misquoted). Instead he deplored communism itself while asserting that whatever elements he admired in the movement dovetailed exactly with "Christianity," boasting that he had raised his children to be devout patriots. He was proud that so few Negroes had joined the party, thereby exhibiting their "common sense," and told *Negro Digest* that the reds had played him for a chump. Naturally, White's old lefty friends were appalled. But when Pete Seeger composed an angry letter, his fellow Weavers proved less judgmental. They understood that White was terrified of jeopardizing the security of his wife and children and that the government might have blackmailed him with revealing photographs. (We now know that in 1950 Frank Sinatra offered to fink for the feds. He was then considered a has-been, and the government declined his services. Either way, "The House I Live In" had become something for its singers to live down.)

Jackie Washington, a folk singer greatly inspired by White, offers the most convincing, if disheartening, analysis: White simply didn't have a dog in the hunt. He hadn't been a committed radical, and finally, he was a black man trying to get over, "taking care of business." If the lefties could say they made him by supplying his first white audience, he could reply that he gave them authenticity and proved that they were more than bourgeois academics.

From cynosure to pariah, White became a despised figure in vanguard circles. Though his career survived, particularly in Europe, American folkies increasingly saw him as a burned-out case. They had loved him singing protest songs, but they savaged his more recent performances of English and Irish ballads. Yet these performances were very fine. In "Molly Malone," he characteristically emphasized the word "crying" and with each reading supplied more inspired blue notes. He took "Barbara Allen" and, with bluesy glissandi, immediately split the difference between Child Ballad and Grand Ole Opry. Two highlights of the 1960s video are "Danny Boy," exactly the kind of ditty that his family would have sung around the piano, and "You'd Be So Nice to Come Home To," wherein he moans whole phrases, perhaps because he has forgotten the words and, as the spiritual advises, was looking to the hills.

The contemporaries he now considered rivals were Harry Belafonte, who had capitalized on his most commercial traits, and Ray Charles, whom he would mimic in the car and, supposedly, out-holler. Why not? Both Charles and White had uncovered the soulful elements in country music.

With suave tact, Wald considers some very intimate matters. We learn that White was a father engaged enough to comfort one daughter during her first period and to introduce his son to a sexual partner when the boy was eleven. The children led middle-class lives, attended private school, never heard him speak ungrammatically, and were stunned by the colloquial slang of his first records. Wald also interviewed two of White's lovers, one of whom reveals that he occasionally sold his favors to rich women. Nor did she blame him: he had a family to support. Most amazing are the interviews with his wife. She knew everything and accepted it, having decided that, in this case, she had to be the greater lover, confident that he would always return home.

To the last, White remained a trouper. In his last popular incarnation, he became the college boy's Johnny Mathis with recordings of love songs that provided all the soundtrack a folkie needed. He played smaller clubs to sparser crowds, traveled circuits in the South that were still largely segregated, was obliged to hock his guitar more than once, was shamed to see his wife go out and get a job. Judging by a photo of his mother, psoriasis ran in the family, and he was tormented by the ailment in, of all places, his fingers. He suffered from ulcers and heart problems, drank and smoked too much, worried always about his position as both a black man and an artist who was dismissed by ignorant latecomers after having, in Wald's fine phrase, "nurtured the aesthetic that now condemned him."

He died at fifty-five in 1969, a victim of "all this hard traveling." Wald lets Carol White have the last words. Despite the infidelities, which extended to feeble attempts on his deathbed, White remained her man. After he died, she tried to hold up and be brave, but once she neared the house he had killed himself to buy, "it was over. It was over." He had wished to be cremated, but for the funeral she selected an open coffin, dressed so that he might be "as handsome in death as he was on the stage." She never failed him.

———

Survival can be a curse. If you die young, like Robert Johnson, you can become a preposterously mythic figure. If you grow old like Josh White— i.e., long enough to undergo the development and, admittedly, the compromises required of a professional musician in mid-twentieth-century America—then you're anything but mythic. The judges have a lot to answer for. What made them so rich and so smart?

That leads to the realization that taste is seldom only personal and not up for dispute. The cultural canon is always up for revision, as is made clear in Marybeth Hamilton's *In Search of the Blues,* an intriguing study of white scholarly attempts to discover and define the Real Blues. Like the figures in that children's story, they kept taking a part for the whole, and most often discovered a distorted version of themselves. But they also convinced a lot of people that they were deeper and wiser than anyone else, and that if you disagreed, you were a shallow, if not a bad, person.

They probably did more good than harm. Although some of the early students were condescending, if not blatantly racist, all of them felt that black music was the most vital element of American culture. This required

some arguing at a time when a critic like Gilbert Seldes could patronize "the negroes' music" as both poignant and mindless—displaying
"little evidence of the functioning of their intelligence"—and academics
found the culture insufficiently steeped in "folklore," a term that became
increasingly nebulous in the age of mass communication. Yet the stunning detail that connects all of Hamilton's subjects—from the plantation nostalgists of the late 1890s to the "Blues Mafia" of the 1960s—is
that honoring the culture meant saving black people from themselves.
The real deal was not now but back then in a mythical past when people
were simpler and their expression more true. This is one of the enduring themes of American culture, both white and African-American.
One of the oldest spirituals laments that "the people don't sing like they
used to sing." The difference lies in the explanation for this decline:
gospel singers would say the people weren't living right; folklorists would
say it was the culture that had gone bad. As early as 1845, Frederick
Douglass discovered the profoundest meaning in "tones loud, long, and
deep . . . Every tone [a] testimony against slavery, and a prayer to God
for deliverance from chains." Fifteen years before the Civil War, he heard
in the sorrow songs a musical code of emancipation.

Over a hundred years later, Alan Lomax would write of the wordless
moans of the black church, "For me, and I believe, for most southerners,
the most magical of all musical sounds is the many-voiced humming of
a lining hymn that arises during quiet moments in the black folk service." Perhaps, indeed, this was the fabled song of the South, the echo
of a musical paradise lost, even if that eden was a product of slavery; as
Hamilton notes, there was a masochistic glee in the way outsiders identified with the sorrow songs. But if everyone agreed that the origins were
uniquely expressive—and that everything from field hollers to bebop
could be traced back to the sisters' wordless moans—what happened
next was up for interpretation. To use the current jargon, it became a
question of conflicting narratives, usually told by outsiders—and always
with the implication that they knew better than the actual participants.

A point would be reached when blue-eyed soul singers and white
bluesmen would behave as if their own years of hard work and disappointment had made them the artistic peers of their idols. Everyone had
a right to claim the blues, or, as Joanna Newsom recently sang, "use"
them. Also a right to determine what was "really real," a church idiom
for those whose faith had proven true, not ersatz. Among the discarded

items would be most black popular music, particularly the work of female artists. Even if blues fans might share Alan Lomax's admiration of the sisters on the mourners' bench, when it came to blues, the word was "Don't bring me no Bessie Smith," a musicians' slang for the great lady's all-purpose epithet. They didn't merely disdain the bullshit, they didn't want the Bessie Smith, either.

Demoting the women also meant a constriction of subject matter and emotional resonance. Hamilton correctly observes that "the world . . . depicted would be pastoral and, with barely a woman in sight. singularly free from the disorganization so evident in the black urban world." The highly subjective dismissal of women's voices and themes from the blues pantheon is a rich topic for Hamilton. An American historian now living in London, the author of *When I'm Bad, I'm Better: Mae West, Sex, and American Entertainment,* she is clearly attracted to episodes of sexual transgression, of a sensuous world ignored by the blues scholars, whom she frequently exposes as humorless prudes. She had initially prepared to write a biography of Little Richard. But instead she was intrigued by the great claims made for country blues singers—e.g., Greil Marcus's description of a Robert Johnson performance as "a two-minute image of doom that has the power to make doom a fact" (and not a moment too soon), or Robert Palmer's rhetorical question "How much history can be trasmitted by pressure on a guitar string?" (If there's a Hall of Shame for such overlistening, many a noted critic would claim pride of place.) Precisely because she didn't share these critics' enthusiasm—even when praising the work of Johnson or Charley Patton, she doesn't sound as if she really means it—she was fascinated by the division in sensibilities. So instead of writing about a black gender bender, she wrote about a world in which blacks and women scarcely figure. While there are references to Langston Hughes (who wrote some weak gospel songs) and Sterling Brown (who wrote some great blues), her scholar-fans are mostly white and male. Even so, the book's most dramatic scene involves a diminutive professor of writing, Dorothy Scarborough, trying to photograph a mass baptism, the sole white person in the crowd. And with a couple of brief, disputatious appearances, Zora Neale Hurston almost steals the book.

Hamilton is steeped in academic methods and terminology: Walter Benjamin's endlessly cited "work of art in the age of mechanical reproduction" makes an inevitable appearance. But she also enjoys dramatizing imagined encounters between scholars and their sources, or—more daringly—the eureka moments when some fan plays some record and figures everything out.

Her first group of researchers bemoaned what has happened to "our Negroes" and their culture. They despised all the jazzy trappings of urban life but were not completely hopeless: "There will be the folk blues," Howard Odom wrote in the late 1920s, "as long as there are Negro toilers and adventurers whose naivete has not been worn off by what the white man calls culture." (This sounds like Norman Mailer's evocation of the White Negro, or—distressingly—like some hip-hoppers' dismissal of "white folks' education.") By the early 1930s Dorothy Scarborough had introduced a more literary take; her shrewdest observation was that the twelve-bar blues resembled an O. Henry story, with the third line subverting what came before. She was both a southern belle and a member of Greenwich Village's literary scene; Carson McCullers was a student. (McCullers's nursemaid in *Member of the Wedding* would become an iconic figure in 1940s literature along with Eudora Welty's neo–Fats Waller in "Powerhouse"—this suggests that southern women made particularly judicious use of their folkloric research.) In her fiction and scholarship Scarborough was also infatuated with the spirit world, with ghosts and "haints." Rural superstitions fascinated her. But, as one friend noted, she was unprepared to enter the office of W. C. Handy, the so-called Father of the Blues, and find an outpost of Tin Pan Alley.

The only blues researchers to become national figures were John Lomax and his son Alan. In a famous March of Time newsreel, John Lomax, a ne'er-do-well (born on "the upper crust of po' white trash") dabbler in folklore, is shown interviewing ex-con Huddie Ledbetter about his good fortune in singing himself out of jail. Nothing about the scene was real; it was staged for the camera with Lead Belly and his friends dressed in striped uniforms. Hamilton laments the "excruciating depiction of Leadbelly as a hapless, hopeless, mindlessly criminal darky, a part that Lomax seems to have set out for him and in which the singer seems to collude." The initial response was more positive. Lead Belly was a brilliantly talented singer and guitarist, a walking repository of American popular music from blues and reels to hymns and ballroom waltzes.

John Lomax was convinced that secular tunes were more uniquely black, free of any debt to white spirituals or the white man's Bible. But they had to be self-contained productions, uncontaminated by popular music or jazz—in other words, hermetically sealed from the worldly influences of radio and, especially, phonograph records. (Like many subsequent critics, Lomax distrusted versatility. His implicit command to Lead Belly was "You're a colored singer, sing colored.")

Lead Belly was visually gripping, an austere, dark-skinned man, who sang and played with a fearful intensity and drifted with remarkable ease from baritone to high tenor, exhibiting the open-throated tessitura of the best gospel singers. YouTube carries a clip of him singing "Take This Hammer" (to the tune of the white hymn "Where He Leads Me"), his back as straight as his guitar is wide.

Initially Lomax did well by Lead Belly and himself; the two appeared at a Philadelphia meeting of the Modern Language Association where Lead Belly, identified as "a Negro minstrel from Louisiana," convinced the academics that black music was folklore too. (Alan Lomax shared his father's respect for the academy's imprimatur. Many years later he would devise a system, "cantometrics," that posited a kind of Chomskian structuralism of musical utterances.) Lead Belly was soon a popular star too, mostly in the Greenwich Village folk circuit, black audiences finding his ways too amateur and "country." Lomax was horrified as his darky became "only an ordinary, low ordinary, Harlem nigger." The relation ended when Lead Belly came around with the reasonable request "I wants my money" and seemed to threaten him with a knife. But their brief union had made both men famous. In the words of Aretha Franklin, who was zooming who?

Besides falling out with Lead Belly, Lomax found himself repudiated by Richard Wright, then a committed leftist, who accused him of "one of the most amazing cultural swindles in American history." (Ultimately this would become a question of copyrights, and of folklorists claiming authorship or co-authorship of songs that most often their informants hadn't composed, either.) Banished by Lomax, Lead Belly became a star of the Communist front—another instance of who's zooming who—though the leftists were embarrassed by some of his more ribald songs.

At this point something astonishing occurred. Zora Neale Hurston, the great folklorist, nursed ideas of cultural nationalism that bordered on the reactionary. For many reasons, personal as much as political, she despised the left, most particularly some of its black literary heroes, and none more than Wright. In the dramatic high point of Hamilton's book, she reports how Hurston wrote John Lomax, both endorsing his right-wing politics and hatred of the (in his words) "largely Jewish" left, and spying on his son Alan's flirtations with the reds, and most particularly with Mary Elizabeth Barnicle, an Irish-American academic who would some years later marry a trade-union leader. In Hurston's view, the left had cast a double spell on Alan, sexual and political. The image of the gifted but tetched Hurston conspiring with the frankly racist Lomax against his son is worthy of a three-act play.

Alan Lomax contested his father on theoretical grounds as well. To his great credit he realized that recordings had not destroyed folklore but amplified it. He had noticed, as would many subsequent folklorists, that singers and musicians who gave dry, lifeless performances when recorded by the Library of Congress would snap to attention before the microphones of a commercial label like Decca or Okeh. While folklorists lamented the loss of a special, spur-of-the moment, improvisatory charm—a forecast of the idea that "mechanical reproduction" changed everything—the artists themselves took it all in stride. They understood that recordings were, in current parlance, merely a "delivery system," an advertisement for what they could do, and promised to do better after their recordings made them famous. Particularly in gospel and jazz, there was a compact between artists and fans that the recording merely initiated an experience that would be completed when the artists appeared in person. Whether single or album or MP3 file, the music remained a calling card, an advertisement for the self. Cantometrics notwithstanding, Alan Lomax's great contribution may be his promotion of commercial records.

Confronting both Lomaxes was Lawrence Gellert, a New York leftist married to a black woman, who in 1936 published *Negro Songs of Protest*. He felt that the Lomaxes had ignored a vital tradition of protest and impiety. *Time* (in an article perhaps written by James Agee, who was freelancing for them at the time) quoted such antinomian lyrics as "Stop foolin' wid pray, / When black-face is lifted, Lord turnin' away." Gellert, a figure barely treated by Hamilton, was similarly audacious in using the politically incorrect language of the people; his fellow Communists were horrified by his abundant usage of obscenities and the N word.

Hamilton does raise the question of obscenity when considering another group of critics, among them Frederic Ramsey Jr., Charles Edward Smith (a very perceptive writer), and the composer William Russell. They helped usher into print the memoir of Jelly Roll Morton, self-proclaimed "Originator of Jazz and Stomps" and "World's Greatest

Hit Tune Writer." Some on the left—particularly Eric Hobsbawm—regarded New Orleans as "a multiple myth and symbol: anti-commercial, anti-racist, proletarian, populist."

But others exhibited the peculiar prudery of the far left. They were discomfited by the frankly sexual nature of Jelly Roll's persona, his very name, his citation of Buddy Bolden's "Funky Butt," his casual observation that his only musical superior on the keyboard was Tony Jackson, a "sissy-man," and, above all, his hilariously blue lyrics. Among the first blues he heard being sung by a woman included the lines "I got a husband and I got a kid man too, / My husband can't do what my kid man can do." The Wife of Bath couldn't have put it better, but Jelly Roll's new audience was mortified. Even coarser by their standards, and buried for years in the vaults of the Library of Congress, was "Winin' Boy Blues," with its boastful line "I fucked her till her pussy stank." (A recent Internet hit, "Smell Yo Dick" by Riskay, a female rapper, could serve as a riposte to Jelly Roll, a hundred years late.)

This was more real than the white blues boys had bargained for. As Hamilton shows, after being accused of vulgarizing the culture, they would be sideswiped by McCarthyism. Dodging attacks on their left-wing sympathies and corrupt morals, they retreated to studying the music of the rural South. The product was a series of Folkways anthologies filled with music undisturbed by a radical thought or sexual impulse. But this attempt to capture a factitious purity was doomed from the start. It has always been emblemized for me by a Folkways recording of a group of country girls singing a song about heaven. The annotators could be forgiven for not recognizing that it was a note-for-note copy of a popular gospel record by the Davis Sisters of Philadelphia. But how could they have transcribed "I'll lay down this old sword and shield" as "I'll lay down this old sewing machine"? And then describe this absurd lyric as "deeply moving"? The recent gospel anthology *Fire in My Bones* drew its title from a recording the annotators misheard as "Fire Shed in My Bones" (the singer actually sang the words "shut up in my bones"). Could the producer really have thought that fires get shed? Read most annotations of blues lyrics and you'll find similar whoppers.

Hamilton's last crew includes a group of men who dubbed themselves the Blues Mafia. Curiously in a world overridden with sexism, two gay men were the dominant figures. In 1964 Blues Mafioso Nick Perls, the son of an émigré art dealer, discovered the great country-blues singer Son House, alive if not quite well in, of all places, Rochester, New York.

Within Perls's affinity group, the dominant sensibility—apparently as much by physical as intellectual bullying—was James McKune, who is probably Hamilton's favorite fan. An impoverished alcoholic who would die the victim of a sexual episode gone horribly wrong, McKune was the Mafioso with the most refined sensibility. While other collectors trafficked in irrelevancies like discolored record labels or scratchy-sounding reprints, McKune's collection was comparatively small but exquisitely chosen. His focus was exclusively aesthetic. Politics didn't signify: "After you've listened to the real Negro blues for a long time," he wrote, "you know at once that the protest of the blues is . . . in the accompanying piano or guitar."

Listening as closely as he could, McKune determined that the ensemble of voice and instrument was most seamless in the country blues of Son House, Charley Patton, Robert Johnson, and Skip James. Patton particularly stirred him: "Only the greatest religious singers have ever affected me similarly." To Hamilton's surprise, McKune abandoned his interest in blues; and Nick Perls, who had rediscovered Son House, switched his allegiances to disco. Others would pick up their obsession. Arguments of a jesuitical precision would follow, denominations as vague as deep blues, country blues, Piedmont blues, Mississippi blues, *und so weiter.* Of course, when everyone had been listening to the same records and had their eyes on the same prize, such distinctions would strike the actual practitioners, the blues singers, as bizarre. (Some academics entertained the French idea that something wasn't real until it was actually named.) When asked whether his music was really folklore, Big Bill Broonzy replied that he hadn't seen any dogs or mules sing it. In one of the most curious developments, blues singers who had never been stars when they were young and strong developed a whole new public when they were old and weak. Hamilton notes the many disappointing encounters between the veterans and their youthful acolytes. The message seemed to be, if they pretend to pay us, we'll pretend to sing.

Later, when generations of white fans would study their records and become virtuoso exponents of their technique, Muddy Waters would shrug, they can outplay me but they can't outsing me. And, ever so often, coming up with the best note, hit exactly where and when, he'd outplay them, too. This was made abundantly clear to me in the late sixties when the Apollo Theater had a spectacular blues show featuring, among others, T-Bone Walker, Muddy Waters, B. B. King, and Big Mama Thornton. All of them sang and played harder than I'd ever seen them perform, whether at folk clubs in Greenwich Village or in Cambridge, Massachusetts. Confronting an audience who took rhythm and improvisation for granted, and expected them to work for their pay, these great artists delivered a blues that was realer than real.

While it's easy to mock the blinkered vision of Hamilton's crew, they also reclaimed a history that might have gone unrecognized. Reading her study, I was struck by the similarities between the moldy figs of yesteryear and the obsessives of today. Once rock and roll was celebrated precisely for its popularity. But now many rock critics would agree with James McKune that the public's taste is to be deplored; a Pazz and Jop poll almost never meshes with the Hot 100. The multiplicity of style from emo to screamo carries us back to the days when blues lovers could locate the fulfillment of their chosen styles within a few miles of country road. No obsessed fan is guiltless. (As the author of the first book on gospel music, I had the chance to define the genre's golden age as running from 1945 to 1960. Now I think I was off by ten years in either direction.)

Hamilton occasionally glances at the reactionary implications of her characters' pursuits. It's not a surprise that champions of the past often end up politically conservative. One of the greatest fans of 1960s soul was Lee Atwater. Remember the image of him doing the soul split at a White House party, surrounded by a group of his aging idols, all his racist demagoguery placed temporarily on hold while he danced to the music? Hamilton includes a devastating quote from Norman Mailer's "The White Negro," in which he praises the black man for "relinquishing the pleasures of the mind for the more obligatory pleasures of the body . . . the infinite variations of joy, lust, languor, growl, cramp, pinch, scream and despair of his orgasm." (Jelly Roll Morton was never so vulgar.) You might be able to hear this as Wilhelm Reich Meets the Blues. But it reminds me of Mailer's many abominable remarks about women and gay men. Ralph Ellison found the essay a shopworn retread of all the blues-boy tropes. He wrote Richard Wright that Mailer was simply offering "the same old primitivism crap in a new package."

But cultural reaction runs in all directions. Hamilton quotes a smart observation of the blues scholar Charles Keil: "I can almost imagine some of these writers helping to set up a 'reservation' or Bantustan for old bluesmen." This is a stunning, if unwitting, echo of something Zora Neale Hurston wrote her professor Franz Boas in 1927: the Negro "is not living his lore to the extent of the Indian. He is not on a reservation, being kept pure. His negroness is being rubbed off by close contact with white culture." That attitude may explain why Hurston joined the John Birch Society in the 1950s. Still atttacking Communists like Richard Wright (sic) and James Baldwin (double sic), she sided with the South's biggest racists in their opposition to integration. Predicting Clarence Thomas's attack on affirmative action, she felt it was patronizing to assume that blacks would benefit from mingling their already superior culture with the outside world. In her despair over a vanished golden age, she was something of a white blues boy herself.

THE FAN WHO KNEW
TOO MUCH

At the end of World War II, observing the ruin of his native land, Thomas Mann lamented that it was impossible to discriminate between the best and worst of Germany. They were precisely the same, and he knew it because both lived in him. This remark haunts me when I consider the blues fans with their benighted claims about a culture they have never inhabited. Hypocrite reader, I address myself. You know these people, you're one of them. And yet, when you begin to think about it, what a peculiar figure is this learned fan, this self-appointed guardian of something he only knows from without. Like one of Thomas Mann's favorite figures, the male wallflower permanently disinvited from the dance, the fan is a melancholy fellow. He's variously condemned as a kook, an exile from adult life, half-mad. But he isn't only that. He's also someone who's discovered an endless storehouse of personal satisfaction. He's the one who anticipated life on the World Wide Web, a prophet without much honor but, all the same, a vanguard figure.

Of all the modern types, he's perhaps the most unprecedented. Before there was a mass media, did he even exist? We know that Charles Dickens's serialized novels became international obsessions, and that people were even trampled to death as they ran wildly to pick up the latest installment, to learn if Little Nell had survived another threat. We also know that artists and intellectuals observed the earlier forms of popular culture with both dismay and envy. In Mann's *Royal Highness*, all the desiccated figures of the court dream that they possessed the effortless command of a vaudeville star, a woman the people call "our Mitzi." Likewise, Marcel Proust makes the sagest observation of popular culture: "The people always have the same messengers, bad songwriters, and a book of old songs should move us like a town or a tomb." This is not disrespectful but it's also pretty grim. It would take a few more cycles before the songwriter would be acknowledged as something more than an idiot savant of the forlorn and distracted. By no later than the 1920s, he had become the man of the hour.

Suddenly, popular culture had the key to all some people needed to know. In *The Magic Mountain*, Mann allows Hans Castorp to become the model of an obsessive fan, basking in his pathetic fallacy. He goes to the movies, and every scene reconfigures his philosophical and sexual ambivalence, each dramatic incident refracts on his political confusion, each glamorous star resembles the latest woman or man of his dreams. Phonograph records give him even more bliss, largely because they can be enjoyed in private. He doesn't listen with the trained ear of a German concertgoer; he hears what he wants to hear, and can turn the most abstruse work into program music. Of course he's too naive and unfocused to be an exact model of the fans who succeed him. But he's also one of the first to assume that all of culture is there for his delectation.

Mann or Proust could not imagine the computer, and the ways it would dissolve all the familiar hierarchies. Yet I like to think they would find it a perfect realization of their fondest dreams. Think how the Web caters to our Castorp-like distractions. Go to YouTube and let yourself wander from one clip to the next; to paraphrase the scripture, each man must work out his own soul's salvation, and what kids once called a "salvation tape" is there for you and you alone, your tastes, your obsessions, your story.

The computer, as we have all learned, can dissolve time. Clips of long-dead performers and politicians can evoke responses that have to be bare approximations of what the original audiences experienced. Yet those same clips extend an immortality that at its best is the apotheosis of democracy, universal, uncensored, and free, at least without financial cost, though the seductive distractions usually come at a price, the anomie lamented by social critics: Donnie McClurkin might well say, "I loose you from the computer!"

Pornographers advertise sexual acts of astonishing novelty, as if the Kama Sutra needed updating. New American chefs bask in permutations and combinations of tastes that seek to revise the palate; once at a table, eating some wild goulash of sweet and savory, a friend complained, "This isn't a dessert, it's a lecture." The computer has revolutionized romance, from the initial encounter to all the subsequent intimacies; I have dear friends who have met the loves of their lives online. Even so, nobody has profited more than a fan basking in the computer's infinite riches. It has allowed the extremest, most intimate self-delight to a point well beyond onanism.

The intense focus can indeed be desocialized, asocial, antisocial. To that extent it has Americanized the world—that is, if we accept D. H. Lawrence's remark that the American soul, for all its attempts to appear homespun and benevolent, is "hard, isolate, stoic, and a killer." These brutal words illuminate the condition of all those transfixed and transfigured by some obsession, and the computer has made that condition universally available. If the fan's condition is usually an isolate one, he often finds safety in numbers. Think of the sports fan, so deafened by his neighbors that he can't even hear himself roar. But then when I think of the true sports fan, I focus on some homebound fellow who calls his local station, providing the most informed exegesis of what they've just seen on the tube or Web. He may have a trick or two up his sleeve; even as he compares today's shortstop to Phil Rizzuto, he may be looking at a clip filmed in the 1950s.

Expertise of the more specialized sort can easily appear to be a monomaniacal obsession. Reviewing Jonathan Lethem's novel *Chronic City,* Charles Baxter exhibits little sympathy for its characters' "torrential specifics," their nerdy command of statistics and factoids: the subject at hand is movies, but it's the disposition that irritates him. The details acquire "the aura of private enthusiasms generated from a core feeling of stifled, adolescent-era loneliness." Take that, you obsessives; your command of the subject is merely a cipher for your immaturity and impotence. Tim Page, discussing the connections between his love of music and his (self-evidently, not very inhibiting) Asperger's condition, confides a secret. "A cluster of facts can be most luminous and lyric, something around which to construct a life." That's why certain obsessives can indeed resemble idiots savants. They know everything about one special thing, and nothing about anything else. To which one response is, "How sad." But may I propose another one: "Really?"

The ruthless obsessiveness of some fans can evoke Lawrence's stoic, isolate killer or Page's advanced Asperger state. But please remember, it can also be a supreme experience, and that too feels new. Randall Jarrell says, "The ways we miss our lives are life." For a great many of us, the outer reaches of fandom have become our most essential selves. We've grown up with them, grown old with them. Our loves may be ineffable, but they're never abstract. For many of us, they have proved more durable and permanent than other attachments. Forget the fact that we may never love some other thing—a movie, a novel, a piece of sculpture, a jazz saxophonist's solo, a gospel moan—so deeply. The more disturbing fact is that we never love someone as deeply as we've loved that thing.

Consider that for many fans, it's possible to insult their parents or partners—but decry their special hero and you become persona non grata. I first noticed this madness in the 1960s, when someone who claimed to be agnostic about the Beatles or Bob Dylan—in particular, someone who derived far more pleasure from J. Robert Bradley and the Roberta Martin Singers—was considered at best an alien, at worst a traitor to his generation. During the 1960s fans made the most apodictic and totalitarian of claims. One fan told me that nothing existed in music between Mozart and Lennon and McCartney; another that excepting W. H. Auden, Dylan was our greatest living poet. When I mentioned other musicians, other writers, I was accused of rank insensitivity. Merely questioning their gods could drive these fans to tears. In other quarters, you would risk more than hurt feelings. Dish a drag queen's favorite diva and she might very well cut you.

I happened to be a graduate student at the time, working sixteen-hour days in order to complete my Ph.D. thesis before I turned twenty-six. Those sixteen hours left barely any time for my jazz and gospel records, so instead they invaded my dreams. And I concluded that there were deep parallels between my roles as aspiring academic and earnest fan. In both identities I found succor and release in statistics. Both demanded jesuitical attention and talmudic scholarship. In both, obsession could never be too limited or too exacting. I heard a story in graduate school about the world's foremost scholar of Aramaic. Why even write in that arcane tongue, somebody asked him, which scarcely anyone understood? "I do not write for everyone," was his dignified reply.

For the Ph.D. orals, students of that day would bone up on an immense history of English literature familiarly known as Baugh. One chapter surveyed the wonders of Victorian fiction. In a footnote the author cited an immensely prolific novelist of herculean stamina; his novels invariably were door stoppers. He wrote close to fifty such monstrosities, and the brave scholar was informed enough to select a few titles as "among his better novels." I loved the mad boldness of that conclusion—more so after reading the novelist, whom I found tedious, quite unlike the invariably delightful Dickens, George Eliot, or Thackeray. It was a dirty job, but someone had to read those books (just as someone had to honor the claims of history enough to even drop the novelist's long-forgotten name). My kind of scholar, my kind of fan.

In those years. the English department was divided into two fiefdoms, two contending approaches to scholarship, represented by the biographically inclined Walter Jackson Bate, who celebrated the great men of literature, their lives almost as much as their works, and Reuben Brower, who represented a precisely delimited form of literary attention that—as would later be claimed—privileged the response almost above its object. "Close reading," the Browerian practice, was very intimate, a transaction that required two participants, the artist and you. Years later, both Bate and Brower would be superseded by other approaches, far more theoretical and, correspondingly, less intimate. Later academics would laugh at Bate's biographical slant, and find Brower's enshrinement of the reader simply irrelevant. But both looked forward to all the ways fans have come to respond. They would love their Marvin Gayes and Kurt Cobains as powerfully as Bate loved Samuel Johnson and John Keats; they would celebrate a musician's artistic decision with an exactitude that would have gladdened Brower, had it been applied to literature.

Now that once-vibrant schools of thought have faded, they increasingly resemble all the other forms, from art to sports to politics, that can command your life, and thereby forever date you. It's indisputable that the academy opened up after World War II, welcoming many people who might not have pursued higher education, much less earned graduate degrees. Once an Ivy League Ph.D. could write his own ticket. Today, like all academics, particularly in the humanities, he's not sure that the train hasn't left the station and won't return. It's my fancy that all the graduate students still pursuing their education despite such uncertain prospects are like the fans of something great and gratifying but no longer popular. With the older professors complaining that nobody knows how to read anymore, and the younger ones complaining that nobody cares to read, the various departments have contracted to a world of downsized intellectuals and lapsed wunderkinder. Many fans know something about that crowd.

I detect a political analogy as well, perhaps because my generation spent so much time on the battlefield. In college I used to argue with a reflexive Stalinist about almost everything. If I liked French food, she preferred Russian; if I praised Oxford or Berkeley, she opted for Moscow University. As a teaching fellow in graduate school I knew self-declared radicals who advised me to have my students in freshman composition read Chairman Mao's Little Red Book. Some of these friends remained steadfast believers: the Stalinist would become the international secretary of the American Communist Party (not, perhaps, a very contested position). But with the fall of the Soviet Union and the capitalist evolution of China, others swerved to the center, becoming ardent supporters of the Clintons or Barack Obama. Yet I've heard a few say that they had been philosophically right even if they had been strategically wrong. Tens of millions may have died, but, as the Star-Spangled Band insists, *their* particular cause, why, "it was just."

They may sound fatuous and callous, but I hear in their desperate apologies another kind of fan, brought low by history. One person says his idol went astray; another says his party imploded. But to question the taste or the political slant is to question their selves at the core. The sadness of a lapsed radical or a betrayed fan rests on a common fear that they wasted the deepest, most imaginative hours of their lives on the wrong object.

For this reason, I find useful Hannah Arendt's distinction between former and ex-Communists, between those who can escape their political misadventures and those doomed to relive them forever. As she noted, many of the latter would become zealous McCarthyites; they took everything personally, *too* personally. There are times I chuckle over my youthful bad taste—how could I have fallen for that book, that record, that painting? What a silly billy, what a dolt! Other times my fury with the artist is self-directed. I wasn't just ignorant, I was dumb, and some kinds of stupidity verge on the immoral. All those wearisome, pointless arguments about good taste, as provincial and doctrinaire as the shout-outs between splinter groups of the left.

The best of fans, with all his exemplary and informed taste, remains just another historical subject, playing a role made possible by forces outside him. Had I not been raised by exceptionally tolerant German Jewish refugees, I might not have started exploring the Apollo Theater when I was fourteen; and, very likely, most of my other aesthetic decisions result from time and chance, the two forces that rule the world, according to Ecclesiastes 9:11. At least the early commitments—and as fans know, they're the ones that count.

—

When we like people, we overlook their faults. When we stop liking them, all we see is their faults. Any fan who stays the course will be prey to melancholy. In his "Ode on Melancholy," contradicting Hazlitt's remark that no young man ever thinks he will die, the quintessentially young poet Keats praises a gorgeous figure, while adding, "She dwells with Beauty—Beauty that must die." It can't be avoided; to love something deeply is to register its impermanence. Even the young gospel fans, discovering Mahalia Jackson or Marion Williams, understand that those are film clips of dead people. But whatever the object of a fan's love, the more he knows, the more he worries. A fan's melancholy partakes of a kind of desperation; and the best description of the artists who evoke the greatest loyalties comes from the late ballet star Rudolf Nureyev: "They pay us for our fear."

Some artists get by. A singer may crack and croak into late middle age; rock or gospel heroes of the 1960s can stir their old fans while leaving youngsters cold. Both artist and fan pretend that the emperor has a brand-new wardrobe, both knowing better while also knowing that any further admission will prove literally fatal. Instead, all the artist has to do is intimate an experience; as long as it's the familiar—if aged—face, singing the familiar lyrics, the fans will fill in the gaps. They hear the complete song and the young voice. Extracting victory from the jaws of defeat is perforce a melancholy experience.

I first understood this in 1967 when I attended an oldies concert headlined by the Five Satins. When they began singing "In the Still of the Night," Madison Square Garden rose to its feet. I linked hands with my date, a pretty college professor newly sprung from Yale, and a churlish neighbor who had irritated us with a series of racist comments. It was clear that many of us fans had nothing in common but our memories of that song, and all it had promised us barely ten years before. Perhaps there had once been a possible community of white kids kvelling to the gorgeous doo-wop, but no more. The unhappy condition of many singers' voices made us even sadder. Or was it the gap between our adolescent verve and our postgraduate ennui? Whenever I watch an oldies concert on PBS, the melancholy is magnified. The music once seemed so young; and now everyone looks and sounds defiantly aged.

The one area where fear and melancholy are ineluctable, and can never be transcended, is sports. Built into the game is its undoing. Even the top batter is lucky no more than forty percent of the time. And while a popular singer can get by with diminished chops, no athlete can. For some reason the obsessions of sports lovers are more acceptable than those of other kinds of fans. People divide their childhoods into the years before and after the Dodgers left Brooklyn. A whole generation of men felt their bodies collapsing when Muhammad Ali retired from the ring. The chutzpah of couch potatoes identifying with a superbly trained athlete escaped attention. Instead, pathos became the signature response. To paraphrase the strictures of Reuben Brower's close reading, it took the mourning of sports fans to complete the tragedy of Ali's ruined body.

Sports fans resemble the customers at oldies concerts. They both take pride from their special historical position. We were the first to attend the Brooklyn Paramount, to hear the Who at the Fillmore East, to see Jackie Robinson play his last game. Ours is the best generation—we had the best politics, best pop songs, best athletes. As I get older, I hear the claim almost every week. And I wonder how long people have been talking like this. Surely every generation has contrasted itself with the next in line, and usually confirmed its own superiority. But how many before 1900 measured themselves by their tastes and their popular idols?

I have been very lucky. As a record producer I had a chance to work with many of my favorite singers. Some sessions didn't go well. One of the saddest remarks came from a great Church of God in Christ diva. After hearing the playback she looked at me: "Well, boy, I don't know whether you were born too late or I was born too soon." Clearly our hours were not in sync. But more often, I got to the singers when they had most of their chops, and even more of their inspiration. In 1973 I was about to produce Sister Rosetta Tharpe's comeback session. Alas, she suffered a fatal stroke the day of the session. But I still have the memories of our rehearsals. In the case of Rosetta's favorite singer, Marion Williams, I had a chance to record her many times, well over two hundred songs, most of them the kind of traditional and folkloric material that nobody cared to record anymore. She proved to be a vocal genius (as would be acknowledged by the MacArthur Foundation when they awarded her their "genius grant"), old enough to remember the songs and gifted enough to perform most of them better than anyone had before.

Once in a while I even struck pay dirt. In 1975 I requested that she perform a cappella the kind of Dr. Watts hymn that had once been the staple of black congregational singing. "Nobody want that," she informed her pianist. "That's just some of Tony mess." But in fact, her version of "Did Christ o'er Sinners Weep?" would go on to win the Grand Prix du Disque. After that, she began singing a cappellas with regularity. To her surprise they still wrecked churches, and one of them, perhaps the most famous, "A Charge to Keep I Have," would be featured in the movie *Fried Green Tomatoes*. This was tantamount to bringing the eighteenth century into the twentieth.

Believe me, I was aware of the fraught task. Not merely was Marion as vocally vulnerable as any singer, but she was constantly sick, and would eventually die of the same leg-amputating diabetes that killed her mother and sister. Her doctor said he'd seldom seen so damaged a body. So there I was, more fortunate than any sports fan could ever be—what good would be hiring an aged Ted Williams to do anything more than doff his cap? At the same time I knew that the great tradition Marion was renewing had long fallen out of favor with the gospel public. It was a quandary, trying to figure how something could be a supreme version of a form that almost nobody cared about.

There were also moments that I was blessed to witness and cursed not to capture. One night, I attended a rehearsal of Claude Jeter, gospel quartet's Father of Falsetto, and a reunited Swan Silvertones. Paul Owens, the quartet's great second lead (and one of Aretha Franklin's mentors), was rehearsing the fellows. I suggested they try some jubilee songs, the kind made famous by the Golden Gates fifty years earlier. It was miraculous. The rhythms were so dazzling that neighbors poured into Jeter's funky flat.

The Swans demonstrated a precisely drilled choreography I had not seen before. If jubilee was like this, it had outmaneuvered Motown, each man stepping precisely to his own cadence, claiming his fraction of the beat. As one song ended, the long, tall Jeter spun to his knees, then twirled counterclockwise to his full height. The fellows were beyond exhilarated; Jeter and Owens looked like their selves in old publicity photos. I returned home, awakened an old friend, and said, high in the Spirit, "Jubilee's not dead, it's only sleeping!" The next day, the eight songs we had rehearsed were reduced to a workaday run-through of the overly familiar "Swing Down Chariot," nothing worth recording, much less releasing. If I said that I had witnessed the consummate power of jubilee quartet, there would have been no reason to believe me.

An equally upsetting event occurred at one of Marion's sessions. I had requested C. A. Tindley's famous hymn "What Are They Doing in Heaven Today," and proposed that she sing it as a super-slow "long meter," the kind of style that had always moved the people in the days when gospel was gospel. Tindley, the composer of "I'll Overcome Some-day" (from which Pete Seeger et al., derived the civil rights anthem), often included politically charged lyrics. Marion chose the verse

There were some who were poor and often despised,
They looked up to heaven, with tear-blinded eyes,
While people were heedless and deaf to their cries—
I wonder what are they doing there now.

It was the greatest, deepest performance I have ever heard, hymn singing worthy of Mary Johnson Davis or J. Robert Bradley, with a folkloric quality unique to Marion, "the barefoot girl come from Florida." She was halfway through the next selection, one almost as fine, when the engineer began to shake. "I don't make too many mistakes, but when I do, it's a beaut. The tape wasn't running."

As a kid, my brother and I would fight so fiercely that our mother would throw buckets of cold water on our entangled bodies. Not since then had I been so driven to smash somebody's face. Marion gave me an alarmed look. "That's all right, baby. Let me rub your hands, and then I'll sing it again." She understood that I had lost something irreplaceable. That she had been the occasion was more my burden than hers. For me it was the performance of a lifetime; for her, part of a gig. She did sing it again, and it was lovely, an A-minus. But Spirit feel is a one-take phenomenon. A-minus was not A-plus-plus-plus, off the charts. A fan can be devastated when something is so foolishly lost. We despair over the might-have-beens, but the should-have-beens are worse.

———

The first times Hans Castorp hears the insidious, proto-fascistic Professor Naphta, he is spellbound; "for as long as he spoke he was right." Even the wisest fan can be seduced into a temporary loss of reason. I think that's because what we admire is so clearly beyond our own reach: a fan is defined by his limits. In Mann's great story *Tristan,* the hero, Detlev Spinell, is a gifted explicator, a sophisticated fan, but fatally untalented. A more gifted pianist, impressed by his analysis (which Mann splendidly refuses to quote) of Wagner's love theme, is perplexed by the discrepancy. "How can you hear it and not play it?" Blushing, physically diminished, the hapless Spinell admits, "The two things seldom go together." As if the gap between knowing and doing were not curse enough, his lack of chops is equated with sexual impotence.

A fan's love is seldom blind. Even Hans Castorp begins to understand that Naphta's words are deadly. Perhaps the most complex situation arises when the figures of our obsession disappoint us, failing us by failing themselves. If we're loyal, we stay with them, trapped in a cycle of agreement and dissent, of adoration and near-hatred. Alan Bennett distinguishes those authors who garner "readers" and those who attract "fans." These fans have a much greater, nearly irrational stake in their heroes' fates. Readers are engaged; fans, haunted. Readers let go of a book; fans dream about it.

But sometimes the dream turns to a nightmare, as the author challenges our initial assumptions and dares us to continue loving him. (At least in literature, such titans tend to be male.) How many times have educated fans tried to reclaim a work from its author. Either they echo D. H. Lawrence's "Trust the tale and not the teller," or they discover a work galloping away from what its author might originally have intended.

Readers from William Blake to William Empson have rebelled against Milton letting the devil have all the good tunes. They have argued for two centuries that the Son of Darkness is his true hero; and considering the poet's majestic defenses of liberty, he might have joined the other side in another time, simply not the one he lived in. Their argument is a loving one; they can't accept a Milton who didn't see the full implications of his text.

Far harder to countenance are the great writers who were total shits. Yet even a Louis-Ferdinand Céline has his defenders, swallowing deeply as they acknowledge that those anti-Semitic utterances are just as vile as they sound. Other writers don't require as much. Even so, the brilliant young critic and science-fiction author China Miéville, analyzing the racist and misogynistic passages in his idol J. G. Ballard, can only admit,

"Those of us committed to Ballard shift in our seats and regret that such tropes were not subject to more assiduous skepticism." In other words, he let himself down along with his disheartened readers.

After World War II there were conspicuous instances of readers upstaging their idols merely by ignoring—effectively canceling—their bias. Thus, despite Norman Mailer's pathetic atttacks on women and gay men, his strongest critic would be Richard Poirier, a gay man who saw his self-proclaimed enemy as "a performing self," thus reducing the bigotry to a literary stunt. In the 1970s I attended an MLA seminar on Henry James featuring three panelists, David Kalstone, Richard Howard, and Cynthia Ozick. You could only speculate how the Master would respond to such close attention from two gay men and a bluestocking intellectual, none of them the lissome beauties of his tales, and each of them Jewish. All three knew that James would not have considered them his kind, and they could handle it. Or, as Stephen Greenblatt says of another ambiguous figure, Wagner the transcendent artist and Wagner the proto-Nazi belong in separate "conversations."

These particular fans may even not suffer. But D. H. Lawrence, the subject of my Ph.D. thesis, has agitated me for years. Nowadays we admirers have it hard. If we take him seriously, we must countenance a lifelong series of repellent statements about women, blacks, Jews, and gays. To be fair is also to recognize that the dreadful Lawrence can, in the space of a narrative clause, transform himself into someone quite different; as a literary quick-change artist, he can make grammar seem downright therapeutic. For instance, in his greatest novel, *Women in Love,* he carries his four leading characters, Rupert Birkin and his wife-to-be, Ursula Brangwen, and Ursula's sister, Gudrun, and her lover Gerald Crich, to an Alpine setting, where they all proceed to drive each other crazy, as Lawrence's prose lurches from inspired poetry to downright hysteria, so close to passages in his more troubling texts that they cannot be dismissed as simply mimetic of his characters' breakdowns. He rescues them and himself with a simple declarative sentence: "Luckily there came a day of snow, they must all stay indoors." How good and practical and *English* for them to do that.

Over forty years ago I attempted with extreme deliberation to distinguish between two kinds of Lawrentian vocabulary: a mystical one with which he celebrates the marital breakthrough of Birkin and Ursula, and a crassly supernatural one—baldly melodramatic—with which he conveys the pathos of Gerald Crich's death and the diabolical nature of Gudrun, who epitomizes all that he despises in modern, emancipated womanhood. I must have convinced my thesis readers. But when I return to the novel I don't convince myself. The mystical passages remain beautiful—Lawrence comes alive outdoors; his landscape passages remain breathtaking. But the ganging up on Gudrun and her ally Loerke (as in the mythic god Loki), a supercilious aesthete, as well as a likely Jew and homosexual, diminishes the novel. To be fair, we read differently now. In the 1960s, many English fans of Lawrence supposedly modeled their marriages on the epithalamium of Ursula and Birkin. (Lawrence's marital strictures can be arduous and shockingly asexual: not even the marriage guides of evangelical Christians demand so heavy a sacrifice of the newlywed.)

Nowadays Gudrun's independence, especially from Gerald Crich, perhaps the earliest Master of the Universe, seems both plausible and right. Lawrence always gave evidence of his own homoerotic temperament, swooning before humpy soldiers though he loathed militarism. Gerald Crich's glamour bewitches Lawrence and his literary stand-in, Birkin. (In the novel's rejected preface, Lawrence writes that Birkin was attracted to women's clothes and men's bodies, precisely what countless students have complained about—to such a degree that when I taught the novel, my students used to rename it *Men in Love*. How that would have repelled his greatest fan, the unerringly homophobic F. R. Leavis!)

And then, just as I'm thinking I wasted a Harvard education on this preposterous fellow, Lawrence writes something that justifies a very great deal. In 1928, two years before his death, he translated Giovanni Verga's *Cavalleria rusticana* (it was most Lawrentian to reconfigure the opera as naturalistic). In his preface he writes that the emotional mind "has its own rhythm, its own commas and colons, and full-stops," but these are neither logical nor chronological. We "can deduce the logical sequence and the time sequence," but only after "the happening." This is a splendid declaration of his own craft. It's also profoundly useful for discovering the cadences and conventions that exist in every unfamiliar form of art.

He is also saying that an inspired teller can predict the future, or at least the next expansion of consciousness. His favored metaphor is literary; he endows the inchoate with its own logic, its own grammar. This is studiously not Freudian; he despises psychoanalysis. And, just to settle another score, he dismisses James Joyce as a contrarian, simply out for sensation. Authors like Verga (and himself) do something better, or so he says; they inscribe the word before it is Word. "Afterwards you can deduce the logical sequence and the time sequence, as historians do from the past. But in the happening, the logical and the time sequence do not exist." Making the largest claims for literature, he demotes all the academics, who plunder an event after the artist, and only the artist, has captured it. There is nothing offensive in these lines. Rather, the pathos is that so few still believe them.

I do understand that I'm as vulnerably inconsistent as a Poirier loving Mailer, or a Cynthia Ozick loving Henry James. I love gospel music without believing a word of it, at least anything beyond the sense of triumphing over impossible conditions; the testimony in lines like "I've come so far, I believe I'll run on some more" remains the deepest one I know. I first met Rosetta Tharpe in the home of Marion Williams. Assuming that I was just another white blues boy, she spoke about her biggest hits, the rollicking tunes that had mesmerized Johnny Cash and Elvis Presley. But I didn't want any upbeat novelties like "This Train" or "Strange Things Happening Every Day." Instead I spoke about her earliest, saddest house wreckers, "I Looked Down the Line and I Wondered" and "The Day Is Past and Gone." (Curiously, the original English hymn with that title and lyric, but without Thomas A. Dorsey's bluesy revision, is cited by D. H. Lawrence, who also wrote a loving essay titled "Hymns in a Man's Life.") Rosetta turned to Marion: "This child ain't right. He like all those *deep* songs." Marion replied, "Ain't he a wreck! He say he an atheist and he only go for those hard songs, the kind that make you bust a gut." I couldn't deny it.

I would find myself playing three roles, fan, scholar, and friend, an ensemble that would raise many eyebrows. When my gospel book appeared, I received hostile glances from black cultural nationalists, who viewed me as an interloper, and white intellectuals, who thought I was slumming. The singers themselves were more welcoming. Shortly after I met Shirley Caesar, I regaled her with my imitation of Reverend Ruben Willingham of the Swanee Quintet. She threw a pillow at me and declared that I was "the jolliest white man" she had ever met. (This was 1961, when such mimicry was less common.)

This doesn't mean that I didn't have some unsettling hours. James Baldwin says that white America doesn't see or know black America. The reverse obtains as well. While I didn't hear more misogynistic, homophobic, or anti-Semitic remarks than I heard, for example, at Harvard, I still heard too many. The ignorance of a Shannon Williams (who used to say that Jews were naturally smarter and greedier than other people) or Alex Bradford (who argued with me for years that Nelson Rockefeller had to be a Jew, since he wasn't "a cracker or Eyetalian") could be appalling. The absence of social consciousness or political savvy was equally distressing. (In retrospect, the achievements of men like Dr. King, Bayard Rustin, and Alfred Duckett seem all the more heroic.)

Among the most politically attuned was Dorothy Love Coates; during its heyday, her group the Original Gospel Harmonettes had featured a narrator, Odessa Edwards, who spoke about civil rights long before Dr. King hit the scene. Dot always introduced herself as a native of Birmingham, Alabama, "the city this nation can't forget," and continued to advise her audience of conditions back home, "where things ain't changed much, not if you look like me." She remained troubled by the conditions of women like her mother, abandoned to raise six children by herself. But she also lamented her own treatment at the hands of record labels and music publishers. "Gave it all away," she said, upon hearing that Johnny Cash had recorded one of her masterpieces, "That's Enough." "They all done robbed me," she'd say. "And they keep on robbing me." Apparently I had convinced her that I wasn't one of them. In 1992 she performed in Central Park. She introduced the final song: "This one is for my brother. He's not a black man, he's a Jew." Not for the first time did I recognize that among southerners of a certain age, Jews are not considered white.

After Dorothy died, I continued to remain friendly with Mildred Miller Howard, the Harmonettes' second-lead singer. Dot always allowed that Mildred had the grander voice; sometimes, her mezzo-soprano in the background would overpower all the other singers, including Dot at the lead mike. The two women also understood that if Mildred had the notes, Dot had the fire. Since Mildred had been the group's original lead, she had essentially sacrificed herself for the Harmonettes. This showed that she was, unlike Dot, not an instinctive fighter; also that she was an extremely sweet person.

One time, shortly before her death, I called Mildred and found her in a depressed state. "What can lift your spirits, Mildred?" "A song." "You know I can't sing." "But you know all the verses," and she requested Fanny Crosby's "I Shall Know Him." Because Mildred was old school, I knew she'd go for the second verse, and I began to recite,

Oh, the soul-thrilling rapture, when I view his smiling face,
And the luster of his kindly gleaming eyes!

She was startled. "How'd you know that, little biddy boy? You're a—you're a—"

"Red, white, and blue, Mildred."

"What do you mean, Tony? Don't you kill me now."

"Well, my politics are very left-wing. In Birmingham, they'd probably call me a red. And unless I get a tan, you'd say my skin is white. And I'm suffering from reality-based depression . . ."

"And that makes you blue, baby!"

"Yes, sweetheart—red, white, and blue."

This fan had found his identity.

—

You might reasonably ask why I should be so attached to a culture so unlike the one in which I'd been raised. I'd been attending shows at the Apollo for two years when some usher took pity on this solitary youth and said, "Boy, you think this stuff is good, you need to see our gospel shows." I started doing so, realized that he was right, and became obsessed with proselytizing for the music. No doubt I took an adolescent pride in my advanced tastes. To this son of refugees from Berlin, everything in America was a cultural novelty. Most Americans did not share my parents' tone, the *Berliner Schnauze* (Berlin lip) with its scrupulous absence of sentimentality and its almost brutal attachment to irony and wit; actually, the impious style of gospel singers was not all that dissimilar.

But on a deeper level, gospel won me emotionally. What I fixed upon was not in any way religious—though I too rejoiced when my favorites shouted the house. There was another reason for my identification with the singers. I had been an isolated child, for years the class bookworm, nerd, outcast. Like so many others, I found school a torment, the arena in which my enemies could exploit my various weaknesses. They were gifted bullies. In particular, the bane of my youth, the class leader, would eventually become a famous right-wing journalist and, according to Max Frankel, the only figure more hated than the forbidding Abe Rosenthal. (In later years, I joked that he was rehearsing over my wounded body.) During those years, I acquired the preternatural alertness of the class pariah. Any corner I turned might bring further ridicule, either from my classmates or from strangers who had been trained to spot me. To paraphrase Madame Ward, I found myself with enemies I didn't know I had.

Those were hard years to get through, and great years to get past, if anything is ever past. They enabled me to identify with the gospel plight, as much as a German jewboy could. For the gospel that reached me, the passion of "How I Got Over," wasn't merely about making it, but about doing so in spite of your enemies. Gospel grounded me and kept me sane, not because "it gets better," but because for most people, it does not. Blues knows this. But gospel won me with its complex balance of the joyous and the grim—or, as I subtitled my first book, its good news and bad times. Dot Love's sister Lillian Caffey gave me a compliment I'll cherish: "Well, buddy, you cracked the code."

Would I have been so drawn to the music if I'd had another kind of youth? Perhaps not. Would I have acquired a key to the code had I not expected so-called friends to smile in my face and cut my throat behind my back? Absolutely not. Did I agree with all the old singers that if you have one true friend, you're rich, and that "if trouble don't come today, it'll surely be here tomorrow?" What else could I have learned? Are these valuable lessons?

"Ach," as my parents would say, "that's an interesting question."

—

There were even times when I could capitalize on my peculiarly earned knowledge of American fundamentalism. From 1977 to 1992 I conceived anthologies of gospel, black and white, that were marketed on television and sold extremely well. My outsider status was often a factor. One time, I created an album of country gospel, the Nashville sound that had inspired the likes of Johnny Cash and Elvis Presley. My boss was unimpressed. "This is the worst shit I've ever heard." "Trust me," I promised. "It'll sell." Acquiring the hits demanded negotiations with the biggest company in the field, Benson Records. I was familiar with the infamous Herman Lubinsky, founder and president of Savoy Records, the equivalent black gospel label, who had recorded the greatest stars of jazz (Charlie Parker), rhythm and blues (Big Maybelle), and gospel (the Ward Singers). He was notorious for stiffing his artists. In truth he simply underpaid them, and took advantage of their temporary needs in order to acquire their best work for the price of a quick fix (jazz) or a lapsed car note (gospel). Lubinsky had frequently driven me back to New York from Savoy's offices in Newark. During our trips he'd proclaim his far-right politics, and boast of running wiretaps for the FBI. My dubious revenge was to describe him in my first book as resembling a cross between Fagin and a shmoo (in fact Al Capp would have endorsed his politics)—a line immediately excised by my publishing company's lawyers. A better revenge occurred when the albums began to sell in the millions, and Savoy's publishing company was obliged to finally pay up, even though in several cases it was the widows and orphans who benefited.

Mr. Benson was a Southern Baptist version of Lubinsky, with an equally wizened view of interlopers. He did seem impressed by my knowledge of his tradition. "I've never spoken to a New Yorker who knew our gospel like you. You know 'Turn Your Radio On and Listen to the Music'? You can't know 'There's a Lighthouse on a Hillside That Overlooks Life's Sea'! How does a New Yorker know that?" New York, New York: I felt like identifying myself as the great-grandson of Rabbi Nathan M. Adler, chief rabbi of Great Britain, but I guess it went without saying.

The work was fun, even if I was surrounded by the far right wing of that era. (My agency, located in Long Island, was staffed by Tea Partiers in vitro: the founder had written and self-published a book entitled *John Kennedy's Thirteen Great Mistakes in the White House.*) I took pleasure in making the music available—my black gospel albums were divided between current hits that I found unappealing and classic records that had changed my life. Because the dross lifted the gold, some composers like Dot Love finally received the royalties they should have earned decades earlier. (Though even then she wasn't totally happy. "My God, the government's robbing all these poor gospel singers!" "Dot! They call it taxes!") One time I even had a chance to let my little light shine. I conceived an anthology of inspirational and neo-gospel music performed by the stars of country music; the televised commercial began with Willie Nelson's performance of "The Uncloudy Day." Usually the commercial included familiar publicity shots of the artists accompanied by snippets of their recordings. But the bosses gave me some leeway. And so, when the fans heard Merle Haggard sing, "Another reason for my mama's hungry eyes," they also saw a photo I had chosen: Dorothea Lange's *Migrant Mother*. The son of German Jewish refugees was trying to remind Haggard's audience of their own hard traveling, and to insinuate that as the WPA's grandchildren, they didn't need to vote Republican. I don't know if anyone picked up on my intentions!

By such means I learned that some fans have been around the block so often that they catch themselves going in the opposite direction.

—

When a fan comes to his senses—or thinks he does—he finds himself wallowing in bad faith. Nobody captured the sensation better than Proust. Charles Swann has devoted years of his life to a vain and idle courtesan named Odette. Suddenly, years of attrition wear down his rationale, and he faces the fact that the greatest love of his life, the object of his abject desire, the ruin of his better self, was "someone who was not my *style*" (italics mine). Yet he doesn't leave her, any more than Captain Dobbin abandons Amelia Sedley in *Vanity Fair,* even after he has determined that she is one silly goose—"not my style."

How much it takes to abandon your former, dearest self! Nietzsche was Wagner's greatest publicist until he claimed to have outgrown him. Now he declared him a "miniaturist," a subtly deflating assessment of the master builder, the kind of remark you expect from the smartest and most objective (does this mean "liberated"?) of fans. But his positive words carried the day, tragically when his sister brought a corrupted Wagnerian sensibility to the aid of Adolf Hitler. Wagner saturates the work of Thomas Mann, even if *Doctor Faustus* draws so greatly on the musicology of Arnold Schoenberg, as relayed to Mann by a third illustrious émigré, Theodor Adorno. He offers a hilarious, unanswerable assessment: as a composer Wagner's a great playwright; as a playwright, he's a great composer. How's that for speaking truth to power? Yet, in a conversation with her children, Katia Mann observed that Mann never outgrew his early love. He would sit dutifully through a concert conducted by their friend Bruno Walter until the first bars of something by Wagner, then purr contentedly, "Ah, yes! Now *that's* music." Just as he knew that good and bad Germany dwelled within him, so he knew that his idol was a charlatan, arriviste, and genius all wrapped into one questionable package. But then this was Thomas Mann, who spent his life worshipping Hermes, the god of thieves, the archetypal rogue and flirt. How could he have released himself from Wagner's hold?

Music can often break a fan's heart. A folkie once confessed to me that he loved the hardscrabble nobility of country music . . . when he wasn't hearing in it echoes of the Klan. Lovers of reggae must live with knowing that some of the most gifted practitioners have glorified the murders of "batty" (gay) men. Rap may include the best vernacular poetry of our time, even if it pours contempt on women and gay men, and reserves its praise for Jesus and bling. A generation of civil rights volunteers, fired up by Bob Dylan's anthems, must deal with the knowledge that his favorite politician of the 1960s was Barry Goldwater, admittedly a libertarian, but also a racist. How do you reconcile your principles with the immense pleasure any of these artists may have given you? Some writers and critics move blithely along, implying that they've beaten their sacred monsters by, if not surpassing them, comprehending them . . . knowing them better than they may have known themselves. But you can't do that with a pop idol: you love him precisely because you *can't* be him. Perhaps, all you can do is echo Jay Gatsby. When informed that somebody he proposes to invite to his next soiree actually hates him, he replies, "That's only personal."

To compare great men with small, I too suffered a vast disillusionment about the art form to which I had devoted years of time and work. Once gospel seemed the most vivid, intimate, and stirring of popular forms. It evolved into contemporary gospel, a form I find almost unlistenable. That might only mean that I too had become a moldy fig, yet another sad case wailing that his youth had been the best youth. But then the gospel church made a terrible turn.

As we saw in "The Children and Their Secret Closet," it became the oppressor of its greatest devotees, the gay men driven out of the choirs, the unmourned sick and dying caricatured as sissies and punks. In years past the bad faith that motivated gospel quartets to pretend that they had gotten happy had just seemed a sanctified form of show business. Now it seemed like the most cynical demagoguery.

Likewise, in an edition of *The Gospel Sound,* I celebrated gospel as the arena that empowered women, even acknowledging their supremacy— though it was mostly gay men who had mounted them so high. But in a recent review of Bettye Collier-Thomas's *Jesus, Jobs, and Justice,* a study of the ways religious faith informed the political roles of women, in both civil rights and labor action, Richard Thompson Ford made the sad but persuasive observation that their commitment was possibly for nought. The male preachers used them, abused them, and still relegated them to second place.

More specifically, there were times when I questioned my own aesthetic. Marion Williams gave me a lifetime's worth of pleasure in the recording studio—everything I could hope for in bluesy moans and raucous shouts. But her performances in person often disturbed me. She seldom chose her best songs, frequently catering to her audience's lowest expectations. She also remained true enough to her sanctified identity to indulge in evangelism when it was most inappropriate; she lost several college engagements after it became known that she would open the doors to the church. Invariably she did it while singing a hymn like "Amazing Grace"—not the most inspired choice, but her version was usually powerful enough to make you temporarily forget all the banalities. Unconsciously echoing Proust, I used to complain, "When she's good, she's better than anyone. When she's bad, she's worse." (Back then I hadn't yet witnessed the altar calls of Donnie McClurkin or Eddie L. Long that would nearly ruin the culture.)

I might have taken to heart the words of Fred Mendelsohn, the A&R director of Savoy Records. One time he managed to get his leading act, James Cleveland and the Southern California Choir, in a big music festival. They were scheduled for two performances, one at midnight, the other at dawn. Of course they killed in the evening. And, perhaps as predictably, Cleveland overslept and didn't even show up the next morning. The promoter was aghast: "That's so unprofessional." Freddie replied superbly, "Of course it's not. He's not a professional, he's a gospel singer." I've caught myself on either side of that divide. Sometimes the gospel singer resembles that Yeatsian ideal, making art instead of rhetoric. Other times I long for a professional discipline that pays only lip service to the concept of Spirit feel. Many a fan can be accused of not even knowing his own mind.

Perhaps I was just doomed to a certain kind of metropolitan angst. And perhaps I, like most besotted fans, no matter how smart, needed a wiser counsel. Some years ago I discussed gospel with Joseph Jennings. Though he was raised in a gospel church, he had traveled long and far. Evelyn Starks Hardy, the original pianist for Dorothy Love and the Original Gospel Harmonettes, attended a Chanticleer concert, and couldn't believe that "one of us" had so aced the highbrow discipline of a Palestrina or Brahms or, for that matter, a Duke Ellington or Benjamin Britten. R&B, Broadway soul, would have been child's play for a gospel bird. But Jennings's direction allowed for no tangents, no Spirit feel, no ad libs, no mile-wide vibrato. She had never heard anyone climb up from a storefront church into high art.

So I asked Jennings to assess various artists. I mentioned a very fine gospel singer, a more-than-adequate veteran of the music's golden age. "Fifth grade," he estimated. Then, what about the new breed of rockers, those upper-middle-class preppies who have heard everything and can produce dizzying collages, accompanied by lyrics that border on the eloquence of rap? "They're good," he allowed, though without enthusiasm. "Junior high school." Then, with some trepidation, I asked him about a singer he only knew on records. "And . . . Marion Williams?"

"Child," he said, lapsing into the drawl of Augusta, Georgia, "she wrote the book."

My eyes filled with sudden tears. To extend my conceit, it was as if Odette had returned to Swann with all her youthful charm, and the contours of his life could be finally revealed as elegant and correct.

Other, more surprising figures had heard something similar. In 1988, shortly after Marion began her dialysis treatment, she was hired to perform on a jazz boat tour. Sick as she was, she was also too poor to turn down the gig. I feared that she would not be up to the challenge. But, upon her return, she informed me that "the Lord blessed and gave me favor with the people." Her only sorrow was that she had neglected to bring any of her CDs. "I feel like kicking myself with pointy-heeled shoes."

In fact, the tour had been a triumph. Whitney Balliett, the jazz critic of *The New Yorker,* wrote that she had outshone geniuses like Dizzy Gillespie, Tommy Flanaghan, Illinois Jacquet, and Joe Williams. (Quite an achievement for a frail old woman who, thirty years earlier, had inspired the likes of Little Richard and James Brown.) Balliett was so enthralled that he would later recommend her for the Kennedy Center Honors. The surprise was that he had previously dismissed her as either brittle or sentimental, all show, no substance, Now, when she was physically and vocally diminished, he found her all heart and mind, America's greatest singer. I had kept her apprised of Balliett's several negative reviews, which bothered me far more than her. That he had become her greatest advocate elicited barely a shrug. "You win some, you lose some. Everyone ain't gonna love you. But child, if *you* ever got saved, I'd shout for a week."

—

An old fan knows a few things—among them, that his fandom has been a major portion of his self, a source of as much pleasure and despair as his love or his work; usually it has saturated both of them. He invariably mellows. To remain a hard, stoic, Lawrentian killer ain't easy when you don't have an affinity group marching by your side. ("Kid," my gospel pal Charles Campbell once said, "the onliest folk who still like us are three hundred quartet hos and seventy-five gospel sissies.") Pierre Boulez once hated any modern music unaffiliated with Berg or Schoenberg, most particularly Stravinsky. A few years ago, aged seventy-nine, he conducted the London Symphony in a performance of *The Rite of Spring* so revelatory that while it lasted, Stravinsky's mastery of rhythm and tonal color seemed to dominate all of the twentieth century, from jazz to classical. Did he ennoble Stravinsky or liberate himself?

Yet many of us remain productively engaged, enraged, and inspired. Just because nobody cares doesn't mean that we surrender. The novelist Dawn Powell said of her late husband that they had undergone so much together, had lived so completely in each other, that the matter of his death was a bagatelle. He was still her companion, their arguments continuing almost as before. That's loyalty, but it could be echoed by many a child still overshadowed by her parent, by many a student still indentured to his professor. The fan who keeps reconsidering his great loves dignifies them and himself—that is, if Randall Jarrell is right and the lives we supposedly miss become our finer lives.

Keats, who dwelled in melancholy, longed for "a life of sensation, and not of thought." That immersion in sensation can be a fan's highest bliss. But then he may aspire to something else; and dream of becoming, in Wallace Stevens's words, "the man who has had the time to think enough." Sensation and thought: that may be an old fan's last reward.

Thomas Mann understood this, better perhaps than anyone else, even Proust. His favorite word, the great theme of his life, was *Sehnsucht,* desire, perpetually rekindled and never satisfied. Some hungry children will never be well fed. He was doomed to burn red-hot, without any release but art. This could break his heart—and contribute unwittingly to the lifetime agonies of five of his six children. But it could also be a source of humor. By his late sixties, even as he had the playful audacity to imagine himself as the second Goethe, he made his definitive pronouncement: "Culture is parody."

This did not mean that history repeated itself as farce; the last paragraph of Mann's *Doctor Faustus* must reckon among the saddest conclusions in all of literature. But it did mean that a comic sensibility applied to any hallowed tradition could tweak it alive. Thus Mann could raid the Old Testament and reimagine it more compellingly than any other modern adaptor, all the while he modeled the beautiful Joseph on the various boys he surreptitiously adored. A banal impetus to literary genius, but Mann would not have considered that a paradox. High tragedy bowed to low comedy. So it was that after *Faustus* came *The Holy Sinner,* in which a medieval pope unwittingly marries his mother, and undergoes a lifetime of disabling torments, only to reveal—in a sheepish, shaggy-dog fashion—that mother and son were always wise to each other's identity. And why all the blood and woe? "We thought to offer God an entertainment." Culture surviving as parody renders even the sacred comic. This novel was the favorite book of Elisabeth Mann Borgese, the author's only happy child.

(Here's a joke that could serve as Mann's parable. A porn-movie actor needs to acquire a full-body tan. He lies down on a beach and covers all of his flesh with sand, except for his privates. Two old women pass by. One turns to the other: "Isn't that just like life? When I was twenty it terrified me. When I was fifty I couldn't get enough. And now that I'm eighty, it's growing wild." That's a capsulized history of popular culture.)

Mann grew very playful with the notion. In his last novel the con-man hero, Felix Krull, is pursued by an extremely dignified and aloof nobleman who is physically and temperamentally the twin of Mann himself. Felix lets him down easy. Recently a woman novelist—Mann in his more familiar disguise—had informed the lad that she wasn't all that crazy about him. He tells the older man, "She loved the entire genre." Mann quickly realized that he had made fun of "the dearest feelings of his heart." A lifetime of sublimation, all for an inspired, final joke that—of course—almost nobody outside of his wife and children would get. He had earned the right to treat the stuff of his life as material suitable for parody, high art, and righteous humor, even if, to paraphrase Lorenz Hart, the last laugh was on him.

The crux of this dilemma is exemplified by Vladimir Horowitz. Four days before his death, he completed a recording of Liszt's transcription of that supreme musical statement of eros and thanatos, the "Liebe-stod" from *Tristan and Isolde*. For me, the performance was a revelation. Largely immune to Wagner's charms—despite my love of gospel—I was thrilled by Horowitz's interpretation. Perhaps it was because the transcription reduced a huge ensemble of soloist and orchestra to a single musician, albeit one in command of all the colors and textures of his instrument: as classical fans would say, his sound was opulently orchestral; as pop fans would say, he could make the piano talk.

But, even more in terms of a fan defying his master, here was Horowitz, the most conspicuously Jewish of pianists, forever tormented by his barely suppressed homosexuality, playing the "Liebestod" with the profoundest emotion, shortly before his own death. Everything he knew of art, of life, went into that last round, literally the final take. You could say Wagner killed him, or rendered him immortal: a story worthy of Thomas Mann's treatment.

So a fan reviewing the highs and lows, the few times he veered right, the many times he steered wrong, is reduced to two options: to laugh or to cry. William Butler Yeats, who like Mann had been enthralled with old age from his youth, chose the former. His wise old men survey all the world's joys and sorrows, the gospel songs and blues, the songs of praise and "mournful melodies." And from their angle of repose, just because culture is parody, "their eyes, their ancient, glittering eyes, are gay."

Acknowledgments

This book could not exist without the counsel and example of the following friends: Margaret Battin, Douglas Bushek, Janet Coleman, Shelley L. Frisch, Vivian Gornick, Brooke Hopkins (my oldest male friend, and the bravest man I know), Andrew J. Humm, Alan Jalon, Margo Jefferson, Stephen Kroninger, Leonard Lopate, Phillip Lopate, Ann Middleton, Peter Minichiello, Amyas Naegele, Edgar Rosenberg, Lore Segal, Steve Wasserman, Donald Wesling, and Hollie I. West. Edwin Kennebeck, William Koshland, and Albert Wertheim did not have a chance to read the finished book, but it would not have been written without their encouragment.

Three men were particularly helpful in the writing of "Brave Tomorrows for Bachelor's Children": Himan Brown, who produced one of the earliest radio soaps, *Marie, the Little French Princess,* as well as the very last, *The Affairs of Dr. Gentry*; Charles Gussman, the most successful of the later soap writers; and Les White, an Irna Phillips scholar (among many other accomplishments), who discovered her unpublished diary.

The male soprano essay is grounded in my interviews with Anthony Roth Costanzo, Robert Crowe, Carl Hall, Joseph Jennings, Richard Penniman (that's Little Richard to you, shaddap), and Don Tatro.

Many, many gospel singers welcomed me into their world. Just a few of those who have enriched this book (and my life) would include Robert Anderson, Inez Andrews, Carl Bean, Alex Bradford, J. Robert Bradley, Shirley Caesar, Charles Campbell, Delois Barrett Campbell, Julius Cheeks, Dorothy Love Coates, Bessie Griffin, R. H. Harris, Mildred Miller Howard, Mahalia Jackson, Claude Jeter, Marie Knight, Sallie Martin, Norsalus McKissick, Paul Owens, Herbert Pickard, Eugene Smith, Willie Mae Ford Smith, Walter Stewart, Sister Rosetta Tharpe, Ira Tucker, Clara Ward, Willa Ward, and Marion Williams. Knowing them was a gift; producing them was a blessing.

My interest in Joseph Roth led me to his cousin Fred Grubel, the former director of the Leo Baeck Institute; Dan Morgenstern, who knew him during his last months in Paris; and Robert Weil, his devoted American publisher.

Victoria Wilson was my wise and patient editor. She forced me to make things better. If I didn't make them right, as the song says, it's nobody's fault but mine. Once again Patrick Dillon has been a meticulous copy editor; his band exists to make writers grateful and humble. Special thanks to the endlessly obliging Carmen Johnson.

"Somebody Else's Paradise" allowed me to update my 1983 book, *Exiled in Paradise*. The story of Hitler's émigrés continues to fascinate me, perhaps because it's my parents' story as well. Otto and Bertha Heilbut were not famous, but they lived exemplary lives. Otto was a relative of the Israel family, owners of Berlin's grandest department store, N. Israel's. Christopher Isherwood called Otto's cousin Wilfred Israel "the greatest man I ever met," largely because he had spent his last years in Europe rescuing his fellow Jews. In the effort he was always assisted by my father. As early as the mid-1920s, when pogroms were targeting Eastern Jews, a few German Jews rallied to their support. Typically, Albert Einstein would be the figurehead; Wilfrid Israel would make the social connections; and my father would do the heavy lifting, intervening with the rare sympathetic government official. My brother Wilfred and I always considered our father the last European gentleman. My mother, Bertha, twenty years Otto's junior, was a Berlin girl, fluent in the city's *Schnauze*. She had attended dancing class with the equally smart and pretty Lilli Palmer, then called Lilli Peiser. (She also swore that Berlin Jews always considered Leni Riefenstahl a particularly unsavory member of their tribe.) During their last years in Berlin, my parents lived down the road from the American embassy. While Wilfrid and Otto were scouting potential havens for the store's Jewish employees, my mother, blond enough to pass, hid thirty of those employees in my dad's apartment. The couple managed to leave Germany in 1939, but they both suffered grievous losses. My mother lost a brother. My father lost a brother and a sister, and several nephews and nieces.

America was harder for my old father—forty-nine when I was born—than my youthful mother. Eventually she was obliged to find work, something that actually liberated her. She completed a B.A. in two years and then earned a master's degree in social work. As a psychiatric social worker, she specialized in single-parent and interracial adoption, thereby offending almost all of her co-workers, black and white, although her haut-bourgeois African-American colleagues would admit that she got along better with the working-class foster mothers than they did. Both parents tolerated my peculiar affection for gospel music; my father would observe, dryly, that the melismatic hymnodists sounded like cantors. My mother would sigh, "My poor son is always discovering areas of American culture that nobody else appreciates." She had my number! My devout father, the grandson of the chief rabbi of Great Britain, would observe the High Holidays. When called to recite my portion, I'd employ the groaning cadences of C. L. Franklin: "Why is this night . . . hmmm . . . not like other nights." My adorable brother would turn crimson and fall on the floor laughing. My impious mother would attend to the matzoh-ball soup, my father would roll his eyes and continue the service, too refined to chastize me in public. They were both wonderfully gracious with my gospel friends. As a result, Dorothy Love Coates called Bertha "Mama"; my father, with an émigré's penchant for wordplay, used to say, "Give my love to Dorothy Love." Marion Williams called Bertha "my Jewish mother."

Even in her last year my mother's political savvy was undiminished. She died shortly after the U.S. invasion of Iraq. If you remember, it seemed to go smoothly, and the general assessment was that it had been an easy victory. But almost her last words were, "This is very bad. This could be the worst thing for America." Once again, in the great tradition of Einstein and Mann, an émigré had seen all too clearly. But, as in the 1950s, what good did that do?

After reading this book, you can see why it's dedicated to their memory. I owe them everything I am.

Anthony Heilbut

Index

Page numbers in *italics* refer to illustrations.

A Note on the Type

This book was set in Adobe Garamond. Designed for the Adobe Corporation by Robert Slimbach, the fonts are based on types first cut by Claude Garamond (c. 1480–1561). Garamond was a pupil of Geoffroy Tory and is believed to have followed the Venetian models, although he introduced a number of important differences, and it is to him that we owe the letter we now know as "old style." He gave to his letters a certain elegance and feeling of movement that won their creator an immediate reputation and the patronage of Francis I of France.

Composed by North Market Street Graphics,
Lancaster, Pennsylvania

Printed and Bound by Berryville Graphics,
Berryille, Virginia

Designed by Iris Weinstein